Teaching in
the American Secondary School

Teaching
in the
American
Secondary
School

Selected Readings

Edited by

Frederick R. Cyphert
The Ohio State University

Earl W. Harmer, Jr.
University of Utah

Anthony C. Riccio
The Ohio State University

McGraw-Hill Book Company
New York   San Francisco   Toronto   London

II

Teaching in the American Secondary School is designed to expedite the development of insights into the theory and practice of secondary school teaching by persons preparing to teach in any subject area. It is a source book of information and ideas and can be used as a text or as a text supplement. It contains representative selections of merit culled from the plethora of recent periodical literature concerning contemporary secondary education. Selections have met the criteria of significance, quality, provocativeness, appropriateness, and readability.

Five main areas of thought are encompassed: (1) American secondary education, its objectives and setting; (2) the adolescent, his learning and development; (3) the teacher, his methodological problems and processes; (4) the secondary school program, its theory and practice; and (5) the major issues confronting secondary educators, together with some promising ways of resolving them. Rather than duplicating material from classes in adolescence, learning theory, methodology, and curriculum, transforming knowledges into professional teaching competencies is emphasized.

Continuity is achieved through the editors' introduction to each part. The introductions provide a frame of reference for approaching the professional considerations involved. The contents are not prescriptive, but are both heuristic and informative. In general, the intent is to let the authors speak for themselves.

The editors are concerned that many students preparing to teach are unable to differentiate between opinion and fact in education. Consequently, major emphasis throughout the book is on clarifying and extending the science of teaching—a process which ultimately increases the effectiveness of teaching's artistic phases. The book contains research findings and sound theory concerning the status and direction of the modern secondary school, the functioning of the adolescent student, the role and task-orientation of the high school teacher, and the pedagogical science which blends these elements into the process called education.

The book provides assistance in acquiring a rational approach to the decisions inherent in teaching. It attempts to answer many of the questions of the prospective teacher, yet it emphasizes his developing techniques for finding answers to problems as they arise. The editors hope that the reader will develop a number of significant questions concerning the educative processes which require further investigation and inquiry.

The editors would like to express their appreciation to the publishing houses and authors who so generously gave permission to have their materials reproduced and to the instructors in the Principles of Secondary Education course at The Ohio State University who tested these materials and many others in their classes.

Frederick R. Cyphert

Earl W. Harmer, Jr.

Anthony C. Riccio

Contents

Preface

part i
Frame of reference

*One phenomenon in present-day America is the pursuit of
excellence. Higher education personnel solicit the bright young
people. Eventually, the bright young people search for companies
and institutions which are looking for new talent and competence.
Once in, the somewhat older bright people look and move again.
Behavioral scientists claim that a pattern has developed.*

*The need for excellence and intelligence has seldom been
more acute. It is unfortunate that comparatively little is known
about how to help someone become an effective teacher, but this is
the case. We professional people want classroom teachers who
are emotionally stable, competent, and confident of their academic
preparation. They should love children without any particular
need for the children to love them. They should be creative,
have an enormous capacity for hard work, and be able to live
with—or above—the vicissitudes of educational criticism and
climate. Most of all, they must understand what they are doing.*

*One of the difficult tasks for the prospective teacher is to
begin to view education and teaching with a trained, unbiased,
objective eye. It is difficult, but necessary, for the teacher-to-be
to step outside the accumulation of years of experience as a
student and see education as a complex phenomenon, a creation
of society, professionalism, politics, and industry.*

*Perhaps no one has the experience and wisdom to wholly
comprehend American education; however, everyone involved,
particularly professional people, must try. We are obligated to
make thorough and repeated investigations into such questions as:*

1

*What are we trying to accomplish? How are we trying to do it?
Who should be involved and for how long? How can we tell
whether we have done what we set out to do?*

The readings in Part I have been selected to help provide a
frame of reference not only to further understanding of the
dimensions of education, but more particularly to provide a
foundation on which the succeeding articles can be read and
understood.

Smith brilliantly synthesizes the relationship of education
and American culture. His thoughts are fundamental for a better
understanding of the remainder of the book. The statement by the
Educational Policies Commission on the function of education
in a democratic society is equally relevant.

"Progressive education" is a term much used and consequently
occasionally abused. Because so much of modern education is a
consequence of the progressive movement and because many of
the goals of progressive education have yet to be fully realized,
the Cremin article "John Dewey and the Progressive-education
Movement, 1915–1952" is "must" reading.

Mehl links the Conant report of 1959 and the work of the
Committee of Ten, published in 1894. Both are major influences
in education. Mehl accurately identifies the parallel relationships
between the two works.

Psychology could use a succession of men of the caliber of
William James. He is one of the intellectual giants of all time,
and Larrabee describes James' contribution to public education.

Values, learning, and meta-knowledge are interrelated with
education. What values does (or should) the prospective teacher
hold? How can he discriminate among the various theories of
learning? What generalizations are sound, understandable, and
applicable for the teacher? What about the structure of
knowledge? What knowledge is of most worth? Allport, Watson, and
Combs discuss certain aspects of these areas of study and their
relevance to teaching.

Bush has contributed a succinct review of the history of
secondary education, with some predictions regarding the future.

The reader should remember that while this section is an
excellent frame of reference for the readings that follow, it in no

*sense constitutes a comprehensive "foundations of education"
reference. Future study will emphasize this important area. On
the other hand, the reader should understand that a fundamental
concept in education is change. Schools exist in order to promote
desirable change, development, and maturity in pupils. Good
schools provide the opportunity for optimal development of all
pupils. In order for this to occur, schools can and must change. That
schools can change and have changed is one of the great strengths
of American education. The readings in this book will extend
and illustrate this concept.*

chapter 1

American education for American culture

Huston Smith

In honoring me with an invitation to address you this morning your Executive Committee generously offered me the freedom to choose any topic which relates to your conference theme. I have been tempted to exercise this freedom and speak to some of my special interests in education, especially those relating to the place of values in the educational process. But in the end I found that there was nothing I wanted to talk about as much as your conference theme itself: "American Education for American Culture." As this is the first general session of the conference it may not be presumptuous to face this theme head-on, to break it open, so to speak, to try to discover the ideas and issues that lie latent within it.

I understand that the theme was chosen in answer to present suggestions from many quarters that education in this country should be patterned after that of Russia. Surely your planning committee is right in assuming that it should not be. We have our own character, our own ideals, our own destiny, and our education should carry their signature. At the same time, we cannot proceed as if Soviet education didn't exist, or as if, existing, it need mean nothing to us—this, I take it, is equally obvious. So we find ourselves with a nice problem: What *should* be the relation of American education to Soviet education, on the one hand, and to our own distinctive culture on the other. This is the question for this hour.

I find that my mind is helped toward an answer to this question by a

From *North Central Association Quarterly*, 34(October, 1959), 155–160.
Reprinted by permission of the author and publisher.

story. It is not irrelevant to our topic that this story comes from a portion of Western culture which Communism has rejected but which continues to shape America, namely the Bible. Nevertheless, just because it is from the Bible I feel somewhat uneasy about introducing it. For though I personally feel that no absolute division between the sacred and the secular is possible or even desirable, and that all our doings, ultimately, should be guided and empowered by faith, I also feel that we ought to be very chary about correlating our panaceas with God's will. For when we do so two unfortunate things happen: first, we tend to immunize our programs from the criticisms they deserve—for who would presume to criticize the divine will to which they have been linked?—and second, we use religion to rally support for what *we* want, demoting it thereby from an end to a means. I'm afraid we have seen both of these processes at work in Washington in recent years and I don't want to compound the phenomenon; certainly the answer to "piety along the Potomac" isn't piosity in the Palmer House. On the other hand I refuse to be deprived of insight and a good story because it happens to appear in the Bible. So I shall use my story, letting it stand wholly on the legs of its self-contained and quite worldly point. For though to millions of Americans the author of this story is the Cosmic Christ, it is enough for this context that he was a great teacher.

The story I have in mind is that of the Swindling Steward as it appears in the Gospel of Luke. It is the story of a man who so badly mismanaged an estate entrusted to him that upon the proprietor's return he is served notice and asked to turn in his accounts. Facing unemployment and personal ruin he suddenly gets an idea; he decides to falsify his master's accounts in favor of his debtors. To the debtors' delight he goes right down the line. Each owed so much according to the books; all accept the chance to alter their accounts. By a scratch of the pen he who owed 100 barrels of oil now owes but 50; he who owed 100 quarters of wheat now owes but 80. Thus all the debtors are under an obligation to the manager. All are now his many friends who will ever be ready to invite him to their houses after his dismissal. With so many friends indebted to him, the future is no longer hopeless or dark. Things are definitely on the uptrail.

If that is where the story had stopped, it would be so much like what we read in the paper every morning that we wouldn't bother with it. It's what follows that gives the story its point. For after painting an authentic portrait of the successful rascal, a man utterly devoid of even run-of-the-mill ethics, this is the way the story ends: "The master *praised* his dishonest steward because he had acted shrewdly, for the children of darkness are wiser in their generation than the children of light."

As I say, I know of no other story that does more to help me set the problem of this hour in perspective. For—and here is the parallel with Russia—the manager's basic philosophy is not one we are asked to accept. He is nothing short of a skinflint, a cheat, and a rascal. Yet the story obviously implies that the manager has something to teach others whose principles may be very different.

And *what* he has to teach is clear. The manager was faced with a crisis. He had to take drastic steps to cope with it. He had to do some hard thinking and some shrewd scheming. Scoundrel though he was, he at least had the merit of taking a realistic and unsentimental view of his predicament and doing something about it. He evaluated the emergency he faced accurately and acted promptly. The concrete steps he took were wrong. Yet his alertness, his immediate and energetic use of opportunity, such as changing the accounts while still in his possession, his aggressive application of the principles he believed in, his resolution to use the present to determine the future—this, says the story, is what the children of light should do with their principles and for their goals.

I apologize for the black and white equation of Communism with the children of darkness and ourselves with the children of light—we all know it's not that simple. But given our conviction that there are values in Western civilization which are universal but which Communism, if triumphant, would destroy, what content pertinent to our topic can be poured into our story? In what ways may Soviet education be wiser in its generation, that is to say within the context of assumptions and principles and circumstances in which it operates, than is our own?

Descriptions of Soviet education are no longer new. The pertinent facts for our purposes are that contemporary Russia provides a picture of (1) educational urgency, (2) mobilized toward world outreach, and (3) motivated by cosmic vision.

Consider first the sense of urgency that appears to characterize Soviet education. Having, in America, known nothing but universal education during our entire lifetime, we take it for granted and treat it casually. By contrast the older generation of Russians who can remember when half their nation was illiterate know directly, by personal recall, the extent to which knowledge is power. So they act on this knowledge. We learn from Dr. William Carr, executive secretary of the NEA, that the Soviets spend 6 per cent of their national income on education compared with our 4.5 per cent; that Russian schools have one teacher for every seventeen students, while ours "struggle to maintain a ratio of one to thirty"; that teaching is one of the highest paid professions in the U.S.S.R. and one of the lowest paid in America. Qualified students are automatically subsidized through the Ph.D. equivalent in the conviction that they will more than repay the nation for what it has invested in them. On returning from an inspectional tour last year, United States Commissioner of Education Lawrence Derthick summarized this entire gestalt as follows:

What we have seen has amazed us in one outstanding particular; we were simply not prepared for the degree to which the USSR, as a nation, is committed to education as a means of national advancement. Everywhere we went we saw indication after indication of what we could only conclude amounted to a total commitment to education. Our major reaction therefore is one of astonishment . . . at the extent to which this seems to have been accomplished. . . . We saw no evidence of any teacher shortage. Teacher workloads and other working conditions are advantageous. Teacher prestige is high. Salaries are at the levels of those of doctors and engineers. . . . Only the best are chosen to teach—one out of six who apply.

But second, this educational urgency is mobilized toward a gigantic world outreach. The Russians give every evidence of thinking of themselves as having a world mission, and of education as one of the primary instruments for accomplishing that mission. In part, Russia's world-thrust roots from historical centrifugal forces that have been pressing outward for a hundred years to the Pacific, the Balkans, and the Middle East. But this is not the whole story: To a very significant degree Russia's outreach springs from a sense of mission. The Communist is convinced that the whole human race is destined to become one Communist brotherhood. Consequently there seems to be no corner of the earth's surface he thinks too insignificant for his attention. Why is it one never even hears of a Communist isolationism? While trade missions are busy in Latin America trading Soviet machinery and oil for wool and coffee, Arab and Asian students are being trained in Moscow, Russian teachers are touring West Africa, and technical advisers are dispatched to India, Burma, and Indonesia.

Third, this world outreach is motivated by a cosmic vision. The thrust in Soviet society is not confined to its international outreach. Visitors report that it appears to pervade its life as a whole. From whence does it come? The answer seems to be: from the cosmic vision in which Communism is rooted. Communism's revolutionary ardor has cooled with the years, but even her very pragmatic political leaders seem to believe profoundly in the truth of their way of life and are quietly confident that it will eventually sweep the world. They seem to be altogether sincere in believing that their methods, aspirations, and dreams make up the final truth about the nature of man and society; that the collective man in the collective state is the ultimate unfolding of human destiny, the end of history, the "far off divine event" for which mankind has been in long travail. Their vision is wrong, but even wrong, it has created a vast powerhouse of energy harnessed to the communal task of building the Soviet dream. The thrust of economic growth that adds 7 per cent increase each year is one aspect of this energy. More pertinent to education are the vast sums available for science and research. But nothing indicates more clearly the resources of energy, work, and skill which their cosmic vision has engendered than the self-discipline and long hours their school children put in to train themselves as scientists, technicians, administrators, and linguists for the new world order they are convinced they are building.

So much for Russia. If, now, we come back to our problem as originally posed, namely, from what within Soviet education may we learn and what ought we to reject as incongruous with American culture, the equipment for a propositional answer is now at hand. The formal features of the Russian educational picture might well be duplicated. But the content should be uncompromisingly our own. We too need an (1) urgent education (2) with world outreach (3) motivated by cosmic vision. But what this cosmic vision should be, how our nation should relate itself to the world, and whence the urgency that needs to infuse our education should derive—the answers to these questions should carry the distinctive stamp of American culture.

This much I'm sure of. From this point on, my thoughts are far more tentative and are intended to be exploratory only. But not wishing to leave you with a formula that is entirely empty, let me try to fill it with at least the beginnings of content. This will involve going for a last time through our three phrases—educational concern, world outreach, and cosmic vision —asking this time how we are doing on each count and what we should be doing.

In the past our educational concern was second to none. What contemporary of Jefferson in any nation was saying, "Education is the keystone of good government"? Never before in the history of the world had a statesman proposed free universal education. Half a century was required before even Europe was to catch up to the idea. And this was just the beginning. Within a century we had extended our educational vision (1) laterally to include Negroes and women, (2) longitudinally to include secondary education and even college, and (3) in its very principle from free, i.e., permissive, education to education as a requirement. When I look back on the record, a record that Mortimer Adler and Milton Mayer have sketched excitingly in their *Revolution in Education,* I am not ashamed. We have not done all things well. But when I review the past I am proud of the history of American education as it has both reflected and invigorated American culture.

The present is a different story. You know it better than I do, for you see more of its ramifications and have to live with it more intimately. It is a story of Presidential apathy as the Administration subordinates everything in its school plan to the demand that nothing be added to the federal budget during the remaining two years of the Eisenhower Administration. With some brilliant exceptions, notably Senator Murray and Representative Metcalf of Montana, it is a story of Congressional apathy as 140,000 needed classrooms wait to be built and 135,000 needed teachers await recruitment. It is a story of state apathy, with eighteen states having no provisions whatever for state aid for school construction. It is a story of community apathy as 250,000 teachers receive less than $3,500 a year (less, often, than the janitors) and their average salary remains under $5,000. (In my own community this year, one of the most favored communities in the most favored nation in the world, the plastic portion of the art program ground to a halt in midyear because no money could be found for clay!) It is a story of parental apathy. When *Look Magazine* last year conducted a nationwide survey asking what kind of courses parents want for their children, a superintendent in Utah answered for the nation: "Courses they can pass—period." But why try to pinpoint the blame? It blankets the entire country as we continue to spend less on the education of our children than we do on alcohol and tobacco.

If American education is to be true to American culture it cannot correct this national languor in Russian style, by turning the whole problem over to the national government for federal support and federal control. Classrooms must be built, and Robert Hutchins and the Secretary of Health, Education, and Welfare may not be far wrong when they say teachers' salaries should be doubled. And a large portion of the help must be federal. But it should not be exclusively that. Consonant with American culture, education's support should be multiple and diverse, a mixture of federal, state, community, and private. And it should be imaginative. One of the nicest recent proposals in this last vein is Robert Frost's suggestion of endowed chairs in primary and secondary schools. Such chairs would honor both the public-minded citizens whose names they would carry and the exceptional teachers who were appointed to them. If American culture indicates that support for education should be diversified, it also requires that control be kept close to the local community as long as standards and civil rights are maintained. The Chamber of Commerce is annually wrong in confusing federal support with federal control; the facts show no such necessary correlation.

Where do we stand in our world outreach? Again in our past we have had it, if not aggressively at least by indirection. America was born dedicated to a proposition whose ingredients—equality, life, liberty, and the pursuit of happiness—brought response from the entire world. Our greatest leaders, our Jeffersons, our Lincolns, our Wilsons, our Roosevelts, were not great because they achieved purely American purposes but because they spoke to humanity at large and extended their vision to the entire family of man. But where is our world vision today? Where are even the slogans of yesteryears—the war to end all wars, the war to make the world safe for democracy, the four freedoms, the century of the common man? Faced with the aggressive internationalism of world Communism, we have, it is true, responded. We have been forced beyond our wish to live and let live, our wish merely to stay home. "Fortress America" isolationism is dead. But our response, I fear, has been primarily a negative one. We have gone forth not to help the world toward goals we believe are relevant for all human living so much as to preserve the world (and often it looks as if by this we mean in the end ourselves) against the advances of our adversaries. Is it possible that whereas our adversaries have something to believe in, Communism, we have something to *disbelieve* in, also Communism?

Personally I am convinced that a negative world vision, epitomized in the phrase Communist containment, is inadequate for the needs of our times. For one thing, a negative vision can never match the appeal of a positive one. Whitehead put this succinctly when he said in another context, "If man cannot live by bread alone, still less can he live by disinfectants." But logic is also against it. When a positive position wins, its position is enlarged; when a negative position wins, it merely holds the dike. As nobody can win all the time, the best a negative position can hope for is to delay its eventual demise.

If America moves to an affirmative world vision consonant with our culture, its content will differ from Communism's. And it is not difficult to see what this content should be. Our vision should be to build a *peaceful* world of *autonomous, prospering democracies*. The order of the four pivotal words in that sentence is important: where, in any specific situation, one of the four objectives must be temporarily subordinated to others, priority should, as a rule, be weighted toward the objective appearing earlier in the sentence. America's methods in working toward these objectives should also differ from the Communist's; they should incline toward evolution rather than revolution; they should be directed toward goals we really share with the nations in question; and they should give greater rein to freedom, individualism, and human rights than do our opponents. But our efforts in behalf of our vision should not be less than theirs. And American education should contribute to these efforts (1) by helping students to understand that the foremost problem in our contemporary world is not Communism but a deeper problem which Communism is riding, namely, the great East-West economic, racial, colonial, and human imbalance; (2) by helping them to understand that the alternative to world domination is not world indifference; and (3) by helping them toward fluency in one foreign language. This last is important in many ways, but not least as a symbol. There is a world image today of Americans as people who expect the world to meet them on their terms. Nothing would do more to correct this image than for every American to assume personal responsibility for bringing himself to the point where he could meet the people of at least one other country, when they come here or when he goes there, on their terms.

Finally there is the matter of cosmic vision. I have said that the Communists seem to have one. This is dangerous, for men possessed can be more terrible than armies with banners. Possessed of good, they are terrible; possessed of evil, worse. But what of men unpossessed? And is this beginning to look like us?

I fear that it may be. Time does not permit me to sketch the outlines of a cosmic vision consonant with our Judeo-Christian tradition, contemporary science, and our democratic leanings even if I were capable of doing so. But two things I think we can say: first, that American education, particularly higher education, should be more concerned with the problem of discovering and clarifying such a vision than it now is; and second, that whatever the metaphysical features of the vision itself, it must provide clearer sanctions for freedom, conscience, and variation than does Marxism. It must be more sensitive to the problem of means and ends, recognizing that the means we use will affect the ends we reap. And it must be cautious about sacrificing present lives, which are actual, for blueprints of a future which may turn out to be largely visionary.

But these are topics for another day. As I have hinged my analysis on a parable, I shall return to it for our close. What the story of the Swindling Steward says to us is that our future depends upon what we do now, and that what we do must be as determined, as relevant, and as imaginative as was the steward's. Let us, then, take this leaf from his notebook, scoundrel though he was. For the children of darkness are wiser in their generation than the children of light.

chapter 2

Education in the American society

Educational Policies Commission

In any democracy education is closely bound to the wishes of the people, but the strength of this bond in America has been unique. The American people have traditionally regarded education as a means for improving themselves and their society. Whenever an objective has been judged desirable for the individual or the society, it has tended to be accepted as a valid concern of the school. The American commitment to the free society —to individual dignity, to personal liberty, to equality of opportunity—has set the frame in which the American school grew. The basic American value, respect for the individual, has led to one of the major charges which the American people have placed on their schools: to foster that development of individual capacities which will enable each human being to become the best person he is capable of becoming.

The schools have been designed also to serve society's needs. The political order depends on responsible participation of individual citizens; hence the schools have been concerned with good citizenship. The economic order depends on ability and willingness to work; hence the schools have taught vocational skills. The general morality depends on choices made by individuals; hence the schools have cultivated moral habits and upright character.

Educational authorities have tended to share and support these broad concepts of educational purposes. Two of the best-known definitions of purposes were formulated by educators in 1918 and 1938. The first definition, by the Commission on the Reorganization of Secondary Education, proposed for the school a set of seven cardinal objectives: health, command of fundamental processes, worthy home membership, vocational

From *The Central Purpose of American Education*, Educational Policies Commission (Washington, D.C.: National Education Assocation, 1961), 1–12. Reprinted by permission of the publisher.

competence, effective citizenship, worthy use of leisure, and ethical character. The second definition, by the Educational Policies Commission, developed a number of objectives under four headings: self-realization, human relationship, economic efficiency, and civic responsibility.

The American school must be concerned with all these objectives if it is to serve all of American life. That these are desirable objectives is clear. Yet they place before the school a problem of immense scope, for neither the schools nor the pupils have the time or energy to engage in all the activities which will fully achieve all the goals. Choices among possible activities are inevitable and are constantly being made in and for every school. But there is no consensus regarding a basis for making these choices. The need, therefore, is for a principle which will enable the school to identify its necessary and appropriate contributions to individual development and the needs of society.

Furthermore, education does not cease when the pupil leaves the school. No school fully achieves any pupil's goals in the relatively short time he spends in the classroom. The school seeks rather to equip the pupil to achieve them for himself. Thus the search for a definition of the school's necessary contribution entails an understanding of the ways individuals and societies choose and achieve their goals. Because the school must serve both individuals and the society at large in achieving their goals, and because the principal goal of the American society remains freedom, the requirements of freedom set the frame within which the school can discover the central focus of its own efforts.

The freedom which exalts the individual, and by which the worth of the society is judged, has many dimensions. It means freedom from undue governmental restraints; it means equality in political participation. It means the right to earn and own property and decide its disposition. It means equal access to just processes of law. It means the right to worship according to one's conscience.

Institutional safeguards are a necessary condition for freedom. They are not, however, sufficient to make men free. Freedom requires that citizens act responsibly in all ways. It cannot be preserved in a society whose citizens do not value freedom. Thus belief in freedom is essential to maintenance of freedom. The basis of this belief cannot be laid by mere indoctrination in principles of freedom. The ability to recite the values of a free society does not guarantee commitment to those values. Active belief in those values depends on awareness of them and of their role in life. The person who best supports these values is one who has examined them, who understands their function in his life and in the society at large, and who accepts them as worthy of his own support. For such a person these values are consciously held and consciously approved.

The conditions necessary for freedom include the social institutions which protect freedom and the personal commitment which gives it force. Both of these conditions rest on one condition within the individuals who compose a free society. This is freedom of the mind.

Freedom of the mind is a condition which each individual must develop for himself. In this sense, no man is born free. A free society has the obligation to create circumstances in which all individuals may have opportunity and encouragement to attain freedom of the mind. If this goal is to be achieved, its requirements must be specified.

To be free, a man must be capable of basing his choices and actions on understandings which he himself achieves and on values which he examines for himself. He must be aware of the bases on which he accepts propositions as true. He must understand the values by which he lives, the assumptions on which they rest, and the consequences to which they lead. He must recognize that others may have different values. He must be capable of analyzing the situation in which he finds himself and of developing solutions to the problems before him. He must be able to perceive and understand the events of his life and time and the forces that influence and shape those events. He must recognize and accept the practical limitations which time and circumstance place on his choices. The free man, in short, has a rational grasp of himself, his surroundings, and the relation between them.

He has the freedom to think and choose, and that freedom must have its roots in conditions both within and around the individual. Society's dual role is to guarantee the necessary environment and to develop the necessary individual strength. That individual strength springs from a thinking, aware mind, a mind that possesses the capacity to achieve aesthetic sensitivity and moral responsibility, an enlightened mind. These qualities occur in a wide diversity of patterns in different individuals. It is the contention of this essay that central to all of them, nurturing them and being nurtured by them, are the rational powers of man.

The Central Role of the Rational Powers

The cultivated powers of the free mind have always been basic in achieving freedom. The powers of the free mind are many. In addition to the rational powers, there are those which relate to the aesthetic, the moral, and the religious. There is a unique, central role for the rational powers of an individual, however, for upon them depends his ability to achieve his personal goals and to fulfill his obligations to society.

These powers involve the processes of recalling and imagining, classifying and generalizing, comparing and evaluating, analyzing and synthesizing, and deducing and inferring. These processes enable one to apply logic and the available evidence to his ideas, attitudes, and actions, and to pursue better whatever goals he may have.

This is not to say that the rational powers are all of life or all of the mind, but they are the essence of the ability to think. A thinking person is aware that all persons, himself included, are both rational and nonrational, that each person perceives events through the screen of his own personality, and that he must take account of his personality in evaluating his perceptions. The rational processes, moreover, make intelligent choices possible. Through them a person can become aware of the bases of choice in his values and of the circumstances of choice in his environment. Thus they are broadly applicable in life, and they provide a solid basis for competence in all the areas with which the school has traditionally been concerned.

The traditionally accepted obligation of the school to teach the *fundamental processes*—an obligation stressed in the 1918 and 1938 statements of educational purposes—is obviously directed toward the development of the ability to think. Each of the school's other traditional objectives can be better achieved as pupils develop this ability and learn to apply it to all the problems that face them.

Health, for example, depends upon a reasoned awareness of the value of mental and physical fitness and of the means by which it may be developed and maintained. Fitness is not merely a function of living and acting; it requires that the individual understand the connection among health, nutrition, activity, and environment, and that he take action to improve his mental and physical condition.

Worthy home membership in the modern age demands substantial knowledge of the role that the home and community play in human development. The person who understands the bases of his own judgments recognizes the home as the source from which most individuals develop most of the standards and values they apply in their lives. He is intelligently aware of the role of emotion in his own life and in the lives of others. His knowledge of the importance of the home environment in the formation of personality enables him to make reasoned judgments about his domestic behavior.

More than ever before, and for an ever-increasing proportion of the population, *vocational competence* requires developed rational capacities. The march of technology and science in the modern society progressively eliminates the positions open to low-level talents. The man able to use only his hands is at a growing disadvantage as compared with the man who can also use his head. Today even the simplest use of hands is coming to require the simultaneous employment of the mind.

Effective citizenship is impossible without the ability to think. The good citizen, the one who contributes effectively and responsibly to the management of the public business in a free society, can fill his role only if he is aware of the values of his society. Moreover, the course of events in modern life is such that many of the factors which influence an individual's civic life are increasingly remote from him. His own firsthand experience is no longer an adequate basis for judgment. He must have in addition the intellectual means to study events, to relate his values to them, and to make wise decisions as to his own actions. He must also be skilled in the processes of communication and must understand both the potentialities and the limitations of communication among individuals and groups.

The *worthy use of leisure* is related to the individual's knowledge, understanding, and capacity to choose, from among all the activities to which his time can be devoted, those which contribute to the achievement of his purposes and to the satisfaction of his needs. On these bases, the individual can become aware of the external pressures which compete for his attention, moderate the influence of these pressures, and make wise choices for himself. His recreation, ranging from hobbies to sports to intellectual activity pursued for its own sake, can conform to his own concepts of constructive use of time.

The development of *ethical character* depends upon commitment to values; it depends also upon the ability to reason sensitively and responsibly with respect to those values in specific situations. Character is misunderstood if thought of as mere conformity to standards imposed by external authority. In a free society, ethics, morality, and character have meaning to the extent that they represent affirmative, thoughtful choices by individuals. The ability to make these choices depends on awareness of values and of their role in life. The home and the church begin to shape the child's values long before he goes to school. And a person who grows up in the American society inevitably acquires many values from his daily pattern of living. American children at the age of six, for example, usually have a firm commitment to the concept of fair play. This is a value which relates directly to such broad democratic concepts as justice and human worth and dignity. But the extension of this commitment to these broader democratic values will not occur unless the child becomes aware of its implications for his own behavior, and this awareness demands the ability to think.

A person who understands and appreciates his own values is most likely to act on them. He learns that his values are of great moment for himself, and he can look objectively and sympathetically at the values held by others. Thus, by critical thinking, he can deepen his respect for the importance of values and strengthen his sense of responsibility.

The man who seeks to understand himself understands also that other human beings have much in common with him. His understanding of the possibilities which exist within a human being strengthens his concept of the respect due every man. He recognizes the web which relates him to other men and perceives the necessity for responsible behavior. The person whose rational powers are not well developed can, at best, learn habitual responses and ways of conforming which may ensure that he is not a detriment to his society. But, lacking the insight that he might have achieved, his capacity to contribute will inevitably be less than it might have become.

Development of the ability to reason can lead also to dedication to the values which inhere in rationality: commitment to honesty, accuracy, and personal reliability; respect for the intellect and for the intellectual life; devotion to the expansion of knowledge. A man who thinks can understand the importance of this ability. He is likely to value the rational potentials of mankind as essential to a worthy life.

Thus the rational powers are central to all the other qualities of the human spirit. These powers flourish in a humane and morally responsible context and contribute to the entire personality. The rational powers are to the entire human spirit as the hub is to the wheel.

These powers are indispensable to a full and worthy life. The person in whom—for whatever reason—they are not well developed is increasingly handicapped in modern society. He may be able to satisfy minimal social standards, but he will inevitably lack his full measure of dignity because his incapacity limits his stature to less than he might otherwise attain. Only to the extent that an individual can realize his potentials, especially the development of his ability to think, can he fully achieve for himself the dignity that goes with freedom.

A person with developed rational powers has the means to be aware of all facets of his existence. In this sense he can live to the fullest. He can escape captivity to his emotions and irrational states. He can enrich his emotional life and direct it toward ever higher standards of taste and enjoyment. He can enjoy the political and economic freedoms of the democratic society. He can free himself from the bondage of ignorance and unawareness. He can make of himself a free man.

The Changes in Man's Understanding and Power

The foregoing analysis of human freedom and review of the central role of the rational powers in enabling a person to achieve his own goals demonstrate the critical importance of developing those powers. Their importance is also demonstrated by an analysis of the great changes in the world.

Many profound changes are occurring in the world today, but there is a fundamental force contributing to all of them. That force is the expanding role accorded in modern life to the rational powers of man. By using these powers to increase his knowledge, man is attempting to solve the riddles of life, space, and time which have long intrigued him. By using these powers to develop sources of new energy and means of communication, he is moving into interplanetary space. By using these powers to make a smaller world and larger weapons, he is creating new needs for international organization and understanding. By using these powers to alleviate disease and poverty, he is lowering death rates and expanding populations. By using these powers to create and use a new technology, he is achieving undreamed affluence, so that in some societies distribution has become a greater problem than production.

While man is using the powers of his mind to solve old riddles, he is creating new ones. Basic assumptions upon which mankind has long operated are being challenged or demolished. The age-old resignation to poverty and inferior status for the masses of humanity is being replaced by a drive for a life of dignity for all. Yet, just as man achieves a higher hope for all mankind, he sees also the opening of a grim age in which expansion of the power to create is matched by a perhaps greater enlargement of the power to destroy.

As man sees his power expand, he is coming to realize that the common sense which he accumulates from his own experience is not a sufficient guide to the understanding of the events in his own life or of the nature of the physical world. And, with combined uneasiness and exultation, he senses that his whole way of looking at life may be challenged in a time when men are returning from space.

Through the ages, man has accepted many kinds of propositions as truth, or at least as bases sufficient for action. Some propositions have been accepted on grounds of superstition; some on grounds of decree, dogma, or custom; some on humanistic, aesthetic, or religious grounds; some on common sense. Today, the role of knowledge derived from rational inquiry is growing. For this there are several reasons.

In the first place, knowledge so derived has proved to be man's most efficient weapon for achieving power over his environment. It prevails because it works.

More than effectiveness, however, is involved. There is high credibility in a proposition which can be arrived at or tested by persons other than those who advance it. Modesty, too, is inherent in rational inquiry, for it is an attempt to free explanations of phenomena and events from subjective preference and human authority, and to subject such explanations to validation through experience. Einstein's concept of the curvature of space cannot be demonstrated to the naked eye and may offend common sense; but persons who cannot apply the mathematics necessary to comprehend the concept can still accept it. They do this, not on Einstein's authority, but on their awareness that he used rational methods to achieve it and that those who possess the ability and facilities have tested its rational consistency and empirical validity.

In recent decades, man has greatly accelerated his systematic efforts to gain insight through rational inquiry. In the physical and biological sciences and in mathematics, where he has most successfully applied these methods, he has in a short time accumulated a vast fund of knowledge so reliable as to give him power he has never before had to understand, to predict, and to act. That is why attempts are constantly being made to apply these methods to additional areas of learning and human behavior.

The rapid increase in man's ability to understand and change the world and himself has resulted from increased application of his powers of thought. These powers have proved to be his most potent resource, and, as such, the likely key to his future.

The Central Purpose of the School

The rational powers of the human mind have always been basic in establishing and preserving freedom. In furthering personal and social effectiveness they are becoming more important than ever. They are central to individual dignity, human progress, and national survival.

The individual with developed rational powers can share deeply in the freedoms his society offers and can contribute most to the preservation of those freedoms. At the same time, he will have the best chance of understanding and contributing to the great events of his time. And the society which best develops the rational potentials of its people, along with their intuitive and aesthetic capabilities, will have the best chance of flourishing in the future. To help every person develop those powers is therefore a profoundly important objective and one which increases in importance with the passage of time. By pursuing this objective, the school can enhance spiritual and aesthetic values and the other cardinal purposes which it has traditionally served and must continue to serve.

The purpose which runs through and strengthens all other educational purposes—the common thread of education—is the development of the ability to think. This is the central purpose to which the school must be oriented if it is to accomplish either its traditional tasks or those newly accentuated by recent changes in the world. To say that it is central is not to say that it is the sole purpose or in all circumstances the most important purpose, but that it must be a pervasive concern in the work of the school. Many agencies contribute to achieving educational objectives, but this particular objective will not be generally attained unless the school focuses on it. In this context, therefore, the development of every student's rational powers must be recognized as centrally important.

chapter 3

John Dewey and the progressive-education movement, 1915–1952

Lawrence A. Cremin

John Dewey had a story—it must have been a favorite of his—about

> . . . a man who was somewhat sensitive to the movements of things
> about him. He had a certain appreciation of what things were passing
> away and dying and of what things were being born and growing. And
> on the strength of that response he foretold some of the things that
> were going to happen in the future. When he was seventy years old
> the people gave him a birthday party and they gave him credit for
> bringing to pass the things he had foreseen might come to pass (1).

With characteristic modesty, Dewey told the story autobiographically,
using it to describe his own place in the history of American life and
thought. And granted the genuinely seminal character of his contribution,
there was a measure of truth to his disclaimer.

Consider, for example, Dewey's relation to the early progressive-education movement; it provides an excellent case in point. We know that the
movement arose during the 1890's as a many-sided protest against pedagogical narrowness and inequity. It was essentially pluralistic, often self-
contradictory, and always related to broader currents of social and political
progressivism. In the universities it appeared as part of a spirited revolt
against formalism in philosophy, psychology, and the social sciences. In the

From *The School Review*, 67(Summer, 1959), 160–173. Reprinted by permission of The University of Chicago Press.

cities it emerged as one facet of a larger program of social alleviation and municipal reform. Among farmers, it became the crux of a moderate, liberal alternative to radical agrarianism.

It was at the same time the "social education" demanded by urban settlement workers, the "schooling for country life" demanded by rural publicists, the vocational training demanded by businessmen's associations and labor unions alike, and the new techniques of instruction demanded by *avant garde* pedagogues. Like progressivism writ large, it compounded a fascinating congeries of seemingly disparate elements: the romanticism of G. Stanley Hall and the realism of Jacob Riis, the scientism of Joseph Mayer Rice and the reformism of Jane Addams. Its keynote was diversity, of protest, of protestor, of proposal, and of proponent; it was a diversity destined to leave its ineradicable mark on a half-century of educational reform (2).

There were, needless to say, numerous attempts to portray this remarkable movement in its early decades; but nowhere is its extraordinary diversity more intelligently documented than in Dewey's volume *Schools of To-morrow*, published in 1915 in collaboration with his daughter Evelyn (3). Over the years, Dewey's continuing interest in pedagogical theory, his widely publicized work at the Laboratory School he and Mrs. Dewey had founded in 1896, his reputation as a tough-minded analyst of pedagogical schemes, and his unfailing support of progressive causes had combined to make him increasingly an acknowledged spokesman of the progressive-education movement. *Schools of To-morrow* did much to secure this image of him in the public mind. Within ten years the book had gone through fourteen printings, unusual for any book, unheard-of for a book about education.

Written neither as a textbook nor as a dogmatic exposition of "the new," the volume is designed "to show what actually happens when schools start out to put into practice, each in its own way, some of the theories that have been pointed to as the soundest and best ever since Plato" (3: Preface). More than anything, the Dewey of *Schools of To-morrow* is the man "sensitive to the movement of things about him." The reader is treated to a fascinating collection of glimpses—into Marietta Johnson's Organic School at Fairhope, Alabama, Junius Meriam's experimental school at the University of Missouri, the Francis Parker School in Chicago, Caroline Pratt's Play School in New York, the Kindergarten at Teachers College, Columbia University, and certain public schools of Gary, Chicago, and Indianapolis. In each instance, the guiding educational theory is given and the techniques by which the theory is put into practice are described. The approach is essentially journalistic; Dewey's enterprise is to elucidate rather than to praise or criticize.

Yet there is a very special kind of reporting here, one that bears closer examination. Richard Hofstadter has observed that the Progressive mind was typically a journalistic mind, and that its characteristic contribution was that of a socially responsible reporter-reformer (4). Certainly this was Dewey's central contribution in *Schools of To-morrow*. For in addition to the who, the what, the when, and the where, Dewey gives us a succession of social whys that quickly transform a seemingly unrelated agglomeration of pedagogical experiments into the several facets of a genuine social movement.

Merely as a record of what progressive education actually was and what it meant to *Dewey circa* 1915, the book is invaluable. The text abounds in vivid descriptions of the physical education, the nature studies, the manual work, the industrial training, and the innumerable "socialized activities" in the schools of tomorrow. There is exciting talk of more freedom for children, of greater attention to individual growth and development, of a new unity between education and life, of a more meaningful school curriculum, of a vast democratizing of culture and learning. Nowhere are the faith and optimism of the progressive-education movement more dramatically conveyed.

Moreover, as the analysis proceeds, Dewey's powers as a "socially responsible reporter-reformer" are soon apparent. He points enthusiastically to the concern with initiative, originality, and resourcefulness in the new pedagogy, deeming these qualities central to the life of a free society. He commends the breadth of the new school programs, their attention to health, citizenship, and vocation, arguing that such breadth is not only a necessary adaptation to industrialism but an effort to realize for the first time in history the democratic commitment to equal educational opportunity. He sees the new emphasis on "learning by doing" as a device par excellence to narrow the gap between school and life; and closeness to life is required "if the pupil is to understand the facts which the teacher wishes him to learn; if his knowledge is to be real, not verbal; if his education is to furnish standards of judgment and comparison" (3: 294). Even more important, perhaps, a school close to life sends into society men and women "intelligent in the pursuit of the activities in which they engage" (3: 249). People educated in this way are inevitably agents of constructive social change, and the schools which educate them are thereby intimately bound to the larger cause of reform (3: 226–227). Indeed, it is this very tie that makes progressive education progressive!

Actually, the dialectic between Dewey the observer and Dewey the reformer is probably the most intriguing thing about the volume (5). On the one hand, we know that many of the pedagogical experiments he describes grew up quite independently of his own theorizing (6). On the other hand, we recognize much in *Schools of To-morrow* that exemplifies the very things he himself was urging in pamphlets going back at least twenty years (7). The only way to reconcile the two Deweys, it seems, is to return to his own disclaimer, that he really was "the man sensitive to the movement of things about him" and to the thesis that his most seminal contribution was to develop a body of pedagogical theory which could encompass the terrific diversity of the progressive-education movement. It is no coincidence that *Democracy and Education* came a year later and wove the diverse strands of a quarter-century of educational protest and innovation into an integral theory (8). The later work has since overshadowed *Schools of To-morrow,* but the two ought not to be read apart. One is as much the classic of the early progressive-education movement as the other. Their genius was to express a pedagogical age. For their very existence, the movement was infused with larger meaning and hence could never be the same again.

World War I marks a great divide in the history of progressive education. Merely the founding of the Progressive Education Association in 1919 would have changed the movement significantly, since what had formerly been a rather loosely defined revolt against academic formalism now gained a vigorous organizational voice (9). But there were deeper changes, in the image of progressivism itself, that were bound to influence the course and meaning of educational reform.

Malcolm Cowley, in his delightful reminiscence of the twenties, *Exile's Return,* describes these changes well. He notes insightfully that intellectual protest in prewar years had mingled two quite different sorts of revolt: bohemianism and radicalism. The one was essentially an individual revolt against puritan restraint; the other, primarily a social revolt against the evils of capitalism. World War I, he argues, brought a parting of the ways. People were suddenly forced to decide what kinds of rebels they were. If they were merely rebels against puritanism, they could exist safely in Mr. Wilson's world; if they were radicals, they had no place in it (10).

Cowley's analysis provides a key to one of the important intellectual shifts of the twenties. With the end of the War, radicalism seemed no longer in fashion among the *avant garde,* particularly the artists and literati who flocked to the Greenwich Villages of New York, Chicago, and San Francisco. It did not die; it was merely eclipsed by a polyglot system of ideas which combined the doctrines of self-expression, liberty, and psychological adjustment into a confident, iconoclastic individualism that fought the constraints of Babbitry and the discipline of social reform as well. And just as prewar progressivism had given rise to a new educational outlook, one which cast the school as a lever of social change, so this postwar protest developed its own characteristic pedagogical argument: the notion that each individual has uniquely creative potentialities, and that a school in which children are encouraged freely to develop these potentialities is the best guarantee of a larger society truly devoted to human worth and excellence.

Now those who had read *Schools of To-morrow* must certainly have recognized this essentially Rousseauean stance; it had been at the heart of several of the schools Dewey had described. Yet readers who had troubled to follow Dewey's argument to the end, and who had accepted his analysis incorporating Rousseau's insights into a larger social reformism, must have noted a curious difference of emphasis here (11). For just as radicalism seemed eclipsed in the broader protest of the twenties, so it seemed to disappear from the progressive pedagogy of the decade (12). For all intents and purposes, the *avant garde* pedagogues expanded one part of what progressive education had formerly meant into its total meaning.

Nowhere is this transformation more clearly documented than in the characteristic exegesis of progressive education during the twenties, *The Child-centered School* (13). Written by Harold Rugg and Ann Shumaker in 1928, the volume attempts for the movement in its time what *Schools of To-morrow* had done a decade earlier. Its pages teem with pedagogical experiments illustrating the new articles of pedagogical faith: freedom, child interest, pupil initiative, creative self-expression, and personality development. And just as Dewey had seen a central connection with democracy as the crux of the earlier movement, so Rugg and Shumaker saw the relationship with the creative revolution of the twenties as the essential meaning of this one. To grasp the significance of the child-centered schools, they urged, one had to comprehend the historic battle of the artist against the standardization, the superficiality, and the commercialism of industrial civilization. The key to the creative revolution of the twenties was the triumph of self-expression, in art and in education as well. Hence, in creative self-expression they found the quintessential meaning of the progressive-education movement.

Dewey, of course, was not unaware of the continuing ferment in pedagogical circles. His interest in education persisted, but as the decade progressed he became less and less the sensitive observer and interpreter of the progressive-education movement and increasingly its critic. As early as 1926, for example, he attacked the studied lack of adult guidance in the *avant garde* schools with a sharpness uncommon in his writing. "Such a method," he observed, "is really stupid. For it attempts the impossible, which is always stupid; and it misconceives the conditions of independent thinking" (14: 37). Freedom, he counselled, is not something given at birth; nor is it bred of planlessness. It is something to be achieved, to be systematically wrought out in cooperation with experienced teachers, knowledgeable in their own traditions. Baby, Dewey insisted, does not know best! (14)

Two years later, the same year *The Child-centered School* appeared, Dewey used the occasion of a major address before the Progressive Education Association to reiterate his point. "Progressive schools," he noted, "set store by individuality, and sometimes it seems to be thought that orderly organization of subject-matter is hostile to the needs of students in their individual character. But individuality is something developing and to be continuously attained, not something given all at once and ready-made" (15: 201). Far from being hostile to the principle of individuality, he continued, some systematic organization of activities and subject matter is the only means for actually achieving individuality; and teachers, by virtue of their richer and fuller experience, have not only the right but the high obligation to assist students in the enterprise (15).

His strictures were not heeded, and in 1930 he leveled them even more vigorously in the concluding essay of a *New Republic* series evaluating a decade of progressive education (16). The formalism and isolation of the conventional schoolroom had literally cried out for reform, he recalled. But the point of the progressive revolt had been not to rid the school of subject matter, but rather to build a new subject matter, as well organized as the old but having a more intimate relation to the experience of students. "The relative failure to accomplish this result indicates the one-sidedness of the idea of the 'child-centered' school" (16: 205).

Then Dewey went on to a more pervasive criticism. Progressive schools, he conceded, had been most successful in furthering creativity in the arts. But this accomplishment, however much it contributed to private sensibilities, had hardly met either the social or the aesthetic needs of a democratic-industrial society. A truly progressive education, he concluded,

> . . . requires a searching study of society and its moving forces. That the traditional schools have almost wholly evaded consideration of the social potentialities of education is no reason why progressive schools should continue the evasion, even though it be sugared over with aesthetic refinements. The time ought to come when no one will be judged to be an educated man or woman who does not have insight into the basic forces of industrial and urban civilization. Only schools which take the lead in bringing about this kind of education can claim to be progressive in any socially significant sense (16: 206).

Dewey's comments seemed particularly *à propos* in the summer of 1930. Already the depression which was to envelop the nation and become the central fact of the thirties was very much in evidence. Breadlines were common in the industrial cities, and women could be seen raking through community refuse heaps as soon as garbage trucks departed. Suddenly radicalism was no longer passè; it was bohemianism that appeared a little out of date (17). Socially conscious notions of progressive education, disparaged by the *avant garde* of the twenties as "social efficiency," were now very much to the point (18).

It should be no surprise that Dewey's formulation of the meaning of progressivism in education came once again to the fore. Early in 1932 he accepted membership on a yearbook commission of the National Society of College Teachers of Education dedicated to producing a statement of philosophy of education appropriate to the times. The volume which emerged, *The Educational Frontier,* is, like *The Child-centered School,* the characteristic progressivist statement of its decade. And while its formulations are essentially collaborative, Dewey's own views are clearly discernible in two chapters he wrote jointly with his student, John L. Childs (19).

The Dewey of these chapters is now the vigorous proponent. His plea is for an educational program conceived in the broadest terms, one which has "definite reference to the needs and issues which mark and divide our domestic, economic, and political life in the generation of which we are a part" (19: 36). As with his educational outlook from the beginning, his call is for a school close to life, one that will send into society people able to understand it, to live intelligently as part of it, and to change it to suit their visions of the better life. Once again, he sees changes through education as "correlative and interactive" with changes through politics. "No social modification, slight or revolutionary, can endure except as it enters into the action of a people through their desires and purposes. This introduction and perpetuation are effected by education" (19: 318).

Dewey held essentially to this position throughout the stormy thirties. To George Counts's provocative question "Dare the school build a new social order?" Dewey replied that in an industrial society with its multiplicity of political and educative agencies, the school could never be the main determinant of political, intellectual, or moral change (20). "Nevertheless," he continued, "while the school is not a sufficient condition, it is a necessary condition of *forming the understanding and the disposition* that are required to maintain a genuinely changed social order" (21). It would be revolution enough, Dewey once told an NEA audience, were educators to begin to recognize the fact of social change and to act upon that recognition in the schools (22).

Dewey steadfastly opposed indoctrination in the form of the inculcation of fixed social beliefs. But he did contend that for schools to be progressive, teachers would have to select the newer scientific, technological, and cultural forces producing changes in the old order, estimate their outcomes if given free play, and see what could be done to make the schools their ally (23). To some, of course, this was as crass a form of indoctrination as any; and Dewey was criticized on the one hand by those who insisted that his notions would cast the school into an indefensible presentism at the expense of traditional values and verities, and on the other by those in the progressive camp who maintained that any social guidance by adults was really an unwarranted form of imposition.

Dewey replied to both groups in what was destined to be his most important pedagogical work of the thirties, *Experience and Education.* The volume is really a restatement of aspects of his educational outlook in the context of the criticisms, distortions, and misunderstandings which had grown up over two decades. There is little fundamentally new, except perhaps the tone. Progressive educators, he suggested, should begin to think

> . . . in terms of Education itself rather than in terms of some 'ism about education, even such an 'ism as "progressivism." For in spite of itself any movement that thinks and acts in terms of an 'ism becomes so involved in reaction against other 'isms that it is unwittingly controlled by them. For it then forms its principles by reaction against them instead of by a comprehensive constructive survey of actual needs, problems, and possibilities (24).

By 1938, Dewey the sensitive observer could already note, probably with a measure of sadness, that the movement was devoting too much of its energy to internecine ideological conflict and too little, perhaps, to the advancement of its own cause.

Frederic Lilge, in a perceptive essay he recently published in a volume honoring Robert Ulich, contends that Dewey's pedagogical progressivism embodies a fundamental inconsistency which Dewey never really resolves (25). A theory which seems to harmonize the school with the larger social environment, Lilge argues, and which casts the school as a lever of reform, inevitably faces a twofold difficulty: first in determining which social goals to serve in the school; and second, in deciding whether or not to embark on an ever broader program of political reform outside the school. Thus

> Dewey was confronted by two equally repellent alternatives: pursuing his basic aim of adjusting the schools to the social environment, he could integrate them with institutions and practices whose underlying values he rejected; or he could attempt to withdraw them from being thus corrupted, but at the cost of sacrificing that closeness to actual life which it was one of the main aims of his educational philosophy to establish (25: 29).

Lilge contends that Dewey accepted neither, and that the thirties saw him and a number of influential followers increasingly thrust into a clearly political program of reform, both via the schools and outside them. Their manifesto was Counts's pamphlet, *Dare the School Build a New Social Order;* their statement of educational principles was *The Educational Frontier;* their intellectual organ was the *Social Frontier,* a journal which appeared regularly in the decade following 1934.

Now Lilge himself grants that his analysis is far more relevant to some of Dewey's disciples than to Dewey himself. Even so, some clarification is needed. For to pose the dilemma in the first place is to misread the relationship between progressive education and progressivism writ large, particularly as Dewey perceived it. Dewey had no illusions about the school changing society on its own; that educational and political reform would have to go hand in hand was the progressive view from the beginning (26). Nor did the notion of adjusting the school to society imply that the school would have to accommodate itself to all institutions and practices. Dewey wanted schools to use the stuff of reality to educate men and women intelligently about reality. His notion of adjustment was an adjustment *of* conditions, not *to* them, a remaking of existing conditions, not a mere remaking of self and individual to fit into them (27). And as for the corrupting influence of life itself, Dewey was no visionary; the problem for him was not to build *the perfect society* but *a better society*. To this he thought a school that educated for intelligence about reality could make a unique contribution.

Dewey restated these faiths in the introductory essay he wrote for Elsie Clapp's 1952 volume, *The Use of Resources in Education;* it is probably his last major statement on education (28). Once again, he returns to the role of sensitive observer. "In the course of more than half a century of participation in the theory and practice of education," he writes, "I have witnessed many successes and many failures in what is popularly known as 'progressive education,' but is also known as 'the new education,' 'modern education,' and so on." He sees the triumph of the movement in the changed life-conditions of the American classroom, in a greater awareness of the needs of the growing human being, in the warmer personal relations between teachers and students. But as with all reform victories, he sees attendant danger. No education is progressive, he warns, unless it is making progress. And he observes somewhat poignantly that in schools and colleges across the country, progressive education has been converted into a set of fixed rules and procedures "to be applied to educational problems externally, the way mustard plasters, for example, are applied." If this ossification continues, he fears progressive education will end up guilty of the very formalism it sought to correct, a formalism "fit for the foundations of a totalitarian society and, for the same reason, fit to subvert, pervert and destroy the foundations of a democratic society."

"For the creation of democratic society," he concludes, "we need an educational system where the process of moral-intellectual development is in practice as well as in theory a cooperative transaction of inquiry engaged in by free, independent human beings who treat ideas and the heritage of the past as means and methods for the further enrichments of life, quantitatively and qualitatively, who use the good attained for the discovery and establishment of something better." Dewey's sentence is involved, complex, and overly long; but it embodies the essence of the movement as he saw it. Those who would understand progressive education would do well to ponder it, as would those who set out to build today's schools of tomorrow.

NOTES

1. *John Dewey: The Man and His Philosophy* (Cambridge, Massachusetts: Harvard University Press, 1930), p. 174.
2. See my essay, "The Progressive Movement in American Education: A Reappraisal," *Harvard Educational Review*, XXVII (Fall, 1957), 251–270.
3. John Dewey and Evelyn Dewey, *Schools of To-morrow* (New York: E. P. Dutton & Co., 1915).
4. Richard Hofstadter, *The Age of Reform* (New York: Alfred A. Knopf, 1955), p. 185.
5. Actually, Evelyn Dewey visited the several schools and wrote the descriptive chapters of the volume; but no pun is intended by the phrase "Dewey the observer." The larger design of the book—both descriptive and analytical—is obviously the elder Dewey's.
6. One need only check some of the independent accounts, for example, Marietta Johnson, "Thirty Years with an Idea" (Unpublished manuscript in the library of Teachers College, Columbia University, 1939), or Caroline Pratt, *I Learn from Children* (New York: Simon and Schuster, 1948).
7. The ideas of *My Pedagogic Creed* (New York: E. L. Kellogg & Co., 1897), *The School and Society* (Chicago: University of Chicago Press, 1899), *The Child and the Curriculum* (Chicago: University of Chicago Press, 1902), and "The School as Social Center" (published in the National Education Association *Proceedings* for 1902) are particularly apparent. See Melvin C. Baker, *Foundations of John Dewey's Educational Theory* (New York: King's Crown Press, 1955) for an analysis of Dewey's pedagogical ideas prior to 1904.
8. John Dewey, *Democracy and Education* (New York: Macmillan Co., 1916).
9. The organization was founded by a young reformist educator named Stanwood Cobb, who had come under the influence of Marietta Johnson. Dewey refused a number of early invitations to associate himself with the group, but later served as its honorary president. The best account of the Association's first years is given in Robert Holmes Beck, "American Progressive Education, 1875–1930" (Unpublished Ph.D. thesis, Yale University, 1942).
10. Malcolm Cowley, *Exile's Return* (New York: W. W. Norton & Co., 1934), chap. ii. Henry F. May contends that the shift toward what Cowley calls bohemianism actually began well before the War. See "The Rebellion of the Intellectuals, 1912–1917," *American Quarterly*, VIII (Summer, 1956), 114–126.
11. The incorporation is most clearly evident in chapter xii of *Schools of To-morrow*. See also Dewey's comments on Rousseau in chapters vii and ix of *Democracy and Education*.
12. Radicalism even tended to disappear from the pedagogical formulations of many political radicals. See, for example, Agnes de Lima, *Our Enemy the Child* (New York: New Republic, 1925), chap. xii.
13. Harold Rugg and Ann Shumaker, *The Child-centered School* (Yonkers-on-Hudson, New York: World Book Co., 1928).
14. His essay, originally published in the *Journal of the Barnes Foundation*, is reprinted in John Dewey et al., *Art and Education*, pp. 32–40.

15. John Dewey, "Progressive Education and the Science of Education," *Progressive Education*, V (July-August-September, 1928), 197–204.
16. John Dewey, "How Much Freedom in New Schools?" *New Republic*, LXIII (July 9, 1930), 204–206. The decade to which the *New Republic* refers is, of course, 1919–1929. The implication, that progressive education really began with the founding of the Progressive Education Association, is oft-repeated but erroneous.
17. Cowley's Epilogue in the 1951 reissue of *Exile's Return* is an interesting commentary on this point.
18. The common cry was that Dewey had been too much the rationalist to develop an adequate theory of creativity. See, for example, *The Child-centered School*, pp. iv, 324–325.
19. William H. Kilpatrick (ed.), *The Educational Frontier* (New York: D. Appleton-Century, 1933). Dewey actually wrote chapters ii and ix, though as joint efforts with Childs. See also "The Crucial Role of Intelligence," *Social Frontier*, I (February, 1935), 9–10.
20. See George S. Counts, *Dare the School Build a New Social Order?* (New York: John Day Co., 1932). The tension between bohemianism and radicalism within the progressive-education movement is dramatically portrayed by Counts in a 1932 address to the Progressive Education Association, "Dare Progressive Education Be Progressive?" *Progressive Education*, IX (April, 1932), 257–263.
21. John Dewey, "Education and Social Change," *Social Frontier*, III (May, 1937), 235–238. Italics mine. See also "Can Education Share in Social Reconstruction?" *Social Frontier*, I (October, 1934), 11–12.
22. John Dewey, "Education for a Changing Social Order," National Education Association *Proceedings*, 1934, pp. 744–752.
23. John Dewey, "Education and Social Change," *op. cit.* and "Education, Democracy, and Socialized Economy," *Social Frontier*, V (December, 1938), 71–72. The latter article deals with an exchange between John L. Childs and Boyd H. Bode in the previous issue of *Social Frontier*.
24. John Dewey, *Experience and Education* (New York: Macmillan Co., 1938), pp. vi–vii.
25. Frederic Lilge, "Politics and the Philosophy of Education," in *Liberal Traditions in Education*, ed. George Z. F. Bereday (Cambridge, Massachusetts: Graduate School of Education, Harvard University, 1958), pp. 27–49.
26. Dewey makes the point on page 226 of *Schools of To-morrow* and in Article V of *My Pedagogic Creed*.
27. This is a central point in view of contemporary attacks on Dewey. See *The Educational Frontier*, p. 312.
28. Elsie Ripley Clapp, *The Use of Resources in Education* (New York: Harper & Bros., 1952), pp. vii–xi.

chapter 4

The Conant report and
the committee of ten:
a historical appraisal

Bernard Mehl

Observing certain historical parallels, which are usually interesting in their own right, may lead to deeper understanding of today's pressing problems. One such problem is the state of our educational system.

For a number of years Americans have been bombarded with articles, books, and radio and television programs whose sole intent is to persuade us that something is radically wrong with the American secondary school. During the same period schoolmen have made a constant though feeble effort to defend the system, but in the main their audience has consisted of fellow school officials and professors of education. In 1959 a report was published by James B. Conant, and with it the issue of public secondary education seems to have taken on a new aspect.[1]

An earlier report, that of the Committee of Ten, published in 1894, was in its time hailed as "the most important educational document ever published in this country."[2] It was shaped by another Harvard president,

[1] *The American High School Today: A First Report to Interested Citizens.* New York: McGraw-Hill Book Company, Inc., 1959. In the Foreword, John W. Gardner, president of the Carnegie Corporation of New York, states: "It would be difficult to overestimate the importance of such a report at this time" (page xii).

[2] W. T. Harris, as quoted in Frank A. Hill, "The Report of the Committee of Ten," *Sixty-fourth Annual Meeting of the American Institute of Instruction: Lectures, Discussions, and Proceedings.* Boston: the Institute, 1894, p. 174.

From *Educational Research Bulletin*, XXXIX(February 10, 1960), 29–38, 56. Reprinted by permission of the author and publisher.

Charles W. Eliot.[3] Like Conant, Eliot had been trained in science and had become president of Harvard at a rather early age. Both Eliot and Conant were concerned with the reform of American public education. Also both were active in political matters. The historical parallel extends beyond the similar careers of Eliot and Conant into the state of secondary education both at the turn of the century and at mid-century.[4]

In 1890 the country was awakening to the fact that the industrial revolution had taken place. That year the Bureau of the Census declared the Western frontier closed. In a comparatively brief span of time, changes were occurring which were altering the lives of most people. The population then, as now, showed a phenomenal growth—from 69,947,714 in 1890 to 105,710,620 in 1920.[5] Approximately one and a half times more immigrants had arrived in the United States during this thirty-year period than in the entire sixty-year period prior to 1890. The growth of inventions and productivity raised the standard of living to a new level, and the list of people's wants was growing. Reflecting this general growth was the remarkable expansion of the public high school. It was seen as fulfilling the American revolution in education by granting more people the opportunity to receive instruction beyond the bare essentials offered by the existing elementary schools.[6] During the nineties, secondary education, particularly the high school, became the center of attention, discussion, and debate among leaders in education as well as interested persons in labor, business, and journalism. The function of this intensive scrutiny was then, as it is now, to establish the aim and direction of secondary education and to determine the exact position it was to occupy in the American educational hierarchy. This scrutiny into the affairs of public secondary education took place at a time of political, social, and intellectual ferment.

The ferment in the nineties concerned itself with conditions similar to those facing us today. Politically the United States was moving toward Theodore Roosevelt's Square Deal and Woodrow Wilson's New Freedom. On the international scene the United States was seeking to enter world affairs as a big power with manifest destiny as the order of the day. In

[3] One of the original members of the Committee of Ten, Oscar D. Robinson, stated in effect that the report represented the work of Eliot. *See* O. D. Robinson, "The Work of the Committee of Ten," *School Review*, II (June, 1894), p. 367.

[4] For a comprehensive treatment of the educational climate of the 1890's, *see* Bernard Mehl, "The High School at the Turn of the Century," 1954 (a doctoral dissertation on file in the library of the University of Illinois), Chapter VI.

[5] Bureau of the Census and Social Service Research Council, *Historical Statistics of the United States, 1789–1945: A Supplement to the Statistical Abstract of the United States.* Washington, D.C.: U.S. Department of Commerce, 1949, p. 25.

[6] *See* M. Adler and M. Mayer, *The Revolution in Education.* Chicago: the University Press, 1952. Part I cites 1850 as the point of no return for the changed attitude toward education.

the social field the air was filled with talk about the eight-hour day and the rise of the common man. Legislation concerning woman and child labor, the rise of the Populist movement, and civil service reform all attest to the intensive social stirrings of the time. In addition, the intellectual tempo of American life was increased by the "new intellectuals"—William Graham Sumner, Frederick Jackson Turner, Thorstein Veblen, Richard Ely, Lester Ward, John Dewey, Josiah Royce, and William James, who were concentrating their energies in the social sciences and philosophy; A. A. Michelson and J. Willard Gibbs were doing fundamental research in physical science.

The nineties set the stage for the next sixty years on these fronts by shaping the intellectual framework for the great debates which were to follow. Here were the beginnings of a new social, political, economic, and philosophical view which was to find its way into the body of contemporary American thought. The element common to the entire decade was the conscious effort to evaluate existing institutions in light of the changes in American life brought on by new technology and industry.

Within the ferment of American life today are conditions not unlike those which characterized the period of the nineties—a boom in population, a revolution in technology brought about by the advent of automation and nuclear energy, a new quest for justice in the struggle for social equality and full employment, and the emergence of the United States as a leader in world affairs. We are also in the process of reexamining our existing institutions including education; again secondary education has our fullest attention.[7]

To force historical parallelism into strict geometric structure would be much too naive and would distort reality. Today we are taking stock of the consequences of what John Galbraith calls our "affluent society," whereas the people of the nineties were entering a new era. Today almost all American youth receive education as far as high school. In 1900 about 11.4 per cent of the high school–age population was attending secondary schools.[8]

We must now weigh the consequences of an educational system which has opened its doors to the bulk of the school-age population. Yet the major questions we are asking of our system are the same that the Committee of Ten asked when it sought to establish an educational system geared to the future. What kind of education is best for all students attending secondary school, regardless of personal goal, was the crucial problem faced by the Committee of Ten and now by James B. Conant. The Committeee of Ten thought that the best terminal education was

[7] The literature on current educational criticism is too voluminous to list here. A good approach to the subject is Cecil Winfield Scott and Clyde M. Hill's *Public Education under Criticism.* New York: Prentice-Hall, Inc., 1954.

[8] *Statistical Summary of Education, 1949–1950.* Washington, D.C.: U.S. Department of Health, Education, and Welfare, Office of Education, 1953, p. 19.

also the best education needed for entrance into college. The high school was to be both terminal and preparatory by offering a program of general education consisting of four areas: language, mathematics, science, and history. The colleges were asked to accept, with only one general stipulation, the graduate of any high school:

> . . . it is necessary that the colleges and scientific schools of the country should accept for admission to appropriate courses of their instruction the attainments of any youth who has passed creditably through a good secondary school course, no matter to what group of subjects he may have mainly devoted himself in the secondary school.[9]

The point to be made here is that the Committee of Ten, especially Charles W. Eliot, the chief architect and defender of the Report, was conscious of the public nature of the secondary school. They wished to make secondary education popular, but at the same time they sought to put it on as high a level as the private school, which served but a small part of the adolescent population. To achieve this dual goal, the Committee of Ten interpreted the phrase "equality of educational opportunity" to mean that high schools should be free, that one course of study should be just as good as another and should be staffed by superior teachers and given the best equipment, that a basic course should be taken by all students, and that a high school diploma from an accredited school should be the key to college entrance. Before the efforts of the Committee of Ten are assessed, the nature of the courses of study which were supposedly equated with one another needs to be explored. The proposition that a bona fide high school diploma be the sole test for college admission rested on the adoption of the program of study recommended by the Committee of Ten.

As stated earlier, the Committee believed that each high school should offer as major subject areas language, science, history, and mathematics. In these areas no rigid list of requirements was set up. Thus in the language area which of the languages to be taught was not specified; in history, political economy was not necessarily included. The Committee further demonstrated the flexibility of its thinking by an attempt to allow for industrial arts in the science area: "If it were desired to provide more amply for subjects thought to have practical importance in trade or the useful arts, it would be easy to provide options in such subjects for some of the science contained in the third and fourth years of the 'English' programme."[10]

Despite this flexibility certain courses were indeed specified. The choice

[9] National Education Association. *Report of the Committee of Ten on Secondary School Studies, with the Reports of the Conferences Arranged by the Committee.* New York: American Book Company, 1894, p. 52.
[10] *Ibid.,* p. 50.

was among four parallel courses of study, though some freedom was allowed within any one of these. As the Committee stated, "numerous possible transpositions of subjects will occur to every experienced teacher who examines these specimen programmes."[11] Four curriculums were suggested: the classical, the Latin-scientific, the modern-language, and the English. The last three were fairly similar; the differences occurred mainly in the language offerings. In order to avoid undue repetition, only the English curriculum will be presented here.[12]

First year	Periods	Third year	Periods
Latin or German or French	5	Latin or German or French	4
English	4	English	5
Algebra	4	Mathematics (Algebra 2 and Geometry 2)	4
History	4		
Physical Geography	3	Astronomy ½ year and Meteorology ½ year	3
	20	History	4
			20

Second year	Periods	Fourth year	Periods
Latin or German or French	5 or 4	Latin or German or French	4
English	3 or 4	English	4
Geometry	3	Chemistry	3
Physics	3	Trigonometry and Higher Algebra	3
History	3	History	3
Botany or Zoology	3	Geology or Physiography ½ year and Anatomy, Physiology, and Hygiene ½ year	3
	20		20

Surprisingly, this English curriculum was considered a compromise in favor of those forces that wanted to denature the strict college-preparatory courses of study dominating many of the existing high schools.

This then was the answer that the Committee of Ten proposed for an expanding high school and an expanding America: four years of foreign language, four years of English, five years of science, four years of history, and four years of mathematics for all students attending high school. The intent of the Committee was to liberalize the offerings in the high school. This liberalizing process was to take place within the framework of the literary and humanistic tradition then prevalent in education. To Eliot, the Report represented an additive process of extending the high school

[11] *Ibid.*, p. 49.
[12] For the four curriculums, see *Ibid.*, pp. 46–47.

curriculums into new areas of knowledge and skills. As conservative as the Report seems to be today, we must remember that, in carrying out its function of seeking to discover "the principles which should govern all secondary school programmes"[13] the Committee took issue with certain established principles.

Charles W. Eliot readily accepted the idea that educational opportunity should not be too narrowly conceived. How, he asked, can an individual really measure up to his inherent capabilities if a prescribed program of education is forced on him? Eliot believed that schools had to diversify their offerings to allow for differences in the abilities of students. Talent, he thought, was universally distributed, but its form differed among individuals. Therefore, if the Jeffersonian tradition to tap talent no matter where it was found was to be kept alive, the high school had to broaden its course of study to account for and unearth differing talents. Eliot seemed to realize that the concept of the universal man had passed away and that the future called for a different image of the educated man. He insisted on the elective system as the wedge to free American education from the shackles of prescribed classicalism:

> Now, if the only school that the youth has attended has had a narrow, uniform programme, containing a limited number of subjects without options among them . . . its range of subjects will be too small to permit the sure fulfillment of this all-important function of a good secondary school—the thorough exploration of all its pupils' capacities.[14]

Eliot's views on education were geared to the doctrine of equivalence. Election was to be permitted among groups of subjects deemed equal in educational significance. Providing for disciplined thought and disciplined judgment based on scientific investigation and keyed to individual differences was Eliot's way of opening up the offerings of the secondary school. Eliot's fundamental doctrine as applied to the instruction of the young was a combination of the theory of formal discipline and faith in the ability of the scientific and historical studies to reveal powers untouched by Greek, Latin, and mathematics.

In spite of all the deficiencies in the Report of the Committee of Ten, and these deficiencies included, as Conant's views include, a limited outlook as to the breadth of high school education, the unmistakable optimism of Eliot and Conant is clear—a belief in the intelligence and maturity of youth combined with an aversion to a prescribed authority. Eliot reflected a general concern which existed among many educators—the fear that the

13 *Ibid.*, p. 50.
14 Charles W. Eliot, "Undesirable and Desirable Uniformity in Schools." National Education Association. *Journal of Proceedings and Addresses: Session of the Year 1892, Held at Saratoga Springs, New York.* New York: the Association, 1893, pp. 83–84.

day would arrive when a two- or three-class system of education would be made part of the American educational scheme. It was Charles De Garmo who sounded this warning in 1894 in his comment on the Report of the Committee of Ten: "The whole scheme of education has been based on the principle that higher education is for a single class. . . . It has been broadened . . . to include another class. . . . It must still farther be broadened to take in all classes. Education cannot remain a caste."[15] In De Garmo's terms the Committee of Ten succeeded in broadening education to include a second class, "those who take the sciences for the basis of their life work."[16]

Conant has faced the same general problem as the Committee of Ten: How can the high school program be broadened so as to account for differing talents and still retain a high-level educational program within the single-track system peculiar to the American heritage? There is, however, an essential difference between the 1890's and 1950's. The Committee of Ten made its pronouncements in the face of an expanding high school population which was just beginning to make itself felt. Generally the 1890's was a decade of educational scarcity. Conant, on the other hand, is addressing his study and convictions to an era of educational affluence. This does not mean that everyone in the high school–age group is in school; there are still pockets of scarcity.[17] Conant is avowedly seeking answers to the questions issuing from the present state of mass education.

Given this important distinction in the historical setting, the two reports necessarily present different views; but their striking similarity should be noted first. Both use the concept of a comprehensive high school. The Committee of Ten sought to maintain comprehension by establishing four parallel courses of study and allowing for options in vocational and business programs. The Conant Report notes that the comprehensive high school is one "whose programs correspond to the educational needs of *all* the youth of the community."[18] It seems as if Conant wished to break the pattern of parallel courses imposed on the high school by the Committee of Ten. His second recommendation is that "there would be no classification of students according to clearly defined and labeled programs or tracks."[19] However, he would have separate patterns of courses for the academic as well as for the vocational students; counselors, who would increase in number, would aid the students in choosing the proper sequences.

---

[15] De Garmo, Charles. "Discussion." National Education Association. *Journal of Proceedings and Addresses: Session of the Year 1894, Held at Asbury Park, New Jersey.* St. Paul, Minnesota: the Association, 1895, p. 512.

[16] *Ibid.*

[17] See John H. Niemeyer, "Splitting the Social Atom," *Saturday Review,* XLII (September 12, 1959), pp. 18–19, 53, for a report on the "alienated" groups in American society who are denied education because of their "social class and minority group status."

[18] *Op. cit.,* p. 12.

[19] *Ibid.,* p. 46.

Here Conant is advocating a flexible parallelism instead of the elimination of parallel sequences. This position does not break radically with the Committee of Ten's Report, for Conant recommends that all students be required to take a program of general education. This would include

> . . . four years of English, three or four years of social studies—including two years of history (one of which should be American history) and a senior course in American problems or American government—one year of mathematics in the ninth grade (algebra or general mathematics), and at least one year of science in the ninth or tenth grade. . . .[20]

This academic program is similar, although diluted, to the English course of study drawn up by the Committee of Ten. This dilution is better understood in the light of the expanded high school. But understood or not, it seems clear that Conant and Eliot agree that the best education for both terminal and continuing students rests within a program of English, mathematics, history, social studies, and science. In fact, at least half of the twenty-one recommendations listed by Conant deal with some phase of the academic core; fewer touch upon the slow learner or the vocationally oriented pupil. The Committee of Ten failed to make direct provision for the development of "marketable skills"; but, as noted earlier, they did clear the way for those skills.

The most striking similarity between the two reports occurs in the ninth recommendation in which Conant lists four years of a foreign language, four years of mathematics, four years of English, three years of science, and three years of social studies as the basic course of study to be taken by the academically talented students. With the exception of science and social studies, this is the same as the English curriculum of the Committee of Ten.

Among the differences between the two reports is the fact that Conant accepts the presence of vocational courses. Also the members of the Committee of Ten did not address themselves to the question of a guidance service since most students who were fortunate enough to get to high school were academically rather than vocationally motivated.

Another significant distinction rises from the fact that Conant has acknowledged the direction of the schools by local boards and their administrators. By addressing himself to the administrators instead of the teachers, Conant implies that teachers are manipulable; they are to have no voice in the programs to be undertaken. Because of this, Conant is in far more danger of failure than were his predecessors in the 1890's. The curriculum advocated by Eliot reflected the desires of schoolmen acting not as agents of the community, but as members of a scholarly group who be-

[20] *Ibid.*, p. 47.

lieved they were bringing fundamental education to the community. The efforts of the Committee of Ten were most successful in those years when the secondary school lay in the hands of liberally trained teachers and administrators who had not yet met the problem of mass secondary education or the power of local control. Their hold on secondary education, however, was weakened by the 1920's.

In 1918 administrators who found greater merit in the needs of the community, the home, and the child than in academic excellence cheered the appearance of the Commission on the Reorganization of Secondary Education. These administrators and the education professors who were allied with them believed that educational quality rested, not in academic excellence, but in the so-called "seven cardinal principles" of the 1918 Report, whose emphasis was on social and personal adjustment.

The writer has no intention of judging either the stand taken by these leaders of public education who were committed to the cardinal principles[21] or the stand taken by Eliot and Conant. What seems clear enough is that Conant, in reiterating the basic views of the Committee of Ten, is trying to use a unique strategy to effect them in a period of mass secondary schooling.

The strategy employed is direct and simple, for he tries to make use of the existing framework of the secondary schools—its ideas, personnel, organization, and program—to reinstitute academic quality. One phase of the Conant strategy calls for the enlistment of the guidance services, which he believes should be given greater and greater power in the schools. But even this tactic may fail him in his attempt to restore the emphasis on intellectual quality. Handing academic responsibility over to the guidance service may be analogous to handing the power to make television quality-minded over to the networks' public relations departments.[22]

With the advent of the Sputniks and the Lunik, Conant's strategy might work, but it should be remembered that in essence he is trying to resurrect both the ghost and the era of Charles W. Eliot. Educational programs in the United States, whatever else they are, are a function of a cultural image of the American people. If that image includes a strong emphasis on intellectual attainment, the public will get Conant's message and find its own means of making sure that the schools carry out that message. On the other hand, if society sees the educational system as fulfilling the diversified functions needed for attaining social status and cohesiveness with a little bit of intellectualism thrown in, then his strategy will fail. Perhaps new leadership is the answer.

[21] Edgar V. Friedenberg in *The Vanishing Adolescent* (Boston: Beacon Press, 1959) points out that the chief function of the high school as seen by schoolmen is to turn out good Americans and not scholars.

[22] Not too long ago a dedicated guidance man remarked that Conant would never get guidance persons to help him regiment students into academic programs. Conant, he said, just didn't have the guidance point of view.

The point has beeen made that the leaders who are now administering high schools are not basically committed to the view of James B. Conant. Therefore it is not surprising to find that there is a move on the part of people outside of education (for example, Rickover, Bestor, Reisman, and Whyte) to criticize that leadership. These critics will not be accepted as replacements for the existing leadership. A return of educational quality in the hands of a reconstituted teaching profession committed to that quality seems to be the only solution.[23]

[23] On this point Myron Lieberman offers the most provocative answer. See *Education as a Profession*. Englewood Cliffs, New Jersey: Prentice-Hall, 1956.

chapter 5

William James' impact upon American education

Harold A. Larrabee

Last year marked the fiftieth anniversary of the death of William James (1842–1910), whose influence upon American education, though over-shadowed by that of John Dewey, was greater than many have supposed. It was an influence exerted not directly through specific writings on educational subjects, but rather through the impact of a vibrant and liberating personality making itself felt in many areas of American life. For it was James' pioneering example which, more than any other single factor, helped "to make the world safe" for the pragmatic reformers who succeeded him.

But the quick fading away of even the strongest personality, once life has ended, was vividly described by James himself in his tribute to Emerson at Concord in 1903, when he said:

The pathos of death is this, that when the days of one's life are ended . . . what remains of one in memory should be so slight a thing. The phantom of an attitude, the echo of a certain mode of thought, a few pages of print, some invention, or some victory we gained in a brief critical hour, are all that can survive of the best of us.[1]

This slipping away of the once-living person has been accentuated in James' case by the turbulence of our century since the outbreak of World

[1] William James, "Memories and Studies" (New York: Longmans, Green, 1917), p. 19.

From *School and Society*, LXXXIX(February 25, 1961), 84–86. Reprinted by permission of the publisher.

War I in 1914. That circumstance has cut us off, psychologically, from what now appear to have been the "innocent" and "confident" decades of the 1880's and 1890's. Unlike John Dewey, who lived on through more than half of our century, William James seems to us to belong irrevocably to the age of McKinley and the Teddy Roosevelt of "the strenuous life."

Today it has become fashionable to disparage James as the outmoded champion of romantic individualism and buoyant optimism in dealing with the concrete issues of daily living. He never hesitated to tackle the difficult questions of *Lebensphilosophie* or to make his teachings available in popular as well as academic form. When he spoke or wrote, it always was with such vital warmth that he had many thousands of listeners and readers outside college and university circles. In the often-quoted words of the late President Lowell of Harvard, "Philosophy is no good unless it is hot. James always made it hot."[2] This was because, in the words of Professor Donald C. Williams, James "cared about philosophy, as he cared about life. If ever the very fire of reality burned in any human mind, it burned in his."[3]

In all things educational James was the enemy of convention and formalism. His colleague, George Santayana, called him "an Irishman among the Brahmins"; and when someone suggested a statue in his memory at Cambridge, it was said that, to be authentic, it would have to show James "trampling on a textbook and looking out the window." For the gifted James had little patience with the cut-and-dried methods of instruction. "Results," he once wrote, "should not be too voluntarily aimed at or too busily thought of."

It was John Dewey who connected James' remarkable versatility and profound interest in all things human with "the nonacademic character of his education," which enabled him to "escape the academic conditions that too often have a benumbing effect." Dewey attributed the latter to "our tendency to exaggerate the phase of technique, of formal skill, in quasi-prescribed lines of thinking."[4]

As is well known, James' childhood tutelage by "educative ladies" was followed by an ever-changing series of tutors and private schools as the nomadic, well-endowed Jameses traveled from New York to London, Paris, Boulogne-sur-mer, Geneva, and Bonn. The greatest educational influence of all, of course, was the animated family circle presided over by "the almost perfect father," Henry James the Elder, whose ample inheritance and domestic tastes enabled him to devote himself to the upbringing of his four sons and one daughter.

When it came to the question of going to college, however, the 16-

[2] Henry James, in "In Commemoration of William James, 1842–1942" (New York: Columbia University Press, 1942), p. 3.
[3] Donald C. Williams, in *ibid.*, p. 97.
[4] John Dewey, in *ibid.*, pp. 48–49.

year-old youth wrote to Edgar Van Winkle, then a student at Union College from which the elder Henry James had been graduated in 1830, "When I left you in Schenectady it was with the almost certainty of becoming a fellow man with you at Union College. When I spoke to my father about it, I found he was not in favor of my going to any college whatsoever. He says colleges are hot beds of corruption where it's impossible to learn anything."[5] This paternal opposition to institutionalism in any form was sufficiently relaxed three years later to enable William to enter the new Lawrence Scientific School at Harvard and later the Medical School, where he received his only "earned" degree.

Later in life, James' detestation of "academicism" displayed itself in his enthusiastic hospitality toward unorthodox educators such as Thomas Davidson and a whole succession of mavericks known as "James's cranks." But the strongest blow which he struck against what he called "the Mandarin disease" was his famous essay, "The Ph.D. Octopus," in which he denounced the possible coming about of a state of things "in which no man of science or letters will be accounted respectable unless some kind of badge or diploma is stamped upon him, and in which bare personality will be a mark of outcast estate."[6]

At the same time that James was throwing down his challenges to formalism in education, he himself was engaged industriously in erecting a new science of psychology that was to have profound effects upon American educational practices. Before James, American psychology had been a branch of philosophy, largely speculative in character, called "Philosophy of Mind." The publication of "Principles of Psychology" in 1890 changed all that by placing the science "foursquare upon a physiological foundation." The frank empiricism of the book came as a shock and a revelation: here was "raw unverbalized life" regarded as "more of a revealer" of truth than "*logos* or discursive thought." It was a radically motor psychology; its base was biological. But James was not engaged in reducing psychology to biology; his concern was with the whole living, acting man. In a style that fairly scintillated, he portrayed "the universe with the lid off," a baffling mixture of the stable and the unstable, the recurrent and the novel, and the rational and the irrational, all "lending poignancy to existence" and giving it "the zest, the tingle, the excitement of reality."

Two years after the "Principles" appeared, James was asked to give "a few public lectures on psychology to the Cambridge teachers," later published as "Talks to Teachers." He warned his hearers that

Psychology is not something from which you can deduce definite programs and schemes and methods of instruction for immediate classroom

5 Ms. in James Collection, Houghton Library, Harvard University.
6 William James, *op. cit.*, p. 334.

use. Psychology is a science and teaching is an art, and sciences never generate arts directly of themselves. An intermediary inventive mind must make the application by using its originality. . . . To know psychology is absolutely no guarantee that we shall be good teachers.[7]

As a Harvard professor, James made many pronouncements concerning the aims of higher education. Pragmatism so often has been criticized for neglecting excellence that some readers may be surprised to discover that James regarded "a sense for human superiority" as the very mark of the educated man. Higher education, he said, should "set up in us a lasting relish for the better kind of man, a loss of appetite for mediocrities, and a disgust for cheap jacks."

In these days, when some educational administrators seem eager to summarize individual children on punch cards to be fed into computers, it may be well to recall James' passionate combination of individualism and pluralism together with his deep antipathy to the sociologist's preoccupation with averages, "with its obligatory undervaluing of individual differences," which he held to be "the most pernicious and immoral of fatalisms." He wrote, in a familiar passage, "I am against bigness and greatness in all its forms and with the invisible molecular forces that work from individual to individual. . . . The bigger the unit you deal with, the hollower, the more brutal, the more mendacious the life displayed."[8]

Long before beatniks had been invented, James diagnosed the creeping paralysis of will that was causing "an irremediable flatness to come over the world," and sought to counteract it by drawing upon fresh sources of energy and moral courage. He clearly recognized, as do the contemporary Existentialists, that life demands decisions and commitments where complete scientific knowledge is not available and where the force of commitments may decide issues. As a militant liberal, he fought against imperialism and war long before such causes were popular. A world calling for moral heroism, as the late Professor R. B. Perry said, "suited his taste in universes" and "made life worth living."

It was this attitude of eagerness in confronting a changing, challenging world full of risk and adventure which was James' greatest contribution to American education, for it altered the orientation of philosophy from past to future, "from abstraction and insufficiency, from verbal solutions, from bad *a priori* reasons, from fixed principles, closed systems, and pretended absolutes and origins . . . towards concreteness and adequacy, towards facts, towards action, and towards power."[9] In education, this meant turning away from tradition and theory toward prac-

[7] William James, "Talks to Teachers" (New York: Holt, 1899), pp. 7–9.
[8] Henry James, "The Letters of William James" (Boston: Atlantic Monthly Press, 1920), Vol. II, p. 90.
[9] William James, "Pragmatism" (New York: Longmans, Green, 1907), p. 51.

tice and experiment. Needless to say, this found a ready response in a people who had shown a long-standing propensity for getting along without theory until after some scheme of theirs had proved to "work."

In the words of Byron S. Hollingshead, "James gave us confidence to go ahead pragmatically, to experiment, to find out what would work, even though we sometimes had to leave theory for later repair."[10] Education was neither something apart from life nor a predetermined program to be unrolled. With James, fresh breezes began to blow through the halls of philosophy, and with Dewey they penetrated thousands of American schoolrooms. It is idle to dispute the relative shares of the two commanding figures in the liberation of both philosophy and education from the stuffiness and irrelevance of the Victorian era. Dewey settled all that long ago by repeatedly acknowledging his indebtedness to his teacher, William James. Many of the battles they fought together have been won, but by no means all. For James summoned his fellow men not only to participation in the conflicts of his own time, but to the endless struggle against ignorance, vulgarity, bigness, pedantry, and moral apathy and inertia. Above all, James set us an example of "that eternal rarity, a great individual."

[10] B. S. Hollingshead, "Education in America," *Educational Record*, 40: 214–215, July, 1959.

chapter 6

Values and our youth

Gordon W. Allport

One aim of education is to make available the wisdom of the past and present so that youth may be equipped to solve the problems of the future. If this is so, then we have good grounds for a feeling of consternation concerning the adequacy of our present educational procedures. The reason is that in the immediate future, the youth of today will have to live in a world very unlike the world of the past from which our store of wisdom has been drawn.

Some Prospects

Think of the vastly changed nature of life in the future, for which we have little relevant wisdom from the past to call upon:

1. The new generation of students will have to face an ever increasing domination of life by science, by technology, and by automation. (One thinks of the story of two cows grazing along the roadside. An immense milk truck passes with the painted legend: Pasteurized, Homogenized, Vitamin B Added. One cow turns to the other and says, "Makes you feel inadequate, doesn't it?")

2. The new generation will have to recognize the impossibility of living any longer in a state of condescension toward the colored peoples of the world (about three-quarters of the world's population). Centuries of comfortable caste discrimination and segregation are from here on impossible to maintain.

From *Teachers College Record*, 63(December, 1961), 211–219. Reprinted by permission of the author and publisher.

Adapted from an address delivered during the 1961 Summer Lecture Series at the Western Washington College of Education, Bellingham, Washington.

3. The coming generation will have to deal with a population explosion whose predicted magnitude staggers our imagination.

4. It will need a completer understanding of world societies and their marked differences in values. In the past, we could be politely ignorant of such places as Africa, Latin America, and Asia in a way that is no longer possible.

5. It will have to create a world government or, at least, an effective confederation to forestall the threat of thermonuclear war.

6. As if a planetary world view were not difficult enough to achieve, the coming generation may have to develop an interplanetary point of view. (I find this prospect especially alarming because we seem to be solving the problems of outer space before those of the inner space of mind, character, and values.)

It is no wonder that this preview of problems confronting our youth throws us educators into a state of self-scrutiny bordering sometimes on panic. Where can youth find the needed equipment? Are they sound enough in mind and morale?

Sometimes our dismay finds an outlet in gallows humor. They tell of the benevolent lady who saw a depressing specimen of the very young generation sprawled on the curb of a city street, swilling down cans of beer. Greatly shocked, she asked, "Little boy, why aren't you in school?" "Cripes, lady," he replied, "I'm only four years old."

And they tell the story of the London bobby. London police, we know, are well trained for social work, even for psychotherapy. This bobby's beat was Waterloo Bridge. He spotted a man about to jump over and intercepted him. "Come now," he said. "Tell me what is the matter. Is it money?" The man shook his head. "Your wife perhaps?" Another shake of the head. "Well, what is it then?" The would-be suicide replied, "I'm worried about the state of the world." "Oh, come now," said the bobby. "It can't be so bad. Let's walk up and down the bridge here and talk it over." Whereupon they strolled for about an hour discussing the state of the world, and then they *both* jumped over.

Humor helps us put our dilemma into sane perspective, but it does not solve the problem. The vague apprehension we feel has led to certain empirical studies of the values of today's youth, with results, alas, that are not reassuring.

Assessing Values

Not long ago, Professor Phillip Jacob undertook to survey (5) all available studies concerning the values held by college students. He found a marked uniformity among them. Fully three-quarters of the students were "gloriously contented, both in regard to their present day-to-day activity and their outlook for the future." Their aspirations were primarily for material gratifications for themselves and their families. They "fully accepted the conventions of the contemporary business society as the context within which they will realize their personal desires." While they will not crusade against segregation and racial injustice, they will accept nondiscrimination when it comes as a "necessary convention in a homogenized culture." They subscribe to the traditional virtues of sincerity, honesty, and loyalty, but are indulgent concerning laxity in moral standards. They normally express a need for religion, but there is a hollow quality in their beliefs. They do not desire to have an influential voice in public policy or government. Their sense of civic duty stops at the elementary obligation of voting. They predict another major war within a dozen years, but they say that international problems give them little concern and that they spend no time on them. Only a minority value their college education primarily in terms of its intellectual gains. They regard it as good because it gives them vocational preparation, social status, and a good time. Such is the flabby value-fibre that Jacob discovers among college students of today.

The picture becomes more vivid when viewed in cross-national perspective. James Gillespie and I, in a comparative study (3) of the values of college youth in 10 nations, asked students to write their autobiographies of the future ("My life from now until the year 2000") and also gave them an extensive questionnaire. The instrument was translated into nine different languages.

In comparison with youth of other nations, young Americans are delightfully frank and open, unsuspicious and cooperative. Their documents had no literary affectation (and, I may add, little literary quality). But the most important finding was that within these 10 nations, American students were the most self-centered, the most "privatistic" in values. They desired above all else a rich, full life for themselves, and showed little concern for national welfare or for the fate of mankind at large. The context of their outlook was private rather than public, passive rather than pioneer. The essential point is made clear by two excerpts, the first drawn from the autobiography of a Mexican girl, 18 years of age, and the second from a Radcliffe student of the same age:

Since I like psychology very much, I wish, on leaving this school, to study it, specializing in it and exercising it as a profession. I shouldn't like to get married right away, although like any woman I am desirous of getting married before realizing all my aspirations. In addition, I should like to do something for my country—as a teacher, as a psychologist, or as a mother. As a teacher, to guide my pupils in the best path, for at the present time they need solid bases in childhood in order in their future lives not to have so many frustrations as the youth of the present. As a psychologist, to make studies which in some way will serve humanity and my beloved country. As a mother, to make my children creatures who are useful to both their country and all humanity.

Now follows the Radcliffe document. Its flavor of privatism is unmistakable:

Our summers will be spent lobster fishing on the Cape. Later we'll take a look at the rest of the country—California, the Southwest, and the Chicago Stockyards. I want the children, when they get past the age of ten, to spend part of the summer away from home, either at camp or as apprentices to whatever profession they may show an interest in. Finally, I hope we will all be able to take a trip to Europe, especially to Russia, to see what can be done about Communism.

Many critics have called attention to the same American value predicament. Our current social pattern, they say, is almost completely geared to one objective alone, namely a profitable, expanding production. To ensure expanding production, there must be more and more consumption. Hence come the expensive glamor of our advertising and its control of our mass media. The sole objective seems to be to stimulate the accretion of goods. Self-respect and status, as well as comfort, are acquired in this way. Someone has called our national disease "galloping consumption." Half a century ago, William James saw the peril and was much worried by what he called "the American terror of poverty." He saw there was truth in the jibes that other countries direct at our "materialism."

Hope in Uneasiness

Now a high standard of living is not in itself an evil thing. All the world wants what we already have. But the single-minded pursuit of production and consumption has brought a dulling of other values. One consequence is symbolized by the scandal of rigged quiz programs. These were in the service of advertising, which in turn was in the service of a profitable expanding economy. Another consequence is the accumulated froth of our TV, radio, and movies. Another is the widely discussed conformity of the organization man, as well as the futile rebellion of the beats. An especially peppery critic, Paul Goodman (4), has shown that the starved lives of juvenile delinquents and of young people caught in the organizational grind are at bottom much alike. Both are attracted to the cult of easiness and aspire to nothing more than amiable mediocrity. Both styles of living fail to prepare youth for the problems that lie ahead for themselves and for the nation.

A somewhat vulgar story seems to me to summarize all this mordant criticism. Moses, a stalwart leader of the old school, said to the Israelites in

Egypt, "Load up your camels, bring along your asses, and I'll lead you to the promised land." By contrast, the modern American prophet seems to urge, "Light up your Camels, sit on your asses, and I'll bring you the promised land."

All this familiar criticism is irritating; yet the fact that it flourishes is a hopeful sign. We suspect it may be too harsh. I am inclined to think so. It is rash indeed to indict a whole generation. At worst, Jacob's gloomy picture held for three-quarters of the college students studied, but not at all for a vital and far from negligible minority. And even though the gloomy generalizations have some truth in them, are the assets given fair attention? I myself have some favorable impressions, although one man's view is not reliable. But youth today appears to enjoy a certain freedom and flexibility that was not common in the more rigid days of our parents and grandparents. I even have the impression that there is less neuroticism among students now than among those of a generation ago. What is more, young people, I find, are not blind to the world changes that are occurring. Their apparent repression of the challenge is due largely to their bewilderment concerning proper paths to take. (And one has the feeling that our own statesmen in Washington are no less bewildered.) All in all, these are hopeful signs that should not be overlooked.

Values and the School

Another hopeful sign is the fact that many teachers are asking, "What can we do to be helpful?" They know, and we all know, that the ability of the school to give training in values is limited. For one thing, the home is vastly more important. A home that infects the child with galloping consumption, that encourages only canned recreation and has no creative outlets, can only with difficulty be offset by the school. Another limitation lies in the fact that the school is ordinarily expected to mirror current social values and to prepare the child to live within the existing frame. It is an unusual school system and an unusual teacher who even *wish* to transcend the current fashions of value.

But assuming that we have an unusual school system and an unusual teacher, what values shall they elect to teach? If they do not choose to follow the prevailing fashions, what standards shall they follow? The ancient Romans were fond of asking, "Who will judge the judges?" and "Who will guard the guardians?" Can the guardians turn perhaps to standard discussions of "the aims of education"? Such discussions are numerous, abstract, and often dull. Their weakness, I feel, is their effort to formulate absolute goals, vistas of abstract perfection. The result is often a series of platitudes or generalizations so broad as to be unhelpful. Of course we want to develop "good citizenship"; we certainly want to "free the child's intellect." These and all other absolutes need to be reduced to concrete, stepwise processes before they can guide us in the strategy of teaching values.

The teacher must start with the situation as he or she finds it and in concrete instances sharpen the value-attributes of the lesson being taught. To a considerable extent, these value-attributes can be drawn from the codified wisdom of our nation. We cannot neglect the value of profitable production and high living standards, for all our vocational and professional education contribute to this end. But the codified wisdom of our unique society extends far beyond the obsession of today. Our values include also such matters as respect for civil liberties. Does the school accent this value? They include approval for individual initiative, for philanthropy, for compassion. And they imply much concerning civic duties that are the reciprocal of civic rights. What must we do to deserve our precious cornucopia of freedom? Vote? Yes. But voting does no good unless the voter is informed above the stereotyped level of the mass media. He must also pay taxes willingly. Do schools and colleges teach the young to pay a glad tax? I wonder. To me the most disturbing finding in *Youth's Outlook on the Future* lay in the elaborate talk about one's right to a rich, full life and in the almost total silence regarding one's duties.

I am saying that in the first instance teachers should choose the values they teach from the whole (not from a part) of our American ethos. Deep in our hearts we know, and most of the world knows, that our national values, derived, of course, from Judeo-Christian ethics, are about the finest mankind has yet formulated. In no sense are these values out of date, nor will they go out of date in the world of tomorrow. Yet many of them are badly rusted. Unless they are revitalized, however, our youth may not have the personal fortitude and moral implements that the future will require.

The Larger Anchor

Excellent as the American Creed is as a fountainhead of values, it does not contain them all. It says nothing explicitly, for example, about intellectual curiosity. And yet surely schools exist to augment this value. The most severe indictment of our educational procedures I have ever encountered is the discovery that a sizeable percentage of graduates of our colleges after completing their formal education never afterward read a single book.

There are other important values that are not spelled out in our American Creed. I am thinking of those details of human relationships that make all the difference between boorishness and brotherhood in the human family. As our population increases, it becomes more and more important to teach the elements of the new science of human relations which go far toward smoothing the roughness of common life by leading us to respect effectively the integrity of the other fellow. I recall a teacher of English whose class was studying *The Merchant of Venice*. She turned a wave of incipient anti-Semitism in her class to a sound lesson in values. Shylock, she explained, was like the resentful, self-seeking portion of every person's nature. We are all potential Shylocks. But while self-love is prominent in all of us, we are so constructed that it need not be sovereign in our natures.

To return for a moment to the relation between home and school—the former, as I have said, is far more important. Recognizing this fact, some people say, "Well, let's leave the teaching of values to the home and to the church. Schools can't do much of anything about the matter."

This position is untenable. If the school does not teach values, it will have the effect of denying them. If the child at school never hears a mention of honesty, modesty, charity, or reverence, he will be persuaded that, like many of his parents' ideas, they are simply old hat. As they grow toward adolescence, children become critical of the teaching of both parents and the church. They are in a questioning stage. If the school, which to the child represents the larger outside world, is silent on values, the child will repudiate more quickly the lessons learned at home. He will also be thrown onto peer values more completely, with their emphasis on the hedonism of teen-age parties or on the destructiveness of gangs. He will also be more at the mercy of the sensate values peddled by movies, TV, and disk jockeys. What is more, some homes, as we have said, give no fundamental value training. In such a case, it is *only* in the school that the child has any chance at all of finding ethical anchorage.

This brings us to the hardest question: How does the teacher, the instructor, the professor, handle his assignment in the classroom? How is it possible to teach values, including the value of intellectual curiosity?

The Meaning of Value

Before tackling this question, we must pause to define what we mean by value. You will recognize that I am using the term psychologically, not in its objective philosophical sense. Values, as I use the term, are simply *meanings perceived as related to self*. The child experiences value whenever he knows that a meaning is warm and central to himself. Values, to borrow Whitehead's term, are "matters of importance" as distinct from mere matters of fact.

So much for definition. Now the hard-pressed teacher is given a solid substantive curriculum to teach. The curriculum in its original state consists of mere matters of fact. And on the number of facts absorbed the pupil's standing depends. It takes virtually all of a teacher's time to convey factual information and grade the pupil on his achievement. There is little time left to transmute these matters of fact into matters of importance, let alone teach all of the moral and social values we have thus far been discussing.

The curriculum itself is not, and should not be, a direct aid. Prescribed instruction in values would be laughed out of court. We have recently been bumped by Sputnik headforemost into core subjects. Get on with science, mathematics, language! Away with courses in folk dancing, personal adjustment, and fudge making! I agree that value-study has no place in curriculum planning, but not because it is a frivolous subject—rather, because it is a subject too hard and too subtle for curriculum makers.

Education for values occurs only when teachers teach what they themselves stand for, no matter what their subject is. If I were to write a treatise on the teaching of values, I would give most of my emphasis to the moral pedagogy that lies in a teacher's incidental comments, to the *obiter dicta*. The hard core is central, but the hard core has a penumbra of moral significance. I mentioned the teacher of English who made a value-lesson out of Shylock. I recall also my college professor of geology who paused in his lecture on diatom ooze to say to us, "Others would not agree with me, but I confess that whenever I study diatoms, I don't see how anyone can doubt the existence of God because the design and behavior of these protozoa are so marvelous." Is it not interesting how we all recall the *obiter dicta* of our teachers, the penumbra of value they point out to us, surrounding the hard-core data? We remember them better than the subject matter itself.

Why does the student remember them so well? No current theory of learning seems able to tell us. I suspect it is because values, being matters of importance to the self, are always warm and central and ego-involved and therefore claim priority on our attention. The child, being value-ripe, cannot help being impressed when the teacher betrays excitement and enthusiasm for a mode of thought or for the content of the subject being studied. True, the youngster does not, and should not, adopt the teacher's values ready-made; but the teacher's self-disclosure leads the student to self-discovery.

What wouldn't we give if we could develop intellectual ardor in every child for hard core subjects? Why is it that for most pupils arithmetic, spelling, physics, remain forever dull matters of fact and never become a meaning perceived as related to the self? One reason, I think, is that the weary teacher fails to convey his own sense of the importance of the subject to the student. If he did so, he would, as I have said, at least fix attention upon the value-potentiality of the subject.

Another reason perhaps is that not all of a teacher's *obiter dicta* are wholesome. Some, indeed, may be deeply damaging, though the teacher may be innocent of any such intent. Sometimes we hear incidental (but still attitude-forming) remarks like this one: "All right now, children. You have had a good time playing at recess; now settle down to your English lesson." Play is recognized as a matter of joyful importance. English, the teacher is saying in effect, is a mere routine matter of fact.

Values and Learning

I think our educational psychology has been mostly wrong about the process of learning—or perhaps not so much wrong as woefully incomplete. At the beginning of his learning career, a young child cannot, of course, be expected to feel adult enthusiasm for the intellectual content of his studies. He does his work in the first instance to avoid a scolding or because he has a habit of obeying instructions. Soon he finds added incentive. The teacher —really in the role of mother—gives praise and love ("Susan, I am proud of you"). There is a great deal of such dependency in the learning situation. Love and social reward (as well as some fear of punishment) sustain the processes of attention and retention. When the child puts forth intellectual effort, he does so in order to obtain a gold star, commendation, or other symbols of love.

All these incentives are extraneous to the subject matter. The youngster does not learn it because it is a matter of importance. When he leaves school or college, he loses these extraneous supports. He finds his love relations directly; they are no longer a reward for intellectual effort. Hence, intellectual apathy sets in, and, distressing to say, no further books are read.

In such a case as this, intellectual curiosity was never tied to independence, only to extraneous supports. At some point in the schooling— and the earlier the better—intellectual activity should become not a secondhand but a firsthand fitting to the sense of self. At the beginning, all learning must be tied, perhaps, to specific reinforcements; but if the dependency is long continued, authentic curiosity fails to develop.

It would be going too far to put the blame for intellectual apathy onto our current teaching of educational psychology. Yet I am inclined to feel somewhat punitive about this matter. Psychology has not yet settled down to the problem of transforming matters of fact—whose acquisition current learning theories explain fairly well—into autonomous matters of importance —which they do not explain at all.

Our emphasis has been on learning by drill and by reinforcement. Such "habit acquisition" receives all the emphasis. But the learning theory involved postulates a continuing dependency relation (extraneous reinforcement). When the relation terminates, the habits of study simply extinguish themselves. I am surprised, therefore, that stimulus-response psychologists do not see this consequence of their own theory. Insofar as teachers employ an educational psychology of this order, they are not likely to break the dependency relation, which belongs properly only to the earlier stages of schooling.

Matters of importance, I strongly believe, are not acquired by drill or by reinforcement. They are transformations of habits and skills from the "opportunistic" layer of personality into the ego-system itself (1). Once inside the ego-system, these habits and skills turn into true interests and utilize the basic energy, the basic spontaneity, that the organism itself possesses. They are no longer sustained as "operant conditionings" by outside rewards. The interest, now being the very stuff of life itself, needs no outer supports.

Functional Autonomy

I have called this process of transforming means into ends, of changing extrinsic values into intrinsic values, *functional autonomy*. Concerning this concept, I am often asked two questions: How do you define "functional autonomy," and how does functional autonomy come about?

For a definition, I offer the following: Functional autonomy refers to any acquired system of motivation in which the tensions involved are no longer of the same kind as the antecedent tensions from which the acquired system developed.[1] To answer the question of how functional autonomy comes about requires a more extended and technical discussion. I can only hint at the direction of my answer. Neurologists are gradually discovering a basis for what I would call "perseverative functional autonomy." I refer to the "self-sustaining circuits," "feedback mechanisms," and "central motive states" that are now commonly recognized to exist in the nervous system. This line of discovery, I find, provides a partial answer to the question. But I believe we have to go further and call on the concept of self. Values, we have said, are meanings perceived as related to the self. Functional autonomy is not a mere perseverative phenomenon; it is, above all, an ego-involved phenomenon. Besides admitting an opportunistic layer to personality, which is the exclusive concern of most current theories of learning, we have no choice but to admit also a "propriate" layer. It is in this layer that all matters of importance reside.

The goal of the educator, then, is to shift the content of the subject he teaches from the opportunistic (matter of fact) layer to the propriate. But there is no sure-fire, mechanical strategy to use. The best general rule, one that John Dewey saw clearly, is to strive ceaselessly to integrate routine matters of act into the growing experience system of the child himself. It would take a long treatise to specify various detailed strategies of teaching that help achieve this goal.

Let me focus on only one aspect of this topic, upon a common mistake that teachers make. I myself am a continual offender. It is to present students with our own carefully thought out conclusions when they themselves lack the raw experience from which these conclusions are fashioned.

This particular error is inherent, for example, in the lecture system. Instead of lecturing on comparative religion, for instance, it would be much better to require all students to attend services of worship that are un-

---

[1] If this definition seems too technical to be immediately helpful, see Ch. 10 of *Pattern and Growth in Personality* (2) for a more extended treatment of functional autonomy.

familiar to them. If raw experience is present, then perhaps a lecture may be effective. Much of the intellectual apathy we complain about is due to our fault of presenting conclusions in lieu of firsthand experience. To us, our well-chiseled conclusion, summing up a long intellectual struggle with a problem of knowledge or of value, seems like a beautiful sonnet. To the student, it may be gibberish.

The fallacy of giving conclusions holds both for subject matter and for values. A lad of 15 cannot profit from the fully fashioned philosophy of life of a man of 50. To register at all, a statement about values must fall precisely on his present growing edge.

Teaching, then, is not the art of offering conclusions, however hard won and valid they may be. No teacher can forcibly enter the student's *proprium* and plant a functionally autonomous motive. He can at best open channels of experience and, by his *obiter dicta*, sometimes lead the student to see the value-potential in the experience.

The theory of personality that we need to guide a more fully developed educational psychology will teach us something important about our basic verb "to educate." It will show us that only at the outset of learning is it a transitive verb. By drill, by reward, by reinforcement, the teacher does indeed educate the child—in matters of fact. But true maturity comes only when the verb is reflexive. For in matters of importance, where values lie, the growing individual alone can educate himself.

REFERENCES

1. Allport, G. *Becoming*. New Haven: Yale Univer. Press, 1955.
2. Allport, G. *Pattern and growth in personality*. New York: Holt, Rinehart, & Winston, 1961.
3. Gillespie, J., & Allport, G. *Youth's outlook on the future*. New York: Random House, 1955.
4. Goodman, P. *Growing up absurd*. New York: Random House, 1960.
5. Jacob, P. *Changing values in college*. New York: Harper, 1957.

chapter 7

What psychology can we feel sure about?

Goodwin Watson

Educators and others who wish to apply psychology in their professional work have long been troubled by controversies among psychologists themselves. Behaviorism arose to challenge the introspective method; Thorndike's connectionism was controverted by Gestalt concepts; psychoanalysts talked an almost completely different language. It was natural for teachers to say, "Let's wait until the psychologists themselves straighten out their various systems!" It looked for a while as if one could support almost any educational practice by choosing which psychologist to cite.

Gradually, however, a body of pretty firm facts has accumulated. While it remains true that research findings will be somewhat differently expressed and explained within different theoretical frameworks, the findings themselves are fairly solid.

A workshop of educators* recently asked me to formulate for them some statements of what we really know today about children and learning. To my own surprise, the list of propositions with which few knowledgeable psychologists of any "school" would disagree grew to fifty.

In no science are truths established beyond the possibility of revision. Einstein modified thinking about gravity, even though Newton's observations were essentially correct. Psychology is much younger and more malleable than physics. New facts are constantly accumulating in psycho-

* The New Jersey State Curriculum Workshop, Atlantic City, Nov. 12, 1959.

From *Teachers College Record*, 61(1960), 253–257. Reprinted as a separate pamphlet under the title, *What Psychology Can We Trust?* New York: Bureau of Publications, Teachers College, Columbia University, 1961. Reprinted by permission of the publishers.

logical research, and these will doubtless introduce some qualifications and modifications—conceivably even a basic contradiction. The educator who bases his program on these propositions, however, is entitled to feel that he is on solid psychological ground and not on shifting sands.

What follows is a listing of fifty propositions, important for education, upon which psychologists of all "schools" would consistently agree. These are presented in twelve classifications.

Nature-Nurture

1. Every trait in human behavior is a product of the interaction of heredity (as determined at conception by genes) and environmental influences. Some traits (preferences in food or clothing, for example) are easily influenced by nurture; others (height, rate of skeletal ossification) seem to be affected only by extreme differences in environment.

2. There are specific stages in individual development during which certain capacities for behavior appear. The manner in which these capacities are then utilized sets a pattern for later behavior which is highly resistant to change. If unutilized then, they are likely not to develop later (for example, visual perception, mother attachment, language pronunciation, sports skills, peer relations, independence from parents, heterosexuality).

3. The significance of the important biological transformations of pubescence (growth of primary sex organs, development of secondary sex characteristics, skeletal and muscular growth, glandular interaction) lies mainly in the *meaning* which cultural norms and personal history have given to these changes.

Learning Process

4. Behaviors which are rewarded (reinforced) are more likely to recur.

5. Sheer repetition without indications of improvement or any kind of reinforcement is a poor way to attempt to learn.

6. Threat and punishment have variable and uncertain effects upon learning; they may make the punished response more likely or less likely to recur; they may set up avoidance tendencies which prevent further learning.

7. Reward (reinforcement), to be most effective in learning, must follow almost immediately after the desired behavior and be clearly connected with that behavior in the mind of the learner.

8. The type of reward (reinforcement) which has the greatest transfer value to other life-situations is the kind one gives oneself—the sense of satisfaction in achieving purposes.

9. Opportunity for fresh, novel, stimulating experience is a kind of reward which is quite effective in conditioning and learning.

10. The experience of learning by sudden insight into a previously confused or puzzling situation arises when: (*a*) there has been a sufficient background and preparation; (*b*) attention is given to the relationships operative in the whole situation; (*c*) the perceptual structure "frees" the key elements to be shifted into new patterns; (*d*) the task is meaningful and within the range of ability of the subject.

11. Learners progress in any area of learning only as far as they need to in order to achieve their purposes. Often they do only well enough to "get by"; with increased motivation they improve.

12. Forgetting proceeds rapidly at first—then more and more slowly; recall shortly after learning reduces the amount forgotten.

Maturation: Life Tasks

13. The most rapid mental growth occurs during infancy and early childhood; the average child achieves about half of his total mental growth by the age of five.

14. Ability to learn increases with age up to adult years.

15. During the elementary school years (ages 6 to 12) most children enjoy energetic activity—running, chasing, jumping, shouting, and roughhouse. For most staid adults this is uncomfortable. Boys are generally more vigorous, active, rough, and noisy than girls.

16. Not until after eleven years of age do most children develop the sense of time which is required for historical perspective.

17. Readiness for any new learning is a complex product of interraction among physiological maturation, prerequisite learning, the pupil's sense of the importance of this lesson in his world, and his feeling about the teacher and the school situation.

Individual Differences

18. No two children make the same response to any school situation. Differences of heredity, physical maturity, intelligence, motor skills, health, experiences with parents, siblings, playmates; consequent attitudes, motives, drives, tastes, fears—all these and more enter into production of each child's unique reaction. Children vary in their minds and personalities as much as in their appearance.

19. Pupils vary not only in their present performance but in their rate of growth and the "ceiling" which represents their potential level of achievement. Some "late bloomers" may eventually surpass pupils who seem far ahead of them in grade school.

20. Gains in intelligence test scores by children are positively related to aggressiveness, competitiveness, initiative, and strength of felt need to achieve.

21. Pupils grouped by ability on any one kind of test (age, size, IQ,

reading, arithmetic, science, art, music, physical fitness, and so forth) will vary over a range of several grades in other abilities and traits.

Level of Challenge

22. The most effective effort is put forth by children when they attempt tasks which fall in the "range of challenge"—not too easy and not too hard —where success seems quite possible but not certain.
23. According to some studies, many pupils experience so much criticism, failure, and discouragement in school that their self-confidence, level of aspiration, and sense of worth are damaged.

Teaching Method

24. Children are more apt to throw themselves wholeheartedly into any project if they themselves have participated in the selection and planning of the enterprise.
25. Reaction to excessive direction by the teacher may be: (*a*) apathetic conformity, (*b*) defiance, (*c*) scape-goating, (*d*) escape from the whole affair.
26. Learning from reading is facilitated more by time spent recalling what has been read than by rereading.
27. Pupils *think* when they encounter an obstacle, difficulty, puzzle or challenge in a course of action which interests them. The process of thinking involves designing and testing plausible solutions for the problem as understood by the thinker.
28. The best way to help pupils form a general concept is to present the concept in numerous and varied specific situations, contrasting experiences with and without the desired concept, then to encourage precise formulations of the general idea and its application in situations different from those in which the concept was learned.

"Discipline" and Learning

29. Overstrict discipline is associated with more conformity, anxiety, shyness and acquiescence in children; greater permissiveness is associated with more initiative and creativity in children.
30. When children (or adults) experience too much frustration, their behavior ceases to be integrated, purposeful and rational. Blindly they act out their rage or discouragement or withdrawal. The threshold of what is "too much" varies; it is lowered by previous failures.

Group Relations

31. Pupils learn much from one another; those who have been together for years learn new material more easily from one of their own group than they do from strangers.

32. When groups act for a common goal there is better cooperation and more friendliness than when individuals in the group are engaged in competitive rivalry with one another.

33. At age six, spontaneous groups seldom exceed three or four children; play groups all through childhood are smaller than school classes.

34. Children learn that peer consensus is an important criterion; they are uncomfortable when they disagree with their peers, and especially when they find themselves in a minority of one against all the others.

35. Groups which feel some need (internal coherence or external pressure) to work together try to influence deviates toward the group norm. If there is no felt need to stay together, the deviate may be ignored and thus excluded.

36. Leadership qualities vary with the demands of the particular situation. A good leader for a football team may or may not be a good leader for a discussion group, a research project, or an overnight hike; leadership is not a general trait.

37. In most school classes, one to three pupils remain unchosen by their classmates for friendship, for parties, or for working committees. These "isolates" are usually also unpopular with teachers.

Subject Matter

38. No school subjects are markedly superior to others for "strengthening mental powers." General improvement as a result of study of any subject depends on instruction designed to build up generalizations about principles, concept formation, and improvements of techniques of study, thinking, and communication.

39. What is learned is most likely to be available for use if it is learned in a situation much like that in which it is to be used and immediately preceding the time when it is needed. Learning in childhood, forgetting, and relearning when needed is not an efficient procedure.

40. Television is the most frequently reported activity of elementary school pupils, occupying about the same number of hours per week as are given to school—far more than would voluntarily be given to school attendance.

Attitudes and Learning

41. Children (and adults even more) tend to select groups, reading matter, TV shows, and other influences which agree with their own opinions; they break off contact with contradictory views.

42. Children remember new information which confirms their previous attitudes better than they remember new information which runs counter to their previous attitudes.

Social Stratification

43. Attitudes toward members of "out-groups" are usually acquired from members of one's "in-group."

44. Children who differ in race, nationality, religion, or social class background, but who play together on a footing of equal status and acceptance, usually come to like one another.

45. Children who are looked down upon (or looked up to) because of their family, school marks, social class, race, nationality, religion, or sex tend to adopt and to internalize this evaluation of themselves.

46. Two thirds of the elementary school children of America come from lower-class homes; the one third who come from the lower-lower class usually find school very uncongenial.

47. Children choose most of their "best friends" from homes of the same socioeconomic class as their own.

48. More girls than boys wish, from time to time, that they could change their sex.

Evaluation

49. If there is a discrepancy between the real *objectives* and the *tests* used to measure achievement, the latter become the main influence upon choice of subject matter and method.

50. The superiority of man over calculating machines is more evident in the formulation of questions than in the working out of answers.

chapter 8

Seeing is behaving

Arthur W. Combs

The social sciences have been discovering some
new ways of looking at human behavior,
and these discoveries seem to have vast
implications for the whole field of education.
Two of these principles are discussed here.

How effective we are in dealing with the great human problems of any
generation will depend in large measure upon the accuracy and scope of
the ideas we hold about what people are like and why they behave as
they do. This is particularly true for what we do as educators. People can
only behave in terms of what seems to them to be so. Hence, the methods
we use to solve our problems of curriculum will depend upon what we
believe about the nature of the people we seek to teach. Whenever, therefore, science changes our ideas of what people are like, it must have
far-reaching implications for our profession.

In recent years, the social sciences have been discovering some fascinating and exciting new ways of looking at human behavior, and these
discoveries seem to me to have vast implications for the whole field of
education. In this article I would like to state just two of these principles
and point out some of the things it seems to me they mean for education.

From *Educational Leadership*, 16(October, 1958), 21–26. Reprinted by permission of the author and publisher.

BEHAVIOR IS A PERSONAL MATTER

The first principle is this: *People do not behave according to the facts as others see them; they behave in terms of what seems to them to be so.* The psychologist expresses this technically as: Behavior is a function of perception. What affects human behavior, we are beginning to understand, is not so much the forces exerted on people from without as the meanings existing for the individual within. It is feelings, beliefs, convictions, attitudes and understandings of the person who is behaving that constitute the directing forces of behavior. In an election, for example, people who vote for the Democrats believe that the Democrats will save the nation while the Republicans will certainly ruin it. The reverse is true of the people who vote the other way. Each side behaves in terms of what seems to it to be so. But what is *really* the fact of the matter we shall never know, for only one party gets elected! In order to understand the behavior of people we must understand how things seem to them.

Our failure to understand this simple and "obvious" fact about behavior is one of the most potent causes of misunderstanding and failure in dealing with human problems. A good example may be seen in the case of the child who feels that people do not like him. Feeling that he is unliked and unwanted, the child is likely to make himself obnoxious in his attempts to get the attention of adults who surround him. When company comes, for example, he is likely to make a nuisance of himself in his attempts to attract attention. Parents seeking to put a stop to this kind of annoying behavior may say, "For goodness sake, Jimmy, stop annoying Mr. Jones and go to your room!" Such behavior on the part of adults simply serves to prove what the child already believes—"People don't like me very well!"

When we fail to understand how things seem to people with whom we are working, we may make serious errors in our efforts to deal with them. The moment, however, we understand an individual's behavior as it seems to him, our own behavior can be much more accurate, realistic, precise and effective. If a child *thinks* his teacher is unfair, it doesn't make much difference whether the teacher is *really* unfair or not. If a child thinks his teacher is unfair, he behaves as though she were. Whether she is *really* unfair or not is, as the lawyers say, "irrelevant and immaterial information" as far as the child is concerned. In this sense, seeing is not only believing; seeing is behaving! To understand behavior we need to understand the personal meanings existing for the people who are behaving.

THE EFFECT OF THE CONCEPT OF SELF

The second important point we are currently discovering is this: *The most important ideas which affect people's behavior are those ideas they have about themselves.* This, the psychologist refers to as the *self concept.* The beliefs we hold about ourselves, we are learning, are among the most important determinants of behavior. People who see themselves as men behave like men; people who see themselves as women, behave like women. Our self concepts even affect the things we see and hear. If you don't think so, try going window shopping with a member of the opposite sex.

The self concept, we are finding, is so tremendously important that it affects practically everything we do. We are even discovering that a child's success in school depends in very large measure upon the kind of self concepts he has about himself. Some years ago, Prescott Lecky observed that children often made about the same number of errors in spelling per page when they were writing free material, despite the difficulty of the material. One would normally expect more errors on harder material, but these children spelled as though they were responding to a built-in quota. It occurred to Lecky that they were behaving more in terms of their beliefs about spelling than in terms of their actual skills. Accordingly, he arranged to have a group of these children spend some time with a counselor who helped them to explore themselves and their feelings about their abilities to spell. As a consequence of these discussions an amazing thing happened. Despite the fact that these children had no additional work in spelling whatever, their spelling improved tremendously, and several of the children took up spelling as a hobby!

We are finding a similar phenomenon in the field of reading. Nowadays we catch children's visual difficulties fairly early so that it is rare these days to find a child coming to the reading clinic with anything very wrong with his eyes. More often than not, when a child is unable to read, the difficulty seems to lie in the fact that he has developed *an idea about himself* as a person who cannot read. Having developed such an idea, he gets caught in a vicious circle that goes something like this: Believing he cannot read, the child avoids reading and thus avoids the very practice which might make it possible for him to learn. Furthermore, believing that he does not read very well, he reads poorly when asked to do so. His teacher, in turn, observing this weakness, says, "My goodness, Johnny, you don't read very well!" which proves what he already thinks! Once having developed the idea that he cannot read, a child's experience confirms his belief, and his teacher, who should know, corroborates it. Just to make sure that the lesson is well learned, moreover, we may also send home a failing grade on his report card so that his parents can tell him too!

We are beginning to discover that the self concept acts very much like a quota for an individual. What a person believes about himself establishes what he can and will do. Once a self concept is established, furthermore, it is a very difficult thing to change, even if we would like to change it in a positive direction. The young man coming to the university believing that he is not very bright, for example, who is told by the test administrator that he has done very well, responds: "Are you sure? There must be some mistake!"

We are even discovering that the question of adjustment or maladjustment is very largely a question of the self concepts people have about themselves. Well-adjusted people, we now observe, are those who see themselves as liked, wanted, acceptable, able—as people of dignity and integrity. People who see themselves so are no trouble to anybody. They get along fine in our society. They are essentially happy people who work efficiently and effectively, and rarely cause difficulty in school or out. The people who cause us difficulty in our society are, almost without exception, those who see themselves as unliked, unwanted, unacceptable, unable, undignified, unworthy, and the like. These are the frustrated people of our generation who frustrate us. They are the maladjusted, unhappy ones who fill our jails, our mental hospitals and institutions.

Some Implications for Education

We have now stated two modern principles of behavior:

1. That people behave according to how things seem to them.
2. That the most important ideas any of us ever have are those ideas we hold about ourselves.

These two very simple ideas have vast implications for education. In some ways they corroborate things we educators have been feeling all along. They also raise questions about some of the things we have been doing. And, finally, they seem to point to some new ways of solving old problems. In the remainder of this article I would like to point out two or three of the important implications these ideas seem to have for me.

EDUCATION MUST DEAL WITH MEANINGS

If it is true that behavior is a function of how things seem to people, then education to be effective must deal with people's *meanings*—not just facts. As educators, we have done pretty well in gathering information and in making information available to people. Where we get into difficulty, however, is in helping people to discover the meaning of information in such a way that they will *behave differently* as a result of the process. When people misbehave it is rarely because they do not know what they should do. Most of us already know a great deal better than we behave. We are like the old farmer who said when they asked him why he wasn't using modern methods, "Heck, I ain't farming now half as well as I know how!"

It is over a failure to understand this problem that we sometimes get into communication difficulties with the public. The public wants the same thing we do. They want kids who *know* something, who *understand* something, but most of all, who *behave* as though they know something. So do we. When the public, however, sees children behaving inadequately, they are likely to assume that the reason they behave so is because they don't *know* any better. But you and I as teachers are aware that this is not the problem. We know that it is very rare that teachers fail because of their lack of knowledge of subject matter. When teachers fail it is almost always because they are unable to bring about the third step we have been talking about—namely, how you get information translated into behavior.

Modern psychology tells us that it is only when knowledge becomes meaning that behavior is affected. If it is meanings that affect human behavior, then it is meanings with which we educators must deal. We will need to concern ourselves with a different kind of facts. We will have to deal with convictions, beliefs, attitudes, feelings, ideas, concepts and understandings. I suspect that we have not always done this in our zeal to "get the facts" from books. Sometimes we have failed to understand that people's behavior is not the result of objective facts, but of *personal* facts, the meaning things have for the behaver himself. I am afraid we have too often said to the child, "George, I am not interested in what you think; what are the facts?" Small wonder that some children conclude that what goes on in school has nothing to do with life in a meaningful way at all.

Since personal meanings lie inside people, they are not open to direct manipulation. To change meanings we must find effective ways of helping students explore and discover for themselves. We have to let personal meanings become an integral part of the curriculum. Many schools and many teachers have already learned to do this with great skill. We need now to push the movement forward.

Teachers Do Not Have to Be Psychiatrists

One of the most exciting implications of these new principles is this: If it is true that behavior is a function of perception, then the causes of behavior lie fundamentally in the present and not in the past. Psychologists for several generations have told us that in order to understand an individual we need to know all that has happened to him in the past. As a result many teachers have often felt helpless to deal with a child because for one reason or other they were unable to acquire knowledge of all his past experiences. Many educators have never been entirely happy with this point of view. We have often felt, as Gordon Allport once expressed it, that "people are busy living their lives forward while psychologists busily trace them backwards!" We are now finding that many modern psychologists are providing support for our suspicion that this preoccupation with the past may not always be essential.

If it is true that behavior is a function of perception, then behavior is a result of how people are perceiving right now, *today, as of this moment!* This understanding opens a whole new world for education. This is not to say that behavior is not *also* the result of what has happened in the past. We can look at the causes of behavior in two ways. A person's behavior is *historically* the result of all the things that have happened to him in the past. It is *immediately* the result of how things seem to him at this moment. For example, a child who has been badly rejected in his youth may come to feel about himself that he is unliked, unwanted, unacceptable, that the world is a pretty tough place, almost too much for what he has to offer. These feelings he has acquired, of course, because of the things that have happened to him. But his behavior today, now, as of this moment, is the result of how he is *feeling* today. This way of looking at behavior opens a whole new frontier for educational practice.

When we believed that behavior was entirely a function of the past, there was, of course, very little we could do. It had all been done. Such a belief leads to preoccupation with the child's history instead of what is going on at the moment. The historical view of causation also encourages the old army game of passing the buck. The college says, "What can you do with youngsters who come so badly prepared from high school?" The high school says, "What can you do for the child who comes to you like this from elementary school?" and the elementary school teachers say, "What can you do with a child from a home like that?" The poor parent in our society is low man on the totem pole. He's stuck with it; he doesn't have anybody he can pass the blame to, except maybe to say, "Well, he gets it from the father's side of the family!"

If we believe that a child's behavior is solely the result of the forces working upon him, there is very little we can do to help, and we are always able to charge off our failures to other people. If, however, behavior is a function of perception, then there are tremendous things we can do in the present. We can help a person to see differently now, even if we cannot change his past. It means that you and I can help children in school without the necessity of having to change their environments. It means that there is something we can do for *every* child no matter what kind of background he comes from. Although we can rarely do much about the past, there are important things we can do about the present.

This new understanding also lifts a great weight from the teacher's shoulders. It means that we do not have to be social workers or psychiatrists, we can just be teachers! It means we do not have to pry, we do not have to know all about a child's background in order to be able to deal with him effectively. This is not to say that knowledge of his past and of his home situation might not be helpful. It does mean that we *do not have to have it* as an absolute essential. I don't know how you feel about this, but this sets me free to do a lot of things I was never able to do before. This simple idea has already caused revolutions in the field of social work, in psychotherapy and in the field of human relations. It seems equally promising in what it may offer to education.

For one thing, teachers do not have to feel defeated. If behavior is a function of perception, then no matter what goes on elsewhere in the child's life, it is still important what you and I do as teachers. People get their perceptions from those who surround them, and that means us. It may be that there are some children with whom we have to deal who are so sick that we cannot make *all* the difference. We may not be able to change a child completely, but neither are we helpless. Fritz Redl once said in a speech, "You know, the difference between a good child and a naughty child is not very great. The difference, however, between a naughty child and a real tough delinquent is a very great distance. Wouldn't it be wonderful if we could just keep them naughty?" I find this sentiment very reassuring. I think that what Redl is trying to tell us is that none of us need feel defeated. That whatever we do is *always* important even though for a particular child it may not be enough to produce immediate results.

Finally, if the self concept is as important as modern psychology tells us, this fact has vast importance for curriculum construction and design. One of the great tragedies of our time is that we have literally hundreds of thousands of people in our society who are the prisoners of their own perceptions. Believing they can only do x well, they only do x much. The rest of us, seeing them do only x much, say, "Well, that's an x much person," and this just proves what these people have thought in the first place! Such people are the victims of their own self concepts. Everyone loses as a result of this great waste of human potential.

But people get their self concepts from the ways they have been treated by the persons who surround them during their growing up. From the minute the child is born we begin to teach him who he is and what he is. Whether we are helpful, or hindering, or of no account at all in the development of children's self concepts will depend upon ourselves. We *can* behave in ways that don't count, ways that have nothing to do with meanings, and they will quickly disregard us. Or, we *can* behave in ways that are important in helping them discover who they are and what they are—in positive fashion. We are, in a sense, the architects of children's self concepts.

Society needs adequate, well-adjusted, informed people as never before in history. What then shall we do to develop these kinds of people? I think the answer lies in the above definitions of the kinds of people we want. Earlier in this article we stated that whether or not an individual was likely to be well adjusted was largely a matter of his self concept. We observed that people who see themselves as liked, wanted, acceptable, able, dignified, worthy, etc., are the kinds who make effective, efficient citizens. People, on the other hand, who see themselves as unliked, unwanted, unacceptable, unable—these kinds of people are the ones who cause us trouble. If this is true, we do not have to be psychiatrists to help children grow.

To be effective in these terms, we need teachers who can understand and perceive how a child is thinking and feeling. We need teachers who can understand the impact of the ways they are behaving and the things they are doing on the perception of children. We need teachers skilled in helping children explore and discover themselves and their relationship to the world in which they live. In the final analysis, the question of curriculum construction boils down to this: How can a child feel liked, unless somebody likes him? How can a child feel wanted, unless somebody wants him? How can a child feel acceptable, unless somebody accepts him? And how can a child feel able, unless somewhere he has some success? In our answers to these questions related to the kinds of self concepts we seek lie the basic criteria for curriculum change and improvement.

chapter **9**

Secondary education: past, present, and future

Donald O. Bush

Is inertia your problem too? The space scientists have been plotting against it for years. First the problem was how to produce enough energy to overcome the forces of gravity and space; now the problem is how to get an object back.

Inertia is defined as that property or quality of anything which resists change. The force necessary to bring about change depends upon the mass and the desired rate or extent of change. In the physical sciences the qualities of inertia can be reduced to qualities of force and can be stated as a law or mathematical formula—$F=MA$. In the social sciences the forces of inertia are very evident, but the derivation of a law or formula is difficult. While the physical scientists were pondering the problems of inertia encountered in placing an object in orbit, the social scientists were pondering the problems of inertia in education. How do you bring about quality education? How do you overcome apathy? Many solutions have been postulated, always with an apology for social resistance to change or recognition of social inertia. The solutions range from reverting to some primitive magic practiced by previous generations to employing futuristic applications such as drugs, automation, and electronic brain activators. Each has promise except for the one common denominator—social inertia.

The American secondary school has undergone a constant and relentless attack from nearly every segment of society since Sputnik I. Out of all

From University of North Dakota *The College of Education Record,* XLVI (April-May, 1961), 102–114. Reprinted by permission of the publisher.

Figure I

PHILOSOPHIC TREND IN AMERICAN HIGH SCHOOLS
First Half of the Twentieth Century

TYPE OF SCHOOL	TRADITIONAL SCHOOL	PROGRESSIVE SCHOOL	COMMUNITY SCHOOL	COMPREHENSIVE SCHOOL
Period	Until about 1900	About 1920-1930	About 1940	Since about 1958
Orientation	Book-centered	Child-centered	Life-centered	Broad opportunities to learn / Accent on individual ability / Articulation from kindergarten to college
Ultimate aim	Literacy and college preparation	Personality Development	Improvement of living	Individual excellence / Expertness, creativity / Specialization
Curriculum pattern	Academic subjects	Interest activities	Social processes and problems (core)	A kindergarten through high school program individualized to ability and interests / Challenge all students
Fundamental method	Exposition / Explanation / Memorization	Problem solving to satisfy personal interests	Problem solving to meet personal and community needs	Problem solving / Reflective and critical thought / Understanding
Learning values	All deferred	All immediate	Both immediate and deferred	Immediate, deferred, and relative
Keynote of discipline	Repressive control	Freedom from restraint	Cooperative responsibility	Responsibility, appreciation
Resources	Study about people places things	Study with people places things	Study with and about people places things / Involvement of the total community	Understand / evaluate / explore / associate / participate / Education is a continuous process for school and society

the confusion of the past five years is emerging a slight evidence of change or direction. In retrospect it appears that secondary schools have changed in some respect during the past half century. In a very generalized sense the high schools have been typified by periods as traditional, progressive, community, and comprehensive. Figure I contrasts the basic characteristics of each as changes have taken place. In spite of these generally recognized philosophical changes which are minor, there are many more common elements persisting in practice. In terms of instruction a vast majority of the schools continue to practice the same methods and organization first employed in mass education; namely, grouping a number of students for a period of time with one teacher to lecture or instruct in a general area of knowledge. The effectiveness of this practice is agreed to be directly proportionate to the effectiveness of the teacher. It is also agreed that the tens of thousands of teachers range from negative to very positive in effectiveness. The problem is identified, but not everyone is agreed as to which is positive and which is negative. It seems that what is considered important to one student is a bore to another.

Secondary education in the United States has also undergone a number of administrative and organizational changes in the past century. About 100 years ago the high school was just beginning to gain recognition as an essential and integral part of the public school system. Prior to this time there was perhaps general acceptance of the grammar school for all and the academy (the forerunner of the high school) for the select. The rapid growth of the American school system in its western expansion, as well as the increased enrollment, resulted in the establishment of a high school in nearly every population center, regardless of size. In 1860 there were, for example, 321 high schools reported in the United States, 167 of which were situated in three states, Massachusetts, 78; New York, 41; and Ohio, 48. It can be noted that the influence of Horace Mann is especially significant in Massachusetts. By 1870 the number of high schools increased to about 500; by 1880, 800; by 1890, 2,526; and by 1900 to over 6,000.[1] The turn of the century brought about almost complete acceptance of the American high school as part of the universal education concept. By 1920 the number of high schools increased to over 14,000 and then gradually increased to the present nearly 24,000, where the number has leveled off. Although there are many new high schools being opened each year to accommodate student enrollment increases in the larger population and surburban centers, there is a marked reduction in small high schools in the rural areas where populations are decreasing and reorganization is decreasing the number of small and inefficient school districts. The recent emphasis on quality education and concern for higher school costs will

[1] Cubberly, Ellwood P. *Public Education in the United States,* Houghton Mifflin Co. Boston, New York, Chicago, San Francisco: 1919.

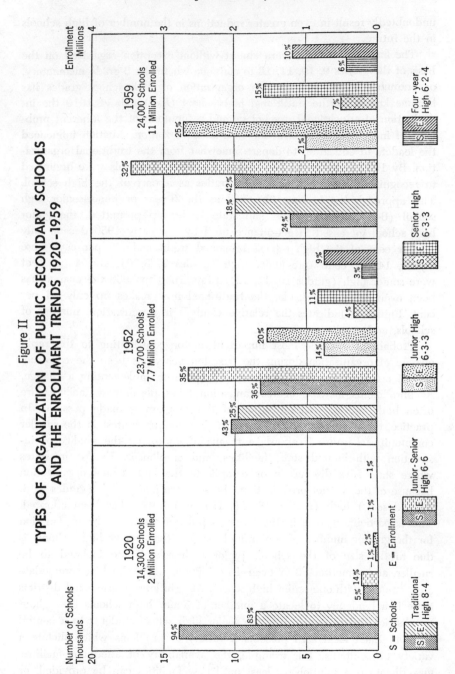

Figure II

TYPES OF ORGANIZATION OF PUBLIC SECONDARY SCHOOLS
AND THE ENROLLMENT TRENDS 1920-1959

Adapted from: Edmond A. Ford, "Organizational Patterns of Nation's Public
Secondary Schools," *School Life,* USOE Journal, Vol. 42, No. 9, May, 1960.

undoubtedly result in even greater reductions in the number of high schools in the future.

The first high schools were almost without exception organized on the basis of the grades 9, 10, 11, 12 to continue where the 8-grade elementary, or grammar, school ended. This organization of high school grades has become known as the traditional high school (8–4). About 1910 the introduction of educational psychology and recognition of the inherent problems of individualized instruction in a mass education situation influenced the leaders in education to depart somewhat from the traditional organization. By 1920 about 6 per cent of the 14,300 high schools were organized to recognize the seventh and eight grades as a part of the high school. This approach has become identified as the 6-year or junior-senior high school (6–6). As state laws and state leadership permitted, the junior high school increased in acceptance until by the early 1950 decade only 43 per cent of the high schools remained traditional, 36 per cent were 6-year, 14 per cent were junior high (grades 7, 8, 9), and 4 per cent were senior high (grades 10, 11, 12). From 1950 to 1960 the change has been even more remarkable; the traditional now makes up only 24 per cent. Figure II indicates the relative changes in organization, number of schools, and enrollments.[2]

Probably the single most important factor contributing to the rapid change of organization during the past ten years has been the construction of new facilities designed for the purpose of implementing a change. As enrollments increase or reorganization takes place, new facilities are often built and the reorganization of the program is made possible. In practice, the popularity of the 6-year high school is greatest in the smaller communities because it affords a means of improving the quality of instruction with limited staff, facilities, and enrollment. Except in states where state laws discourage or complicate the high school organization because of the district organization, the separate junior high (grades 7, 8, 9) and senior high (grades 10, 11, 12) organization has been adopted. This is particularly true in the larger population centers. The explanation for the greater number of junior high schools than senior high schools is due to the size of the school. Junior high schools are inclined to be smaller, and sometimes 3 or even 4 or 5 junior high schools accommodate a community with one senior high school. Also, in large reorganized districts there is a tendency to locate a number of junior high schools throughout the district and transport only the senior high school students to a central location. Each local area presents a variety of problems which dictate a variety of solutions. For example, the availability of adequate facilities may dictate one solution, at least until new facilities can be provided, or

2 Ford, Edmund A. "Organizational Pattern of the Nation's Public Secondary Schools," *School Life,* Official Journal of the Office of Education, Department of Health, Education, and Welfare, Washington 6, D.C.: May, 1960.

the transportation may influence the decision to either centralize or localize attendance centers. The organization is important only as an administrative means of facilitating an improved educational program from kindergarten through high school.

Aristotle, writing in the fourth century B.C., said: "All men do not agree in those things they would have the child learn. From the present mode of education we cannot determine with certainty to which men will incline, whether to instruct a child in what will be useful to him in life, or what tends to virtue, or what is excellent, for all these things have their defenders." After 2,300 years the argument still goes on. While only a very few question the propriety of any public education at all, or would confine it only to the elementary grades, many are quick to challenge the aims and methods of education used in public schools today.

Perhaps H. G. Wells best summarized the present dilemma when, commenting on the subject of provincialism in education, he stated: "The survival of humanity is a race between education and catastrophe, a race in which education must keep up with technological change or civilization will perish." To send a rocket on a trip to the moon may be little compensation on the scientific front if in doing so we lose our liberty on the political and social battlefield.

It is difficult if not foolish to try to discuss the role of secondary education without consideration of the role of the total education process. The secondary school is only a small segment of time in our total educational life, particularly when we consider education a lifetime process. However short it may be, it is important to everyone and perhaps crucial to some, particularly those who do not continue their formal education beyond high school, because life goes on for another fifty years or more for the average person and opportunities in life are greatly affected by our formal education background. We have come to accept the school as simply a social invention for facilitating the educational process of the mentally young more efficiently.

An examination of future inevitabilities and predictable consequences should give some insight into the role of our school system. It seems that three levels of concern need to be examined; namely, the individual, the nation, and the international. Assuming that the individual does have some inherent responsibility to the national and international situation, we might look first at national concern for education as it relates to the international situation. It is reasonably clear that the potential of a nation is neither more nor less than the sum performance of its citizens. It is also reasonably clear that the latent human potential may be as great in one nation as in another, but performance can vary greatly depending in large part on the average level of education of the citizenry. As technology (particularly in transportation and communication) brings people of nations closer together on the time-space continuum, disparity of performance between nations becomes more and more in conflict and a common problem. This it seems is the present impending and increasingly more crucial international problem. In any event, it is recognized as a problem worthy of writing about by more national and international authorities than has been true at any period in our past history. It is probably the number one priority now. As a nation of people we feel the impact more intensely than ever before because some of the less-educated neighbors are nearly in our back yard. As we recognize the problems inherent in this international situation we begin to search for solutions. Our attention is immediately directed to the one institution recognized as basically responsible for the improvement of our national performance—the American school system. At this time, in the various state legislatures and at the national level, much time and attention is being directed toward legislative reform to improve education. Upgrading the performance level of the citizenry is vital to national progress and important to international prestige. Although it is a national and international concern, the only approach is through the education of individuals. In the final analysis the solution requires that each individual be given the opportunity to develop his potential to perform at the maximum for the mutual benefit of himself and society. In precise words, as expressed in the statement of *Goals for Americans*,[3] "The central goal, therefore, should be a renewal of faith in the infinite value and the unlimited possibilities of individual development," or stated as the first national goal, "The development of the individual to his fullest potential." This is based on the philosophy that "No limits are known to the degree to which, by the expenditure of adequate time, energy, skill, and money, the human mind can be developed at various levels of ability." This seems to be the challenge and the solution to the gravest of individual, national and international problems. They must be considered inseparably important and interdependent if we are to avoid catastrophe.

In looking ahead to the time when the products of our schools today face the practical problems of life, several eventualities seem probable. Will enough of today's students be properly prepared for useful purposes in the world of tomorrow? Already the unemployment problem looms as a major national concern. At the same time, competition increases for the services of the technically and professionally prepared.[4] Nearly every trade and professional official publication emphasizes the gross shortage of prepared employees and predicts even more critical shortages in the future.[5] Figure III illustrates the trend and predicted manpower needs by 1975.[6]

[3] "The Report of the President's Commission on National Goals," *Goals for Americans*, Prentice-Hall, Inc., 1960, p. 57.
[4] "Shortage of Skills—It Grows Despite Unemployment," *Time*, March 10, 1961, p. 90.
[5] "The Fabulous Fifteen Years Ahead," *Changing Times*, The Kiplinger Magazine, Washington, D.C., January, 1961.
[6] "The Coming Boom in Good Jobs," *Changing Times*, The Kiplinger Magazine, Washington, D.C., December, 1957.

Figure III
NOT MUCH FUTURE FOR THE UNSKILLED
Employment Trends 1910-1975

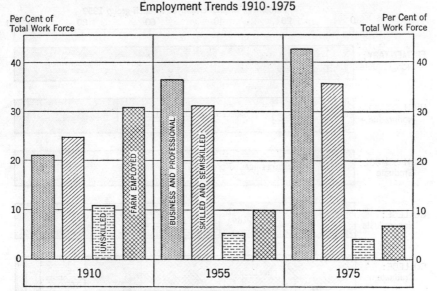

Percentage of U.S.A. work force by employment classification
for the years 1910, 1955, and predicted for 1975

Adapted from: *Changing Times,* "The Coming Boom in Good Jobs," December, 1957.

Figure IV indicates the relationship of occupations to education level for the year 1959.[7] The best evidence available indicates that only about 50 per cent of the labor force has completed high school and that about 10 per cent is prepared with college degrees. In the decade ahead the predicted manpower requirements needed to adequately meet the classification of technological and professional alone will approach nearly 40 per cent. With only the 10 per cent of college-prepared workers available and no clear trend indicating a marked increase in the immediate future, the critical future need for a more highly educated population is dramatically pointed up.

One important implication of the problem of educating the individual (and consequently the potential of the total population) to meet the labor force requirements is illustrated on a normal distribution curve in Figure V. This attempts to show the ability range and relative percentages as now employed. In terms of the basic potential of people this is the present relationship between ability and jobs. As human potential will remain constant, so the challenge facing our educational system is to find

[7] *The Conference Board,* "Road Maps of Industry," National Industrial Conference Board, Inc., New York, No. 1268, April, 1960.

Figure IV
EDUCATION AND OCCUPATION

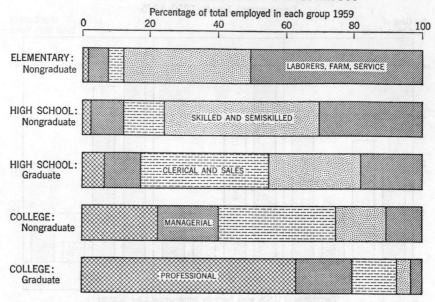

Percentage of total employed in each group 1959

Reproduced with permission of: *The Conference Board,* "Road Maps of Industry," No. 1268, National Industrial Conference Board, Inc., New York, April 15, 1960.

ways to shift considerable numbers of the future work force into positions requiring higher degrees of skill and competence. The alternatives are quite clear. Unless through education a greater percentage of the population is prepared for more technical jobs, the dead weight or inertia of unemployment due to an overabundance of the insufficiently trained will level off or possibly cause a recession in American progress. However, if we can meet the challenge educationally we can progress as a nation and a bright future will lie ahead for the citizen.

Education Pays
Average yearly earnings of employees by labor classification, 1960

Labor classification	Average yearly salary
Laborers	$ 4,100
Semiskilled	5,200
Proprietors and Clerical	6,000
Technical-Managerial	7,600
Professional	11,000

Figure V
HOW PEOPLE OF THE U.S.A. WERE EMPLOYED TO EARN A LIVING IN 1955

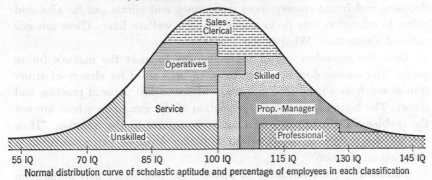

Normal distribution curve of scholastic aptitude and percentage of employees in each classification

Employment Classification	Per cent	IQ Range
Professional	9	110-140+
Prop.-Manager	17	105-135
Skilled	13	110-120
Sales-Clerical	19	90-110
Operatives	20	85-105
Service	10	75-105
Unskilled	12	70-100

Adapted from: Ray Bryan, "Creating Understanding," U.S. Census and AGCT scores.

The secondary school does represent a particularly critical period in each student's educational life. It is during this short period that the student's interests and potentialities must be fully explored, and it is during this period that he needs maximum encouragement and assistance to determine the available optimum opportunities for future success in accordance with his interests and abilities. In terms of the individual the role of the secondary school is to provide through a very comprehensive program and individualized instruction the maximum opportunity for each student to progress toward his goals—the achievement of excellence in the performance of his chosen occupation.

It is our national concern that this educational goal be achieved. It is our concern that the secondary school do its part. Most state laws, through compulsory attendance age limitations, require students to be in school through at least part of the secondary program. As a nation it appears that we can tolerate neither an appreciable dropout of the less able nor the termination of education for those more able at any point short of full expression of their potential capabilities and capacities. With a national capacity for future useful employment of less than 10 per cent in the unskilled worker classification, the present dropout rate of nearly 30 per cent of the students before high school graduation will pose a real unemployment problem for the future. Stated in terms of present decisions and future consequences our money and efforts can be allocated either to education now or to unemployment welfare later. These are our national alternatives. What is our choice?

Does the secondary school need changes to meet the nation's future needs? The answer does not seem to point up a need for change of structure so much as a need for application of sound instructional practice and theory. The basic concept and organization of the secondary school are not the problem. The problem seems to be in answer to the question, "How can all the people be educated to a higher level of performance in a shorter span of time?"

Admittedly, great advances in knowledge, technology and application have been made in recent years. It has been stated without too much argumentation that our accumulation of recorded knowledge has been doubling each decade or so since the turn of this century. This implies that the schools should have imparted a comparably greater amount of knowledge for each generation of students if, as adults, they are to take a relatively equal position in a changing society. Increases have been made in the dispensation of knowledge, but apparently not enough. The process, we agree, is extremely complex. Children begin their formal education at age five, and in the twelve years of schooling they not only must acquire the basic skills of the "3 R's" as always but they must, in addition, accumulate from five to eight times as much knowledge and skill as the children of fifty years ago. Hence the need for more efficient and effective methods of teaching.

Our dilemma today can be likened to the development of our transportation conveniences. Until about one hundred years ago the quickest and most convenient method of transportation was by animal, the horse. Then came the railroad. About fifty years ago the automobile was introduced and improved, and it replaced the animal. The first automobiles were soon declared obsolete because of inherent performance limitations, namely, speed. The early models were retired because 35 mph was not fast enough. About thirty years ago new models were designed to double that speed, which seems to be maximum for land vehicles because of traffic safety. People then turned to the air, first with slow model planes, later faster models, and now supersonic models are being fabricated. With each change of speed because of limitations, the old models have been discarded for new designs. The actual changes have been insignificant; the old designs have merely been technically improved through engineering efficiency and performance.

We face much the same problem in education except that society is reluctant to scrap the old chassis in favor of more effective and efficient methods of instruction. Compare the engineering technology of the first automobile fifty years ago with that of the modern one or with that which produced a supersonic jet of today. Now compare the teaching technology of fifty years ago with that of today. In the case of engineering technology and transportation the change is almost incomprehensible; in the case of education it is only minor. Very little improvement has been made in teaching technology. If we are to break through the educational sound barrier society must recognize the need for the application of more efficient and effective teaching technology.

How do we greatly speed up the process of instruction and at the same time improve the performance of every child? The solutions may not be simple or inexpensive, but to find them and put them into practice is critical. The following suggestions are made because they are basic and of universal concern:

1. Individualize instruction at all levels, elementary through college, so that well-prepared teachers can deal with the interests and talents of each child as he progresses at his predestined rate. This implies a much smaller ratio of students per teacher—perhaps six or eight students per teacher.

2. Organize the instructional staff to utilize their greatest teaching potentialities where they are most valuable. This implies organization of schools and school districts into effectively sound and efficient units. It also implies efficient use of teachers' time for professional purposes.

3. Initiate steps to prepare professionally capable teachers. This implies the minimum of a six-year college teacher preparation program with several years of internship. Also, this implies salaries commensurate with the professional investment and performance of these teachers.

4. Utilize automation, instructional machines, and actual student experiences to facilitate teaching and learning. This implies considerable improvement of facility and equipment and perhaps a complete redesign of some buildings. It also implies use of services and facilities available in the community.

5. Carefully articulate the educational program for the student to progress efficiently and effectively from kindergarten through school and his life work. This implies the kind of differentiation of students and program to take each as far along the educational road as is feasible.

6. Education is a lifetime process and our schools need to be designed for continuous education of the citizenry throughout life. This implies a considerable expansion of the present curriculum both in content and in scope, particularly at the adult level. As the demands of society change, the schools need to provide the means for citizens to advance their skills and technology in order to continue to be worthwhile contributors.

To try to look at the problems without visualizing the ultimate goals and total situation can result in nothing but confusion. When the ultimate implications are carefully considered, then decisions can be made in terms of alternatives. The alternatives are to progress or to regress. To stand still for a minute in the international situation today is to regress.

Let us for once approach education from the student's point of view. How can a student be assisted toward the greatest development of his potentialities? Assume that one teacher and one student were to undertake the task of learning a subject. The teacher is a specialist; the student may be slow, average, or talented. What would take place? Given an allotment of time each week the teacher would work with the student proceeding from the student's understanding and mastery of the subject into new material step by step as the student gained new mastery of skills and understanding. The rate of progress would be determined entirely by the interest and capabilities of the student and, of course, the skill of the teacher. Some will say, "Yes, this would be an ideal situation." Admittedly, in this manner students could be moved through subject matter much faster and with much greater mastery. No two students would move at exactly the same rate; hence, the time necessary to cover a given lesson or develop skills would vary in terms of the student's potential to progress. Teachers' opinions indicate at least a belief on their part that this approach, working with one individual, could easily result in coverage of the yearly quota of subject matter with much greater mastery in easily less than one-half the usual time. Teachers generally agree, also, that there would be further gains with certain tasks if there were several students rather than one. However, the advantages of individualized instruction would be lost for most situations if many more than five students were tutored at one time. Teachers explain that the methods they would use would depart quite radically from the traditional. The departures would include, of course, capitalization on the individual's interests and natural motivation, real and practical problems, field trips, and follow-up of individual questions and problems through reading and research. On the individual approach, if possible, much use would be made of such teaching devices as teaching machines, particularly for the efficient mastery of facts and rote skills. The use of proper and adequate instructional materials would, in some instances, extend a teacher's effectiveness to a larger group of students (perhaps seven to ten). It is generally agreed that the potential of a class of high school students developed thus individually by professional teachers could result in achievement almost beyond comprehension.

Several problems can immediately be thrown up as a smoke screen to this approach. However, the individualizing of instruction has such great promise in terms of meeting the present and future national manpower need that the challenge should be to give our energies to make it possible instead of making excuses for it not being practical. It will be expensive. There are not enough professional teachers now and this would require at least three for each one now in service. Our present buildings would have limited usefulness and so the problems can be identified on and on without end. This is, however, quite similar to the problems facing the space scientists. Let us take a lesson from them. They have spent their time working out the problems and overcoming the failures. It is extremely expensive, they have a shortage of trained personnel, and they are not patching up old models. They are using their technology to design new models and problems are identified in order to work on solutions. Let us set our sights on some practices which, when accomplished, will mean a major breakthrough. We must make a major breakthrough, but our goals are worthy of our best efforts. Man's potential has only been sampled to date. Or do you disagree with this last statement?

Education is the key to survival or to catastrophe. To argue the merits of schedules, discipline, grouping, subject matter, and other similarly moot matters as relating to the goals of education at this time would have about the same relationship to the real problem as to argue the merits of modernizing the Model T by installing new plugs, a new timer, new tires, and new seat covers as sufficient to keep pace on the superhighway or in the race for exploration of outer space. It will take more than superficial remodeling. We need a sound basic design.

We need some new educational designs which will hold together. We have the research, we have the experience, we have the goals, and we have the national and financial resources. Yes, we have inertia in education too, but once we break through the barrier of educational tradition as the space scientists have broken through the gravity barrier, inertia can maintain our society in orbit as inertia keeps our satellites in orbit. The choice rests with society, but society depends on the educational technology and advice of professional educators. What is your problem with inertia? Are you permitting inertia to hold you back, or are you utilizing it to move yourself forward—in orbit!

part ii

The secondary school student

The purpose of all education is to bring about changes in behavior. First, the school attempts to change ignorance to knowledge. When we educators realize how rapidly vast areas of knowledge are becoming available to us, we begin to see the gigantic task which confronts the school. We know that an informed and intelligent citizenry is necessary if our democratic way of life is to survive. We know that the school has been entrusted with the responsibility of helping students make sense out of what is happening around them daily. The school should help the citizens of tomorrow to evaluate the newspapers they read, the speeches they listen to, the commercials that are forced upon them, and the meaning of life itself. But we also realize that knowledge is powerful, and that unless it is directed toward noble ends it is dangerous. An intelligent demagogue is a far greater threat to our way of life than an illiterate thug. For this reason the school must be concerned with more than the mere development of the intellect.

This leads to the second kind of change the school must endeavor to effect. The school must develop students who act on the basis of ideals rather than on the basis of impulses. And what is an ideal if it is not loyalty to an idea? We want our schools to develop citizens who will put their intelligence to good use; we want citizens who will strive mightily to use their intelligence to improve the world into which they have been born; we want to develop citizens who will be able to cooperate effectively with other citizens who differ from them in race, religion, and nationality.

We want to produce Americans who are so proud of being American that they will abhor the use of totalitarian methods in their daily lives. We do not want to produce citizens who are distrustful of other citizens who disagree with them on political or religious matters, for in this day and age America cannot afford discrimination in any of its ugly forms.

An effective citizen also makes a positive contribution to the nation's economy. He has a salable skill, which enables him to support himself and his loved ones while contributing to the economic community. To assist students in this area, the school must effect another kind of change. It must help students change their capacities to abilities. To do this, the school must have some means of learning what the aptitudes of individual students are. It must have more than a single-track program; its curriculum must provide for those who are going on to college and for those who are employed immediately after high school. The school must help students to identify and develop their talents—as diverse as these talents might be.

In sum, then, the school must effect three kinds of changes in the students it serves:

1. It must help them to become less ignorant and more knowledgeable.

2. It must help them to act less on the basis of impulse and more on the basis of ideals.

3. It must help them to transform their capacities into abilities, their potentials into actualities.

Of course, the kind and extent of behavioral change that actually takes place in school are dependent upon the crucial characteristics of the student, the potentials each student has which make specific changes possible. Although all students are equal in their rights before the law, this is the only way in which all students are equal. All students have certain basic needs, love and security, for example, but they differ greatly in the extent to which they have fulfilled these needs, as well as in the manner in which these needs have been met. It follows that before a teacher can hope to effect desirable behavioral changes in students—and this is what true learning is—he must be aware of the differences existing among students in his classes. Since students differ in intellectual capacity, emotional security, and physical development, this is no small task. The problem is confounded by social forces which are constantly impinging upon the student. A teacher must take account of the significant differences among students, for these differences are intimately related to the aspirations of students and help determine the extent to which students will profit from their educational experience.

The selections in Part II are concerned with the differences among students in public secondary schools. Thompson's article deals with the psychological and social characteristics of freshmen and seniors in rural and urban secondary schools in California.

The contributions of Taylor, Havighurst, Dale, and French and Steffen are concerned with specific kinds of students. Taylor discusses creativity and suggests some means for identifying creative individuals. Havighurst describes the characteristics and developments of students who are classified "hard to reach." Dale writes about students who drop out of high school, whereas French and Steffen are concerned with gifted adolescents who are planning to become teachers.

Coleman's paper is one of the most insightful contributions on the adolescent subculture to appear in the professional literature. His concern for the dispersion of the energy of the adolescent has many implications for the secondary school program.

The student of education who reads and reflects upon these selections should gain an appreciation of the tremendous complexity involved in helping students acquire desirable patterns of behavior. These articles should help the prospective teacher bridge the gap between simple knowledge of student behavior and the transformation of this knowledge into effective teaching behavior.

chapter 10

What is the high school student of today like?

O. E. Thompson

What is the high school student of today like? What is his home situation? Does his mother work? With whom does he live? Does he attend church regularly? Has he made an occupational choice? What is important to him in selecting a vocation?

Answers to these and similar questions about the high school student should be of interest not only to the general public but particularly to those in curriculum planning, pupil personnel work, and educational and vocational guidance, and those responsible for the over-all administration of the school.

It is often stated that the high school student of today is different from one of a decade ago. Undoubtedly this is partially true, for as our society progresses, the occupational values, personal values, and attitudes of students will reflect the culture of the particular era.

Today the family situation is in transition. The general economic level of the American family is near an all-time high. Education in general is undergoing critical evaluation. Atomic energy and space research are forging ahead at an unbelievable pace. The conflict in ideologies among world powers is at fever pitch. These and many other developments and problems cannot help but influence and direct the thinking, action, and general characteristics of the modern teen-ager.

From *Journal of Secondary Education*, 36(April, 1961), 210–219. Reprinted by permission of author and publisher.

THE PROBLEM

The problem under study was—what are some of the sociological and psychological characteristics of the modern high school student and how do these characteristics relate to his vocational choice and his reaction to selected vocational values and desires?

PROCEDURE

The questions already listed, plus others, were posed to freshmen and seniors in five central-California high schools—two small ones in rural areas, one medium-sized school in an industrial area, and two moderately large schools, one in a semirural community and the other in a strictly urban center. Thus, this is a cross section of the various kinds of high schools, and might well be considered a sample of typical California high schools.

Each freshman and senior completed a survey form asking for personal information and reactions to certain occupational values plus a personal differential values inventory. A random sample of 100 boys and 100 girls from each of the classes was drawn for analysis from the total population of about 1,400 students. This report deals with only the personal information and occupational values of the students.

DISCUSSION

Home Situation

The home situation is often a factor with mentally disturbed children as well as with those who exhibit tendencies toward delinquency. Here, the idea was not to try to correlate family situation with any other characteristics but merely to find the proportion of high school students that came from atypical home situations.

It was found that about one in eight students came from an abnormal home. About two-thirds of those not living with both parents were living with the mother. Home situation differed little between boys and girls, and between freshmen and seniors.

In some areas the place of residence is known to influence the opportunities students have in high school, their attitudes and values, and the curriculum they follow. This study, however, found little difference between rural students and their city cousins. In this study at least, rural students did not necessarily live on farms. Thus, only one-third of the parents of rural students were farmers. About one-fifth were in each vocational class, skilled and unskilled, whereas over one-tenth were in the professional-managerial category, only slightly less than the proportion for the parents of city students. This perhaps accounts for the lack of major differences between rural and city students.

The only stratification showing significant differences between rural and city students was whether the mother worked outside the home for pay. Significantly fewer (at 1 per cent level) of the rural mothers worked outside the home. That is logical when one considers items such as employment opportunity and child care facilities.

No differences were apparent between rural and urban students in high school curriculum, vocational choice, academic achievement, church attendance, or occupational values and desires.

High School Curriculum

Although the curriculums followed by rural and urban students were very similar, the same is not true for other stratifications of the sample. It will be noted in Table 1 that slightly over two-fifths (43.5 per cent) of the entire group were taking a program designed for entrance into college. Almost one-fourth were in each curriculum, business and general. About one-tenth didn't know what curriculum they were enrolled in. Probably it was a general curriculum, for they likely would have been aware of any special choice they might have made.

Table 1 Curriculum followed in high school
(All figures are in per cent.)

Curriculum	All boys $N = 200$	All girls $N = 200$	Freshmen $N = 200$	Seniors $N = 200$	Total $N = 400$
College preparatory	48.5	38.5	43.5	43.5	43.5
Business-commercial	6.5	38.5	19.0	26.0	22.5
General	32.0	16.0	23.0	25.0	24.0
Don't know	13.0	7.0	14.5	5.5	10.0

chi square $= 62.074$ chi square $= 10.442$
(significant 1% level)   (significant 5% level)

Differences between boys and girls in curricular choice were large enough to be significant at the 1 per cent level. Significantly more boys than girls were in the college preparatory curriculum, whereas the reverse was true in the business field. Likewise, more boys than girls were in the general major.

Differences in curricular choice were also large enough to be significant between freshmen and seniors, but not as great as between boys and girls. More seniors were in the business and general curriculum, whereas more freshmen than seniors did not know what curriculum they were in.

The decrease in the number of seniors unsure about their major could mean one of two things—either a proportion had settled upon a specific major or had withdrawn from school.

Academic Achievement

Academic achievement was measured by the grades students stated they received. Although the grade distribution for all the students does not follow a normal curve, it is probably quite typical for the average high school. Failures because of deficient grades are generally quite rare.

Grades earned by students during the 1959–1960 school year were compared with the grades students indicated they received. There was no demonstrable difference between grades earned and grades indicated. Girls proved to get better grades than boys, enough so to be significantly superior at the 1 per cent level. Likewise, grades for seniors were enough higher than those of freshmen to be significant at the 1 per cent level. Undoubtedly the dropping out of some of the low-ability students had upgraded the average for the seniors. See Table 2.

Table 2 Academic level of achievement
(All figures are in per cent.)

Grades	All boys N = 200	All girls N = 200	Freshmen N = 200	Seniors N = 200	Total N = 400
Mostly A's	4.00	12.06	8.54	7.50 .	8.02
Mostly B's	27.50	35.17	23.11	39.50	31.33
Mostly C's	54.50	44.72	52.26	47.00	49.62
Mostly D's	13.50	8.04	15.57	6.00	10.78
Below D	0.50	....	0.50	....	0.25
	chi square = 14.675 (significant 1% level)		chi square = 17.796 (significant 1% level)		

It was also found that, in general, students with high ability were in the college preparatory majors, and the less-capable students were in the less-demanding majors. Of the 32 students in the A grade category, 87 per cent were in college preparatory work. Likewise, B students tended to be oriented toward the college preparation majors. Actually, about two-thirds of this group were preparing for college and one-fifth were in the business major.

Students earning mostly C grades were about equally distributed among the majors, whereas the D students were primarily in the general curriculum group. It is evident that students in general, either on their own or with the assistance of counselors, are seeking the kinds of educational preparation that are in line with their abilities. Naturally, there are minor departures from this.

When students whose mothers worked outside the home were compared with those whose mothers did not, the differences in grades were significant at the 5 per cent level. Students whose mothers worked received significantly higher grades than those whose mothers did not.

Church Attendance

Studies of student characteristics ordinarily omit consideration of the spiritual side of the students' lives. Since this one aspect may be a factor influencing others, it is included in this study. The frequency with which a student attended church was used as an indicator of his religious interest.

It is obvious from Table 3 that there is a difference in the frequency with which the different groups attended church. Girls were by far the most regular in attendance, with the differences between boys and girls significant at the 1 per cent level. Freshmen attend church more frequently than seniors, though the difference was not as great as between boys and girls (5 per cent significance). It can be concluded that boys, and senior boys in particular, have poor church attendance records.

Table 3   **Frequency of church attendance**
(All figures are in per cent.)

Frequency	All boys N = 200	All girls N = 200	Freshmen N = 200	Seniors N = 200	Total N = 400
More than once weekly	7.00	12.50	11.00	8.50	9.75
Once a week	36.00	52.50	49.00	39.50	44.25
About once monthly	15.00	15.50	16.50	14.00	15.25
Seldom	42.00	19.50	23.50	38.00	30.75

chi square = 25.741   chi square = 9.933
(significant 1% level)   (significant 5% level)

A comparison of the church attendance of A, B, C, and D students showed a distinct relationship. Over 71 per cent of A students attended church at least once a week, compared with 54 per cent of B students, and 51 per cent of C and D students. Only 6 per cent of the A students seldom attended church, whereas this percentage was respectively 32, 30, and 41 for the B, C, and D groups.

Occupation of Father and Vocational Choice of Students

Each student was asked to state what his father did to support his family. These jobs were then classified into seven major categories by the Dictionary of Occupational Titles.[1] Student vocational choices were classified similarly. Table 4 compares the occupations of the fathers and vocational choices for boys, girls, and both.

Students in general aspire to occupations that are higher on the socio-economic ladder than those of their fathers. For example, over three times as many boys chose professional-managerial kinds of vocations as there were fathers in these occupations. Many girls were interested in clerical-sales vocations. The vocation with the closest relation between fathers and students was agriculture-forestry. Here, almost as many boys (14.5 per cent) planned to enter the vocation as there were fathers presently in the vocation.

Table 4   Comparison of the vocational choices of students with the occupation of the fathers
(All figures are in per cent.)

Kind of occupation	Father's occupation All boys N = 200	Choice of boys	Father's occupation All girls N = 200	Choice of girls	Father's occupation Totals N = 400	Choice of students
1. Professional-Managerial	11.50	38.00	17.00	36.00	14.25	37.00
2. Clerical-Sales	11.50	3.00	8.00	32.50	9.75	17.75
3. Services	5.00	9.00	7.50	11.50	6.25	10.25
4. Agriculture-Forestry	16.00	14.50	19.00	0.50	17.50	7.50
5. Skilled	27.50	13.50	17.50	....	22.50	6.75
6. Semiskilled	6.00	1.00	5.50	1.00	5.75	1.00
7. Unskilled	13.00	4.00	17.00	....	15.00	2.00
8. Unemployed, retired, undecided	9.50	17.00	8.50	18.50	9.00	17.75

It is readily apparent that most high school students have made at least tentative vocational choices. When freshmen were considered separately, only 22 per cent were undecided, some 8.5 per cent more than for seniors. This refutes the contention of some educators that students of this age are too immature even to consider this important decision.

Also, it is interesting to note that girls were as vocation conscious as were boys. On the data sheets many girls indicated that being home-makers was their ultimate goal. Nevertheless, most were planning for another vocation first.

Some interesting inferences can be drawn when the vocational choices of students are compared with academic achievement. Three-fourths of the

[1] U.S. Department of Labor, Bureau of Employment Security, *Dictionary of Occupational Titles: 1949*, Vol. II, Occupational Classification and Industry Index.

students in the A group were interested in professional-managerial vocations, with none choosing semiskilled or unskilled work. The C students, which included about one-half of the entire group, were interested in a wider range of vocations. Slightly over one-fourth chose the professional types of vocations, and about 15 per cent were interested in clerical work. About 10 per cent were interested in service, agricultural, and skilled kinds of vocations. The D students likewise chose a wide range of vocations, with some one-fourth (the largest group) interested in service kinds of vocations.

It is interesting to note that the undecided students were primarily in the C and D groups: over 20 per cent in these groups, compared with 10 per cent in the A and B groups. In one sense it can be said that students are reasonably realistic in choosing vocations that are in line with their academic achievement.

One might observe, however, that far too many of the C and D students are considering vocations that require a four-year college degree. Also, too many are avoiding the semiskilled, skilled, and unskilled occupations.

Over 43 per cent of the fathers were employed in these categories, yet only 9 per cent of the students showed an interest in these areas. Granted, there has been a decrease in the need for unskilled laborers; but the same is not true for semiskilled and skilled workers. The missile industry has created a terrific demand for such technicians.

It is highly desirable to have students raise their levels of aspiration, but care must be taken to ensure that these are in line with the students' mental and physical abilities. One might conclude that a number of these students, particularly those with average academic accomplishments and below, are being oversold on the "prestige vocations."

Occupational Values and Desires of Students

Interesting information resulted from findings on student values regarding a job or vocation. Student values were assessed by having each student record whether each of the items below was important or not important to him in deciding on the vocation of his choice:

1. A job where you could be a leader.
2. A very interesting job.
3. A job where you will be looked upon very highly by your fellow men.
4. A job where you could be boss.
5. A job you are absolutely sure of keeping.
6. A job where you could express your feelings, ideas, talents, or skills.
7. A very highly paid job.

8. A job where you could make a name for yourself or become famous.
9. A job where you could help other people.
10. A job where you could work more or less on your own.

The above statements were adopted from items developed by Center.[2] The sincerity with which students responded to the ten items is exemplified by the fact that there were only six omissions out of a possible 4,000 responses.

It is apparent in Table 5 that the high school student of today places high emphasis on a vocation that provides interesting experiences, a means of self-expression, security, and an opportunity to give social service. Also important to him, though less so, is independence, esteem of fellow workers, and a high salary.

The values and desires given very little importance, and in a way almost rejected, were drive to be the leader, desire to be the boss, and desire to become famous. It is disturbing to see so many young people reject the values and desires that many would attribute to the successful man of today. The three low-rated values are an integral part of our emphasis on freedom of the individual.

One might wonder if students are reflecting the emphasis that schools may be placing on the fact that the things we do should benefit society as a whole and not be for personal gain or recognition. In any event, these interesting findings deserve study with more refined instruments. These results compare favorably with the findings of Center[3] and Wilson,[4] who used similar measuring instruments.

There was general agreement among stratifications in the responses of students to individual values and desires, but significant differences did appear. Boys rated leadership important to them significantly more times than did girls, even though both rated this item rather low. Likewise, boys were significantly more interested than girls in positions giving power and a high salary. Girls were significantly more interested in providing social service. Freshmen were significantly more interested than seniors in having security, high salary, and recognition in their vocations.

A comparison of the occupational values and desires of students, stratified by academic achievement, showed some definite trends. As grades went from A to D, interest in being boss, high salary, and job security increased substantially. The opposite was true of interest in self-expression. Others showed practically no variation among grade categories.

Stratification by frequency of church attendance showed that student interest in being boss, getting a high salary, or becoming famous increased

[2] Richard Center, *The Psychology of Social Classes*, Princeton: Princeton University Press, 1949, 152.

[3] *Ibid.*, 152.

[4] W. Cody Wilson, "Value Differences between Public and Private School Graduates," *The Journal of Educational Psychology*, Vol. 50, No. 5, October, 1959, p. 213.

Table 5 Student reactions to various occupational values and desires
(Per cents stating that this value or desire was important to him personally.)

Values, desires	All boys N = 200	All girls N = 200	Freshmen N = 200	Seniors N = 200	Total N = 400
1. Leadership	38.5*	21.5	33.0	27.0	30.0
2. Interesting experiences	95.5	98.0	96.5	97.0	96.7
3. Esteem	64.0	58.5	64.0	58.5	61.2
4. Power	33.5*	9.0	23.0	19.5	21.2
5. Security	92.0	83.0	91.0*	84.0	87.5
6. Self-expression	88.0	91.5	87.5	92.0	89.7
7. Profit	69.5*	52.0	68.5*	53.0	60.7
8. Fame	25.0	18.0	27.0*	16.0	21.5
9. Social service	72.5	91.5*	84.5	79.5	82.0
10. Independence	65.0	60.5	61.0	64.5	62.7

* Significantly different from its counterpart at the 5% level.

as regularity of church attendance decreased. No other categories were correlated with church attendance.

CONCLUSIONS

There are certain recognized dangers in attempting to arrive at a composite picture of the high school student of today by a study of any kind. This study was intended to give some insight into this problem and not necessarily to arrive at any conclusions. Even so, from these data we might venture to describe the modern high school student as follows:

1. Chances are seven to one that he is living with both parents.

2. Whether he lives in the country or in the town or city will not noticeably influence his high school program.

3. If he is a high-achieving student, the chances are that he is taking a college preparatory major, plans to enter a professional field, and attends church at least once a week.

4. If he is a low-achieving student he is probably enrolled in the general major, may be undecided about vocational plans or is interested in a service kind of vocation, and is quite irregular in church attendance.

5. If the student is a boy his grades are probably lower than the average for the girls.

6. If his mother works outside the home, chances are he gets higher grades than if she did not work.

7. He has made at least a tentative vocational choice, and this decision will conform in general to his academic ability as measured by achieve-

ment. The vocation of his choice will probably be on a higher socio-economic level than that of his father.

8. When considering a vocation he will place high emphasis on a job that offers interesting experiences, a means of self-expression, job security, and an opportunity for social service.

9. He will place moderate emphasis on a vocation that provides for independence, esteem of fellow workers, and a high salary.

10. He will attach only minor importance to a vocation that will enable him to be a leader, to be a boss, or to become famous.

The reader is reminded that these are group characteristics and may not be representative of a single individual. Perhaps the most important outcome of the study is that patterns do appear to exist among certain of the sociological and psychological characteristics of freshmen and seniors in high school.

chapter 11

A tentative description of the creative individual

Calvin W. Taylor

Recently a researcher in education wrote that "if anything is needed in our educational system, it is a way to speed up the application of research findings to educational procedures." We all have some responsibility in this area. Some of us who have been doing basic research must communicate our findings and our suggested new leads while those in education, in my opinion, have a responsibility for testing out these findings in their setting and incorporating into their system those that prove to be relevant and effective.[1] At best I feel only partly adequate in my attempt to transmit some of the many ideas and findings that have emerged from research on creativity to date.

In discussing the topic of creativity at this time, I would rather err by exaggerating differences and unsolved problems and by stirring thought and counteractions than by debunking these problems and differences. My approach will be more to stir research and thinking than to attempt prematurely to find a perfect stance and to make perfect statements in this relatively young scientific field.

[1] We are currently engaged in a research project with support from the U.S. Office of Education in which we are searching for and assembling relevant research findings from psychology and other fields that have implications for education.

From a paper presented at the University of Minnesota, October, 1959. Reprinted by permission of the author.

This paper is a revised version of a report given at the Fifth ASCD Research Institute (Eastern Section) in Washington, D.C., in December, 1959, which in turn was a modification of a paper presented at the Second Minnesota Conference on Gifted Children held at the University of Minnesota in October, 1959.

Several Different Types of Gifted

In order to stir such thinking I have recently been stating to others that they may want to seek the gifted, but I am interested in seeking the creative. Then I indicate that the word "gifted" as typically used is closely tied to the current intelligence tests, but that I will be using quite different tests in a search for the creative. The word gifted has also been tied to high academic performance in school-like activities, not often very creative in nature. The implication is that there may be essentially two different worlds, the academic world with its current school-like activities, and an almost different world on the job calling for creative activities as well as other activities which may not overlap very much the nature of the activities in school.

In your thinking you may already be giving me some difficulties in using this recently adopted approach, because you may be expanding your concept of gifted to include creativity. This type of expanding of the meaning of the word "gifted" usually emerges quite rapidly, as a counteraction to my attempts to make a sharp distinction between the gifted and the creative. However, some points should be made by contrasting intelligence, as measured by the traditional type of IQ tests, with creative talent. The traditional intelligence tests cover only a *very few* of the *large number of dimensions of the mind* that we have been discovering to date. Consequently, there may be several other types of intellectually gifted than the IQ type, even though the IQ type may be closely tied to our current academic activities and to the grades that measure success in our present academic world.

I will focus on the creative type of gifted rather than on the IQ type. My current thought is that there may be not only several different types of creativity, but also *several other types of gifted,* relatively separate from the IQ type and the creative types. Some of these other types may be planning, evaluation or decision making, and communication types. Before focusing on creative types of gifted, I will comment on the total field of high-level talent.

Certain Concepts May Deter Future Progress

A friend once said that we would make further progress in a particular area when we became sufficiently dissatisfied with the shortcomings of the current categories in that area, even though they had served valuable purposes up to that time. In considering giftedness, we may now need to recognize the difficulties in many of the current categories and concepts that have quite wide usage in order to make better progress. For example, with the discovery of fifty or more dimensions of the mind, only a handful of which are currently included in our IQ tests, we find it difficult to refer to these other forty or so dimensions in customary terms. They are *not* a part of intelligence (as traditionally measured) though they are *intellectual* activities. Consequently, we could describe these many other important dimensions of the mind as *nonintelligence intellectual activities.* Undoubtedly you will admit that this is a clumsy and confusing type of statement. This statement illustrates our difficult predicament in trying to communicate many new research findings on the complexity of the mind.

Another example of current terminology limitations is that we now might say that a certain person does not particularly have high intelligence even though he does have a certain *special ability,* such as merely the special ability to do scientific research, or the special ability to be creative in one or more fields such as composing new music, or the special ability to pioneer new ventures, or the special ability to emerge as a leading executive in our world of work. You can readily see that I am not particularly fond of the current, almost completely preeminent position of the initial set of dimensions of the mind which have formed our concept of intelligence.

I do not like to see *other really parallel things actually* relegated to an implied lesser category called "special abilities." Instead, I have often felt that the human characteristics that we are able to measure first are *not necessarily the most important* characteristics. Some of the remaining characteristics which have been postponed for later measurement may often be extremely important characteristics. We have just not known how to measure them earlier.

To me it is highly inconsistent to conceive of the mind as being represented by a single score or even by only a handful of scores or dimensions that are present in our current intelligence tests. The brain which underlies the mind is far, far too complex to hope that all of its intellectual activities can be represented by only a single score or by only a handful of dimensions. In fact, it might be considered an insult to the brain and human mind to continue to do so. Consequently, I would like to see these other dimensions *receive parallel treatment* to the first set of dimensions that we have combined (in many different combinations, incidentally) to form our current intelligence tests.

For a long time I have similarly been troubled about the readiness which some persons conclude that everything in an activity that is not measured by our current intelligence tests is *therefore nonintellectual* in nature. Too many new and potentially important intellectual factors have now emerged for this type of reasoning to be tolerated any longer.

Another concept that I would like to mention is the one of *overachievement-underachievement.* This concept is frequently tied to our current intelligence testing and it undoubtedly has some real merits. But when carried to an extreme it suggests that something is wrong with a student when he is located some distance either below or above his predicted score and that some corrective steps should be taken. In its extreme form, this thinking and action suggests an underlying belief, even a deep conviction, that the particular test score should truly be an almost perfect predictor of success. The action often taken has the implication that this score contains *all* the necessary ingredients within it. This approach would lead to the ultimate revision of both our academic and counseling program to make the nature of school and of success in school more highly parallel to the activities measured in our intelligence tests. I, for one, do *not believe* that changes in the nature of school programs should follow this guideline.

Let us alternately consider a group called the academically gifted. It is quite true that some of our most successful predictions have been made by predicting success in college from measures of success in high school. Such predictions usually work quite well across several years of college work. To me it seems possible that these predictions may work too well and too long. In other words, one possible conclusion from such relationships is that college work is very, very much like high school work and perhaps resembles high school *far too much*. My preference would be to try to make high school more like graduate school rather than vice versa.

In this regard a recent study by Guilford and Allen seems relevant. They selected some 28 dimensions of the mind which they felt were relevant to success on the job in the physical sciences. Then they prepared plain English descriptions and also a sample item of a best test for each of these 28 intellectual characteristics. A sizable number of scientists on the job were interviewed by Allen after which he asked them to arrange these 28 characteristics in terms of importance on their job. The 28 characteristics were arranged in rank order according to their judged importance by the total group of scientists. Traditional intelligence tests have included about 5 or 6 of these characteristics, such as general reasoning, vocabulary ability, number ability, memory for ideas, ability to visualize spatially, and perhaps perceptual speed. All but one of these traditional intelligence factors ranked below twentieth in the list. In other words 19 of the 20 intellectual characteristics ranking at the top on the job in science were *nonintelligence intellectual characteristics*. Some examples are intellectual flexibilities, fluencies, originality, penetration, redefinition ability, sensitivity to problems, etc. This finding suggests that the nature of our educational program, at least in science, as well as the nature of our measures of success in school should move in the direction of more emphasis on these abilities. Incidentally, as one moves farther and farther through school one finds that the predictive value, especially of the vocabulary part of intelligence tests, tends to decrease. Some will say, "Well, that is because of the criterion problem, the measure-of-success problem." You will find, however, that the nature of the task is changing to some degree away from the characteristics in intelligence tests, as you get into graduate school and particularly as you get on the job. This trend also suggests that we should be seriously concerned with searching for other kinds of high-level talent, other kinds of gifted, in addition to the current academically gifted or the current IQ type of gifted.

There have been two studies in the field of science on relatively large samples which have shown that the total undergraduate grade point average in college correlated zero with overall ratings of success on the job in large research organizations in our nation. In one of these studies some people were placed on the job even though their total grade point average had been less than "C" (they had been granted a degree with this average). Those with low grades had succeeded on the job with some being found at each rated level of success. The top grade-getters likewise spread out across all levels of success on the job. Although there are other studies with smaller samples that have yielded somewhat more positive findings along this line, it is suggested that we seriously consider some modifications in our academic program in view of these results. Then other dimensions of the mind which are important in certain work on the job will *no longer be largely ignored* in our school-like activities where presumably we are trying to develop the mind. At least this would be one new approach in education.

We have finished a first large project on our campus on a study of human communication abilities as *required frequently on the job* in large organizations. Though these communication abilities tests might be classified by some persons as nonintellectual in nature, we feel that practically all of them have a high degree of intellectual features. For example, the ability to sense that something is wrong with a communication, then to raise effective questions about what is wrong, and to get answers to the questions are all activities that could be called intellectual in nature.

Our sample of college students found these communication activities to be very challenging and highly interesting. They stated that they had rarely been asked before to do anything like the nature of most of these activities. In fact they called them parlor games. We think that their main motivation for returning on three successive Saturdays (in spring weather) was to find out about the nature of the remaining tests. From this testing experience we again conclude that there are many important intellectual activities in the world of work for which our current students are not receiving any particular training or experience. Perhaps one reason why our society does not give very much moral and tangible support to education is that persons leave the academic world and find, to some degree at least, that characteristics in which they are highly trained are not called for as much as they expected in the world of work. Contrarily, other intellectual characteristics in which they have had little experience and training may be some of the more crucial characteristics that determine success in their part of the world of work.

In our tightening manpower predicament it will be advantageous to find that there are several different types of high-level talent and that a somewhat different set of persons emerge in successive groups as we seek different types of high-level talent. This prospect is very heartening. We are properly concerned about the percentage loss of high IQ students across the various levels of our total educational system. We should similarly be concerned about the loss of other types of high-level talent. We have strong reason to believe that the loss of those with high creative ability is greater than the loss of the highly intelligent and may even exceed the dropout rate for students in general.

Strategy for Progress in Research on Creativity

It may be that more rapid progress will be obtained in a complex area, such as communication abilities or creative abilities, by admitting early that the area is highly complex and by taking the stand that things are really different until demonstrated otherwise. If the initial package is highly complex, then researchers, as well as users and the public at large, might be more enthusiastic in seeking simpler approaches than those initially offered. The other extreme approach is to give an initial impression to the consumers and public that an area is much simpler than it actually is, as has been done in the case of representing intelligence by a single score. In this latter approach (in contrast to the former one) there might be *considerable reluctance and resistance* to move toward the middle ground of moderate complexity from this initial ground of extreme simplicity. My best guess is that we will have more support to *make rapid progress* by initially viewing the field of creativity as highly complex than by starting at the other oversimplified extreme.

Creative Talent Not Measured Well by IQ Tests

For those who have the idea that IQ tests measure creative talent with at least some degree of validity, I would like to cite a few results. In factor analysis studies by many research workers across the country, the factors which get at the ability to sense problem areas, to be flexible, and to produce new and original ideas tend to be *unrelated* or to have only low relations with the types of tests entering into our current measures of intelligence. Getzels and Jackson, in the College of Education at the University of Chicago, as well as Torrance, in the Bureau of Educational Research at Minnesota, have reported that if an IQ test is used to select top-level talent, about 70 per cent of the persons who have the highest 20 per cent of the scores on a creativity test battery will be missed. (Or stated otherwise, more cases with high creativity scores are missed than are identified by using an IQ test to locate creative talent.)

In our Utah conference reports on creativity there has been more than one indication that creativity scores and IQ scores are essentially unrelated or at least are only lowly related. The nature of traditional intelligence tests does not directly involve the ability to create new ideas or things. Another bit of evidence on this point is that Chorness studied civilian personnel in the Air Force who made suggestions in the organization which were officially accepted. He obtained approximate IQ scores on them and found that these suggestors of good ideas were spread out across the entire gamut of IQ scores found for civilian personnel.

Let us be flexible and toy for a moment with our present situation. If a creativity index had been established first in our schools we might now be putting forth the same type of arguments to make room to add an intelligence type of index if it had been largely ignored to date. Lest the reader misunderstand my message, let me state that my viewpoint is definitely for measurement of human beings as well as for research on people.

My attempt will be to open wide the problems in identifying creative talent in science and in other fields rather than to give any strong impression of closing up and wrapping up this field at the present time. This may be a time more appropriate for *divergent* (expanding, elaborating) thinking, with a variety of attempts, than for *convergent* (reducing, abstracting, shrinking, extracting) thinking with firm crystallization. Some convergent thinking, some reduction attempts, can and should be occurring, but any crystallization should certainly be considered as tentative at the present time in this field. The ability to uncrystallize as further research findings emerge is an important counterpart for any crystallization process. As we consider creativity in individuals, we must never forget that an unexpected idea that emerges from a student may be as good as and occasionally much better than the more commonplace idea that we expected from him.

I am pleased that there is a growing awareness in the nation of the importance of the topic of creativity. I am deeply concerned about trying to *speed up the rate of this growing awareness*. I am also cognizant of the similar progress being made in European countries on this topic as a result of correspondence with persons from Belgium, Holland, France, Switzerland, and Sweden. You may be interested to know that the National Academy of Sciences in Poland is initiating a large study in their universities of the creative talent of their students, especially in science. In some respects our nation has had a lead in this vital research on creativity, but challenges may arise to close the gap on that lead, too.

Early Identification, Development, and Encouragement of Creativity

Our nation is currently spending several billion dollars on research and development activities. With such a vast expenditure of money it seems obvious that at least a minute percentage of it should be channeled into research on how to identify, develop, and encourage those who will be most fruitful in science if their research is supported. I doubt if more than

2/1,000 of 1 per cent of the nation's R&D[2] budget is currently being spent this way.

I am also aware that many of our present organizations and systems, including the key people in them, are not necessarily encouraging creativity. For example, in a study in our 1959 conference report by Frank Jex of the College of Education on our campus, a group of high school science teachers in our region were tested with an "ingenuity" battery (which probably measure creativity more than ingenuity) when they came to our university for graduate study. Their ingenuity scores were correlated with their principals' or supervisors' ratings of their overall teaching ability made during the previous year. The correlation was —.38. This result from one study suggests that the present academic system may be looking with some disfavor upon teachers who show certain ingenuity and creativity characteristics. It may be possible that these teachers are developing ingenuity traits in their students more than other teachers are.

We all recognize that it would be to our advantage if we could identify creative talent very early in life. However, the creative process in its greatest degree is one of the highest, if not the highest, activity to which man can aspire and is currently a relatively rare phenomenon. Consequently, the prediction problem is very difficult if we try to identify in the very early ages those persons who, 15 or 30 years later, might be the ones most likely to have a rare, high-level creative process occur within them. The difficulty of these early prediction attempts can be further realized from the fact that society has often failed to recognize creative products until a generation or two after the persons who created them have lived. Even when creative persons are recognized, organizations in our nation may reward them by making them supervisors and by also increasing the number of essentially noncreative activities for which they are responsible. Many of our present academic programs are stressing noncreative activities so that the work habits which are being developed are strongly ingrained and are valuable in accomplishing noncreative things. Some of these successful persons may show real resistance and perhaps emotional disturbances if relatively late in their education, or anytime afterwards on the job, they are asked to be creative. They may resist this late change "in the nature of the ball game" even though they may have high, though uncultivated, potential to be creative. Such conflicts might be avoided if creativity training and encouragement had occurred much earlier or even throughout their entire academic training.

On this issue we have heard from more than one source that there is another degree beyond the academic Ph.D. degree. This is called the *on-the-job* Ph.D. degree. We are told that three or four additional years are required for this degree, partly because this amount of time is needed to wear off certain bad effects in the academic doctorate and also to develop

2 R&D: research and development.

new abilities required on the job. These emerging comments increase one's suspicions that there are not only important variables missing in our searches for talent but also many important high-level abilities being largely ignored in the education and development of our youth.

Early State of Knowledge about Creative Talent

Scientific knowledge about creative talent is in a very early stage, but I hasten to add that some real progress has already been made—the surface has unquestionably been scratched. We are currently at the state where it can *no longer be said* that research cannot be done on creative talent. In fact, there are currently too many leads to follow rather than too few leads. There have been a small number of studies to validate certain creativity tests (predictors of creativity) and a few criterion studies to measure the degree of creativeness in a contribution. Many other available tests have not yet been validated to any degree and many new ideas have been proposed for which tests have not yet been developed. Cross-validation studies are largely missing to date as are parallel studies of creativity across different fields of science and across nonscientific fields, except for recent work by Lowenfeld. There are a few beginnings on how different educational and training programs as well as different working environments might modify our predictions of creativity. Anything that can be done to modify our educational programs and our environmental conditions to increase the emergence of creative activity will reduce the burden of identifying the creative individual. This last point cannot be overstressed.

The reason for this lengthy background treatment in this paper is to break down unnecessary restrictions in current thinking that might reduce the quality and quantity of creativity research as well as lengthen the lag of acceptance and implementation of such research findings.

Findings in the Three Utah Research Conferences on Creativity

My remarks will be based largely on our own research and on research reported in the three University of Utah research conferences on the *Identification of Creative Scientific Talent*. In each of these research conferences held in 1955, 1957, and 1959, the steering committee selected those participants throughout the nation who had done the best research and who the committee felt would make the best contribution to the conference topic. In total there were 37 different nationally selected participants in the three conferences who presented a total of nearly 50 reports. These research papers covered various subareas of creativity, such as criteria of creativity, predictors of creativity, education and training of creativity, and working environments that affect creativity. The last day of each conference was spent in subgroup sessions that took stock of the knowledge and of needed research in subareas of creativity. These three conference reports are available through the University of Utah Press.

The emphasis has been on a broad approach to the identification of creative talent, somewhat in contrast to the identification of the so-called gifted *by means of a single measuring device* such as an IQ score. *Nonintelligence intellectual* characteristics are being stressed in the search for the creative individual. In other words this treatment will include intellectual, motivational, biographical, sociometric, and other personality characteristics in trying to understand the nature of creative talent and how to identify it. We (in our study of Air Force scientists) and other researchers have been attempting to measure creative talent from any angle possible.

More studies on creative characteristics have been done on adults than on children. There are now many challenging tasks of redesigning the measuring devices on adults, where necessary, so that they can be used on children of all ages. I sense that those doing this type of work are finding it to be filled with fun and at the same time are coming up with new ideas of their own to try. In fact, as a result of his experiences in training children in creative activities, Wilson of the Portland, Oregon, studies said that children would be eager to go to school if they found it all to be as interesting as their experience in these creative activities. Torrance also recently wrote that when he went into a group of fourth graders recently to test them further with creativity tests, "he received a thunderous welcome. Not even the coming of recess time dampened their motivation. Instead they said that this is more fun than recess!" We had a somewhat similar type of favorable reaction from the young adults who took our communication abilities tests.

Teachers who have tried to help students learn to generate and express ideas of their own have often found some excitement for themselves, too, in the process. For example, I had lunch recently with an experienced scientist who told me that one of his graduate students had been a straight "A" performer in typical academic work but was now proving to be well below average in his ability to produce new ideas. This teacher considered it a challenge to try to teach his graduate student how to produce new ideas. They are now having weekly sessions together just for this purpose. These sessions have been more fruitful than expected. Not only has the student started to produce some ideas, but the teacher also got a topnotch idea during these exchanges which he feels is far better than any of the ideas on which he is already doing research with good support.

As stated above, the main research approach to date has been to study creativity in more full bloom in adults with the hope of tracing these characteristics back to their earlier budding stage. An alternative approach which may be at least equally promising, is to study creativity "in its more natural state" in children before it may get curtailed, distorted, and even blotted out by various features in our world.

Criterion Studies of Creativity

First, I would like to look at studies of creativity on the job. Sprecher was interested in the novelty and the value of the ideas and other products produced by scientists as well as their work habits. He also was concerned about differences in opportunity to be creative in their working situation. Lacklen has indicated that the Space Agency attempts to assess the creativeness of the contribution of scientists by determining *the extent of the area of science which each contribution underlies,* so that the more basic a contribution the wider its effects. Chiselin of our campus has suggested that the measure of a creative product should be *"the extent to which it restructures our universe of understanding."*

In our criterion studies of scientists on their jobs,[3] products as well as processes of people have been judged and overall ratings of creativity have been obtained using various types of measuring devices.

We actually analyzed about 50 measures of different contributions of scientists. We found 15 different meaningful dimensions of the contributions of scientists, at least five of which involve some aspect that could be called creative. These five were overall work output which included patent rate; creativity rating by supervisors; creativity rating by lab monitor; originality in written products including patents and suggestions; and organizational awards (which were slightly negatively related to originality ratings of research reports).

We also found some unexpected but intriguing and meaningful results in our criterion study pertaining to working conditions for researchers in scientific laboratories. The number of published scientific *articles* was negatively related to ratings by supervisors on cooperation and flexibility. In other words, those who go the "extra mile" and publish their completed research may pay a price of being judged uncooperative and inflexible by their supervisor. The second finding is the one which is more directly concerned with creativity than with productivity. Those who have the fastest promotion rate have been credited with very few official suggestions and rate themselves below the average rating in their desire for discovery. Stated otherwise for this one situation studied, those with a strong desire for discovery, who also make good official suggestions to the organization, have a below-average rate of promotion.

Group Aspects of Creativity

In seeking the creative one may find some important leads by looking somewhat away from instead of directly toward the target. Clues for spot-

[3] This project is being accomplished on Contract AF 41(657)–158 with the Personnel Laboratory, WADC, of the Air Force. Dr. A. Carp is the monitor having replaced the initial monitor, Dr. Robert M. W. Travers. Our communication project was supported earlier by the same organization with Dr. Travers as the monitor.

ting creative talent may be obtained by watching the reactions of others around a person. There is some support for this hunch from the work at Minnesota. If some persons in a group appear excited, disturbed, or threatened, *perhaps* there is a creative person around whose ideas and work are being at least vaguely sensed as threatening the present scheme of things. Some group behaviors may occur as an attempt to eliminate or reduce this threat, such as by developing *sanctions against* the person and by overorganizing and building other controls into their world. An experimental approach may be tried here by removing one person at a time from the group to see in which case the group tensions are reduced the most. Unfortunately (and this is true with other selection devices), one may locate other types in addition to some creative individuals by this procedure.

In group discussion sessions (including brainstorming sessions), individuals differ widely in their contributions to the flow of ideas. Some persons help to set the stage while others make crucial leaps ahead in the discussion. Some persons do *not* slavishly follow the flow of the discussion. Instead, they think "at right angles" on an unusual train of thought. Later they may speak up to send the discussion down new and fresh alleys. One person did this several times during a tape-recorded session to which I listened, whereas the contribution of others seemed to be merely minor variations or refinements around already existing themes. In creativity training sessions, one similarly might build measuring devices to identify those with the greatest readiness initially for such training as well as those who show the greatest gains during the training.

Bloom has indicated that science students who truly become involved in research work and in the research role during graduate training, tend to become the productive researchers afterwards. Contrarily, those who do *not* get really involved in research as they finish their advanced degree requirements but somehow get by this hurdle without becoming involved, usually manage *not* to produce research afterwards and also usually manage to avoid research opportunities. If the creative are to be found somewhere among the productive, then in science we can reduce our problem by finding those students who truly become involved in research problems during their academic career. Some analogous situations entailing student involvement could also be sought in nonscientific fields. We might seek out such persons at almost any academic level if we set up the situation properly and ask for the right type of performance.

The results from Torrance's descriptions from one's fellow students seem promising. Consequently, well-designed confidential reports including ratings, check lists, and written descriptions from peers and from appropriately selected teachers and supervisors (as well as ratings on oneself) should not be overlooked as possibilities for identifying those with above average promise of being creative. One basic question here is to what degree a rater must have creative characteristics himself in order to be able to judge whether another individual has a high degree of these characteristics.

Some Intellectual Characteristics

Based upon insights derived from factorial findings of many workers, Guilford has evolved and listed the following specific factors or intellectual characteristics as most likely to be valid measures of creative talent: originality, redefinition, adaptive flexibility, spontaneous flexibility, associational fluency, expressional fluency, word fluency, ideational fluency, elaboration, and probably some evaluation factors.

Speaking more broadly, some components of memory, cognition, evaluation, and more particularly convergent production and especially divergent production are involved in creative work. The divergent production area is possibly the one which has been most overlooked to date in our efforts in psychological measurement. It is probably the most important area in creative talent since it includes production of ideas in quantity and in quality, originality, flexibility, sensitivities, and redefinition abilities. Pictorial fluency may be an example of a characteristic needed more in creative work in art than in science.

Convergent (reduction) thinking undoubtedly also has a role in creative work. Our communication research would suggest that the ability to converge and recognize a correct answer on a multiple choice task is probably not sufficiently similar to be used as a substitute for an open-ended task of extracting a fresh generalization from a mass of data or otherwise expressing one's own product as a result of convergent thinking. While we can accomplish many fine things by using separate answer sheets and multiple choice questions, let's not conclude that we can measure everything by using them.

Mainly as a result of Guilford and Wilson's particular factor study on creativity, certain batteries of tests usually including mainly divergent thinking tasks are being used in some industrial and educational settings to identify creative talent. Persons selected by this type of creative battery have shown a higher degree of certain intellectual characteristics, such as more fantasies and more ability and tendency to toy with ideas, than found in comparison groups selected on the basis of high IQ scores. They also tend to be more able to suggest solutions when problems arise with gadgets, than to merely "curse the gadgets." The research leaders in the educational setting are Getzels and Jackson, and Torrance.

Ability to sense problems is another intellectual characteristic that is usually included in creativity. It may also lead to motivational features. The capacity to be puzzled may be a very important characteristic. A keen observer once said that part of Einstein's genius was his inability to understand the obvious. Thus the rejection of superficial explanations of one's own as well as of others is a prerequisite to understanding and *to know when you don't know* may be a crucial ability needed in making original contributions.

From our communication abilities research we feel that the ability to sense ambiguities, plus effective questioning ability, may be important in creative activity. This may alternately be described as curiosity in action. Thus, I sense that many of the components of curiosity and of motivation are of an intellectual nature.

Our revision test, even though it involves only verbal revision, is at least analogous to the manipulation, restructuring, and reworking of ideas found both in the earlier and later stages of the creative process. It is probably also related to the ability and tendency to strive for more comprehensive answers or solutions or products, another feature that has emerged in on-the-job studies of creativity. Unfortunately, we find too few occasions in our academic programs requiring such revisions and strivings for a higher quality or for more original and workable products. Likewise, most of the other creative characteristics are often ignored or not particularly stressed in present academic programs.

Somewhat in contrast with this reworking and thoroughness characteristic, we found a verbal superficiality factor. At least in science and perhaps in certain other fields it seems unlikely that either creative or profound contributions will come from dilettantes.

At least two response-set factors, which we have found, may measure characteristics functioning in creativity. The first one is called *"broadly diffused attention."* This type of attention has often been a part of the description of the crucial moments preceding the insight stage of the creative process. The second response set factor is described as a "resistance to idea reduction." The opposite end of this trait of willingness to reduce ideas may be valuable in creating broad new generalizations. In contrast are the persons who make second-order corrections on such generalizations; they may be resisting what they sense as an overreduction in ideas represented by the broad initial generalization. Of course, both types of contributions have some value.

Creative persons in several fields usually state that they work intermittently across long periods of time (though perhaps almost continually below the conscious level) on their key problems. Consequently, Ghiselin has suggested that we try take-home aptitude tests to find those who continue to be involved and who jot down additional responses whenever and wherever they occur. Similarly, the ebb and flow of ideas in the creative process suggest the need for tests which show variability of performance within an individual across time. Presumably the person sought often functions at a low level, but occasionally functions at a very high level. Maybe the person with the greatest variability across time has more creative potential.

Other tests or test ideas that may have validity include the abilities to form and test hunches (hypotheses), to foresee consequences, to infer causes, to evaluate revisions in a product, and to be able to toss one's ideas into the arena of ideas. Our finding of a verbal originality factor leads us to hope for an analogous measure of *nonverbal originality*. Another hunch, expressed in the Utah conference, is that one needs to be able to manipulate several ideas concurrently in one's mind. We lack a good test which will determine how many-idea-man each individual is. An interesting side question is whether we can increase such idea power by forming and training teams of workers.

Thurstone suggested that a creator has good rapport with his prefoca thoughts. We also need measures in the areas of imageless thought, pre verbal thought, preconscious thought, and in the relations between think ing and the formulations of expressions for this thought. The ability to make good intuitive decisions on the basis of incomplete information may be relevant. Barron has suggested that we need to test the ability to express the heretofore unexpressed experience or phenomenon. He feels that creatives are more observant (seeing both what others do and what they do not), that they place high value on truthful reporting and testifying of their observations, and that they have the ability to make them explicit. They also make richer syntheses and note their own impulses more. We might add here the possible importance not only of an *ability* to sense but also of the ability to question the implicit. We suspect there are some important unmeasured characteristics in the ability to pioneer in an unexplored area.

To summarize my current understanding of the intellectual aspects of creativity, I believe that there are many relatively separate intellectual components. It is therefore quite possible that multiple types of creative talent may exist. Another general hunch is that certain of these intellectual components may underlie some of the motivational forces in the creative person and may also be linked significantly to certain personality characteristics.

Motivational-Interest Characteristics

Many relevant characteristics have been suggested in this area. The great need is for good measuring instruments (for all ages) that will demonstrate the widespread belief of practically everyone that motivation is a strong component of creativity. Some motivational characteristics suggested are curiosity or inquiringness of mind, liking to think, liking to manipulate and toy with ideas, intellectual persistence, need for recognition for achievement, need for variety, need for autonomy, need for preference for complex order and for challenges therein, tolerance of ambiguity, resistance to closing up and crystallizing things prematurely coupled with a strong need for ultimate closure, need for mastery of a problem, insatiability for intellectual ordering, and a need to improve upon currently accepted orders and systems. High energy with vast work output through disciplined work habits is usually found.

Other traits suggested are a willingness to take greater and more long range risks for greater gain, and the tendency to accumulate an overabundance of raw stuff plus a willingness ultimately to discard some of it in forming final products. One provocative idea of McClelland's is that the creative person is willing to take a calculated risk larger (though not unrealistically large) than others and that his judgment of the odds in research areas is actually smaller than the average judgment from other persons. The creative individual presumably does not want to deal in a sheer gamble situation but rather to engage in a risk situation where his own efforts are involved so that they may make a difference in the odds.

Barron reports that the creatives have an intense aesthetic and moral commitment to their work. They may also sense at least vaguely, a distinct sexual meaning to their act of creating.

Younger persons with creative talent, according to Getzels' findings, have a much greater variety of occupational choices, with greater interest in and awareness of unconventional careers, than do their fellow students. They sense that their views are not the predominant ones of what success in adult life is. They are also willing to be nonconforming and consequently to be in the small minority.

Other Personality Characteristics

Some evidence to date on personality characteristics suggests that creative persons are more devoted to autonomy, more self-sufficient, more independent in judgment (contrary to group agreement, if needed, to be an accurate judge), more open to the irrational in themselves, more stable, and more capable of taking greater risks in the hope for greater gains, more feminine in interests and characteristics (especially in awareness of one's impulses), more dominant and self-assertive, more complex as a person, more self-accepting, more resourceful and adventurous, more radical (bohemian), more controlling of their own behavior by self-concept, and possibly more emotionally sensitive, and more introverted but bold.

Other personal characteristics which may differ in relevance across different fields are: liking for ideas versus people versus things, socialization and interpersonal involvement tendencies, introversion-extroversion, surgency-desurgency and impulse control (suppression versus expression). In many fields there is often an incubation period though differences may occur in the insight period. For example, one view is that whenever a person has an inspiration in certain fields like art, he had better get to his canvas quickly before this feeling vanishes.

The Biographical Inventory Approach

Our research team is currently studying samples of scientists locally, in the Air Force, and in the Space Agency with this biographical approach. Nearly every time that even a brief biographical inventory has been tried on scientists, it has been found to have promising validity in the initial sample studied. However, we are uncertain about the amount of loss in validity that will occur in second and third studies. We recognize that indirectly these items are getting at a hodgepodge of motivational and personality traits such as work habits, attitudes, interests, values, family and academic history, and several personality characteristics. As persons have various experiences through life and are exposed to different problems, ideas, training, treatments, environments, etc., they are *"being programmed"* in different ways so that their probability of eventually being creative is changing either favorably or unfavorably. This program within each individual probably becomes less modifiable as time passes so it provides one basis for predicting future characteristics and performance. Many of our 600 biographical items being tried on scientists would be suitable for trial use on high school and possibly junior high school students.

Some Final Comments

As we look at this total challenging field, we believe, until shown otherwise, that quite different psychological processes are involved when we learn existing knowledge and systems than when we produce new ideas, new knowledge, and new systems. Education may teach people to recite the past and repeat past performances more often than to prepare them to develop new things or even to be ready for new developments by others. As a result, the perspectives of educated persons may be more backward than forward. People are probably being far better prepared to perpetuate the past than to take new steps in the future that might improve upon the past. Certainly, one does not find a wide readiness for progress. Too often, strong fears rather than positive abilities emerge when the opportunities arise to take a new step forward, to pioneer at the frontiers. And the sheer amount of education may not be a good basis for identifying those ready to take a new step.

We may need to identify and develop people who can learn the past without taking it too seriously (as some unfortunately do even to the point of almost worshipping it). We need people who can mentally toy with and manipulate man's knowledge and ideas and products of the past, who can use the past as a springboard for the future developments and who can find new leads and do something with those leads to improve upon the past. In other words, maybe our task is to produce more minds that are "tomorrow minds" than "yesterday minds."

I am repeatedly concerned with restrictions, inhibitions, and deterrents within a person as contrasted with freedom within him. I am saddened when I find within myself or in others that some of these inhibitors are really self-imposed restrictions that reduce the possibility of generating new, fresh solutions in problem areas. These built-in restrictions can thus reduce the freedom and potentialities of a person and may even block his efforts that would otherwise lead to successful performance.

I am also concerned when I sense that many administrators, who presumably have the responsibility to facilitate good, new developments, often seem to be much more interested in controls than in progress. On this point of organizational controls, the creative persons may be the ones who will most appreciate the necessity of a few very good rules in an organization. Contrarily, they may be most sensitive to unnecessary rules that are built in by people. The creative may be those who attempt to work their way out of such needless restrictions.

One of our conference participants reflected upon those *rare* persons who had made contributions that had truly *reshaped* the world. He observed that nearly all of these individuals had eventually done their work outside of an existing organization—they were neither supervisor nor supervised. At the same time I am aware that a recent speech called "The Greatest Invention of All" was recently delivered at the Franklin Institute in Philadelphia. The message was that the organization has been the greatest invention, because it has proved to be so effective in implementing new ideas. However, we should certainly *not* assume that organizations that are effective either in implementing ideas or in other kinds of assembly-line production tasks are therefore the types of organizations that are best suited for creative work. Unfortunately, there are some cases where scientific and other creative work have been merely plugged into existing organizations, apparently without any question or serious concern about the suitableness of the organization for such work.

This report has been much more based upon thinking and research on creative talent in science (especially physical science) than in the arts and other fields (though creative writers have been studied). I have stated more than once before that science may have more to learn about creativity from the arts than vice versa. I am also aware that most of the research work to date has been done on adults instead of children.

It will be much healthier when we can sharpen and reduce this long list of characteristics and also tie the appropriate ones to different types of creative talent. Nonetheless, it is good at this stage to have so many tangible and suggested leads to try. And plenty of these leads can be readily tried on children. My last comment is one of encouragement to whoever is willing to work on any of the several gifted types with a hope that it will be an exciting adventure. Persons willing to do research in this area will find that there are many, many things that should be tried.

BIBLIOGRAPHY

1. Taylor, Calvin W., editor, *The Identification of Creative Scientific Talent*, essentially verbatim report of the 1955 University of Utah national research conference, University of Utah Press, 1956, 268 pp.
2. Taylor, Calvin W., editor, *The Identification of Creative Scientific Talent*, essentially verbatim report of the 1957 University of Utah national research conference, University of Utah Press, 1958, 255 pp.
3. Taylor, Calvin W., editor, *The Identification of Creative Scientific Talent*, essentially verbatim report of the 1959 University of Utah national research conference, University of Utah Press, 1959, 334 pp.
4. Taylor, Calvin W., Smith, William R., Ghiselin, Brewster, Sheets, Boyd V., and Cochran, John R., *Communication Abilities in Military Situations*, Technical Report WADC—TR-58-92, Pers. Lab., Wright Air Development Center, 1958.

chapter 12

The hard-to-reach adolescent

Robert J. Havighurst

Educators and social workers talk nowadays of a type of teen-ager whom they call "hard-to-reach." In school, these boys and girls have a record of poor or failing work. They are unresponsive or hostile to teachers and other adults who try to be of help. Out of school, the record may show theft, traffic violations, and sexual misbehavior. Ranging from fourteen to seventeen years of age, these students contribute to most of the discipline problems in junior and early high school.

My colleagues and I found several hard-to-reach boys and girls during a study we were making of a group of children as they grew from childhood through adolescence (1). Our finding was not new. Others have met hard-to-reach teen-agers. Although the problem is most acute in big cities, it is affecting more and more smaller communities.

Hard-to-reach boys and girls are sometimes called "slow-learning" because they do poorly in school and have a relatively low measured intelligence. However, they should not be confused with young people of very low intelligence—the 3 or 4 per cent who score below 75 on intelligence tests. Such boys and girls are now generally taught in special classes for the educable mentally handicapped. In general, if they find simple work to do, they seem to make a fairly good adjustment in adolescence and adulthood—a better adjustment, on the whole, than that made by children with intelligence quotients ranging from 75 to 80. This difference is largely due to the fact that school programs for the educable mentally handicapped have rather adequately met the academic needs of these children. On the other hand, the schools are still trying to teach children who have a slightly

From *The School Review*, 66(June, 1958), 125–133. Reprinted by permission of The University of Chicago Press.

higher intelligence quotient as if they were well-motivated middle-class children who merely need to be taken through the usual academic curriculum a little more slowly.

Most of the "hard-to-reach" children have intelligence quotients between 75 and 90. In an average population, about 15 per cent have intelligence scores in this range. It should be pointed out that many boys and girls in this range get along quite well in school and community. Depending on the type of community and the type of school, half to three-quarters of the children in this group do passable schoolwork and grow through adolescence without much trouble for the community. The remainder, who make up from 5 to 10 per cent of the total age group, constitute the hard-to-reach group. While children of greater intelligence also have difficulty in growing up, the hard-to-reach adolescents are the major problem group in the ordinary high school and community.

In the study that we have been making, four-fifths of the students with intelligence scores between 75 and 90 came from families in the lowest third of the community in socioeconomic status; 37 per cent came from broken homes. Half the boys considered severe discipline problems by school authorities were in this group; 60 per cent dropped out of school before eleventh grade. The names of boys and girls from this group were at least twice as likely to appear on police records as the names of others in this age group.

Dick was the toughest youngster in the fourth grade of a slum-area school. A year older than most of his classmates, he was a bully on the playground and a constant source of irritation to his teacher. He had an intelligence quotient of 90, and, though he was not interested in schoolwork, he impressed his teacher as being brighter than his score would suggest. He was singled out in fourth grade as an aggressive, maladjusted child, one who would need a good deal of help if he was to avoid trouble and delinquency in adolescence.

Dick's father, a truck driver, was often away from home. For long intervals he neglected the boy. From time to time, particularly after a drinking spree, the father would beat Dick severely. After Dick reached school age, his mother worked in a tavern as a waitress. She paid little attention to Dick, leaving to his older brothers the responsibility of getting him to school and back.

Dick moved up through the elementary school, barely passing from one grade to another, though his teachers believed that he could do better work if he tried. In junior high school he began to get into difficulty with his teachers, usually for fighting with other boys and for being unruly in class. In eighth grade, an English teacher asked the class to write a paragraph on "What I Think about the School and Myself." Dick turned in this response: "The old school can go and jump in the lake if its deep, and I don't like most all the teachers in school. And I like to take the car hub caps off and throw them away. It's all right if the school blow up with a hand grenade, or the school would burn up. That's all I can say for now. Signed, Nobody."

In ninth grade Dick began going with a gang of boys a year or two older than he. His chums rode about in rattletrap cars purchased at junkyard prices. The boys' big hope was to qualify for membership in an informal club called the "Heaven Hounds." Members in good standing were expected to drive at least fifty miles an hour inside the city limits, a rule that brought the young motorists into constant trouble with the police. Though speeding was a popular sport among the Heaven Hounds, their favorite game was "chicken." To play it, members assembled in their cars in an empty field and tried to outdo one another in dangerous stunts. Each driver was out to prove that he was not afraid, that is, not "chicken." The game culminated in a dash at full speed toward the edge of a cliff. The first driver to slow down was "chicken." Two cars actually went over the edge, though at the last possible moment before the plunge, the drivers leaped out.

Dick, who was not quite sixteen, could not legally drive. Even so, one evening he and a friend "borrowed" a car parked near their home. They picked up two girls, went riding, and wound up in a ditch. Though driver and passengers escaped injury, they were picked up by the police, who found a stolen gun on Dick. The boy was taken into court with considerable publicity, which made him the center of attention at school. After the clash with the law, Dick became more hostile and more unruly than ever in his classes. Eventually he was sent to the state school for delinquent boys.

Myrna first came to our attention when a sociometric test in fourth grade identified her as a "withdrawn" child. A pretty, blonde, blue-eyed girl, she was extremely shy, afraid to speak in class, and, according to her classmates, afraid to play games. Her teachers felt baffled in their attempts to help her. Reading was very difficult for Myrna. Twice she had failed in school because she could not read. In spite of individual tutoring by a remedial-reading teacher, Myrna's work showed little improvement. To add to her distress, she was not well. She was absent a great deal because of stomach upsets, though the doctor could find nothing physically wrong with her.

Myrna lived at home with her mother and a small sister. The father, a factory worker, was a fairly steady man, though harsh to Myrna and sometimes cruel to his wife. The mother had many complaints. She complained about Myrna's health and encouraged her to stay home when she felt ill. She complained about the school, which she blamed for Myrna's poor reading.

The school provided a great deal of special tutoring in reading for Myrna. A volunteer, interested in helping children who were having difficulty, coached Myrna and became very much attached to her. The work seemed to help. The teachers came to feel that Myrna was making progress and passed her along from year to year. Actually it would have added to Myrna's difficulties to fail her. She was already two years older than her classmates and big for her age. She had matured early, and, by the age of twelve, when she was in fifth grade, she was growing into an attractive woman.

Eventually, at sixteen years of age, Myrna reached ninth grade. She was now grown up physically but quite incapable of doing high school work. Her reading was at about fourth-grade level. Discouraged and unsure of herself, she was convinced that she was stupid. She was so fearful that she avoided talking to adults at school lest they make demands on her that would prove too great. For example, she did not report the theft of a sweater from her locker. She thought the office secretary would ask questions she could not answer. She said to her counselor, "Oh, I'm so dumb I don't like to talk to people because they'll find out how dumb I am." In home-economics class when she had trouble with a piece of sewing, she made no move to get help. Rather than seek out the teacher, she did nothing for several days and finally took a failing mark for the grading period.

At home, things were going poorly for Myrna. Boys were asking her for dates, but her mother, suspicious of all of them, made it unpleasant for any who came to the house. One boy, a senior in high school, persisted in going with Myrna, but when the boy came to her home, her mother made it extremely difficult for them to be alone together. She watched them closely and accused Myrna of misconduct if the pair so much as stepped out into the hall to be alone. If Myrna and her friend went to a movie, her mother would set a time for her daughter to get home. She would be waiting for them when they came back, and as soon as they returned she would send the boy away.

Speaking to her counselor, Myrna confided that she was all mixed up and tired of life. What was there to this business of living anyway? You were born. You grew up. You got married. You had children. What did it add up to? Was life anything more than tiredness? Did life amount to anything more than disgust?

Dick's story and Myrna's follow in essence the story of hard-to-reach youth. These boys and girls fall into two groups. One group is made up of young people like Dick. They are discontented, aggressive, hungry for excitement, and hostile to school and to legal authority. In this group, boys outnumber girls. The other group is made up of young people like Myrna.

They are the fearful, the shy, and the apathetic. In this group girls are in the majority.

Both types of maladjustment grow out of one general cause. The boy or girl is failing to grow up successfully. These young people feel the physical strength of adulthood and the stirrings of manhood or womanhood. They are no longer children. But they are not becoming adults. And there lies the trouble. For these boys and girls, the pathways to adulthood are blocked.

There are three such pathways. School is one. School is an avenue to better jobs. School is also an avenue to places of prestige and privilege among the young people of the community. The leaders in school activities are high school juniors and seniors. They are the athletes and the social leaders. They have the highest prestige in the world of teen-agers. But the youth who is failing in school—the youth who will probably never be a junior or a senior—knows that he cannot hope to achieve prestige and win privileges through school.

Another pathway to adulthood is work. For the fourteen- or fifteen-year-old, this avenue is blocked by child-labor laws, which prevent him from getting a steady job unless he lives on a farm and works at home. Even the sixteen- or seventeen-year-old who drops out of school has difficulty in finding a path to adulthood through a job because employers are reluctant to hire young people under eighteen and because apprenticeships are scarce on the American labor scene.

The third pathway to adulthood is marriage, a pathway sought by many girls who are blocked in their progress in school. For some girls, marriage at fifteen or sixteen is actually a satisfactory solution of the problem of growing up. But for an inexperienced girl, who is all too likely to make a mistake, marriage is a dangerous answer. This pathway is blocked for many girls who would like to take it. Well-meaning but fearful parents may object. Or the girl may have to wait until her prospective husband has completed his military service.

Thus a dangerously large proportion of boys and girls meet roadblocks in the path of growing up. These young people have little choice but to wait several years, until society acknowledges their readiness for adulthood. During this waiting period, the aggressive ones seek excitement and sensual gratification, acting out their fantasies of being grown up. The passive ones live out the interval in apathy, hopelessness, and daydreaming.

The plight of these hard-to-reach boys and girls is the result of three failures. Their families have failed them. The school has failed them, and society has failed them.

Nearly every one of these boys and girls comes from a poor family environment. They have grown up to an accompaniment of fighting and disagreement between the parents; often the family has been broken by desertion or divorce. The father or mother may have been given to drinking, law breaking, or sexual promiscuity. The mother may have had to work outside the home. Her long hours and her weariness spelled neglect for her children. One or both parents have presented a poor model to the children.

The crucial need is to improve family life. But this task is exceedingly difficult since it means changing the outlook and behavior of mothers and fathers whose own childhood and youth followed the pattern of the boys and girls described here. Somehow the vicious circle must be broken.

Whether or not family life is improved, many children will still be slow learners. For many of them, school, under present circumstances, will be a place of discouragement, frustration, and punishment. Somehow schools must find a way to work with slow-learning children. Schools must find a way of helping these children get as much as possible out of classes. Schools must offer these boys and girls an experience of accomplishment and reward for constructive work. Otherwise, the school has no business keeping these boys and girls in classes at all.

Here and there, good ideas are being put into practice to help the slow learner. Special work with these children should probably be started as early as first or second grade. They should be in the care of teachers who are interested in helping slow children. The ungraded primary room is one useful device. Children from six to eight years of age may remain in the room for as long as three or four years. When the pupils have the necessary skills, they are passed to a regular third or fourth grade. In this way, slow children are not punished by obvious failure, nor are they promoted to classes where work is beyond their comprehension.

Still, there are bound to be some boys and girls who reach eighth or ninth grade although their reading is at a fourth- or fifth-grade level. For these students, junior high school will continue to be crucial. For this reason, the junior high school should also have a program for slow learners, a program geared to their ability, yet a program that at the same time gives them a reasonably clear pathway for growth. Work opportunity and work experience are essential for these boys and girls. By earning money and doing useful work, they can generally get the feeling of successful growing up even if their school performance is a source of discouragement to them. In a rural area, work experience can usually be obtained on a farm or in a farm household. But in towns and cities, patient and persistent programs should be set up to find jobs and to supervise the work of these young people.

Society in general, apart from its influence on home and school, can take steps to clear the path to growing up for hard-to-reach youth. Some measures, of course, have been taken. The program of Aid to Dependent Children has enabled some responsible mothers to stay at home and care for their children. Family-service agencies in larger cities have helped many husbands and wives to work out their family problems. Mental-health clinics, which are growing in number, are helping disturbed children and their parents.

Society can help hard-to-reach youth directly by taking two other important steps. The first is to examine child-labor laws carefully to find out whether, under present industrial conditions, the laws may not unnecessarily limit the opportunity of boys and girls fourteen years old and over to get wholesome work experience. The other is to develop and expand recreation programs that will give teen-agers a chance to get, under wholesome circumstances, the excitement and adventure and pleasure that many young people crave.

There is no easy cure-all for the dangerous social malady of the hard-to-reach youth. But we do know enough about the problem to take useful measures to reach these young people through the home, the school, and the community. We can, if we will, set aside many obstacles that stand astride the pathways to growth and responsible adulthood.

REFERENCE

1. Paul H. Bowman and Others, *Mobilizing Community Resources for Youth.* Supplementary Educational Monographs, No. 85. Chicago; University of Chicago Press, 1956.

The forgotten third

Edgar Dale

In this fifth year after Sputnik we still deplore the neglect of the gifted and are avidly searching for hidden and underdeveloped talent. Dr. Conant and others have spoken thoughtfully and eloquently about the need for nurturing the talents of the upper 15 or 20 per cent of high school students.

True, we have neglected the gifted child. But the larger truth is that we have failed to help all children reach their full potential. I wish here to speak for the forgotten third, most of whom do not now graduate from high school.

In many of our reports about the educational health of the nation, our prospects for the future, there is at best a thoughtful, but brief mention of the less able one-third, and then a swift movement to a discussion of the talents of those pupils who most closely resemble the authors of the report.

But the neglected children are also a part of the precious human race. To ignore them, to speak disrespectfully of them, to sort them *out,* to look down upon them as inferiors is basically undemocratic and will eventually corrupt and corrode rejector and rejected alike.

Many who teach the forgotten third enjoy them as I did. Indeed, when these youngsters realize that someone really cares about them, that they will not be punished by more flunking and more failure, their response is sensitive and inspiring. They must be taught concretely, they need lots of encouragement, but they can and do learn. Many of them make up in graciousness and good-heartedness what they lack in scholastic competence. Some sorely try the patience of overworked teachers and reveal our inadequacies in school guidance.

From *The News Letter,* XXVI(April, 1961), 1–4. Reprinted by permission of the author and publisher.

Let us look more closely at these students, discover what they are like, their competencies and handicaps.

The forgotten third are the ones who either drop out of grade and high school before they graduate or finish at the bottom of their graduating class. The NEA reports that slightly more than half of all fifth-grade pupils finish high school; less than two-thirds of those in the ninth grade remain through grade 12. One study showed that 46 per cent of the dropouts had IQs below 90 as contrasted with 21 per cent of those who graduated. Six per cent of dropouts had IQs of 110 or above.

The forgotten third would have included 716,000 men rejected by the army in World War II because of illiteracy. "Out of every 1,000 Negroes in the Southeast 202 were rejected because of educational deficiency, as contrasted with 10 whites in the Middle Atlantic and Far West."

Further, there is a 20-year lag between the average years of schooling of white and nonwhite. "Negro workers on the average have about 3½ years less schooling than the rest of the labor force."

The unemployment rate for the dropout is double that for the high school graduate. A report from the AFL–CIO states that:

A boy who is good with his hands and not much interested in "book learning" could in the past drop out of school and learn a trade. No longer. Not only are the skill requirements higher in themselves, but most companies will not touch a boy for skilled job training or an apprenticeship—whether on a formal or informal basis—without a high school diploma.

There are increased opportunities for highly skilled workers. "For every 100 skilled workers that the nation had in 1955, it will need 122 in 1965 and 145 in 1975. Yet the nation's spotty training programs are not even turning out enough new craftsmen to replace those who retire." Could some of the forgotten third become skilled workers? One study says: "A good share of the dropouts . . . might have made the grade as skilled, highly trained, blue collar workers if they had stayed in high school until graduation and had thus become eligible for training programs in these fields." A guidance expert told me that he believes the expression "a good share" was overoptimistic.

But certain jobs are getting scarcer and there will be more competition for them. Automation is erasing certain kinds of low-skill jobs and setting higher qualifications for the jobs which remain. Further, competition for these jobs will increase. "By the late 1960's three million new young workers will enter the labor force each year, as compared with two million a year now starting their work careers." Forty per cent more young workers will enter the labor force in the 1960's than entered during the 1950's. The unskilled dropouts, the forgotten third, will find job competition very tough.

We cannot dismiss or evade the job problem by suggesting that the less able work on farms, become truck drivers or ditchdiggers. Our overflowing granaries dramatically highlight the need for fewer not more farmers. One writer predicts that eventually farmers will make up only 4 per cent of the labor force. One national trucking company employs only high school graduates and pays them $5,250 to start. Dig ditches? The pick and shovel is as outmoded as the cuspidor or the mustache cup.

The forgotten third are not only the culturally deprived in our large cities. Remember that some of them came with their parents from depressed areas in various parts of the country. Many still remain in those areas living with parents who are suffering from chronic unemployment.

Low educational levels in these depressed areas further aggravate the problem of unemployment because factories do not wish to locate in such areas, thus accelerating the drift of the undereducated to the large cities. Charles Drake notes in *Mountain Life and Work,* published quarterly at Berea, Kentucky, that

> . . . a large manufacturing concern selected an Eastern Kentucky county seat town as a prime location site. . . . Everything was set to build until representatives from the company gave out job application blanks in the county. After examining the completed forms, the company quickly called everything off because of the low educational levels and the language disabilities that the forms revealed. . . .

The unemployables of the future are now in our schools. What can and must we do for this forgotten third?

First, some of them can with guidance move successfully into the regular channels of the high school. Their talents overlap with and are sometimes superior to some students who do graduate. However, we must take seriously what John W. Gardner has said in the *1960 Annual Report of the Carnegie Corporation of New York:*

> Youngsters in the lowest 25 per cent of the population in terms of ability often have capacities so limited that they cannot enter even the vocational courses leading to skilled work. The average high school really doesn't know what to do with such boys and girls. For the most part it simply bears with them until school-leaving age and then turns them out into the streets. There is a great need for the development of practical courses that will prepare these young people for the simple tasks that they can perform.

Second, we can equalize the instructional materials for all children and young people in the United States. The National Defense Education Act has demonstrated what can be done by providing rich materials of instruction in science, foreign languages, and mathematics. We must now move into the fields of reading, literature, social studies, fine arts, and others to provide needed teaching materials including books, films, television, tape recordings, reference materials, and the like. It is shameful that over 66 per cent of our elementary schools with 150 or more pupils do not have a library at all, as noted in a recent *Saturday Review.*

Third, we can begin a rescue operation for those children who are potential dropouts by sharply increasing the quality of their school experiences and the quality of their guidance. We can already point to the success of the Higher Horizons projects in New York City and similar efforts now going forward in perhaps a dozen of our larger cities. Good education for the forgotten third will be expensive but never as expensive as ignorance.

Fourth, we can begin the planning necessary to put the curriculum for these less able students on an attainable and functional level. I do not refer to the makeshift methods often used, in which diluted English, diluted social science, diluted mathematics provide a thin gruel for the already underfed. Programmed teaching, rich experience through field trips, drama, motion pictures, television, and the like will put ideas at a level where they can be grasped and used.

We can bring together what we know about the forgotten third, see what we need to find out, and go ahead. Pitifully meager sums are now being spent in the United States on research and developmental activities concerning reading materials for the reluctant, the underdeveloped reader. Most high schools do not have a developmental program for teaching reading. There are seriously retarded readers for whom we have no program of remediation.

I trust I have made it clear that the schools alone cannot solve the problem of the forgotten third. It is much too big for them. The development of a basic policy regarding the education of all children, no matter who they are or where they live, is imperative. Industrial developments of the future will signally affect these young men and women. It will make a difference to them where future factories are located, whether automation is introduced humanely or inhumanely, whether we see clearly enough that future job possibilities lie chiefly in expansion of the "services" sector as contrasted with the "material goods" sector.

But there is a difference between being responsible for the *solution* of the problem and bearing responsibility for illuminating the problem, diagnosing it, calling it to the attention of influential leaders in many fields. The superintendents of our large city school systems have begun thoughtful experimentation and have warned about the growing cultural and economic disintegration at the heart of these big cities. We must listen carefully to them and plan a program of study and action.

This can be no piecemeal approach. The study need not and should not deal only with the forgotten third. It should be a part of a nation-wide movement to study the junior and senior high school curriculum with special emphasis on those students below the 15 to 20 per cent who are highest in scholastic ability. It must be seen as a study of all the key environmental factors in the lives of these boys and girls—the influence of home, church, community, peers, social and economic factors.

In *Peoples Speaking to Peoples,* White and Leigh note that "Learning, knowing and understanding must reach beyond the few to the many, lest the many, through ignorance, undo the labors of the few." We would do well to remember too that "the stone which the builders rejected" may indeed become the chief cornerstone.

chapter 14

Interests of gifted adolescents

Joseph L. French and Hans H. J. Steffen

Counseling of the gifted may not differ in nature from counseling of other students, but it does vary in its demands on the counselor. The demands in vocational counseling are enlarged because the educational and occupational opportunities are believed to be greater for the gifted than for others (4).

Educators and psychologists know less about the interests of the gifted than of any of the other major characteristics such as special talent, achievement, or personality. It is the purpose of this paper to open the door for further consideration of the interests of gifted adolescents—specifically collegiate freshmen with majors in education.

Background

In determining what role the assessment of interests should play in the total talent-identification program, Passow suggested that school personnel should consider "in what way, if any . . . students with outstanding ability in a given field differ in their interest patterns from less talented students active in the same field" (2, p. 27).

Vocational interests have received sporadic treatment in the growing maze of literature pertaining to gifted students.

Super believes that vocational interests "are best defined in terms of the methods used to assess them" and that of these methods, interest inventories "have so far proved best" (9, p. 224). He also states that "vocational interest is important largely in determining direction and persistence of effort but not, apparently, the amount of effort."

From *The Personnel and Guidance Journal*, 38(April, 1960), 633–636. Reprinted by permission of the senior author and publisher.

In summarizing a number of studies concerned with the relationship between intelligence and interests, Roe reports "correlations ranging from about —0.40 to +0.40. The relation is affected by sex, age, amount of education, occupation, the type of intelligence test, and the type of interest" (*3, p. 93*). Strong (*5*) reports higher positive correlations occurring between scientific and linguistic interests and intelligence; and negative correlations between intelligence and social welfare, business contact, and business detail interests.

Later Strong (*6*) questioned the appropriateness of correlational technique for showing true relationships between interests and intelligence. Despite the low correlations he felt that ability must be important in the development of vocational interests. Although not specifically concerned with interests, Naomi Stewart (*8*) indicated in her study of World War II Army personnel records that there is a clear occupational hierarchy with respect to Army General Classification Test Scores. Her report was consistent with World War I data and other studies including standardization data for most intelligence tests.

In reporting an analysis of scores from the Strong Vocational Interest Test used with National Merit Scholarship Corporation winners and runners-up, Lawrence Stewart (*7*) found the scholars to possess interests which were less intense and consequently spanning a wider range than those recorded by a more representative sample of college students. Stewart postulated a less intense interest because the subject recorded fewer primary and reject patterns than are normally found. This observation supports Strong's (*5*) report on Terman's gifted group. The Terman group had fewer A's than a more representative student group.

Terman (*10*) used Strong's Vocational Interest Test with 627 men who had been identified in childhood as being in the top 1 per cent of the population intellectually and who as adults continued to be classified as gifted by the Concept Mastery Test. The men were divided into seven academic occupational groups and one noncollege group. The patterns of interest revealed by the test differentiated the subgroups more clearly than most of the other variables investigated. A large number of A and B+ scores is assumed to indicate a wide range of interests. To have seven or more such scores out of the 24 scored occupations is indicative of a rather extreme range. Terman found three subgroups to be rated quite high by this standard in that 55 to 57 per cent of the subjects had seven or more A or B+ scores while no group had less than 37 per cent of its members with such a wide variety of significant scores.

Stewart feels that a "reasonable explanation is that the interests of the high-ability students are less clearly differentiated from those of men in general than are the interests of more typical student groups, or . . . that high-ability students have a large number of interests which are spread over different areas" (*7, p. 138*). Another possible explanation for Stewart's scholars is that to qualify for inclusion in the NMSC group the "students had to be more 'well rounded' than those in the more representative groups." He concluded that "the findings indicate that special pattern norms are necessary to describe the interests of high-ability students."

Preceding the Study

Little information exists regarding the relationship between Kuder interest test scores and intelligence.

The senior author (1) observed that gifted freshmen enrolled in a midwestern state teachers college tended to have more interests as reflected by the number of high Kuder Vocational scores than their randomly selected, less intellectually able peers. (A "high" Kuder score is one falling above the 75 percentile.) The number of high scores obtained by the intellectually capable students did not span a significantly greater range than those of their classmates and significant differences between the sexes in either means or standard deviations were not found.

The mean number of high Kuder scores of the random sample was 2.56 while the mean of the intellectually superior group was 2.87. The standard deviations for the groups were 0.97 and 1.01 respectively. The observed mean difference in the distributions was statistically significant at the 1 per cent level when the conventional t test of the difference between means was applied ($t = 3.99$).

An exploration of the data reported for the entire population cited above seemed desirable to determine (1) the distribution of high scores recorded by freshmen enrolled in a midwestern state teachers college and (2) how students with outstanding ability in this setting differ in their interest patterns from less talented students in the same setting.

A Central Hypothesis

The intellectually superior group of future teachers consisted of 278 entering college students whose total score on the American Council on Education Psychological Examination or the School and College Ability Tests placed them in the top 25 per cent of the standardization sample whereas the less talented group numbered 1,663 students and included all of the remaining entering freshmen in a two-year period who took the scholastic aptitude test and a Kuder.

A number of hypotheses were tested but all of them centered around the following null hypothesis: There is no difference between the gifted and less gifted members of the freshmen class in one midwestern state teachers college in their patterns of interest.

A total of 97 males and 181 females met the criteria of giftedness, and 640 males and 1,023 females composed the comparison groups.

To obtain a population of nearly 2,000, the freshman classes for two years were combined. Before combining the groups the hypothesis was formulated that there is no difference between the classes in number of significant areas. A chi-square value of 0.321 was obtained and the tested hypothesis was not rejected.

The hypothesis that there is no significant difference between the number of significant areas for males and females was tested. The resulting chi-square value of 0.053 led to the retention of this null hypothesis also.

A third null hypothesis was tested. It was hypothesized that no significant difference existed between the gifted males and females and the less gifted males and females. The resulting chi-square of 11.329 was significant at the 1 per cent level of confidence and led to the rejection of the third hypothesis. Gifted students in a teachers college seem to express a preference for a greater number of areas than do the less gifted students.

Appropriate null hypotheses were formulated to determine whether differences existed between the gifted males and less gifted males and also between the gifted females and less gifted females. A chi-square value of 7.968 for the males was significant at the 1 per cent level of confidence, and the chi-square value of 4.398 for the females was significant at the 5 per cent level of confidence. It was concluded that a real difference probably existed between the gifted and less gifted students of either sex in the number of recorded high areas.

On the basis of the rejection of the last three null hypotheses, the gifted and less gifted of either sex were considered separately in the following analyses. The significantly different areas for freshmen students as classified by sex and intellectual level with the resulting chi-square values are presented in Table 1.

Study Findings

For this population of male future teachers, the areas classified as literary, artistic, and computational contributed greatly to the differences between

Table 1 Significant interest areas and chi-square value for freshmen students as classified by sex and intellectual level

Area	Males	High group	Females	High group
Mechanical	. . .	. . .	6.796†	Gifted
Computational	6.029*	Gifted	5.775*	Gifted
Artistic	6.911†	Gifted	4.699*	Gifted
Literary	9.423†	Gifted	17.898†	Gifted
Social service	. . .	. . .	4.164*	Less gifted

* Indicates significance at the 5 per cent level.
† Indicates significance at the 1 per cent level.

gifted and less gifted in number of high interest areas recorded. More than the expected number of gifted males recorded high scores in each area.

In considering the female population, the areas classified as literary, mechanical, computational, artistic, and social service contributed greatly to the differences in number of high interest areas. More than the expected number of gifted females recorded high scores in each area except social service.

Less than the expected number of gifted future teachers expressed significant scores in the social service area. A similar but nonsignificant trend was noted among gifted males.

Although the data are not statistically significant, it is interesting to note that neither the gifted males nor the gifted females recorded as many high scores as expected in the persuasive area. The gifted males were also slightly below expectancy in the clerical area. In all other areas the gifted males and females posted more high scores than would be predicted from the patterns of their less gifted peers.

The finding in regard to the literary and social service areas supports some of Strong's work. The other findings neither support nor oppose the data reported by Strong or Roe.

These data must remain descriptive of this specific population and should not be generalized to all potential teachers. However, the diversity of interests expressed by these 1,941 students warrant further consideration and investigation of interest patterns recorded by groups with various collegiate majors as well as groups in other colleges of education.

These data substantiate the belief that the gifted possess a greater range of interests and that gifted students differ in their interest patterns from their less gifted occupational peers. Adequate interpretations of these patterns have not been developed. These findings also support the belief that the educational and occupational opportunities for the gifted are usually greater than for others.

REFERENCES

1. French, Joseph L. Interests of the gifted. *Vocational Guid. Quart.*, 1958, 7, 14–16.
2. Passow, A. H., Goldberg, Miriam, Tannenbaum, A. J., & French, W. *Planning for talented youth.* New York: Bureau of Publications, Teachers College, Columbia University, 1955.
3. Roe, Anne. *The psychology of occupations.* New York: J. Wiley & Sons, 1956.
4. Rothney, J. W. M., & Koopman, N. E. Guidance of the gifted. In Henry, N. B., *Education for the gifted.* Chicago: National Society for the Study of Education, 1958.
5. Strong, E. K., Jr. *Vocational interests of men and women.* Palo Alto, California: Stanford University Press, 1943.

6. Strong, E. K., Jr. *Vocational interests 18 years after college.* Minneapolis: University of Minnesota Press, 1955.
7. Stewart, Lawrence H. Interest patterns of a group of high-ability, high-achieving students. *J. counsel. Psychol.*, Summer, 1959, *6*, 132–139.
8. Stewart, Naomi. AGCT scores of Army personnel grouped by occupation. *Occupations*, October, 1947, *26*, 5–41.
9. Super, Donald E. *The psychology of careers.* New York: Harper & Bros., 1957.
10. Terman, Lewis M. Scientists and nonscientists in a group of 800 gifted men. *Psychol. Monogr.*, 1954, *68* (7), No. 378, 1–44.

chapter *15*

The competition for adolescent energies

James S. Coleman

important
very good

> *Adolescent energies can be successfully*
> *captured for learning if those responsible for*
> *the high school program will plan it that way.*
> *This study shows, alas, that many of America's*
> *schools are rigged against such an outcome.*

When a child is a small child, he must learn if he is to stay alive. His energies must be fiercely concentrated toward understanding the world in which he lives, toward becoming what he is not. When a man is a grown man, he may distribute his energies as he sees fit. His security and shelter are often assured, and when they are not, the activities which make them so have little to do with learning. I saw my young son recently, intensely concentrating on cutting a paper in the shape of a circle. He *must* do that, and he would do it, trying until he someday pulled himself to an "adult" level of competence. In the meantime his father, who could already cut a circle reasonably well, sat, newspaper in hand, mind wandering, eyes scanning, energies dissipated in a multitude of directions. The young son, having to fight his way out of the ignorance and incompetence of childhood, has his energies focused by that fight. The father, having won that battle, can relax his energies.

Somewhere in between is the adolescent—old enough to make his way in the physical world, yet too young to manage the complexities of modern industrial society. He can handle himself in the society of his peers, and, to be sure, in the company of adults as well. A boy can hold a job if he

From *Phi Delta Kappan*, XLII(March, 1961), 231–236. Reprinted by permission of the publisher.

likes, he can own and drive a car; a girl suddenly finds herself able to hold her own in the world of womanly competition—in the same league with adult women, if she so chooses. And adolescents today have more of the equipment of adult life than ever before. Cars are the most important, but there are other things. Adolescents have become an important market not only for popular music (where they have always constituted the major part of the audience), but also for movies, which have turned more and more to adolescents, since television diverted the mass adult audience. Similarly for many other commodities, particularly clothes and sporting goods, adolescents now constitute a very important market, with their own considerable buying power. For several years they have even had their own special market researcher, discovering their tastes and locating their weaknesses for wide-awake entrepreneurs.

In short, the adolescent no longer faces the barriers of illiteracy, inarticulateness, and inability to comprehend which focused his energies and forced him to learn as a child. These fundamental hurdles overcome, his energies may spread themselves in the diverse directions toward which our affluent society pulls. For the first time, "learning" has serious competitors for his attention and energy. The primacy of the school can no longer be taken for granted, and formal education must take its place alongside the other activities which compete for an adolescent's energy. If formal education can successfully compete with these other matters, well and good, but compete it must, for learning no longer has the unquestioned primacy it once had when the child was unable to cut a paper into the shape of a circle.

Not so very long ago in our society, and even yet in most other societies, the natural hurdles offered by the child's environment were quickly followed by others just as natural. Children were thrust into a man's world when they had reached a man's size: they quickly went into an occupation, whether on the farm, or in their father's shop, or as a houseservant, or into academic training for a specific occupation such as law, medicine, ministry, or teaching. In every case, the occupation offered its specific and very visible hurdles, whether physical or mental, hurdles which continued to focus energies until some security was gained.

The Limbo We Call Adolescence

These immediate hurdles leading to a specific occupation which once existed for a boy or girl of fourteen or fifteen are no longer in evidence. The requirements of industrial society have greatly extended the period of general education, and have created a state of limbo which we know as adolescence. The adolescent is no longer child, not yet adult; he is uncommitted to any specific occupation with its specific hurdles, yet he is "committed" to an institution which is devoted to educating him. That institution, of course, is the high school.

If that institution is to succeed, it must manage to capture the energies and attention of the inmates who are committed to it. It must compete "in the open market," so to speak, for the energies which are no longer focused on learning by the natural hurdles of the environment. It has some advantages over other competing activities, for it has physical control over adolescents for a large portion of each day, and it has a stamp of approval, in the form of a diploma and records for college admission, which it can give or withhold.

These are important weapons in the competition for adolescent energy, and they are used implicitly or explicitly by every high school, and by every teacher. But these weapons are of a coercive sort, reminding one of the dictum, "You can lead a horse to water, but you can't make him drink." The horse is under the external control of the master, and the adolescent under the external control of the adult, but the horse and the adolescent will drink at their respective fountains only if they want to do so—disdaining the master's or adult's plea that it is in their own interest.

That such external control is not highly effective is obvious to any observer of our society. The casual observer of modern "youth culture" might easily wonder whether these weapons are at all effective in the competition for adolescent energy. Adolescents' lives are filled with many things, their energies flow in many directions, and much as adults might wish that the flow toward learning be great, the hard facts of the case suggest otherwise.

I have just finished a detailed study of ten high schools—city, suburban, and small town; upper class, middle class, and working class—and some of the results of the research are relevant here, to answer the question: "What, in fact, *are* adolescents interested in? What captures their collective and individual attention and directs their energy?"

The schools I have studied are extremely diverse. The smallest has an enrollment of 100, the largest 2,000. The poorest is a parochial school in big city slums, with a dark, dingy, and tiny building. The richest is in a very well-to-do suburb, with a new building in a country club atmosphere. In the former, only 4 per cent of the fathers have finished college; in the latter, 40 per cent have finished college. In two schools, farmers are the largest occupational group; one school in a new suburb contains almost nothing but blue-collar workers' children, and in the well-to-do suburban school, managers and owners of large businesses are the largest occupational group, closely followed by professionals.

Importance of Athletics, "Right" Crowd

These schools, in short, were selected for their very diversity. Yet most striking to the naive adult observer are the similarities from school to school in the directions teen-agers' energies flow. In a questionnaire, we asked several questions which show this well. Each boy was asked to rank several items according to their importance in making a boy "looked-up-to" or important in the eyes of other boys. In every school—small town, suburban, and big city; working class, middle class, and upper class—being an athlete ranked highest, when compared with numerous other things (getting good grades, being an activities leader, having a car, etc.). And in every school "being in the leading crowd" ranked second highest. Girls, asked a similar question, ranked being in the leading crowd *highest* by far in every school, surpassing activities leadership, good clothes, good grades, and other goals.

Anyone who has had any contact with high schools is well aware of this powerful element in the social system of the school. Schools larger than the ones I have studied (that is, larger than about 2,000) may be able to support more than one leading crowd, just as large adult communities are able to support more than one social elite. However, in schools of the size I studied there is one leading crowd, and it exerts a powerful force in focusing the energies of adolescents. Its activities and interests constitute the norm of the adolescent society, toward which others strive. Though some students reject the leading crowd, most do not, but strive to be part of it. If they cannot, then the psychological consequences are far from trivial: they more often say they would like to trade and be someone different from themselves when they are asked such a question; their self-confidence is undercut in various other ways, and they spend considerably more time watching television and listening to records than do the others (a fact which strongly reinforces the oft-suggested theory that television is used as an escape from a disturbing situation).

Energy Goes in Jockeying for Status

Thus a great amount of the energy of adolescents goes toward purely social matters, toward a continuous jockeying for status in the adolescent society or in some subsection of it; or, in cases where this status is not forthcoming, to a more rewarding fantasy life such as television and popular music provide.

Now we as adults may bemoan this fact, this continual struggle for status and recognition, and the powerful hold of "the group" among adolescents. But in this, adolescent societies are not different from adult societies, where status is equally important, and the struggle for status, recognition, and respect is equally great.

This is not to say that high schools are invariant in the importance of "the crowd": some high schools constitute societies more nearly than do others. In city schools which are not built around distinct geographic communities, "the group" and the "leading crowd" are less powerful than in suburbs and in small towns. The leading crowd was of *most* importance, and social acceptance of highest importance, in the well-to-do suburban school. For example, all students in the ten schools studied were asked to rank several items according to importance "among the things you strive for during your high school days." One item was "learning as much as possible in school," another was "being accepted and liked by other students." The way these two items were ranked gives some indication of the relative importance "learning" and "social" matters have among these teen-agers. On the average, these two items were ranked about the same; but in the well-to-do suburban school which encompassed the greatest part of an adolescent's life (the school where 40 per cent of the fathers completed college, and where 75 per cent of the students were planning to go to college), social acceptance ranked considerably higher than did learning. In fact, social acceptance was accorded more importance relative to that of "learning as much as possible" in this school than in *any* of the other nine schools.

This was true despite the educated parents of these children, despite the excellent school facilities, despite the fact that their teachers were far better trained and could offer far more challenge than those in other schools, despite the fact that they were preparing for college, and despite the fact that their actual preparation was undoubtedly the best of all these schools. (This school is no peculiar deviant; it is on several current lists of "best" schools in the country, lists based not upon the interest in learning which these schools generate in their students but on physical facilities, curriculum, and teacher salaries.)

It is interesting to note that in this school, as in most of the others, the importance of social acceptance *rises* over the four years from freshman to senior, while the importance of learning *drops;* and in this school these shifts were more marked than in any other.

Parents Make School a Social Cosmos

There are several reasons for the great importance attached to social matters, but one is quite clear: in this school, as in many other well-to-do suburban schools, the parents have expanded the functions of the school to encompass the total social life of the students: dancing classes before and after school, parties, extracurricular activities, and various diversions to keep them busy, off the street, and out of their parents' lives. In other words, the parents have created of the school a true social system (so that two of the outstanding items in the school newspaper are the gossip column and the social events column, which reports on recent houseparties). This has the desired effect of pulling a greater and greater part of the adolescents' energies and interests into the school, but it does so in such a way that the "school" toward which the adolescents' energies are directed is hardly recognizable to the adult whose conception of school is a more traditional one.

This is not to say, of course, that classes do not go on as usual (and under far better instructional techniques and far better trained teachers than in schools of some years ago, or than in more traditional schools today); it is to say, rather, that the classroom activities are embedded within a powerful culture whose interests are diverse. The sweater a girl wears to class takes on great significance, overshadowing the significance of the algebra lesson to be learned; apparently casual conversations become loaded with the significance of getting into a certain clique; a boy's response to a teacher is fashioned with regard for the impression it makes upon other boys in his group; between-class conversation centers around recent social events.

The strategy, then, of this community and many other modern upper middle class suburbs in making "adolescent social centers" of their schools has somewhat unanticipated consequences: though it captures energies within the school, it does so by changing the school into a very different institution.

But, one might argue, these highly social activities are themselves preparation for life, adjustment to life. I would certainly agree that boys and girls learn more about the hard realities of social life through their cliques and crowds than through their social studies courses. A girl comes to learn that discrimination is bad, not through the moral preachments of her social studies classes, but in "learning by living" when she is excluded from the group she aspires to. Another girl, on the other end of the excluding process, also learns by living; but she learns that discrimination does a pretty good job of enhancing the status of her clique.

That such training for life is effective no one will dispute. What is questionable, however, is whether it is adjustment to a civilized society or to a society of the jungle, where the war of all against all rages at its fiercest.

A Solution That Is No Solution

I'm suggesting, then, that one solution, one way in which adolescents' energies are incorporated within the school, is not a solution at all. Every evidence from my research suggests, in fact, that it diverts energies even further away from learning than they usually are. How, then, is learning to capture the energies of teen-agers, to effectively compete against the other activities which struggle for an adolescent's attention? If it cannot do so by incorporating those outside activities, what is the alternative?

Some Alternative Solutions

One alternative is exemplified by the parochial boys' school in the city, a school which was stripped down and barren in both its physical aspect and its extracurricular and social activities. Many of the boys did not know each other outside school, for the school drew boys from many neighborhoods. In this school the social system of adolescents was hardly admitted into the school—partly by the absence of girls, partly by the absence of community or neighborhood, partly by the lack of extracurricular activities.

As a consequence, these boys were at the opposite extreme from the well-to-do suburban school in the relative importance they gave to "learning as much as possible in school" and "being accepted and liked by other students." The rank of social acceptance, relative to that of learning, was lowest of all in this school. There was, in short, far less infiltration of social relations into the classroom here. The jungle of dating activities and of social maneuver was excluded by the very barrenness of the school program. As a consequence, prestige among the boys in school depended almost solely upon two things: athletic achievement and scholastic achievement. The athletes and the scholars were admired and envied here, the athletes somewhat more than the scholars. It was evident in numerous ways that the energies of the parochial school boys were more nearly directed toward learning, less infused with extraneous matters.

Is this, then, the answer—that learning can best compete for an adolescent's energies by shedding itself of external allures (the opposite sex, extracurricular activities, clubs, and the like)? It would seem so but for one slight omission in the above description of the parochial boys' school: The total energies which these boys brought to school were far less than in the other nine schools. Of those energies which the school captured, a great many were directed toward learning, but the sum total of these energies was not high. For many of these boys lived their real lives, and had their greatest interests, outside the school. After-school jobs—or more frequently, street corner gangs—constituted some considerable part of their interests.

These, then, appear to be the two horns of the dilemma: to incorporate adolescent social life into the school and see it pervade every corner of scholastic activity, or to keep it outside and see the adolescent energies stay outside as well. The first alternative is the modern one, taken on by more and more schools, as parents force the schools into taking their adolescents off their hands. The second is the more traditional one, the one which kept schools to a single pure function, that of teaching and learning.*

A Familiar Dilemma to the Sociologist

To a sociologist, this dilemma is similar to problems faced by many other institutions. To cite just one example, the TVA found itself with these

---

* Speaking conjecturally, I suspect that the traditional, single-sex, single-function barren schools are better for the bright, college-bound boy or girl whose energies are already directed toward learning; the modern, luxurious, multi-function school most typified by Scarsdale in New York or New Trier in Illinois is best for the boy or girl whose energies wander away from learning. That is, most of the students in the well-to-do surburban school I studied would have been better off in the boy's barren parochial school; more of their energies would have been captured by *learning* and by a desire to learn. In contrast, the boys of the slum, uninterested in school, would have had more of their energies captured for learning in the enticing suburban school.

alternatives: to keep its goals intact but face possible destruction at the hands of vested local interests, or to gain the support of these powerful farmers and give up one of its goals, the goal of developing conservation areas surrounding its lakes. It chose the latter course.

But is this the best an institution can do—to choose one of the two evils facing it? I think not. There are a number of hints to the contrary. One such hint comes from some peculiar results in my research concerning the girls in the well-to-do suburban school. By all evidences, these girls (and the boys as well) are more socially mature than those in any of the other schools. Their parents have given them dancing lessons, have taught them manners, have often treated them as equals. In other ways they have been brought to a level of social assurance and independence greater than that of students in other schools. It is a surprise, then, to find that among these girls the brilliant student's popularity with boys, relative to that of the girl who is an activities leader, is *lowest* of all schools. Consistent with this, girls in this school shy away from the label of "brilliant student" and are drawn to the label of activities leader more often than those in any other school. Why? The reason seems in part to be this: These adolescents are no longer children, and the girl who is admired and sought after by boys is the *active* girl, not the girl who is still conforming to adult standards by her concern with studies and good grades.

That is, "good grades" and concentration upon studies are seen by the adolescent community, and rightly so, as acquiescence and conformity to adult constraints. By contrast, social affairs, extracurricular activities, and athletics are activities of their "own," activities in which adolescents can carry out positive actions on their own, in contrast to schoolwork, where they carry out "assignments" from teachers. Such assignments are galling to any community which feels itself at all autonomous. It is no wonder that the acquiescent girls, who are still conforming to parental and school "assignments," are not more popular with boys.

It needn't be this way, of course, for academic achievement is inherently no more passive than is any extracurricular activity. It is only that academic matters in school are still largely presented to adolescents as something to be received, as prescribed "exercises," as "assignments"; that is, they are matters which require more receptivity than positive action.

The first hint, then, is this: Adolescent energy is not going to be successfully won for learning by keeping the learner in a passive role, one in which "grades" dispensed by the teachers (like gold stars to kindergarteners) are the only mark of achievement. The energy needs somewhere to *go*, some goals to be won. Many extracurricular activities have such goals, goals which involve active effort, sometimes creative effort: dramatic presentations, music concerts, putting together a newspaper or a yearbook, and (as the best example) winning an athletic game.

Athletics provides, in fact, a second hint, for athletics has a peculiar role in most high schools. For boys it far outdistances any other school activity in the energy it captures. The time and effort expended by high school athletes are phenomenal. It subjects boys to a rigid discipline, yet captures nearly all the energies not only of school-oriented boys but also of those for whom the pull of cars and gangs is strong. How and why does it do this? To even a casual observer the answer is straightforward, and research only reinforces it: People are willing to work very hard when they're sufficiently rewarded. An athlete who helps win a game is a star and a hero. He is rewarded by his fellows, and by the adult community as well. He receives the kind of personal rewards—the prestige, attention, and popularity—for which adults strive in their own ways. No other achievement in school gives a boy the same amount of immediate recognition and respect from others. If we wonder why boys work so hard at athletics, we should wonder why men work so hard at becoming successful businessmen, for the successful athlete gains as many of the rewards that accrue to adolescents as the successful businessman gains of the rewards that accrue to adults.

Why Do We Reward the Athlete?

But this does not explain why the adolescent community—and, to be sure, the adult community as well—gives such extra rewards to the star athlete, lifts him on its shoulders, symbolically or in fact, and makes of him a popular hero. Why is the student who achieves highly not acclaimed in the same way, rather than being seen as a grind or a bookworm? The answer is that once in a while he *does* receive such acclaim, but only under special circumstances: When the star student achieves something for the *school*, as does the star athlete in winning his game, he too becomes a popular hero. A star debater who wins his contests, a National Merit Scholarship winner who brings attention to the school, such boys gain attention and prestige in their school as the ordinary scholar does not. The reason is simple: These boys' achievements are not solely for themselves; they are winning for the school as well, just as is the star athlete. In contrast, the boy or girl who simply gets high grades is achieving for himself alone—he's in competition only with his classmates. His efforts do nothing to give his classmates a sense of communal pride; they only force everyone else to work harder, to keep up. It's no wonder he's often seen by his fellows as a "grind" and a "curve-raiser," whose efforts must be stifled rather than encouraged.

Thus the peculiar fact emerges that the very structure of education acts to *hold down* the adolescent's expenditure of energy toward learning. To be sure, he receives encouragement from teachers and sometimes from parents, and his efforts are sharpened by the classroom competition—but that very competition sets in motion the forces which hold down efforts, forces which "restrict production," so that no one will have to work too hard. In contrast, these same institutions—that is, high schools—have found a marvelous device to capture energy, not for learning but for athletics. The device is interscholastic games, which give an athlete a chance to achieve not only for himself, but for his team and school and community—and receive his just rewards in return. The struggling student, who's often regarded as a little queer because his goals are purely selfish and individual, is deprived of such a chance—not by the nature of intellectual activity, but by the way this activity is structured in the schools.

There exist intellectual games of numerous sorts, and others could easily be invented. Games of strategy can have any content imposed upon them, from mathematics to football. An excellent example is provided by a recent development in executive training. It's called "management games," and involves several teams representing firms competing in a market. An electronic computer serves as the market and responds to the decisions made by each firm. Those firms whose economic knowledge is not sharp slowly lose their share of the market as their competitors' strategies and knowledge overcome them.

One result is already clear from these games: They create an intense involvement among usually staid businessmen, and keep them up till all hours, plotting charts and calculating the market. The game itself, plus the encouragement one receives from teammates, creates such involvement and captures the energies which ordinarily lie dormant as the executives yawn through training films and other audio-visual aids.

Let Good Students Achieve for the School

The point, then, is this: Adolescent energies can be successfully captured for learning, intellectual activities can come to captivate their interest, if they are allowed to do so. If a good student is given a chance to achieve for his school and receive the rewards attendant upon doing so, more adolescents will be interested in becoming good students. If interscholastic games were not only athletic games but contained the contents of mathematics and English and sewing and bricklaying, the distribution of adolescent energies would be very different than it now is. If schools in a city or county competed in a "scholastic fair," with teams, exhibits, and tournaments, the impact on adolescents' distribution of energies would be impressive. The solution is not simple in its execution, for it consists of something more than a new course in the curriculum, or graded classes, or sifting out the "gifted children." Yet if it is carried out, and carried out well, it could pull adolescent energies into those directions of learning, of creativity, and of intellectual excitement for its own sake toward which a democratic society aims.

forces which "restrict production," so that no one will have to work too hard. In contrast, these same institutions—that is, high schools—have found a marvelous device to capture energy, not for learning but for athletics. The device is interscholastic games which give an athlete a chance to achieve not only for himself but for his team and school and community—and receive his just rewards in return. The struggling student, who's often regarded as a little queer because his goals are purely self-ish and individual, is deprived of such a chance—not by the nature of intellectual activity, but by the way this activity is structured in the schools. There exist intellectual games of numerous sorts, and others could easily be invented. Games of strategy can have any content imposed upon them, from mathematics to football. An excellent example is provided by a recent development in executive training. It's called "management games," and involves several teams representing firms competing in a market. An electronic computer serves as the market and responds to the decisions made by each firm. Those firms whose economic knowledge is not sharp slowly lose their share of the market as their competitors' strategies and knowledge overcome them.

One result is already clear from these games. They create an intense involvement among usually staid businessmen, and keep them up till all hours, plotting charts and calculating the market. The game itself, plus the encouragement one receives from teammates, creates such involvement and captures the energies which ordinarily lie dormant as the executives yawn through training films and other audio-visual aids.

Let Good Students Achieve for the School

The point, then, is this: Adolescent energies can be successfully captured for learning, intellectual activities can come to captivate their interest, if they are allowed to do so. If a good student is given a chance to achieve for his school and receive the rewards attendant upon doing so, more adolescents will be interested in becoming good students. If interscholastic games were not only athletic games but contained the contents of mathematics and English and sewing and bricklaying, the distribution of adolescent energies would be very different than it now is. If schools in a city or county competed in a "scholastic fair", with teams, exhibits, and tourna-ments, the impact on adolescents' distribution of energies would be im-pressive. The solution is not simple in its execution, for it consists of something more than a new course in the curriculum, or graded classes or sifting out the "gifted children." Yet if it is carried out, and carried out well, it could pull adolescent energies into those directions of learning, of creativity, and of intellectual excitement for its own sake toward which a democratic society aims.

part iii

The secondary school teacher

*The teacher is the ultimate factor in the development of the
educational well-being of learners. This generalization is not only
currently valid, but it has always held and will continue to hold
true. Furthermore, it is substantiated by knowledge gained from
experience and research. A fundamental attitude for the prospective
teacher is to recognize that the prime responsibility for learning
is his.*

*1. The teacher may defer to the text as a primary influence.
Textbooks today are well organized, efficient, and usually attractive.
It is easy to follow an assign-study-write-test pattern, all dependent
upon the text. That the text cannot be all-knowing, or responsive,
or meet individual interests or problems is obvious.*

*2. The teacher may defer to some teacher-surrogate, such as
TV, films, recorders, syllabi, or teaching machines.*

*3. The teacher may abdicate his responsibility to the demands
of his student group, to a department tradition, or even to the
philosophy, materials, and pattern of his college.*

*4. The teacher may abdicate his responsibility simply by not
assuming it. When a teacher "keeps" school, rather than teaches,
he no longer promotes learning.*

*On the other hand, a person who creates situations in which
adolescents can learn, who stimulates inquiry, understanding, and
enthusiasm, who is well informed and professionally competent, and
who recognizes that his function is to work for the optimal*

*development of each adolescent can be called teacher. There are
some compelling reasons for this kind of responsible professionalism.
For example:*

*1. The teacher who accepts the responsibilities of his task
is most likely to continue to develop, learn, and grow as a person.*

*2. The teacher who really teaches has the greatest potential
for personal satisfaction, fun, and pleasure.*

*3. The teacher who assumes his role, who produces, is likely
to be the person who advances professionally and monetarily.*

*The articles in Part III are especially chosen for their bearing
on the professional role of the teacher. What is "classroom climate"?
What concepts and understandings are necessary to foster learning?
What professional skills are needed by the teacher in his relationship
with pupils? Flanders and Hughes discuss teaching as interaction
with pupils. It is reasonable to assume that the student-teacher
interaction, in both character and quality, may be the most significant
aspect of the teaching-learning phenomenon.*

*There is a growing demand in our society for schools to provide
an individualized program for each child. Cook discusses the
teacher's task in providing for individual differences, particularly
for gifted and retarded pupils.*

*Inevitably, however, teaching requires skills in working with
groups. Just what is the influence of the peer group? How can
the teacher organize in order to capitalize on peer groups?
Jeep and Hollis believe that group dynamics is especially conducive
to good learning. Their article is an explicit delineation of the
learning situation, the implementation of group dynamics,
and a statement of basic principles.*

*Rogers explores the area of personal helping relationships.
In education the relationship of person to person is crucial, and
Rogers' knowledge and experience are invaluable.*

*Gifted teachers have long recognized that a key to successful
teaching is to have students learn to ask intelligent, insightful
questions and then to seek legitimate, verifiable answers. In a school
situation, where the teacher is an obvious power figure,
how can the teacher encourage a questioning attitude? Thelen
and Aschner deal with this question.*

The teacher's responsibility is multidimensional. While it is not possible to discuss every aspect, Cyphert details library skills, McCleary answers some pertinent questions regarding homework, Alexander reviews reporting to parents, Nordberg discusses teaching machines, and Tyler, TV.

Finally, an article by Kerins is included for his clever analysis of the "way to the top" for academicians. Although Kerins talks about college teachers, his wit and wisdom have universality.

While the articles in Part III cannot purport to include all the dimensions of the secondary teacher, they constitute a broad, fundamental base from which the reader can move to other studies.

The teacher's responsibility is multidimensional. While it is not possible to discuss every aspect, Gopbert details history skills, McClean answers some pertinent questions regarding homework, Alexander reviews reporting to parents, Nordberg discusses teaching machines and ploy TV.

Though . . . an article by Kerins is included for his clever analysis of the "road to the top," for academicians. Although Kerins talks about college teachers, his wit and wisdom have universality. While the articles in Part III cannot purport to include all the dimensions of the secondary teacher, they constitute a broad fundamental base from which the reader can move to other studies.

chapter 16

Teacher influence in the classroom

I. Research on classroom climate

Ned A. Flanders

Introduction

The present article is the first of a series reporting research on the teacher's influence in the classroom. The general purpose of the series is to develop tentative principles of teacher influence that someday may contribute to a theory of classroom instruction. A theory of instruction would be broader in scope than a theory of learning and involve concepts describing both the pupil's and teacher's behavior. Such a theory would be quite apart from the various subjects taught and would be concerned with the effects of the teacher's behavior on motivation and attitude formation. The first article begins with a review of research on classroom climate and then presents tentative hypotheses of teacher influence.

Most of the research reviewed in this article makes use of observational techniques to assess the spontaneous behavior of the teacher. The analysis of spontaneous teacher behavior involves the development and standardization of a system of categories that an observer can use to note the frequency of quantitatively different acts. Systematic observation produces a frequency distribution within discrete categories that can be drawn as a histogram profile covering short or long periods of observation. Profiles from long

From a paper presented at Columbia University, April, 1962. Reprinted by permission of the author.

periods of observation ignore variability of teacher influence that is easily seen if profiles of the same teacher over short time periods are compared.

The ultimate goal of studying teacher influence in the classroom is to understand teacher-pupil interaction and, in particular, to specify conditions in which learning is maximized. The research on classroom climate that is reviewed in the next section contributes to a general understanding of teacher influence over long time periods, but ignores short-term influence patterns of the teacher and changes in classroom conditions that occur as a result of learning.

Research on Classroom Climate

The words *classroom climate* refer to generalized attitudes toward the teacher and the class that the pupils share in common in spite of individual differences. The development of these attitudes is an outgrowth of classroom social interaction. As a result of participating in classroom activities, pupils soon develop shared expectations about how the teacher will act, what kind of person he is, and how they like their class. These expectations color all aspects of classroom behavior creating a social atmosphere or climate that appears to be fairly stable, once established. Thus the word *climate*[1] is merely a shorthand reference to those qualities that consistently predominate in most teacher-pupil contacts and contacts between pupils in the presence or absence of the teacher.

The earliest systematic studies of spontaneous pupil and teacher behavior that relate directly to classroom climate are those of H. H. Anderson, his colleagues Helen and Joseph Brewer, and Mary Francis Reed (1, 2, 3, 4) and are based on the observation of "dominative" and "integrative" contacts. It is essential to understand the qualitative differences between an integrative and a dominative social contact because most of the research on classroom climate makes similar behavioral distinctions.

A preliminary study showed that it was possible to devise reliable measures of behavior of young children. Behavior was recorded as "Contacts" and divided into two groups of categories. If a child snatched a toy, struck a playmate, or commanded him, or if he attempted to force him in some way, such contacts were included under the term "domination." By such behavior he ignored the rights of the companion;

[1] Climate is assessed either by analyzing teacher-pupil interaction—and inferring underlying attitudes, or by the use of a pupil attitude inventory—and predicting the quality of classroom interaction. Its precise meaning, when commonly used, is seldom clear just as its synonyms "morale" "rapport" and "emotional tone" are also ambiguous. To have any meaning at all, the word is always qualified by an adjective and it is in the choice of adjectives that researches confuse objectivity, e.g., Lippitt and White's choice of "authoritarian" and "democratic" to describe climate. In later articles the word "climate" will not be used; it is used in the present article because it appeared in the research being reviewed. "Direct" and "indirect" have difficulties also.

he tended to reduce the free interplay of differences and to lead toward resistance or conformity in responding or adapting to another.

Other contacts were recorded which tended to increase the interplay of differences. Offering a companion a choice or soliciting an expression of his desires were gestures of flexibility and adaptation. These tended in the direction of discovering common purposes among differences. Such contacts were grouped under the term "socially integrative behavior" (4, p. 12).

The findings of Anderson *et al.* are based on the study of preschool, primary and elementary school classrooms involving several different teachers and extending over several years. Taken altogether, their imaginative research has produced a series of internally consistent and significant findings. First, the dominative and integrative contacts of the teacher set a pattern of behavior that spreads throughout the classroom; the behavior of the teacher, more than any other individual, sets the climate of the class. The rule is that when either type of contact predominates, domination incites further domination, and integration stimulates further integration. It is the teacher's tendency that spreads among pupils even when the teacher is no longer in the room. Furthermore, the pattern a teacher develops in one year is likely to persist in his classroom the following year with completely different pupils. Second, when a teacher has a higher proportion of integrative contacts, pupils show more spontaneity and initiative, voluntary social contributions and acts of problem solving. Third, when a teacher has a higher proportion of dominative contacts, the pupils are more easily distracted from schoolwork, and show greater compliance to, as well as rejection of, teacher domination.

A year or so after Anderson started his work, Lippitt and White (10), working with Kurt Lewin, carried out laboratory experiments to analyze the effects of adult leaders' influence on boys' groups. The laboratory approach used had certain advantages (or disadvantages, depending on your point of view) in studying the effects of the adult leader's behavior. First, the contrasting patterns of leader behavior were purified and made more consistent as a result of training and role playing. Second, differences in the underlying personality and appearance of the adult leaders were minimized through role rotation. Third, the effect of the pattern of leader behavior was intensified, compared with a classroom, since there were only five boys to a group. Roughly speaking, the pattern Lippitt and White named "authoritarian leadership" consisted of dominative contacts; "democratic leadership" consisted of integrative contacts; and "laissez-faire leadership" consisted of irregular and infrequent integrative contacts with an element of indifference to the total group that is seldom found in a classroom and was not present in the Anderson *et al.* studies.

Most of the conclusions of the Lippitt and White study confirm or extend the general conclusions of Anderson *et al.* with some semantic modification but very little change, if any, in behavioral meaning. From the point of view of classroom teaching one interesting extension was the conceptualization of "dependence on the leader" by Lippitt and White. This is a state of affairs in which group members were unable to proceed without directions from the leader. Anderson *et al.* used the category "conforming to teacher domination" and thus noted its occurrence, but in the more concentrated social climates of the laboratory experiments it was clearly seen that extensive compliance occurs when there is a generalized condition of dependence.

As a result of these two basic and independent studies that produced mutually supportive results, the notion of social climate was established. Additional research revealed minor variations of the central theme already established. Withall (16) showed that a simple classification of the teacher's verbal statements into seven categories produced an index of teacher behavior almost identical to the integrative-dominative (I-D) ratio of Anderson *et al.* A sustained dominative pattern was consistently disliked by pupils, reduced their ability to recall, later on, the material studied, and produced disruptive anxiety as indicated by galvanic skin response and changes in the heartbeat rates. The reverse trends were noted as pupil reactions to integrative contacts. Perkins (12), using Withall's technique, studied groups of teachers organized to study the topic of child growth and development. He found that greater learning—about child growth and development—occurred when group discussion was free to focus on that topic; groups with an integrative type of leader were able to do this more frequently than were groups led by a dominative type of leader. In a large cross-sectional study that did not use observation of spontaneous teacher behavior, Cogan (6) administered a single paper-and-pencil instrument to 987 eighth-grade students in 33 classrooms that contained three scales: (*a*) a scale assessing student perceptions of the teacher; (*b*) a scale on which students reported how often they did required schoolwork; and (*c*) a scale on which students reported how often they did extra, nonrequired schoolwork. Cogan's first scale assessed traits one would associate with the behavior patterns observed in the research already cited although it was developed in terms of Murray's list of major personality needs (6, p. 326). The items of one pattern were grouped as "dominative," "aggressive," and "rejectant"; these correspond to Anderson's dominative and integrative patterns. Cogan found that students reported doing more assigned and extra schoolwork when they perceived the teacher's behavior as falling into the integrative pattern rather than the dominative pattern.

Altogether these research projects support the statements about classroom climate that appear in the first paragraph of this section. The two teacher behavior patterns that create the contrasting classroom climates have been well established.

The integrative pattern[1]	*The dominative pattern*[1]
a. Accepts, clarifies, and supports the ideas and feeling of pupils	a. Expresses or lectures about own ideas or knowledge
b. Praises and encourages	b. Gives directions and orders
c. Asks questions to stimulate pupil participation in decision making	c. Criticizes or deprecates pupil behavior with intent to change it
d. Asks questions to orient pupils to schoolwork	d. Justifies his own position or authority

Associated attitudes of teacher (suggested by Cogan)

Outgoing	Trustful
Good-natured	Patient
Friendly	Self-effacing
Cheerful	Self-submissive
	Responsive

Associated attitudes of teacher (suggested by Cogan)

Antisocial	Impatient
Surly	Self-centered
Spiteful	Self-assertive
Dour	Aloof
Hostile	

These research results should be interpreted with caution. They do not suggest that there is a single pattern of teacher behavior that should be continually maintained in the classroom. Anyone with teaching experience recognizes that there are situations in which an integrative teacher behavior pattern is less appropriate than a dominative pattern; furthermore, it is possible that identical acts by the teacher may in one situation be perceived by pupils as dominative and in another situation as integrative. These research results do show that over a period of time, more integrative than dominative teacher-pupil contacts will establish desirable pupil attitudes and superior patterns of work. The work of Anderson *et al.* and Cogan presents evidence that a desirable climate results in more learning, although additional evidence is needed to confirm the conclusion.

The Implication of Research on Classroom Climate for a Theory of Instruction

Research on classroom climate is incomplete because it does not contribute to the question, "why and when should a teacher react in either a dominative or integrative manner?" An adequate theory of instruction should specify the effects of integrative or dominative contacts for different types of

[1] Most of the researchers cited have their own favorite words to describe essentially the same behavior patterns. Anderson *et al.*: "dominative versus integrative"; Lippitt and White: "authoritarian versus democratic versus laissez-faire"; Withall, Flanders, Perkins: "teacher-centered versus student-centered"; and Cogan: "preclusive versus inclusive." For the sake of simplicity, Anderson's terms have been used in the first section of this paper; the concept "direct influence" and "indirect influence" will be introduced later.

situations that occur frequently in the classroom. Stated another way, there is a need for a dynamic explanation of how short-term patterns or teacher influence affect momentary situations so that the flexibility of the teacher's behavior is taken into account.

One clue that supports the notion that teachers probably are flexible in exerting dominative and integrative influences over short periods of time appears in the work of Mitzel and Rabinowitz (11), who used Withall's technique to assess the classroom climate of four teachers. Their observation data were organized to permit an analysis of variance between teachers, visits, and observers. Since the median length of an observer's visit was of the order of twenty minutes, the finding of statistically significant, wide variability among visits for the same teacher suggests that teachers adapt their influence to the immediate situation. There may be several reasons for the flexibility of teacher influences.

Teachers may adapt their influence to fit different phases of problem solving that probably occur in the classroom. Bales and Strodtbeck (5) have found that the quality of verbal interaction changes, in group problem-solving discussion, as the discussion progresses through phases of orientation, evaluation, and control.

Teachers may also adapt their influence to fit the needs of the individual pupil in contacts with single pupils. In two different studies involving college-age students, Wispe (15) and Smith (14) have shown that psychologically different types of students, identified by personality tests, have different reactions to the same teacher behavior patterns. This was equally true of the two contrasting patterns used in each study and while the patterns were by no means identical to Anderson's dominative-integrative contrast, they were in many ways similar. Gage (8), in a study of elementary school children, found that pupils' perceptions of the same teacher were different according to whether the pupil could be classified as tending to seek "affective" or "cognitive" responses from a teacher.

Even though research on climate tends to ignore flexibility of teacher-influence and is restricted to generalized, broad patterns of teacher behavior, it does make a fundamental contribution to a theory of instruction. This contribution consists of identifying general patterns of the teacher influence that produce predictable responses of pupils and thus establishes cause-and-effect principles that are true in the long run. However, the task of investigating flexibility of influence remains uninvestigated.

Tentative Hypotheses of Teacher Influence

The purpose of this section is to develop hypotheses of teacher influence that are consistent with generalizations about classroom climate which also account for flexibility of teacher influence. Most of the hypotheses are not yet supported by research evidence. If future experimentation provides evidence in support of the hypotheses, they may contribute to a theory of instruction.[1]

In the classroom teacher-pupil relationships are essentially superior-subordinate in quality. The responsibility for classroom activities is the teacher's and both the teacher and the pupils expect the teacher to take charge, to initiate and to control the learning activities. The freedom to direct or not to direct the activities of others is initially given only to the teacher; whatever freedom pupils have in this respect results from the actions of the teacher. No pupil can consistently ignore the authority of the teacher and it is most difficult and sometimes impossible for a pupil to escape from the teacher's control. In the discussion that follows, the word *dependence* will be used to refer to these essential qualities of a superior-subordinate relationship. The presence of dependence has already been noted in the work of Anderson and Lippitt and White.

The opposite of dependence is *independence* and since various degrees of dependence or independence exist, they must be distinguished in the discussion that follows. *High dependence* will refer to a condition in which pupils voluntarily seek additional ways of complying to the authority of the teacher. This condition has aptly been described by Lewin (9, p. 132) as, "at every point within his (the pupil's) sphere of action he is internally controlled by the wishes of the adult (teacher)." He adds later "that a pupil might even anticipate these wishes." *Medium dependence* will refer to the average classroom condition in which teacher direction is essential to initiate and guide activities but the pupils do not voluntarily solicit it. When it occurs they comply. *Low dependence* refers to a condition in which pupils would react to teacher directions if they occurred but their present activities, usually teacher initiated, can be carried on without continued teacher direction. In the face of difficulties pupils would prefer the teacher's help. *Independence* refers to a condition in which the pupils perceive their activities to be "self-directed" (even though the teacher may have helped create the perception) and they do not expect directions from the teacher. In the face of difficulties pupils would prefer to at least try their own solutions before seeking the teacher's help. If teacher direction is given, pupils would feel free to evaluate it in terms of the requirements of the learning activities.

Underlying the entire discussion that follows is the basic assumption that the learning potential of pupils is inversely related to their level of dependence within reasonable and practical limits of classroom organization. In a condition of high dependence a pupil is too concerned with his relationship to the teacher to be completely objective about the learning task. "Objectivity cannot arise in a constraint situation; it arises only in a

[1] For an initial consideration of a "theory of instruction" the author is indebted to Professor Herbert A. Thelan, University of Chicago. See "Toward a Theory of Instruction" (entire issue), *J. of Ed. Res.*, October, 1951.

situation of freedom" (9, p. 178). No doubt there are philosophical values at issue here, but it is psychologically sound and logically self-evident to point out that the learning experience is distorted to the extent that the dependence present in the learning situation is not present in the situation in which the learning is applied. No pupil is ever completely independent of the teacher's authority, nor is anyone completely independent in society, but there are certain types of desirable educational objectives that can be achieved only in a situation involving the degree of independence defined in the preceding paragraph. It is equally true that there are some limited objectives that can best be achieved in a condition of medium dependence, also defined above.

Conditions of dependence or independence are created by the teacher's choice of influence. One can conceive of *direct influence* and *indirect influence* which, under appropriate circumstances, determine the degree of dependence. These two kinds of influence can be defined, in terms of verbal behavior, as follows.

Direct influence consists of stating the teacher's own opinions or ideas, directing the pupil's action, criticizing his behavior, or justifying the teacher's authority or use of that authority.

Indirect influence consists of soliciting the opinion or ideas of the pupils, applying or enlarging on the opinions or ideas of the pupils, praising or encouraging the participation of pupils, or clarifying and accepting the feelings of pupils.

It will be shown in later articles that the teacher's direct and indirect influence can be reliably assessed by observation in spontaneous classroom situations and that the dependence of pupils can also be assessed by observation or paper-and-pencil techniques.

If the flexibility of teacher influence is to be understood, a theory of teacher influence should explain why direct influence may, in one situation, increase or maintain dependence, and in another situation may increase or maintain independence. The cues used consciously or unconsciously by a teacher to guide his choice of influence may arise from a *Gestalten* so complex as to defy conceptualization. In order to be parsimonious, the theory about to be conceptualized will employ the fewest number of variables that seem necessary to predict and understand the teacher's choice of influence.

One aspect of the classroom situation that should make a difference in the pupil's reaction to teacher influence is his perception of the learning goal and the methods of reaching that goal. One can conceive of a situation in which the goal and the methods of reaching the goal are clear to the pupil and another situation in which these are unclear. Certainly the reactions of a student to teacher influence when he knows what he is doing and when he isn't sure of what he is doing will be different. In the discussion that follows, reference will be made to clear goals and unclear goals in order to distinguish between these two situations.

Another aspect of the goal in a learning situation is whether or not the goal is perceived by the student as desirable or undesirable. The attraction of a goal determines motivation[1] and this attribute of a goal has been designated by Lewin (9, p. 77) as *positive valence* or *negative valence*. In the discussion that follows, a positive valence is assigned to goals that satisfy the interest of pupils AND require goal activities that match their abilities. A negative valence is assigned to goals that fail to satisfy the interests of pupils AND/OR require activities that do not match their abilities.

By logical convention, an unclear goal has an unknown or neutral valence.

It should now be clear that the theory about to be developed will suggest that direct and indirect influence will have a different but predictable effect in situations where (a) the goal is unclear, (b) the goal is clear with a positive valence, and (c) the goal is clear with a negative valence. The operational differences between these three situations necessary for experimentation are (a) the pupils do not know what goal will develop, (b) the pupils know what the goal is, know what steps they will take to reach the goal, see necessary actions as matching their ability, and are very interested and satisfied to be working toward that goal, and (c) the pupils know what the goal is, what steps are necessary to reach the goal, may or may not see necessary actions as matching their ability, and are very uninterested and dissatisfied to be working toward that goal.

Situation in Which Goals Are Unclear. Suppose one assumes that:

Assumption A. There exists a drive in both the teacher and the pupils to establish a learning goal in the classroom and work toward that goal.

Assumption B. When the goal is unclear, the behavior of pupils participating in identifying and clarifying a goal is determined by the real or imagined restraints of the teacher's control.

This is to say that most pupils expect to work on "schoolwork" in the classroom; that in order to get started, they expect the teacher to initiate activities that will clarify a learning goal and spell out the steps required to reach the goal. In short there exists in a classroom with unclear goals a state of medium dependency.

(*H* will refer to hypothesis; *SH* to subhypothesis.)

H 1.00   Indirect influence increases independence, when goals are unclear, by reducing the real or imagined restraints[1] of the teacher's control.

---

[1] "Restraints" is a word originally used by Lewin to refer to barriers. Here it refers to barriers the teacher sets to pupils' behavior or that pupils imagine that the teacher sets. Included would be prohibitions, admonitions, and imposed directions. The author recognizes that every teacher must set "minimum restraints," but he believes that if they are set reasonably, pupils will perceive a degree of freedom that permits disciplined self-direction. Technically, restraints refer to forces which exist in the pupil's social environment (life space).

SH 1.10   When restraints are at the barest minimum needed to coordinate class activity, pupils will have the maximum opportunity to express their interests in the goals suggested and to compare their abilities with the activities required.

SH 1.20   Pupils who tend to be uncomfortable with minimum teacher restraints will need considerable support and encouragement, as part of the teacher's indirect influence, in order to continue to express their interests and to compare their abilities.

These hypotheses suggest that the effect of indirect influence, when goals are unclear, is to stimulate the expression of the pupil's interest, curiosity, and appreciation of several possible learning goals and to evaluate these goals in terms of the methods required to reach them. To be realistic, the goal requirements should be within range of the abilities of the pupils. During this activity the teacher takes an active part by asking questions, praising and encouraging pupil participation, and expressing his own opinions primarily in terms of pupil ideas. In practice, the more mature judgment of the teacher is expressed by what he chooses to praise and the particular ideas he chooses to question or develop.

H 2.00   Direct influence increases dependence, when goals are unclear, by maintaining or increasing the restraints of the teacher's control.

SH 2.10   With high dependence or increasing medium dependence, direct influence results in overt compliance.

SH 2.11   If the goals subsequently prove interesting and match the pupil's ability, the overt compliance will occur with inner acceptance.

SH 2.12   If goals subsequently prove uninteresting or do not match the pupil's ability, the overt compliance will occur with inner resistance.

SH 2.13   Either type of compliance maintains the restraints of the teacher's control and pupils will be more dependent throughout the entire process of reaching the goal, compared with goals identified with direct influence.

SH 2.20   Pupils who are more comfortable in a dependent teacher relationship will actively solicit the teacher's direct influence when goals are unclear.

These hypotheses suggest that the effect of direct influence, when goals are unclear, is to increase, or at least maintain, the existing dependence of pupils on the teacher's control. Under these circumstances, direct influence restricts the alternative reactions of pupils to overt compliance. Festinger (13) has suggested that public compliance to group pressures can occur with private acceptance or without private acceptance; with a slight change in words, his analysis is adapted here as a reasonable outcome of direct influence. The notion that either type of compliance maintains a dependent relationship is, perhaps, most questionable in the case of overt compliance with inner acceptance. However, it can be argued that compliance is less a matter of working on an interesting or uninteresting goal, and due more to a perception of the pupil that he must work on that goal only, if he is to receive the approval of the teacher who holds ultimate authority. The consequences of this perception will be discussed later.

Both *SH 1.20* and *SH 2.20* are tentative extensions of the work of Wispe, Smith, and Gage, whose studies of individual pupil reactions to various types of teacher influence have already been mentioned.

The hypotheses stated are presumed to hold whenever goals are unclear either for individual pupils or for the class as a whole, whether this occurs at the beginning, middle or near the end of a particular learning cycle. Goals are most likely to be unclear for the total class during the initial phases of a learning cycle. However, it is a common experience to be working toward what appears to be a clear goal only to find, after some progress, that the original picture of the goal has become unrealistic. Barriers to progress lower goal clarity by changing the steps required to reach the goal. The incidence of unclear goal perceptions among pupils may be far more frequent at the beginning of a school year when pupils, teacher, subject, and methods are less understood. In general, unclear goals become clear with the passage of time, either suddenly or gradually, so long as efforts to reach the goal are maintained. Since perceptions of the goal are subject to individual differences and some goals are more difficult to understand than others, a teacher must assume that there is a range of goal perceptions in a class at any given moment.

The development of positive or negative valence occurs simultaneously with the clarification of goals and methods of reaching goals. As soon as a pupil imagines a relationship between his interests and abilities and the nature of a goal, positive or negative valence is anticipated. Many pupils bring into the classroom a generalized anticipation of goal valence based on past experience, the previous class, or their attitudes toward the teacher. Indirect influence is particularly useful for clarifying such feelings and relating them to the present goal activities.

In the next two sections consideration is given to situations in which the goal and the goal activities are sufficiently clear for pupils to have definite positive or negative reactions toward the goal. But before these situations are discussed, it is necessary to examine more closely the meaning of dependence and independence when goals are clear.

As a goal becomes clear with a positive valence, a force toward the goal develops, action becomes rewarding, and the resultant pupil behavior is usually classified as "self-motivated." As a goal becomes clear with a negative valence, a force away from the goal develops, action becomes unrewarding, and if the resultant pupil behavior is oriented toward the goal, it is usually the result of a force created by the teacher through the use of reward or punishment. In this latter situation medium or high dependence exists and pupils comply to forces that stem from the teacher's authority. In the case of a clear, positive goal dependence exists to the extent that the pupil reacts, either consciously or unconsciously, to forces that stem from the teacher's authority. This latter case is most clearly illustrated by the pupil who senses that his present enjoyment in working on a rewarding task is a "gift" or is permitted by the teacher. He expresses his dependence by appreciating the teacher as well as the nature of the task. In a practical problem-solving sense, his objectivity is distorted since his decisions include judgments of what the teacher will approve or disapprove, as well as the more objective requirements of the problem. His behavior is the resultant of both the restraining forces set by the teacher and the force that results from the positive goal valence.

Situations in Which the Goal Is Clear with a Positive Valence. With a clear, positive goal there is a strong force toward the goal which will be stable as long as the action satisfies the pupil's interests and his ability permits him to proceed. If the restraining forces set by the teacher are small, compared with the valence force, the pupil's behavior will be relatively independent. If the restraining forces approach significance, compared with the valence force, the dependence of the pupil will increase. The proportional balance of these two sets of forces depends on the use of direct or indirect influence when the goals are initially clarified and upon subsequent influence that the teacher provides.

H 3.00   When the initial positive valence of a goal is clarified with indirect influence, the effect of subsequent direct or indirect influence on the existing independence is insignificant.

SH 3.10   The tendency of subsequent direct influence to increase dependence, and indirect influence to decrease it, is greater when the influence is initiated by the teacher, compared with being solicited by pupils.

SH 3.20   Independent progress toward a clear, positive goal reinforces the valence and provides pupils with objective criteria with which to evaluate teacher influence.

These hypotheses emphasize the primary goal orientation of an independent pupil moving successfully toward a clear, positive goal. Teacher influence solicited by pupils is likely to have a goal orientation and, as such, will not affect independence. Influence initiated by the teacher is unlikely to affect independence unless the pupil fails to see a relationship between such influence and the goal, e.g., when the teacher attempts to change to a completely different goal. Under these conditions which include a maximum of independent goal orientation and a minimum of teachers' restraints, barriers to progress are more likely to appear as an intellectual challenge. With proper teacher stimulation and direct challenge there would be an opportunity to enrich the problem-solving experience by stretching the goal requirements to the limit of pupil ability, without loss of positive valence.

In the case of a clear goal with a positive valence that was developed with direct influence, the restraining forces set by the teacher would be of sufficient magnitude to affect the pupil's behavior. However, successful progress toward a positive goal may modify the original dependence. This modification is probably due to the development of the valence force and not due to a decrease in the restraining forces; on this point, however, there is certainly the possibility of different interpretations. Lewin (9, p. 169) would suggest that the decrease in restraining forces would be more likely to occur with younger children, providing the goal activities are truly rewarding. With older children, the realization that the original direct influence was, in a sense, unjustified would increase the pupil's awareness of the restraining forces. Although the dynamics of this situation are not yet clear, the author is disposed to suggest the following hypotheses primarily because dependence is easier to create, during initial stages, than it is to diminish, in later stages.

H 4.00   When the initial positive valence of a goal is clarified with direct influence, subsequent direct influence maintains or increases existing dependence and subsequent indirect influence decreases existing dependence only slightly, if at all.

    SH 4.10   If a goal that is initiated with direct influence develops a positive valence, the existing dependence of the pupils is reenforced by the rewarding experience.

    SH 4.20   Direct influence during initial clarification of positive goals, followed by indirect influence, maintains existing dependence if pupils become aware of the inconsistency in the teacher's influence.

These hypotheses suggest, in effect, that once dependence is established, under conditions of *H 2.00*, it is not likely to decrease even if the learning goal develops a positive valence.

Situations in Which the Goal Is Clear with a Negative Valence. In this situation the actions of both the teacher and pupils are limited. The teacher usually attempts to maintain the restricted learning possibilities by exerting direct influence through either reward or punishment. The only other alternative is to attempt to change the valence of the goal. This second alternative will be considered first.

Dislike of a goal or the activities required to reach a goal depends on the total perceptual field of the pupil. He may think the task is too difficult, too tedious, of no future value, or he may simply dislike the teacher. The reorganization of the pupil's perceptual field is best facilitated by indirect influence that clarifies and supports the pupil's diagnosis of his own difficulties. Successfully carried out, the process is very similar to initiating a new goal. A resourceful teacher recognizes that it is the pupil's perception that must be changed, that only he can change it, and that the change can often occur with only minor alterations in the nature of the goal or goal activities. In fact, the same task, imbedded in a different perceptual organization, may take on a completely different valence (9, p. 168).

H 5.00 A shift from negative to positive goal valence is most likely to occur in response to indirect influence by the teacher.

The analysis of situations involving reward and punishment has already been carried out by Lewin (9, pp. 114–170 and an analysis of compliant behavior has been published by Festinger (13, pp. 232–256). In both references there are many principles which apply directly to the classroom and are related to direct influence, compliance, and dependence. In nearly every classroom, reward or punishment is never used alone, instead, the two are used in combination. The essence of direct influence with the threat of punishment or possibility of reward is the creation of a conflict situation which restricts the pupil's freedom and narrows the alternative actions of the pupil to one or two that the teacher desires. The maintenance of these restrictions requires alert and active surveillance of pupil behavior by the teacher because there are usually a few pupils who are willing and able to test the limits of their freedom in imaginative and unusual ways. With negative goal valence, if the threat of punishment is relaxed or if rewards are unfulfilled, action toward the goal decreases or stops. Thus, high dependence is maintained at all times.

Summary and Conclusions

The major purpose in reviewing research on classroom climate and in developing hypotheses about the effects of direct and indirect teacher influence is to explain variability of teacher influence. In considering, first, situations in which goals are unclear, and second, situations in which goals are clear, different effects of the same teacher behavior were hypothesized. Other articles in this series will be concerned with testing these hypotheses in either field studies or laboratory experiments.

A general assumption underlying the discussion is that there are times when direct influence and other times when indirect influence is most appropriate in the control of classroom learning. At first glance, this assumption may appear to conflict with the findings of research on classroom climate. However, a careful study of the data collected indicates that in all types of classroom situations both direct and indirect influence occurred. A widespread misinterpretation of research on classroom climate has been that direct influence should be avoided in the classroom. *H 3.00* suggests that there will be no change in dependence when direct influence is exerted during periods when goals are clear. In fact, direct influence related to a clear goal may provide opportunities to challenge the ideas and conclusions of the pupil and to enrich the learning process.

The contrast between predictions of *H 1.00* and *H 2.00* with those of *H 3.00* provides a tentative explanation of why direct or indirect influence may in one situation have one outcome, and in another situation a different outcome.

Many factors have been ignored in this initial statement of teacher influence. Some data have already been collected (and will be reported in later articles) suggesting that younger pupils, ages five through seven, do not react to direct influence in the same way as older pupils. If this trend is supported some modification of *H 1.00* and *H 2.00* will be required that takes into account the age of the pupils. Data from the classroom of older pupils also suggest that certain kinds of learning activities can be introduced into classrooms with what appears to be almost instantaneous goal clarity. If this is true, such activities may be unrelated to *H 1.00* and *H 2.00*. Data from high school classes suggest that certain topics such as mathematics and science are normally associated with a higher proportion of direct influence although, at the moment, this should be considered as no more than a commentary on current school practice.

No effort has been made in the present article to indicate how patterns of direct influence can be modified by using group activities in the classroom. It may be that the teacher who uses group methods can control dependence by making appropriate shifts in the classroom group organization. Finally there are certain obvious relationships between the hypotheses of teacher influence, principles of counselling, and the trainer's role in group therapy that have not been developed.

REFERENCES

1. Anderson, Harold H. "The Measurement of Domination and of Socially Integrative Behavior in Teachers' Contacts with Children," *Child Development*, Vol. 10, No. 2, June, 1939, pp. 73–89.
2. Anderson, Harold H., and Brewer, Helen M. *Studies of Teachers' Classroom Personalities, I: Dominative and Socially Integrative Behavior of Kindergarten Teachers*, Applied Psychology Monographs, No. 6, 1945.

3. Anderson, Harold H., and Brewer, Joseph E. *Studies of Teachers' Classroom Personalities, II: Effects of Teachers' Dominative and Integrative Contacts on Children's Classroom Behavior,* Applied Psychology Monographs, No. 8, 1946.

4. Anderson, Harold E., Brewer, J. E., and Reed, M. F. *Studies of Teachers' Classroom Personalities, III: Follow-up Studies of the Effects of Dominative and Integrative Contacts on Children's Classroom Behavior,* Applied Psychology Monographs of The American Psychological Association, No. 11, December, 1946, pp. 1–156, Stanford University Press.

5. Bales, R. F., and Strodtbeck, F. L. "Phases in Group Problem Solving," *J. of Abnormal and Soc. Psychology,* Vol. 46, October, 1951, pp. 458–496.

6. Cogan, M. L. "Theory and Design of a Study of Teacher-Pupil Interaction," *The Harvard Educational Review,* Vol. XXVI, No. 4, Fall, 1956, pp. 315–342.

7. Flanders, Ned A. "Personal-Social Anxiety as a Factor in Experimental Learning Situations," *Journal of Educational Research,* Vol. 45, October, 1951, pp. 100–110.

8. Gage, N. L., et al. "Teachers' Understanding of Their Pupils and Pupils' Ratings of Their Teachers," *Psychological Monograph: General and Applied,* No. 406, Vol. 69, No. 21, 1956, p. 37.

9. Lewin, Kurt. *Dynamic Theory of Personality,* McGraw-Hill, New York, 1935, pp. xi–286.

10. Lippitt, R., and White, R. K. "The 'Social Climate' of Children's Groups," in Barker, R. G., Kounin, J. S., and Wright, H. F. (eds.), *Child Behavior and Development,* McGraw-Hill, New York, 1943, pp. 458–508.

11. Mitzel, Harold E., and Rabinowitz, William. "Assessing Social-Emotional Climate in the Classroom by Withall's Technique," *Psychological Monographs, General and Applied,* No. 368, Vol. 67, No. 18, 1953, pp. 1–19.

12. Perkins, H. V. "Climate Influences Group Learning," *Journal of Educational Research,* Vol. 45, October, 1951, pp. 115–119.

13. Sherif, M., and Wilson, M. O. (eds.). *Group Relations at the Crossroad.* "An Analysis of Compliant Behavior," by Leon Festinger. Harper Bros., New York, 1953, pp. 232–256.

14. Smith, D. E. P. "Fit Teaching Methods to Personality Structure," *High School Journal,* Vol. 39, December, 1955, pp. 167–171.

15. Wispe, Lauren G. "Evaluating Section Teaching Methods on the Introductory Course," *Jr. Educational Research,* Vol. XLV, No. 3, November, 1951, pp. 161–186.

16. Withall, John. "The Development of a Technique for the Measurement of Social-Emotional Climate in Classroom," *Journal of Experimental Education,* Vol. XVII, March, 1949, pp. 347–361.

chapter 17

Teaching is interaction

Marie M. Hughes

With the advent of Sputnick, public attention is once again focused on American education. The tiny ball coursing through space blazoned an urgent message across the globe. Without trying to decipher the deep-deep signals coming from the small whirling moon, an eminent educator gave his version of the message broadcast by the first earth satellite: "Nothing is as important as the trained and educated mind. . . . The sphere tells, not of the desirability, but the urgent necessity of the highest quality and expanded dimensions of the educational effort" (10).

American concern about education predates Sputnick. The mounting costs of education, the need for engineers and scientists, the tragic facts of juvenile delinquency and mental illness are among the portents that have led us to question the quality of education offered in our public schools. In our concern we have raised questions that have ranged from phonics and spelling to gifted children and creative expression.

We would like to believe that the resurging interest in our public schools creed—a creed that embodies the dream of individual fulfillment and recognizes the right of every child to an opportunity to develop his talents to the utmost. With this creed prompting our concern, we may well wonder whether we are asking appropriate questions or offering appropriate solutions.

Are we urging expedient measures? Are we advancing theories that are little more than opinion and prejudice? How should we go about improving education? Where do we start? What do we really know about the teaching act?

From *The Elementary School Journal*, LVIII(May, 1958), 457–464. Reprinted by permission of The University of Chicago Press.

The conclusions of A. S. Barr, a persistent investigator in this field, may be summed up succinctly: We do not yet have an adequate definition of teaching efficiency (1). However, he suggests that "teaching effectiveness may be essentially a relationship between teachers, pupils, and other persons directly concerned with the educational undertaking . . ." (2). What he says makes us wonder whether we have been looking in the wrong places for the crucial elements of effective teaching.

Nathaniel Cantor, a thoughtful student of the teaching process, wrote: "What occurs psychologically in the interaction . . . between teacher and pupil determines the quality of teaching and learning" (5).

It is our assumption here that the most crucial aspect of teaching is the interaction between teacher and children. The interplay may occur in the classroom or on the playground, in the lunchroom or any other place in the school where the teacher has recognized status as a teacher.

Starting with this belief that the teaching process can be defined as the interaction between teacher and children, we shall in this discussion present the major components of this interplay. These components or forces deserve scrutiny, for they are at work in all relationships between teacher and pupils, in all relationships among the pupils themselves.

The Teacher Has Authority

The most pervasive force of all is the status of the teacher. His status and power derive in part from his age and adulthood in contrast to his pupils' childhood and youth. His power also derives from the institutional authority bestowed by society at large. The teacher is expected to control. This fact is impressed on children every day. It may be wrapped in warning, a reproach, or a threat, but the teacher's authority is an ever-present reality, imbedded in such remarks as these:

When you go to school the teacher will get after you for that.
Have a good time at school, and be sure to do what the teacher asks.
The teacher will make you keep your desk at school neat.

Even the adult who gleefully recalls how he outwitted or defied his teachers acknowledges their authority.

Throughout the years, the power and the authority of the teacher have been upheld by the courts. In their rulings the courts have contended that the teacher is a parent surrogate or substitute, acting for the good of the child.

There is no denying that certain controls must exist if school is to keep at all. Quiet and attention to the business at hand are essential. The teacher is expected to act in a way that will ensure control. Children, parents, and the teacher himself share this expectation.

The Impact of Daily Decisions

The teacher's authority is expressed in sanctioned ways—in his decisions, for example. Actually, whatever a teacher does requires a decision of some kind on his part. He says to Mary, "Read that sentence again." To Johnny, "Yes, you may sit with Melvin." To Ben, "You must finish the problems on this page before you can go home."

Teachers' decisions are the very essence of what goes on in school. They determine to a large degree the life space of the child so far as school is concerned. They indicate what he can and cannot do, the subjects to which he may give attention. The teacher may present his decisions casually enough. For example, Roger was leafing through a book he had chosen from the library shelf. Noting his choice, the teacher said, "That book is too easy for you." Indirectly the teacher ruled out the child's choice. After such a comment, few children could continue to read a book and feel comfortable about it. This teacher used an indirect way of getting Roger to set aside the book. The teacher might have ruled out the child's choice directly by saying to him, "Don't take that book. It's too easy for you."

Another incident illustrates how teachers' decisions can restrict children's attention. During the height of the Suez crisis, a child in sixth grade asked a question about Egypt. The teacher dismissed the query with the reply, "We're studying the Scandinavian countries now. Egypt comes next year." The teacher's response determined the direction of that day's lesson. The response may have done more; it may have dampened the child's curiosity about the larger world.

The teacher's decisions can play a large part in determining the kind of thinking a child does. Important in this respect are the questions a teacher decides to ask. Do they call for comparison and contrast? For the sorting out of relationships? The assessing of consequences? Imagination? Or do his questions require only memory?

What responses does the teacher permit his pupils to make? Do the children dare to exercise merciless logic? Do they dare challenge an alleged truth?

The teacher's authority is expressed, not only through decisions, but also through the system of rewards and penalties. The system operates day in and day out, subtly perhaps but nonetheless persistently (8). A teacher in the primary grades may say, "John is sitting up straight. I'll choose him to take the lunch money." A teacher in the junior high school may announce, "If you forget to bring the right paper to class, I'll take two points off your mark."

Teachers have been known to use classroom seating arrangements to reward and to punish. In one classroom the children who make a perfect score in arithmetic are seated next to the windows; the children who score the lowest are seated farthest from the windows.

The system works in other ways. In English class, the children write letters asking for information to help them in a science project; the letter in the best handwriting is chosen for mailing. In art class, the children paint pictures of the first Thanksgiving; the best paintings are chosen for the hall exhibit. The decisions bring rewards to children whose work is chosen. For the boys and girls who had hoped for recognition and failed to win it, the decisions may spell punishment.

Children know that a system of rewards and punishments is at work. Pupils have it in mind when they rate fairness high as a quality they prize in teachers.

How fair are teachers? How evenly do they distribute rewards and punishments? De Groat and Thompson (6) studied the responses of several teachers to their pupils. From 35 to 70 per cent of the teachers' expressions of approval were directed to four or five pupils. Four or five other children bore the brunt of 37 per cent of the teachers' disapproval.

The ultimate in school punishment is failure or expulsion or both.

The teacher's power is expressed in the decisions he makes, the rewards he bestows, and the punishments he metes. This power is a dominant component in the interaction of teacher and pupils.

New Data in the Interactive System

Interaction is far from static or simple. On the contrary, it is dynamic and complex. New elements constantly enter the situation. One act begets another. The teacher acts; the pupils respond. The pupils act; the teacher responds. The children respond to one another, and the teacher, in turn, responds to their interaction. Even an act that ignores the act of another is still a response and has its effect on the initiator.

The ebb and flow of actions and reactions constitutes a feedback system. The children's responses to what a teacher does or says offer clues to their feelings and understandings, their needs and perceptions. Again, the power of the teacher is exercised as he responds to the data the children place into the situation.

The child who puts away his drawing immediately after the teacher makes a few changes on it is saying something about his feelings. The child who protests, "I'm new here," when the librarian scolds him for not replacing a book on the proper shelf is also saying something about his feelings.

Flanders tells of an incident in a fifth grade where the class was launching a study of weather in the United States. A lively discussion was going on. The children were offering useful suggestions from their own experience. Suddenly the teacher thrust in a proposal of her own: "Let's make up committees on the Rockies, the Far West Coast, the Central Plains, the Southeastern States, and the Gulf States." The lively discussion ended abruptly. Few children volunteered for committee work. The reason for their lack of enthusiasm escaped the teacher completely. She was unaware that she had imposed a structure that ignored the children's suggestions (7).

By his responses to the data of action and reaction, a teacher legitimatizes certain processes and procedures. If, for example, the teacher seriously considers his pupils' suggestions, he encourages initiative. If he ignores his pupils' suggestions, he dampens initiative. The children learn not to act on their own. They learn, instead, to wait until they are told what to do.

One day during an early snowfall a third-grade boy bounced into the room and called out, "Let's make a poem." The teacher's reply? "I think we ought to write a song."

In another room, another teacher said, "Mary, will you take charge this morning?" Bill, who had been ill and out of school for several days, spoke up, "I haven't had a chance to take charge." The teacher replied, "It takes a long time for everyone to get a turn. Why don't you help Mary? Will that be all right, Mary?" Mary accepted the suggestion and made an addition of her own: "You call on someone, then I'll call on someone." This teacher took into account the meaning of the situation to Bill. The teacher also took care to ask Mary's permission before assigning Bill as her assistant.

How do teachers respond to the data that enter the interactive situation? Are they aware of the feedback? Do they understand a child's responses? Can they read the language of behavior? Do they feel free to respond to it? Responsiveness, especially on the part of a person who has status to a person of less status, says, in effect, "You count. You are worthwhile. What you know, think, and feel are important." The psychological significance of responsiveness cannot be overestimated, for teachers' responses affect the quality of living and learning in the classroom.

To understand more fully the dynamics at work in the classroom, it is necessary to take a closer look at the teacher and the child as individuals.

The Teacher as a Person

The teacher brings his status and his authority to his interaction with the child. He cannot avoid doing so. What other factors condition his behavior in this relationship?

The teacher brings to the situation his own experience with teachers. As a child dreaming of the day when he would be a teacher, he may have said to himself, "I'll be able to tell kids what to do." Or, "I'll never make a child come up in front of the class if he doesn't want to."

A sixth grader, explaining why she wanted to teach, disclosed her mental picture of teachers: "A good understanding of people and their personality. A grasp of all subjects. A strong voice. A firm will." Katherine went on to tell why she thought she would make a good teacher: "I have studied hard on all subjects. I have tried to get along with teachers and put myself in their place. I have learned how to correct, score, and record papers. I am reasonably well read."

If Katherine goes on to get professional preparation, she may change her picture of teachers. At best, however, professional study simply reorganizes and adds to the image the student already has of teachers, an image based on previous experience with them. As a student teacher, Katherine may identify strongly with the teacher with whom she works. She may find it congenial to adopt certain educational goals and to slight others. She may be strongly influenced by research findings on patterns of human growth. On the other hand, it is entirely possible that professional preparation will have little effect on the major expectations she has of herself as a teacher.

The teacher, then, brings to the classroom his own experiences in professional preparation. The teacher also brings with him whatever traditions, biases, and ways of looking at teachers and teaching he learned from the social class and the subculture of America into which he was born. He may come from a family of teachers and enter the profession because he is expected to do so. He may choose teaching because of the alleged security it offers. A woman may choose teaching out of the belief that it is a proper vocation for a woman, though "sissy" for a man.

We need not describe in detail the varying attitudes and expectations that individuals bring from their families and communities. The important fact is that these attitudes and expectations are part of the teacher as a person.

What, then, determines an individual's actions when he becomes a teacher? First, he acts as he believes that others—parents, children, principal—expect him to act. Moreover, he acts as he believes a teacher should act with children. What he expects of children will influence what he does in the classroom. Does he believe that all third graders should know the multiplication tables? Then he will approach third graders differently than he would if he did not associate third grade and multiplication tables quite so closely. Does he believe that children, in general, try to get away with as much as they can? Then he will be less accepting of their mistakes and inexperience than he would otherwise be. Does he believe that routines and schedules are made to help people live together? Then he will be more flexible than if he believes that rigid schedules build character. The teacher's attitudes and expectations—those he has of himself and those he believes that others have of him—define "his participation in the interactive process" (11).

The teacher, no less than the child, brings all of himself to school. The teacher is a person with unique experiences and personal needs. His behavior, like that of children and other adults, is influenced by his efforts to meet those needs. Clearly, the classroom offers teachers many possibilities for using their power for this purpose.

For example, the teacher's need to punish may create a relationship of extreme punitiveness. The teacher's need for affection may lead to an overly affectionate, smothering relationship. Whatever the relationship, the teacher can rationalize that what he is doing is "for the good of the child."

Because of the teacher's status, the psychological mechanism of projection may have full sway. If the teacher is filled with resentment and anger at the world, he may think that the children are filled with anger and resentment at him. He may, accordingly, take out his feelings on them.

Bush, in his clinical case study of some twenty high school teachers, was impressed with the uniqueness of each teacher-student relationship. No teacher was rated high by all students, and no teacher was rated low by all students. Since students' liking for teachers is one of the most forceful factors in creating effective conditions for learning, he suggests that:

> A strategic task for the teacher is a cultivation on his part of personal liking of his pupils for him. This requires a teacher who is skillful, sensitive and adjusted in the area of personal relationships and who is able to handle his relations with pupils objectively rather than as a source of meeting his own personal inadequacies (4).

We have suggested here some of the influences that shape the expectations a teacher has of himself, expectations that influence what he does as a teacher. Each teacher will meet some of his own needs in the classroom. The most competent and effective teachers learn to handle their personal needs in a constructive manner, remaining warm, receptive, and humane individuals.

The Child in the Interactive Situation

What influences affect the child's participation in the interactive situation? Of course he reacts to the teacher's status. He also brings to his responses his attitudes, feelings, and ways of reacting to adults and their authority. He may consistently see adults as adversaries with whom to do battle. Or his outlook may be quite matter of fact, now friendly, now unfriendly; for the child brings to school his dependence on adults as well as his struggles for independence, his anxieties as well as his self-confidence. The combinations of attitudes and feelings toward the teacher held by thirty or more children show infinite variety and intensity. Their effect is considerable. Moustakas says: "All emotions influence the child's attitudes toward himself, other children, and his teachers. They affect his ability to read, to spell, and to think" (9).

The classroom has been called an arena, a jungle. Why? Here the child compares himself with others of his own age. He may discover, for example, that he is taller or shorter than most of his age mates. He may find that in arithmetic he is quicker or slower than they. He may make discoveries about his family and its "place" in the community. He gets answers to questions that are critically important to him, such questions as:

> Will these kids like me?
> Will I be chosen first?
> Will I be able to chin myself ten times today?
> Will I get to collect the lunch money?
> Will the kids laugh at me when I read?
> Will Jim and Pete ask me to sit at their table for lunch?
> Will my spelling paper be put on the bulletin board?

The child also brings his own personal goals to school:

> Today I'll finish the big book on dinosaurs.
> If I get a chance, I'll push Bill in the nose.
> I won't sit by a girl for reading.
> I'm going to ask to sing "Drill Ye Terriers Drill."
> I'll ask Mike to help me take the milk to the kindergarten.
> Me and Mike and Pete will play in our cave at noon.
> I'll ask the teacher if I can bring the big globe to our room.

Every child feels a certain amount of inner tension and pressure, and each situation he enters brings additional pressure as well as possibilities for satisfaction. The actual satisfaction that can be gained from a given situation varies greatly from child to child and from classroom to classroom. For example, in a classroom of thirty boys and girls, 435 paired interactions are possible (3).

This potential may not be realized, as a recent study points out. The study compared mutual choices in two sixth-grade classes across the hall from one another (12). In one classroom, 90 per cent of the children made mutual choices. In the other, only 36 per cent of the choices were mutual. For the children and teacher, the quality of the interaction in these two classrooms must be different.

Further understanding of the child's reactions in school may be gained from a study by Stendler (13). She questioned mothers about the attitudes of two hundred first graders. Although 92 per cent of the children viewed school favorably, 39 per cent had at some time during the first two months of school disliked it to the point of wishing they did not have to attend; 42 per cent had openly criticized the teacher or the school.

Obviously the child, no less than the teacher, has his own aspirations, his own way of reacting, his own expectations, satisfactions, and fears. He does his own learning for his own purposes.

To the children, and probably to the teacher as well, the classroom is a dynamic blend of victory and defeat, of satisfactions and frustrations, of fear and safety, of conflict and serenity, of attractions and repulsions, of boredom and challenge, of hope and despair, of love and hate, of friendliness and enmity, of fairness and injustice, of clarity and confusion.

We have defined teaching as the interaction of teacher with children, individually or as a group. We have noted, as the dominant element in the relation, the power of the teacher. This power, bestowed by society, is expressed in decisions, rewards, and punishments. We have noted that interaction between teacher and pupil is complex and changing, that new elements constantly enter in, elements that may or may not be used by teacher and pupils. Response—and lack of response—to these elements have a strong influence on interaction. Other elements also have their effect—the array of expectations, purposes, and personal needs that teacher and pupil alike bring to a situation and seek to fulfill through it.

What bearing does our analysis have on understanding good teaching? We offer the following propositions:

An understanding of the factors in the interactive situation is essential to an evaluation of good teaching.

Every act of the teacher has a function in the interactive situation.

The good teacher recognizes his status and acts to ameliorate, rather than to maximize, his power.

The good teacher is expert at reading the language of behavior. He responds to the feelings and attitudes expressed in the children's reactions and uses them as constructively as possible.

The good teacher, recognizing his decision-making power, strives to base his decisions on sound knowledge.

The good teacher understands himself and his needs and does not exploit his power over children for his own purposes.

The good teacher recognizes the importance of interpersonal relations. He strives for teaching that will have positive rather than negative results.

The good teacher provides pupils with opportunities for making choices and for using a wide range of mental processes.

The good teacher recognizes that children need opportunity to practice initiative as they work at their own problems of learning and growing.

REFERENCES

1. Barr, Avril S. "Teaching Competencies," *Encyclopedia of Educational Research* (1950 ed.), p. 1453.
2. Barr, Avril S. "Measurement of Teacher Characteristics and Prediction of Teacher Efficiency," *Journal of Educational Research*, XXII (June, 1952), 174.

3. Bossard, James. "The Law of Family Interaction," American Journal of Sociology, L (January, 1954), 292–294. (Quoted by Willard Olson in *Child Development*, p. 370. Boston: D. C. Heath & Co., 1949.)
4. Bush, Robert N. *Teacher-Pupil Relationships*, p. 189. New York: Prentice-Hall, Inc., 1954.
5. Cantor, Nathaniel. *The Teaching-Learning Process*, p. 270. New York: Dryden Press, 1953.
6. De Groat, Albert, and Thompson, George G. "A Study of the Distribution of Teacher Approval and Disapproval among Sixth-Grade Pupils," *Journal of Experimental Education*, XVII (Spring, 1949), 57–75.
7. Flanders, Ned A. *Teaching with Groups,* chap. iv. Minneapolis: Burgess Publishing Co., 1954.
8. Hollingshead, A.B. *Elmtown's Youth*. New York: John Wiley & Sons, 1949.
9. Moustakas, Clark. *The Teacher and the Child*, p. 37. New York: McGraw-Hill Book Co., Inc., 1956.
10. Murphy, Franklin D. Address in Washington, D.C., on the occasion of his retirement as chairman of American Council on Education. *College and University Bulletin*, X (October 15, 1957), 3.
11. Parsons, Talcott, and Shils, Edward A. *Theory of Action*, p. 23. Cambridge: Harvard University Press, 1954.
12. Squires, Boyd. "The Process Used by an Elementary Principal to Help Teachers Identify Children with Problems and to Work Constructively with Them," pp. 109–111. University of Utah, 1956.
13. Stendler, Celia Burns, and Young, Norman. "The Impact of Beginning First Grade upon Socialization as Reported by Mothers," *Child Development*, XXI (December, 1950), 241–250.

chapter 18

The gifted and the retarded in historical perspective

Walter W. Cook

The current tide of public interest in public education is welcomed by all competent schoolmen—even the panic-striking books, pamphlets, and journal articles crying that we are neglecting our gifted children, that Johnny can't read, that children can't spell, that schools have no discipline; written with sweeping generalizations made from two or three horrible examples and showing no more psychological insight than is commonly apparent at a supermarket or over the bridge table; blaming the whole sorry mess on that overworked, underpaid, and unappreciated group of men and women who have dedicated their lives to the improvement of public education.

Even these articles can leave some good in their wake, if we are not panicked into indefensible patterns of school organization and procedure. It is important in these times that we keep our eyes on the goal—*at least twelve years of schooling for all the children of all the people; that we take every child where he is and develop his capacities to as high a level as possible in the time we have.* Let us resolve to make certain that this tumult and shouting leads to more skillful ways of providing for individual differences; more enriched programs for all children; enough classrooms for every child; a wealth of instructional materials—books, books, and more books in the school library, in every classroom, and in every home; a class size that is manageable; a work load that does not leave the teacher too physically and emotionally exhausted for good teaching; and above all, educational procedures based on greater insight into how the creative

From *Phi Delta Kappan*, XXXIX(March, 1958), 249–255. Reprinted by permission of the publisher.

power, imagination, and the thrill of learning can be released in all children.

Reactions which some schoolmen make to the flood of criticisms indicate no greater depth of psychological insight than that shown by the admirals, journalists, history professors, and businessmen who criticize. The articles in lay journals and newspapers, both pro and con, rarely get above the emotional level. The layman never has an opportunity to learn: how great is the range of ability in the common schools; why retardation and acceleration are not an answer to the problem of variability; why general ability grouping is not an answer; how the concept of the passing mark and the textbook distort educational processes into mere mechanical memorization; how and under what conditions the teacher is able to maximize individual development in heterogeneous groups; what the equipment and library resources of an adequate classroom should be; and, above all, the personality and intellectual qualifications of an adequate teacher.

Despite space limitation, some historical perspective seems necessary. Perhaps the most important factor in shaping our attitudes and policies in education is the graded textbook. *American schools are predominantly "textbook" schools.* The majority of teachers feel lost without a uniform textbook in the hands of every pupil. Education is conceived by many as a process of memorizing the content of textbooks. Limited goals are set in terms of the content of textbooks. Examinations are based upon the content of textbooks. Educational progress is measured in terms of pages covered in the textbook, and the intellectual ability required for success at a given grade level or in a given subject is determined by the textbook. The basic assumption underlying textbook procedure is that pupils can be classified into homogeneous groups and taught uniform material by a standardized procedure. The textbook has a place in education, but these assumptions inhibit the process of making "schooling" truly educational.

Planned for the Assembly Line

Plans devised to make assembly-line educational procedures operate successfully have had a long history. The first set of graded textbooks in America, the *McGuffey Readers,* came from the press in 1837. In 1848, the first eight-room building was constructed to house a graded elementary school. By 1870, the schools of the United States—even the one-room rural schools—had been graded. Achievement standards—*determined by the difficulty of the graded text, which in turn was determined by the subjective judgment of textbook authors—served as the basis for promotion. The rate of failure was high.* Even in 1920, it was common to fail over 30 per cent of the pupils in the primary grades; and by the time the children had finished the intermediate grades, over 50 per cent had failed at least once. During the early 1900's "laggards in our schools" became a matter of national concern. Unfortunately the chief argument against it was the great expense of keeping slow-learning pupils in school so long. Early research in education dealt with this problem. Early remedies consisted of establishing minimum essentials in the various subjects, eliminating useless material from textbooks, and graduating the difficulty of textbooks on a more objective basis.

Perhaps it is desirable to mention the panaceas for variability recommended and adopted in the early years of the century, lest we repeat the same mistakes. All forms of acceleration and retardation were tried—semiannual promotion, quarterly promotion, subject promotion, and special promotion. In some schools an attempt was made to hold standards constant and to get uniformity of achievement by increasing the amount of instruction for the slow pupils, as in the Batavia Plan, the Assisting-teacher (Teacher-aide) Plan, and the Vacation-classes Plan. Other schools received recognition by holding the course of study constant and differentiating the amount of time required for slow-, medium-, and fast-learning pupils, as in the North Denver Plan, the Cambridge Plan, and the Portland Plan. Other schools got their names in print by holding time constant, and differentiating the course of study for slow-, medium-, and fast-learning pupils, as in the Santa Barbara and Baltimore Plans. Still other schools tried dividing the course of study into units of specified activities and achievement, permitting each pupil to advance at his own rate in each subject, as in the Pueblo Plan, the Winnetka Plan, and the Dalton Plan. By 1920, group intelligence tests had been developed to the place where Detroit attempted to attain homogeneous instruction groups through X, Y, and Z grouping, on the basis of capacity as revealed by group intelligence tests. Other schools used achievement tests and teachers' marks for homogeneous grouping. In 1936, the National Society for the Study of Education devoted Part I of its *Thirty-fifth Yearbook* to a critical evaluation of practices in the grouping of pupils. General ability grouping was criticized and defended on educational grounds, philosophical grounds, social grounds, and psychological grounds—all questions were raised except: *How homogeneous are the groups in the particular subject being taught?*

Before we try more administrative panaceas for making our assembly-line type of school machinery operate more effectively, let us examine the facts of individual differences, trait differences, and the process of intellectual development.

The Extent of Variability

When a random group of six-year-olds enters the first grade, 2 per cent of them will be below the average four-year-olds in general mental development, and 2 per cent will be above the average eight-year-old. Disregarding the extreme 2 per cent at the higher end, there is a four-year range in general intelligence. By the time this group has reached the age of twelve (seventh-grade level), the range will have increased to almost eight years. As long as all the children of all the people remain in school, the range continues to increase. When the educational achievement of a typical sixth-grade class is measured, we find a range of approximately eight years in reading comprehension, vocabulary, arithmetic computation, mechanics of English composition, and other forms of achievement. In almost any sixth-grade class will be found a pupil with first- or second-grade reading ability, and another with eleventh- or twelfth-grade reading ability. In any grade above the primary level will be found the complete range of elementary school achievement.

At the high school and college levels, Learned and Wood have given us an answer. When the *General Culture Battery*, consisting of achievement tests in general science, foreign literature, fine arts and social studies, was administered to high school and college seniors in Pennsylvania, it was found that the upper 10 per cent of high school seniors were above the college senior median and could have been given B.A. degrees without lowering the intellectual standards of such degrees. It was also found that the lower 10 per cent of college seniors were below the high school senior median.

The Public Should Learn the Facts

Although these facts should be basic data in educational thinking and call for a revision of our postulates, they are largely ignored. The idea that the process of schooling *must* consist of homogeneous groups of pupils receiving uniform instruction by mass educational techniques from uniform textbooks is the axiom which prevents constructive approaches to the problem of variability in the classroom. It leads to the further assumptions that grade levels should signify rather definite states of educational achievement; that the course of study is for all pupils, that a pupil should not be promoted to a grade until he is able to do the work outlined for that grade; that when individual differences are provided for by good teaching, all pupils can be brought up to standard, that maintaining a passing mark results in homogeneous instructional groups; and that when relative homogeneity does not prevail, it is a result of poor teaching or lax standards. These assumptions are contrary to fact. *It is time the public learned the facts. The range of ability in the classes of the elementary and high school is so great that if the slow learner in the eighth grade were demoted to the fourth, he would still be a slow learner in the fourth, and below the median of the class. It the top pupil of the fourth grade were accelerated to the eighth, he would still be a bright pupil in the eighth, and above the median of that class.*

The Acceleration Fallacy

What happens when the bright pupil is accelerated, and the slow pupil is retarded? *The bright pupil—the one who profits from an educational environment—is eliminated from school first. He spends less time there,*

*while the slow pupil who can profit least from educational environment
spends the most time there.* If the educational procedure of a class is such
that the bright pupil is bored and unstimulated, we may be certain that
the pupils of median ability and of low ability are equally bored. A teacher
who understands modern methods of instruction, working with a class of
limited size and with adequate instructional material—especially books,
books, and more books—makes a class exciting for the bright, the dull, and
the average.

What happens in a school system with strict policies of promotion is
revealed by two instructional surveys of the Austin, Minnesota, Public
Schools, one in 1921 and the other in 1951. The same tests were used in
both surveys. In 1921, 54 per cent of the pupils entering the seventh grade
were overage and had been retarded at least one year. The median IQ of
the elementary school at that time was 94. In 1951, 4 per cent of the
children entering the seventh grade were overage. The median IQ on the
same tests was 111. This IQ was checked by another test—a modern test—
and found to be correct. Hence, the intellectual level of an elementary
school was reduced from a potential median IQ of 111 to a median IQ of
94 simply by hoarding the dull pupils. At the time when the median IQ
of the elementary school was 94, the median IQ of the high school graduating class was 129. The overage pupils dropped out of school in the seventh,
eighth, and ninth grades. There was no one beyond the tenth grade with
an IQ of 100 or less. Of course, the highly select group of seniors with a
median IQ of 129 could do college work successfully. In 1951, when the
median IQ of the elementary school was 111, the median IQ of the high
school graduating class was 117. Still some selection, but most of the
children finished high school. It is true that the high school graduate of
1951 was not as able to do collegiate work as his counterpart in 1921.
High school graduation is no longer an adequate criterion of ability to do
college work, nor should it be. This is not to deny the colleges the responsibility for establishing standards of entrance which will ensure a
college level of intellectual work. Unless we adopt a policy denying intellectual development to a large group of our citizens, this must be the
policy. The surest way to lower the standards of the common schools is to
hoard the dull pupils; to eliminate them is hardly recommended by even
our most aristocratic critics.

The effect of promotion policies on the variability of classes and achievement standards is also commonly misunderstood. It is generally believed
that the trend toward universal promotion has increased the variability
of upper-grade classes, lowered their average achievement, and reduced
the incentive of pupils to work hard. Research reveals the contrary to be
true. The excess of slow pupils in the school with high promotion standards
lowers the intellectual level of the classes, and achievement is significantly
less. The excess of retarded pupils in the upper grades aggravates the
range of ability problem, and the variability of classes is as great as when

universal promotion is practiced. Furthermore, studies have consistently shown that the slow-learning pupil achieves more when promoted regularly than when retarded.

Trait Differences and Ability Grouping

The effectiveness of general ability grouping depends upon the relative magnitude of trait differences, that is, the variability of the individual from his subject of highest achievement to that of his lowest. *Ability grouping is based on the hypothesis that the pupil varies little in achievement from subject to subject.* Evidence from several overlapping fields of investigation refutes this hypothesis. The first is concerned with basic theories of mental organization and primary mental abilities; the second with studies of the so-called "idiot savant"; the third with asymmetry of development in normal and gifted individuals; the fourth with direct measures of trait variability; the fifth with evidence of correlation between traits and areas of achievement; and the sixth with overlapping in educational achievement of groups which have been made homogeneous with respect to some measure of general ability. Tentative generalizations drawn from the research of Hull may be stated as follows: *Trait variability in the typical individual is 80 per cent as great as individual variability in his age group. Trait differences are normally distributed. Some individuals are twice as variable as others, and there is no relationship between general level of ability and of the amount of trait variability.*

Under the most favorable circumstances, that is, when pupils are grouped in X, Y, and Z fashion on the basis of an achievement test battery, which is heavily weighted in favor of reading and arithmetic scores, we may expect a reduction of about 20 per cent in reading and arithmetic variability. The extreme X and Z groups will overlap approximately 80 per cent. Instead of a range of eight years in reading ability at the sixth-grade level, the teacher has, after grouping, a range of six and four-tenths years. In other subjects, such as art, music, handwriting, and spelling, the reduction of range approaches zero. *Consequently, when grouping is practiced, it must be on the basis of status and needs in specific subjects. Pupils should be grouped differently in each subject area. In the elementary school, such groups should be flexible in organization and specific in purpose. At the high school and college levels, grouping for mathematics, science, English, and other areas can be more permanent and have the nature of honors courses.* The pupil should enter an honors class and remain there only on the basis of achievement. To label a child as either retarded or gifted on the basis of an intelligence test is to do him a gross educational disservice; if low, he is discouraged from trying; if high, he feels hard work is a reflection on his superiority. *Prognosis should be based on specific achievement in a given area and only on that basis.* The time for scrambling different types of achievement in varying amounts and calling it intelligence should have passed by now.

It is widely believed by laymen that instructional groups can be made more homogeneous in achievement through effective teaching. Education is conceived to consist of learning such things as are found in textbooks— spelling words, type problems in arithmetic, causes and results of wars, names of the states and their capitals, explorers and where they explored, countries and their products, and the seven basic food groups. To such, good teaching is conceived to consist of assigning, threatening, drilling, rewarding, and punishing, until the pupils can verbalize these facts. The process of providing for individual differences is assumed to mean getting all pupils to memorize the facts required by the examination in sufficient amount to exceed the passing mark. What is the harm in this simple conception of the schooling process which substitutes information for education?

Complexity of Task Affects Variability

This question concerns us with the effect of a period of learning upon individual differences. Are individuals more alike or less alike with respect to a given ability after a period of instruction? The research on this problem leads us to the following generalization: *If the responses to be learned are sufficiently simple that a high proportion of the group can master them during the period of learning, the variability of the group becomes less; but if the task is complex, involving the higher mental processes to the extent that the abilities of the most apt members of the group are taxed during the period of learning, then the variability of the group increases.*

Limited educational goals in the form of lists of facts and type problems which enable the pupil to answer examination questions of the *name, describe, define, who, what, when, and where* variety and which may be memorized in a rote sense for examination purposes to give a semblance of uniformity of achievement in meeting the requirements of a passing mark, result in highly temporary learning. Our early objective tests tended to emphasize this type of learning. *Tests of retention administered from three months to three years after a course such as this was completed revealed from 30 to 90 per cent loss. The forgetting curves of such learning closely approximate those of nonsense materials.*

Although rapid forgetting is the rule when factual tests are repeated, it has been demonstrated that tests of problem-solving ability, reading, comprehension, the application of principles to new situations, organizing ability, and the interpretation of new data show an *increase* in ability with the passing of time. *When learning is structured and meaningful and involves problem-solving mental processes, the learning is relatively permanent.* Such learning involves unlimited goals, and when the abilities of all members of a group are taxed, individual differences increase during the period of learning. The conclusion seems justified that the emphasis on the process of striving for limited goals, homogeneity of achievement, and getting all pupils over the passing mark tends to encourage teachers to set limited goals for instruction which results in temporary factual learning. *Our conclusion must be that the more effective the instruction—the more adequately we meet the needs of all pupils—the more heterogeneous groups become.*

The central problem of meeting the needs of the slow pupil and the gifted pupil, as well as the average pupil, is how best to meet the needs of individuals in groups of widely varying ability. Since all instructional groups vary widely in interests and ability, it seems wiser to attempt to develop techniques for meeting the needs in such groups instead of constantly striving for a homogeneity which cannot be achieved. This calls for changes in beliefs, attitudes, and understandings which will result in more defensible administrative and curriculum policies. Let us suggest some of them.

Administrative Policies

The administrative policy should have two purposes: (1) to make it possible for the teacher to know the pupil well enough to meet his needs and (2) to provide instructional material with a range of difficulty and interest appeal commensurate with the needs of the instructional group:

a. The size of classes must be reduced to not more than twenty-five pupils. The practice of giving each elementary teacher a class of from thirty to forty pupils and having the high school teacher meet from 150 to 250 different pupils a day, with instruction based on a uniform textbook, precludes the possibility of meeting individual needs.

b. A systematic testing program revealing status and growth in *the basic intellectual skills and abilities (not facts)* required for optimal adjustment in the culture must be instituted, with the results for each pupil from kindergarten to college graphically portrayed. The purposes of these tests are not the traditional ones—those of holding teacher and pupils to standards or as a basis for promotion or marking; the purpose is rather to enable the teacher to know more about the pupil, the books he can read, the type of problems he can solve, the amount of improvement that can be expected—in short, to know the educational experiences that he needs.

c. A permanent record folder, containing in addition to the superimposed profiles of the test results, the health record, samples of handwriting, creative written work, and other evidences of achievements showing the pupil's development from kindergarten on, should be in the hands of each teacher.

d. Each teacher should have an opportunity for a personal conference with the parents of each pupil not less than twice each year in order that both the parents and teacher may understand the pupil better.

e. The primary basis of grouping children should be physical and social development (probably best indicated by chronological age), since these are the most obvious criteria of status in childhood groups. A child should live and work with the group he most obviously belongs with—one which accepts him and which he accepts.

f. There must be grouping within classes on the basis of status and needs in specific learning areas. These groups should be flexible as to size and duration and specific in purpose.

g. The practice of labeling school books by grade should be discontinued. A code number indicating to the teacher the difficulty of the material is sufficient.

h. In both the elementary and high school, the practice of having a teacher instruct the same group of pupils from three to six years should be encouraged.

i. At the high school level there should be special honors courses for students who demonstrate unusual ability in mathematics, science, language, and other subjects.

j. In the high school the practice of integrating English and the social studies in a four- to six-year coordinated sequence with two- or three-hour daily periods in a laboratory workshop should be encouraged.

k. A wealth of instructional material should be provided in each classroom. It should have a range of difficulty, interest appeal, and content commensurate with the range of abilities and interests of the class. It must be placed in the classroom and not in the library or other special room. Perhaps the best way to meet the needs of the potential geniuses in our classes is to place them in intellectual contact with the geniuses of the ages. This can be done through books. This should be an item of first priority in any school system. The most serious indictment that can be brought against public education today is its failure to furnish the teacher with adequate books and instructional material and to surround every pupil with a wealth of reading materials of both a literary and factual nature. *Textbooks are necessary, but they are far from sufficient as instructional material.*

Curriculum Policies

An understanding of individual and trait differences is essential for determining adequate curriculum policies. Such policies should: (1) provide flexibility of requirements in order that the potential unskilled laborer and the potential research physicist will not be held to the same requirements; (2) free the teacher to plan for the welfare and optimal development of each pupil; and (3) broaden the curriculum sufficiently to recognize and reward the great variety of aptitudes and combinations of aptitudes and interests of students, enabling each to discover his strengths and weaknesses and preparing him to find his place in our complex society with its multiplicity of demands.

a. Curriculum content should be organized around large units or problems in the social science and natural science areas. Each unit should be organized and developed with the following purposes in mind: (1) to make possible an appeal to many different interests and to utilize to the maximum the great variety of abilities; (2) to make possible the utilization of a wealth of reading materials selected to ensure a wide range of difficulty, content appeal, and points of view; (3) to provide possibilities for use of a wide variety of stimulating materials from books, both literary and factual, moving pictures and other visual aids, field trips, museums, journals, and observations from the world of work; (4) to stimulate and make meaningful a wide range of activities in reading for different purposes, use of reference materials, writing reports and letters, interviewing people with special knowledge, preparing and presenting oral reports, planning, organizing materials, seeing relationships, developing generalizations, dramatization, construction projects, appreciation of music and the arts in their proper relation to life, quantitative thinking, designing graphic portrayal of data, evaluating evidence, reading maps and diagrams, assuming individual responsibility, cooperating in group activities—all to the purpose of developing understandings, ideals, beliefs, attitudes, and above all, sustaining intellectual interests.

b. The grade levels at which certain knowledge, skills, and abilities should be learned cannot be determined with any degree of specificity. The graded lists of skills and knowledge commonly provided in textbooks serve to provide a helpful sequence of materials in developing skills in the various subgroups of abilities: they furnish material which should be emphasized as limitation in a skill becomes evident, and they should be used as a check list for diagnostic purposes. It should not be assumed that these listed and itemized goals are to be achieved in a 1, 2, 3 fashion, out of their functional setting and natural context, once and for all time, and that all instruction should be organized around these piecemeal itemized goals. Perhaps half the school time should be devoted to a systematic development of the skills necessary in the development of units and related to them as much as possible. The other half of the time should be devoted to the meanings and relationships involved in understanding the social sciences and natural sciences.

c. The pupil should have a large share of responsibility in setting the immediate goal toward which he strives and for evaluating his own work in terms of this goal. This will help ensure that the pupil develops high ideals of performance and will focus attention on the next step in his progress.

REFERENCES

Anastasi, A. *Differential Psychology.* New York: Macmillan Co., 1937.
———. "Practice and Variability: A Study of Psychological Methods," *Psychological Monographs,* XIV (1934), 1–55.
Burr, Marvin Y. *A Study of Homogenous Grouping.* ("Contributions to Education," No. 457.) New York: Teachers College, Columbia University, 1931.
Cook, Walter B. *Austin School Survey: Part II, The Instructional Program.* Minneapolis: University of Minnesota, 1952.
———. *Grouping and Promotion in the Elementary School.* ("Individualization of Instruction," No. 2.) Minneapolis: University of Minnesota, 1941.
———. "The Functions of Measurement in the Facilitation of Learning," Chap. I in *Educational Measurement,* ed. by E. Lindquist. Washington, D.C.: The American Council on Education, 1950.
Hollingshead, A. D. *An Evaluation of the Use of Certain Educational and Mental Measurements for the Purpose of Classification.* ("Contributions to Education," No. 302.) New York: Teachers College, Columbia University, 1928.
Hull, Clark L. "Variability in Amount of Different Traits Possessed by the Individual," *Journal of Educational Psychology,* XVIII (1927), 97–104.
Klene, Vivian, and Branson, E. P. "Trial Promotion versus Failure," *Educational Research Bulletin* (Los Angeles Public Schools), VIII, 11.
Learned, William S., and Wood, Ben D. *The Student and His Knowledge.* New York: The Carnegie Foundation for the Advancement of Teaching, 1938.
McNemar, Quinn. *The Revision of the Stanford-Binet Scale.* Boston: Houghton Mifflin Co., 1942.
Terman, Lewis M., and Merrill, Maud A. *Measuring Intelligence.* Boston: Houghton Mifflin Co., 1937.
Tyler, R. W. "Permanence of Learning," *Journal of Higher Education,* VIII (1937), 136–140.
West, J. E. "Twin Examination Assumptions," *Journal of Higher Education,* VIII (1937), 136–140.

chapter 19

Group dynamics in action

H. A. Jeep and J. W. Hollis

The fear is often expressed that the mutual understanding and sharing between the individual and the group which usually result from the use of group dynamics will bring about conformity and common thinking on the part of all members of the group. From our experience, just the opposite is true. In a healthy group dynamics situation the individual maintains his individuality and is encouraged by the group to do this. In fact, each member of the group is helped to realize that he can contribute more if his views are different from those of other members of the group. It is the responsibility of each individual not to conform but to share, and to make available to the group his unique contributions.

Group dynamics is sometimes erroneously referred to as an easy, lazy man's way of teaching. Such an understanding suggests that group dynamics is merely letting or permitting the learners to do pretty much as they please and that it is more a question of what the instructor does not do than a question of what he does do. Nothing could be further from the truth, as the term group dynamics is used in this article. Group dynamics is not the absence of something; it is the presence of a very positive thing. The philosophy of group dynamics is not *laissez faire*. We contend that group dynamics requires more skill and confidence and a more thorough knowledge of the subject field, on the part of the instructor, than most other teaching methods.

Group dynamics is successful to the extent that the instructor is skillful

From *The Clearing House,* 32(December, 1957), 223–229. Reprinted by permission of the publisher.

enough to create and maintain an atmosphere within which the group can experience purposeful learning with progressively emerging group goals and objectives and with continuous self-evaluation and reevaluation. These phenomena are unique in group dynamics because they are "group-individual" orientated, rather than instructor orientated or group orientated. The energy of the instructor is used in creating and maintaining among the group and the individuals within the group a mutual feeling of responsibility for these phenomena.

The Learning Situation

We believe that group dynamics is especially conducive to good learning. Out of the many elements which could be identified as characterizing a good learning situation, we have selected the following four as having particular significance:

Learning takes place as the needs of an individual are met.

Learning is an active expression rather than a passive absorption.

Learning should build and strengthen such commonalities as the learner must have in order to be an accepted member of his society.

In a modern democratic society the emotionally healthy learner seeks more and should seek more for the acceptance of his peers than for the acceptance of the teacher.* In fact, teacher approval of the learner often tends to weaken peer approval. Peer approval is generally much more potent as a motivating need than is teacher approval.

We hasten to add that we do not contend that group dynamics is the only method by which the foregoing objectives could be realized. Nor is it argued that group dynamics should be used by all teachers. We believe teaching to be an individual art, which is to be expressed by each teacher as he feels he can do it most effectively. This article is not an argument for the general adoption of group dynamics as a method but is merely a description of what happened when two instructors who believe in group dynamics used it as a method.

Implementation of Group Dynamics

During the summer of 1956 we met with each other's class for the purpose of observing and studying how group dynamics may be used to establish a learning situation consistent with the four premises set forth above. Each of us met in class with the other for a total of ten hours each week for a five-week term. [The two classes involved were: (1) a graduate class of sixteen in mental hygiene, taught by Jeep and observed by Hollis and (2)

* An exception must be made for the very young learners—preschool, kindergarten, and possibly the early primary-grade children. Arthur Jersild, *Child Psychology.*

a graduate class of twenty-six in organizing the pupil personnel program, taught by Hollis and observed by Jeep. This information is of minor significance because we believe that group dynamics as a teaching method can be used with equal success and with only slight modifications in all subjects, with all grade and age levels, and within broad limits in groups of all sizes.]

Each of us felt comfortable with the content of the course he was observing. This is important because it enabled us to feel free to spend all of our time observing procedure and process without becoming involved in the content. Alfred Adler once said, "We are concerned not with the possession of truth, but with the struggle for it." Regarding these classes, we should like to feel that we were at least as much concerned with the individual who was learning, with what happened to the individual as he learned, and with how learning took place, as we were with what was learned.

Neither of us spoke at any time while observing in the other's class until the last day of the term. Each of us felt that he was in the class to observe the other instructor and the class members at work. We could not do this if we became involved in the discussion. Only in the last meeting of the class, which was given over to evaluation, did either teacher speak in the other's class. In this last meeting both of us participated in both classes.

To establish the emotional climate consistent with group dynamics and the premises of a good learning situation as set forth above, each of us developed with his students the methods to be used. The following ideas and their implications were discussed during the first or second meeting of each course:

a. The class members were encouraged to be informal and relaxed in expression of ideas, attitudes, and beliefs.

b. An attempt was made to accept any and all statements made by any member of the group. Different viewpoints were considered as challenges for further study.

c. Everyone was encouraged to "think out loud." No one was to hesitate to speak because he had not thought through and carefully formulated the exact phrasing of his contribution. All were encouraged to speak first and then to think through what they had said. This would be especially true if the point had not been made before. When a person spoke, it would not follow that he necessarily felt any need for defending what he had said. It merely meant that he had brought up a point for consideration.

d. To understand the implications of statements made by various class members the students were encouraged to get acquainted with one another. It was their responsibility to become acquainted. They were encouraged to change their seats every day and sit next to someone they did not know very well. As much importance was placed upon becoming acquainted with one another as upon getting to know the teacher. They were encouraged to break up cliques and "buddy buddy" relationships.

e. Each student was encouraged to introduce himself. This was more than merely giving names and home addresses. The students were encouraged to talk about themselves at some length (as much as fifteen minutes) in these introductions, answering such questions as "What makes me different from others?" "If I had only one wish, what would that wish be?" These introductions were voluntary. No one gave an introduction until he was ready. There were seldom more than one or two introductions on any one day and on many days there did not seem to be time for anyone to introduce himself. As a consequence, these introductions were scattered throughout the five weeks and were not all completed until the last week of the term.

f. The processes operating were frequently discussed by the group. In some instances certain individuals served as process observers. As such, they did not allow themselves to become involved in the "content" being considered but gave all their attention to the consideration of group and individual feelings and attitudes. Sometimes such process observers were appointed by the instructors and at other times certain individuals in the group took it upon themselves to serve in this capacity.

g. Reading was not assigned or required. Each member was provided with an extensive bibliography and encouraged to go beyond this if he felt the need. They were encouraged to do as much or as little reading as their individual needs seemed to require and to read purposefully rather than with the objective of filling the requirements of an assignment.

h. Note taking, of the traditional sort, was not encouraged but was actually discouraged. Students were encouraged to use pencil and paper whenever they felt the need to jot notes for their own future reference, to organize thinking, or to draw up discussion work sheets, always remembering that such notes were taken for the individual notetaker's benefit. Such notes were not necessarily to be shared with the instructor or with other members of the group.

Statement of Principles

The authors recorded statements each day based upon observations and evaluation made by us in these two classes. Space will not permit the use in this article of all recorded observations. We have listed only those statements which seem to emphasize the characteristics of good learning as stated above and which will give a picture of our thinking and insights as the group progressed through the five weeks. Little or no editing was done on these statements. Furthermore, little change was made in the order in which the statements were originally written.

1. The teacher who wishes to use group dynamics need not do so at the first meeting of the class. The traditional teacher may move toward group dynamics as the term progresses.

2. When certain individuals have difficulty in participating in the total group, dividing the larger group into smaller groups (numbering from four to six) results in more participation on the part of everyone.

3. Participation in small groups results in more participation when the groups reunite.

4. Participation in small group discussions tends to encourage the "we feeling" in both small groups and large groups.

5. When teachers show ego involvement, they often stop class participation and discussion.

6. Teachers need to supply information at times and can do so without interfering with group dynamics provided it is factual information needed for clarification of problems on which the students are already working and provided there is a readiness on the part of the students to receive it. The teacher may interfere with group dynamics if he attempts to communicate opinions, attitudes, ideas, and so on.

7. Group dynamics is furthered when students know and understand one another. Considerable time can be profitably used in introducing and discussing individual backgrounds in getting acquainted.

8. Attitudes cannot be determined or changed by voting.

9. Process should be discussed as close as possible to the time when it is operating.

10. Through group dynamics each person feels compelled to help anyone who needs help. Cooperation, not competition, is the spirit of group dynamics. The only way a person can "cheat" in a group dynamics situation is to fail to cooperate; that is, by failing to share what he has with the group.

11. The discussion often has to do with the consideration of personal problems. All of the students feel a responsibility to aid one another in working on individual problems. The group assumes responsibility for clarifying and solving the needs of each individual within the group.

12. The teacher is a resource person who "sparks" sharing or supplies material at a psychological time.

13. Responsibility of the individual for the group is normally understood and expected. With group dynamics, the group has a definite responsibility for the individual. If any individual "withdraws" from the group, the group feels the responsibility to draw him back.

14. Group dynamics helps and motivates a student to express himself when his usual pattern of behavior might be to remain silent.

15. Care must be taken to see that insecurity on the part of certain individuals is not increased as a result of group dynamics. The transference from more traditional types of instruction to group dynamics may be a

threat to some students. Once this transference has been accomplished, these same students may need help to adjust back to a more traditional type of instruction in other classes.

16. The teacher welcomes criticism by any member of the group. In group dynamics self-analysis of the teacher's process or even his admission of a feeling of insecurity may increase classroom rapport.

17. The person who doesn't talk may not only evidence the fact that he is threatened by the group but in turn his silence may be a threat to the group.

18. Silent periods are a desirable part of group dynamics. To avoid the threat of these to members of the group and also to the instructor, the value of silent periods in group dynamics should be discussed as soon as possible after the first threatening silent period occurs.

19. As the term progresses, the emphasis shifts from "I" to "we" and from "me" to "us" and there are frequent comments beginning with "Here is something we might want to consider."

20. As cohesiveness is established in group dynamics, the individual member begins to feel a need to explain to the group his reason for being absent. This explanation may be made either before or following the absence. The individual offers to do more than his share for the group as a result of feeling that he has not done his part in aiding the group discussion because of absence. This action is looked upon by the group as a natural thing to do.

21. In group dynamics the individual can afford to be, and is encouraged to be, different and even feels obligated to bring differences into the open for group consideration.

22. Most activities, "assignments," and plans are made by the group and they feel committed to the proposed action with full understanding of what is to be done.

23. As the term progresses the emphasis on content is rapidly accelerated. It is felt that this is due to the groundwork which has been laid in process during the early meetings in such things as attitudes, better acquaintance, mutual acceptance, and respect of students and teachers.

24. Formal assignments in content can be made by the teacher at various times during group dynamics without interference with the process. Care must be taken in making these assignments to see that they are in line with the content covered and in the frame of reference of each individual learner at the time the assignments are made.

25. Group dynamics tends to bring out personal attitudes on the part of the individual students, such as his ability or inability and/or willingness or refusal to accept responsibility for himself or his group, his need for acceptance by the group, his need to dominate, and so on. The important thing is to bring such attitudes to the surface and to do so in an environment where neither approval nor disapproval is shown.

26. Group dynamics can perhaps be justified because of the fact that it tends to bring learning down to the "visceral level"; i.e., the constant attention to process and its effect upon students causes the individual to feel the importance of each action and/or work and its effect upon the cohesiveness of the group. Thus, facts (content) become important as they have a place in the behavior and growth of the class. It is only under such conditions that "real" learning takes place.

27. In group dynamics the unstructured reading tends to encourage the student to do reading which is at the same time meaningful to him in light of his immediate frame of reference.

28. Group dynamics does not just happen; it is caused. Group dynamics results from a positive something. Group dynamics cannot be created by subtracting autocratic techniques, lectures, and teacher centeredness from the traditional method.

29. In effective group dynamics there is not just one teacher—every member of the group is a teacher. Group dynamics creates an environment in which the individual feels secure enough to be an individual.

30. The student lives the content rather than recording the content in a notebook. This may result in reducing the bulk of note taking but perhaps makes more meaningful for the individual the notes which are taken. The same is true of the amount and kind of reading which are done during the course.

31. Group dynamics places the importance of individuals and student responsibilities ahead of the feeling that certain content must be covered uniformly by each member of the group. This should not suggest that content is slighted, but it does mean that content is individualized.

32. Leadership, as most of us know it, is using one person as a chairman and letting him carry the responsibility. If we are realistic, however, we know that some would make better leaders in some areas and others would make better leaders at other times. This, group dynamics strives to accomplish. Leadership shifts spontaneously with the discussion. In fact, if there is not this continual shifting of leadership, group dynamics is not effective.

33. Evaluation is the learning edge of experience. Experience without evaluation is merely time-consuming busywork and there is little or no learning taking place. It is therefore important that the experience be evaluated. It is also important to remember that if evaluation is to be a part of the learning process, who does the evaluation is important. In group dynamics evaluation is primarily self-evaluation. The encouragement group dynamics gives to continuing self-evaluation may be one of the major arguments for use of it as a teaching method.

34. In group dynamics every individual and the group as a whole should have the privilege and should assume the responsibility of evaluating all contributions by any participants. Any member of the group

should feel responsible for getting his own contributions and the contributions of all others before the group for consideration regardless of whether he agrees or disagrees with these contributions. Frequently the best contributions from the group's point of view are made by a person who at the moment is in intellectual disagreement with what he is saying.

35. In effective group dynamics, students soon come to realize that they are in the group to "learn"—to learn rather than to be taught.

36. In group dynamics the instructor's major responsibility is to help the student create the environment (emotional climate) in which learning takes place.

37. As the group members create or grow in the "we feeling," they accept more completely the importance of the feeling underlying the contributions of the various members of the group.

38. The notebook is not used mainly as a means of recording facts and truths expressed by others; it is merely a tool used to record or write or place symbols of ideas gained while others talk. These ideas are to be expressed to the group at the first opportunity. The notebook is only a means of temporary retention of ideas—ideas are flighty and need momentary capture if ever to be meaningful. Once the idea is captured on paper the mind of the individual is free to follow the trend of discussion of the group.

39. As individuals gain satisfaction from the group situation, their interests broaden and their capacities for appreciation of others deepen.

40. For group dynamics to remain effective the reactions and comments of the members (and teachers) must be straightforward and honest. Flattery and ridicule have no place in group dynamics.

41. Group dynamics seems to work best in a group with greatest heterogeneity—people of different standards, values, attitudes, and abilities. In the truly homogeneous grouping, group dynamics may have relatively little to offer.

42. Group dynamics operates primarily on the feeling and attitude level. We need to help individual members realize that the attitudes and deep feelings of various members have been formed over a long period of time. If these attitudes and feelings are to be changed, days or weeks, not minutes, must be required. In other words, if the teacher and group members are not willing to use the necessary time to consider, accept, and respect the feelings or attitudes of one or all participants, they should not accept group dynamics as a method.

43. In the group dynamics situation the overt tools or devices of thinking are the same as those used with any other method. These are such tools and devices as written and oral expression, reading, note taking, and periods of introspection. The objectives for which these devices are used in group dynamics differ, however, from the objectives for which they are used in traditional methods. For example, in group dynamics, they are

seldom used to satisfy the requirements of daily course assignments as made by the instructor. In group dynamics such devices are more likely to be used for the purpose of clarification, for the exploration and development of the individual or group interests and ideas. In group dynamics such devices are likely to leave the learners with more questions than answers and also to leave them with a desire to go further in their study. At the end of the course in which group dynamics is used there is not so much a feeling of having finished the course as a feeling of how much more there is to learn.

44. Intrapersonal relationships are important in group dynamics. Who participates is important. It is also important to know what caused the participation and who caused it, and to what and to whom the participation is a reaction. It is the responsibility of each person in the group not only to accept all contributions when they are made but also to see that each person is given sufficient "sparking" and encouragement to cause him to participate.

45. Group dynamics assumes mutual respect for the dignity of the individual on the part of all concerned. A teacher should never expect or ask a student to tell anything about himself unless the teacher is willing to let the same information be known concerning himself. No teacher should assume the privilege of criticizing students unless he is willing to accept the same from the students.

46. As the group develops a strong "we feeling" and gains experience in group process, the teacher moves more and more out of the function as a leader. The ultimate is when the teacher is no longer the leader and becomes a resource person whose function is to supply information. At this point each member will feel free to discuss what is important to him and what he thinks will help the group. Each member will feel that he is part of the group and that he is responsible for the group and the individual members of the group. Each member will enjoy the group.

Conclusions and Implications

Group dynamics as a method of teaching helps individuals to grow toward independence and self-security while at the same time learning that in a society one member depends upon another.

We feel that group dynamics enables students to release their feelings and aggressions and thus increases their chances for individual and social adjustment. This in itself is reason enough for our students' having some contact with this method.

Because group dynamics creates a situation in which the individual is responsible and is ego involved, the motivation for learning, for constructive action, and for self-evaluation is always present in effective group dynamics.

The teacher must be secure in his position, confident in his subject matter, and skillful in the psychology of human relations before attempting group dynamics.

Group dynamics is an energy-consuming, but very rewarding, method for both students and teacher. Soul searching and deep learning are always energy consuming.

chapter *20*
The characteristics of
a helping relationship

Carl R. Rogers

My interest in psychotherapy has brought about in me an interest in every kind of helping relationship. By this term I mean a relationship in which at least one of the parties has the intent of promoting the growth, development, maturity, improved functioning, improved coping with life of the other. The other, in this sense, may be one individual or a group. To put it in another way, a helping relationship might be defined as one in which one of the participants intends that there should come about, in one or both parties, more appreciation of, more expression of, more functional use of the latent inner resources of the individual.

Now it is obvious that such a definition covers a wide range of relationships which usually are intended to facilitate growth. It would certainly include the relationship between mother and child, father and child. It would include the relationship between the physician and his patient. The relationship between teacher and pupil would often come under this definition, though some teachers would not have the promotion of growth as their intent. It includes almost all counselor-client relationships, whether we are speaking of educational counseling, vocational counseling, or personal counseling. In this last-mentioned area it would include the wide range of relationships between the psychotherapist and the hospitalized psychotic, the therapist and the troubled or neurotic individual, and the

From *The Personnel and Guidance Journal*, 37(September, 1958), 6–16. Reprinted by permission of the author and publisher.

This address was delivered during the APGA Convention, held at the Sheraton-Jefferson Hotel, St. Louis, Missouri, March 31–April 3, 1958.

relationship between the therapist and the increasing number of so-called "normal" individuals who enter therapy to improve their own functioning or accelerate their personal growth.

These are largely one-to-one relationships. But we should also think of the large number of individual-group interactions which are intended as helping relationships. Some administrators intend that their relationship to their staff groups shall be of the sort which promotes growth, though other administrators would not have this purpose. The interaction between the group therapy leader and his group belongs here. So does the relationship of the community consultant to a community group. Increasingly the interaction between the industrial consultant and a management group is intended as a helping relationship. Perhaps this listing will point up a great many of the relationships in which there is the purpose of promoting development and more mature and adequate functioning.

The Question

But what are the characteristics of those relationships which *do* help, which do facilitate growth? And at the other end of the scale is it possible to discern those characteristics which make a relationship unhelpful, even though it was the sincere intent to promote growth and development? It is to these questions, particularly the first, that I would like to take you with me over some of the paths I have explored, and to tell you where I am, as of now, in my thinking on these issues.

The Answers Given by Research

It is natural to ask first of all whether there is any empirical research which would give us an objective answer to these questions. There has not been a large amount of research in this area as yet, but what there is is stimulating and suggestive. I cannot report all of it but I would like to make a somewhat extensive sampling of the studies which have been done and state very briefly some of the findings. In so doing, oversimplification is necessary, and I am quite aware that I am not doing full justice to the researches I am mentioning, but it may give you the feeling that factual advances are being made and pique your curiosity enough to examine the studies themselves, if you have not already done so.

Studies of Attitudes

Most of the studies throw light on the attitudes on the part of the helping person which make a relationship growth-promoting or growth-inhibiting. Let us look at some of these.

A careful study of parent-child relationships made some years ago by Baldwin and others (1) at the Fels Institute contains interesting evidence.

Of the various clusters of parental attitudes toward children, the "accept-ant-democratic" seemed most growth-facilitating. Children of these parents, with their warm and equalitarian attitudes, showed an accelerated intellectual development (an increasing IQ), more originality, more emotional security and control, less excitability than children from other types of homes. Though somewhat slow initially in social development, they were, by the time they reached school age, popular, friendly, nonaggressive leaders.

Where parents' attitudes are classed as "actively rejectant" the children show a slightly decelerated intellectual development, relatively poor use of the abilities they do possess, and some lack of originality. They are emotionally unstable, rebellious, aggressive, and quarrelsome. The children of parents with other attitude syndromes tend in various respects to fall in between these extremes.

I am sure that these findings do not surprise us as related to child development. I would like to suggest that they probably apply to other relationships as well, and that the counselor or physician or administrator who is warmly emotional and expressive, respectful of the individuality of himself and of the other, and who exhibits a nonpossessive caring, probably facilitates self-realization much as does a parent with these attitudes.

Let me turn to another careful study in a very different area. White-horn and Betz (2, 18) investigated the degree of success achieved by young resident physicians in working with schizophrenic patients on a psychiatric ward. They chose for special study the seven who had been outstandingly helpful, and seven whose patients had shown the least degree of improvement. Each group had treated about 50 patients. The investigators examined all available evidence to discover in what ways the *A* group (the successful group) differed from the *B* group. Several significant differences were found. The physicians in the *A* group tended to see the schizophrenic in terms of the personal meaning which various behaviors had to the patient, rather than seeing him as a case history or a descriptive diagnosis. They also tended to work toward goals which were oriented to the personality of the patient, rather than such goals as reducing the symptoms or curing the disease. It was found that the helpful physicians, in their day-by-day interaction, primarily made use of active personal participation—a person-to-person relationship. They made less use of procedures which could be classed as "passive permissive." They were even less likely to use such procedures as interaction, instruction or advice, or emphasis upon the practical care of the patient. Finally, they were much more likely than the *B* group to develop a relationship in which the patient felt trust and confidence in the physician.

Although the authors cautiously emphasize that these findings relate only to the treatment of schizophrenics, I am inclined to disagree. I suspect that similar facts would be found in a research study of almost any class of helping relationship.

Another interesting study focuses upon the way in which the person being helped perceives the relationship. Heine (11) studied individuals who had gone for psychotherapeutic help to psychoanalytic, client-centered, and Adlerian therapists. Regardless of the type of therapy, these clients report similar changes in themselves. But it is their perception of the relationship which is of particular interest to us here. When asked what accounted for the changes which had occurred, they expressed some differing explanations, depending on the orientation of the therapist. But their agreement on the major elements they had found helpful was even more significant. They indicated that these attitudinal elements in the relationship accounted for the changes which had taken place in themselves: the trust they had felt in the therapist; being understood by the therapist; the feeling of independence they had had in making choices and decisions. The therapist procedure which they had found most helpful was that the therapist clarified and openly stated feelings which the client had been approaching hazily and hesitantly.

There was also a high degree of agreement among these clients, regardless of the orientation of their therapists, as to what elements had been unhelpful in the relationship. Such therapist attitudes as lack of interest, remoteness or distance, and an overdegree of sympathy, were perceived as unhelpful. As to procedures, they had found it unhelpful when therapists had given direct specific problems. Guiding suggestions mildly given were perceived in an intermediate range—neither clearly helpful nor unhelpful.

Fiedler, in a much-quoted study (7), found that expert therapists of differing orientations formed similar relationships with their clients. Less well known are the elements which characterized these relationships, differentiating them from the relationships formed by less expert therapists. These elements are: an ability to understand the client's meanings and feelings, a sensitivity to the client's attitudes, a warm interest without any emotional overinvolvement.

A study by Quinn (15) throws light on what is involved in understanding the client's meanings and feelings. His study is surprising in that it shows that "understanding" of the client's meanings is essentially an attitude of *desiring* to understand. Quinn presented his judges only with recorded therapist statements taken from interviews. The raters had no knowledge of what the therapist was responding to or how the client reacted to his response. Yet it was found that the degree of understanding could be judged about as well from this material as from listening to the response in context. This seems rather conclusive evidence that it is an attitude of wanting to understand which is communicated.

As to the emotional quality of the relationship, Seeman (15) found that success in psychotherapy is closely associated with a strong and growing mutual liking and respect between client and therapist.

An interesting study by Dittes (4) indicates how delicate this relationship is. Using a physiological measure, the psychogalvanic reflex, to measure the anxious or threatened or alerted reactions of the client, Dittes correlated the deviations on this measure with judge's ratings of the degree of warm acceptance and permissiveness on the part of the therapist. It was found that whenever the therapist's attitudes changed even slightly in the direction of a lesser degree of acceptance, the number of abrupt GSR deviations significantly increased. Evidently when the relationship is experienced as less acceptant the organism organizes against threat, even at the physiological level.

Without trying fully to integrate the findings from these various studies, it can at least be noted that a few things stand out. One is the fact that it is the attitudes and feelings of the therapist, rather than his theoretical orientation, which is important. His procedures and techniques are less important than his attitudes. It is also worth noting that it is the way in which his attitudes and procedures are *perceived* which makes a difference to the client, and that it is this perception which is crucial.

"Manufactured" Relationships

Let me turn to research of a very different sort, some of which you may find rather abhorrent, but which nevertheless has a bearing upon the nature of a facilitating relationship. These studies have to do with what we might think of as manufactured relationships.

Verplanck (17), Greenspoon (8), and others have shown that operant conditioning of verbal behavior is possible in a relationship. Very briefly, if the experimenter says "Mhm," or "Good," or nods his head after certain types of words or statements, those classes of words tend to increase because of being reinforced. It has been shown that by using such procedures one can bring about increases in such diverse verbal categories as plural nouns, hostile words, statements of opinion. The person is completely unaware that he is being influenced in any way by these reinforcers. The implication is that by such selective reinforcement we could bring it about that the other person in the relationship would be using whatever kinds of words and making whatever kinds of statements we had decided to reinforce.

Following still further the principles of operant conditioning as developed by Skinner and his group, Lindsley (12) has shown that a chronic schizophrenic can be placed in a "helping relationship" with a machine. The machine, somewhat like a vending machine, can be set to reward a variety of types of behaviors. Initially it simply rewards—with candy, a cigarette, or the display of a picture—the lever-pressing behavior of the patient. But it is possible to set it so that many pulls on the lever may supply a hungry kitten—visible in a separate enclosure—with a drop of milk. In this case the satisfaction is an altruistic one. Plans are being developed to reward similar social or altruistic behavior directed toward another patient, placed in the next room. The only limit to the kinds of behavior which might be rewarded lies in the degree of mechanical ingenuity of the experimenter.

Lindsley reports that in some patients there has been marked clinical improvement. Personally I cannot help but be impressed by the description of one patient who had gone from a deteriorated chronic state to being given free grounds privileges, this change being quite clearly associated with his interaction with the machine. Then the experimenter decided to study experimental extinction, which, put in more personal terms, means that no matter how many thousands of times the lever was pressed, no reward of any kind was forthcoming. The patient gradually regressed, grew untidy, uncommunicative, and his grounds privilege had to be revoked. This (to me) pathetic incident would seem to indicate that even in a relationship to a machine, trustworthiness is important if the relationship is to be helpful.

Still another interesting study of a manufactured relationship is being carried on by Harlow and his associates (10), this time with monkeys. Infant monkeys, removed from their mothers almost immediately after birth, are, in one phase of the experiment, presented with two objects. One might be termed the "hard mother," a sloping cylinder of wire netting with a nipple from which the baby may feed. The other is a "soft mother," a similar cylinder made of foam rubber and terry cloth. Even when an infant gets all his food from the "hard mother" he clearly and increasingly prefers the "soft mother." Motion pictures show that he definitely "relates" to this object, playing with it, enjoying it, finding security in clinging to it when strange objects are near, and using that security as a home base for venturing into the frightening world. Of the many interesting and challenging implications of this study, one seems reasonably clear. It is that no amount of direct food reward can take the place of certain perceived qualities which the infant appears to need and desire.

Two Recent Studies

Let me close this wide-ranging—and perhaps perplexing—sampling of research studies with an account of two very recent investigations. The first is an experiment conducted by Ends and Page (5). Working with hardened chronic hospitalized alcoholics who had been committed to a state hospital for 60 days, they tried three different methods of group psychotherapy. The method which they believed would be most effective was therapy based on a two-factor theory of learning; a client-centered approach was expected to be second; a psychoanalytically oriented approach was expected to be least efficient. Their results showed that the therapy based upon a learning theory approach was not only helpful, but was somewhat deleterious. The outcomes were worse than those in the control group which had no therapy. The analytically oriented therapy produced some positive gain, and the client-centered group therapy was associated with the greatest amount of positive change. Follow-up data, extending over one and one-half years, confirmed the in-hospital findings, with the lasting improvement being greatest in the client-centered approach, next in the analytic, next the control group, and least in those handled by a learning theory approach.

As I have puzzled over this study, unusual in that the approach to which the authors were committed proved least effective, I find a clue, I believe, in the description of the therapy based on learning theory (13). Essentially it consisted (1) of pointing out and labeling the behaviors which had proved unsatisfying, (2) of exploring objectively with the client the reasons behind these behaviors, and (3) of establishing through reeducation more effective problem-solving habits. But in all of this interaction the aim, as they formulated it, was to be impersonal. The therapist "permits as little of his own personality to intrude as is humanly possible." The "therapist stresses personal anonymity in his activities; i.e., he must studiously avoid impressing the patient with his own (therapist's) individual personality characteristics." To me this seems the most likely clue to the failure of this approach, as I try to interpret the facts in the light of the other research studies. To withhold one's self as a person and to deal with the other person as an object does not have a high probability of being helpful.

The final study I wish to report is one just being completed by Halkides (9). She started from a theoretical formulation of mine regarding the necessary and sufficient conditions for therapeutic change (14). She hypothesized that there would be a significant relationship between the extent of constructive personality change in the client and four counselor variables: (1) the degree of empathic understanding of the client manifested by the counselor; (2) the degree of positive affective attitude (unconditional positive regard) manifested by the counselor toward the client; (3) the extent to which the counselor is genuine, his words matching his own internal feeling; and (4) the extent to which the counselor's response matches the client's expression in the intensity of affective expression.

To investigate these hypotheses she first selected, by multiple objective criteria, a group of 10 cases which could be classed as "most successful" and a group of 10 "least successful" cases. She then took an early and late recorded interview from each of these cases. On a random basis she picked nine client-counselor interaction units—a client statement and a counselor response—from each of these interviews. She thus had nine early interactions and nine later interactions from each case. This gave her several hundred units which were now placed in random order. The units from an early interview of an unsuccessful case might be followed by the units from a late interview of a successful case, etc.

Three judges, who did not know the cases or their degree of success, or the source of any given unit, now listened to this material four different times. They rated each unit on a seven-point scale, first as to the degree of empathy, second as to the counselor's positive attitude toward the client, third as to the counselor's congruence or genuineness, and fourth as to the degree to which the counselor's response matched the emotional intensity of the client's expression.

I think all of us who knew of the study regarded it as a very bold venture. Could judges listening to single units of interaction possibly make any reliable rating of such subtle qualities as I have mentioned? And even if suitable reliability could be obtained, could 18 counselor-client interchanges from each case—a minute sampling of the hundreds or thousands of such interchanges which occurred in each case—possibly bear any relationship to the therapeutic outcome? The chance seemed slim.

The findings are surprising. It proved possible to achieve high reliability between the judges, most of the interjudge correlations being in the 0.80's or 0.90's, except on the last variables. It was found that a high degree of empathic understanding was significantly associated, at a 0.001 level, with the more successful cases. A high degree of unconditional positive regard was likewise associated with the more successful cases, at the 0.001 level. Even the rating of the counselor's genuineness or congruence—the extent to which his words matched his feelings—was associated with the successful outcome of the case, and again at the 0.001 level of significance. Only in the investigation of the matching intensity of affective expression were the results equivocal.

It is of interest too that high ratings of these variables were not associated more significantly with units from later interviews than with units from early interviews. This means that the counselor's attitudes were quite constant throughout the interviews. If he was highly empathic, he tended to be so from first to last. If he was lacking in genuineness, this tended to be true of both early and late interviews.

As with any study, this investigation has its limitations. It is concerned with a certain type of helping relationship, psychotherapy. It investigated only four variables thought to be significant. Perhaps there are many others. Nevertheless it represents a significant advance in the study of helping relationships. Let me try to state the findings in the simplest possible fashion. It seems to indicate that the quality of the counselor's interaction with a client can be satisfactorily judged on the basis of a very small sampling of his behavior. It also means that if the counselor is congruent or transparent, so that his words are in line with his feelings rather than the two being descrepant—if the counselor likes the client, unconditionally, and if the counselor understands the essential feelings of the client as they seem to the client—then there is a strong probability that this will be an effective helping relationship.

Some Comments

These then are some of the studies which throw at least a measure of light on the nature of the helping relationship. They have investigated different facets of the problem. They have approached it from very different theoretical contexts. They have used different methods. They are not directly comparable. Yet they seem to me to point to several statements which may be made with some assurance. It seems clear that relationships which are helpful have different characteristics from relationships which are unhelpful. These differential characteristics have to do primarily with the attitudes of the helping person on the one hand and with the perception of the relationship by the "helpee" on the other. It is equally clear that the studies thus far made do not give us any final answers as to what is a helping relationship, nor how it is to be formed.

How Can I Create a Helping Relationship?

I believe each of us working in the field of human relationships has a similar problem in knowing how to use such research knowledge. We cannot slavishly follow such findings in a mechanical way or we destroy the personal qualities which these very studies show to be valuable. It seems to me that we have to use these studies, testing them against our own experience and forming new and further personal hypotheses to use and test in our own further personal relationships.

So rather than try to tell you how you should use the findings I have presented I should like to tell you the kind of questions which these studies and my own clinical experience raise for me, and some of the tentative and changing hypotheses which guide my behavior as I enter into what I hope may be helping relationships, whether with students, staff, family, or clients. Let me list a number of these questions and considerations.

1. Can I *be* in some way which will be perceived by the other person as trustworthy, as dependable or consistent in some deep sense? Both research and experience indicate that this is very important, and over the years I have found what I believe are deeper and better ways of answering this question. I used to feel that if I fulfilled all the outer conditions of trustworthiness—keeping appointments, respecting the confidential nature of the interviews, etc.—and if I acted consistently the same during the interviews, then this condition would be fulfilled. But experience drove home the fact that to act consistently acceptant, for example, if in fact I was feeling annoyed or skeptical or some other nonacceptant feeling, was certain in the long run to be perceived as inconsistent or untrustworthy. I have come to recognize that being trustworthy does not demand that I be rigidly consistent but that I be dependably real. The term congruent is one I have used to describe the way I would like to be. By this I mean that whatever feeling or attitude I am experiencing would be matched by my awareness of that attitude. When this is true, then I am a unified or integrated person in that moment, and hence I can *be* whatever I deeply *am*. This is a reality which I find others experience as dependable.

2. A very closely related question is this: Can I be expressive enough

as a person that what I am will be communicated unambiguously? I believe that most of my failures to achieve a helping relationship can be traced to unsatisfactory answers to these two questions. When I am experiencing an attitude of annoyance toward another person but am unaware of it, then my communication contains contradictory messages. My words are giving one message, but I am also in subtle ways communicating the annoyance I feel and this confuses the other person and makes him distrustful, though he too may be unaware of what is causing the difficulty. When as a parent or a therapist or a teacher or an administrator I fail to listen to what is going on in me, fail because of my own defensiveness to sense my own feelings, then this kind of failure seems to result. It has made it seem to me that the most basic learning for anyone who hopes to establish any kind of helping relationship is that it is safe to be transparently real. If in a given relationship I am reasonably congruent, if no feelings relevant to the relationship are hidden either to me or the other person, then I can be almost sure that the relationship will be a helpful one.

One way of putting this which may seem strange to you is that if I can form a helping relationship to myself—if I can be sensitively aware of and acceptant toward my own feelings—then the likelihood is great that I can form a helping relationship toward another.

Now, acceptantly to be what I am, in this sense, and to permit this to show through to the other person, is the most difficult task I know and one I never fully achieve. But to realize that this *is* my task has been most rewarding because it has helped me to find what has gone wrong with interpersonal relationships which have become snarled and to put them on a constructive track again. It has meant that if I am to facilitate the personal growth of others in relation to me, then I must grow, and while this is often painful it is also enriching.

3. A third question is: Can I let myself experience positive attitudes toward this other person—attitudes of warmth, caring, liking, interest, respect? It is not easy. I find in myself, and feel that I often see in others, a certain amount of fear of these feelings. We are afraid that if we let ourselves freely experience these positive feelings toward another we may be trapped by them. They may lead to demands on us or we may be disappointed in our trust, and these outcomes we fear. So as a reaction we tend to build up distance between ourselves and others—aloofness, a "professional" attitude, an impersonal relationship.

I feel quite strongly that one of the important reasons for the professionalization of every field is that it helps to keep this distance. In the clinical areas we develop elaborate diagnostic formulations, seeing the person as an object. In teaching and in administration we develop all kinds of evaluative procedures, so that again the person is perceived as an object. In these ways, I believe, we can keep ourselves from experiencing the caring which would exist if we recognized the relationship as one between two persons.

It is a real achievement when we can learn, even in certain relationships or at certain times in those relationships, that it is safe to care, that it is safe to relate to the other as a person for whom we have positive feelings.

4. Another question the importance of which I have learned in my own experience is: Can I be strong enough as a person to be separate from the other? Can I be a sturdy respecter of my own feelings, my own needs, as well as his? Can I own and, if need be, express my own feelings as something belonging to me separate from his feelings? Am I strong enough in my own separateness that I will not be downcast by his depression, frightened by his fear, nor engulfed by his dependency? Is my inner self hardy enough to realize that I am not destroyed by his anger, taken over by his need for dependence, nor enslaved by his love, but that I exist separate from him with feelings and rights of my own? When I can freely feel this strength of being a separate person, then I find that I can let myself go much more deeply in understanding and accepting him because I am not fearful of losing myself.

5. The next question is closely related. Am I secure enough within myself to permit him his separateness? Can I permit him to be what he is— honest or deceitful, infantile or adult, despairing or overconfident? Can I give him the freedom to be? Or do I feel that he should follow my advice, or remain somewhat dependent on me, or mold himself after me? In this connection I think of the interesting small study by Farson (6) which found that the less well-adjusted and less competent counselor tends to induce conformity to himself, to have clients who model themselves after him. On the other hand, the better adjusted and more competent counselor can interact with a client through many interviews without interfering with the freedom of the client to develop a personality quite separate from that of his therapist. I should prefer to be in this latter class, whether as parent or supervisor or counselor.

6. Another question I ask myself is: Can I let myself enter fully into the world of his feelings and personal meanings and see these as he does? Can I step into his private world so completely that I lose all desire to evaluate or judge it? Can I enter it so sensitively that I can move about in it freely, without tramping on meanings which are precious to him? Can I sense it so accurately that I can catch not only the meanings of his experience which are obvious to him, but those meanings which are only implicit, which he sees only dimly or as confusion? Can I extend this understanding without limit? I think of the client who said, "Whenever I find someone who understands a *part* of me at the time, then it never fails that a point is reached where I know they're *not* understanding me again. . . . What I've looked for so hard is for someone to understand."

For myself I find it easier to feel this kind of understanding, and to communicate it, to individual clients than to students in a class or staff members in a group in which I am involved. There is a strong temptation to set students "straight," or to point out to a staff member the errors in his thinking. Yet when I permit myself to understand in these situations, it is mutually rewarding. And with clients in therapy, I am often impressed with the fact that even a minimal amount of empathic understanding—a bumbling and faulty attempt to catch the confused complexity of the client's meaning—is helpful, though there is no doubt that it is most helpful when I can see and formulate clearly the meanings in his experiencing which for him have been unclear and tangled.

7. Still another issue is whether I can be acceptant of each facet of this other person which he presents to me. Can I receive him as he is? Can I communicate this attitude? Or can I only receive him conditionally, acceptant of some aspects of his feelings and silently or openly disapproving of other aspects? It has been my experience that when my attitude is conditional, then he cannot change or grow in those respects in which I cannot fully receive him. And when—afterward and sometimes too late—I try to discover why I have been unable to accept him in every respect, I usually discover that it is because I have been frightened or threatened in myself by some aspect of his feelings. If I am to be more helpful, then I must myself grow and accept myself in these respects.

8. A very practical issue is raised by the question: Can I act with sufficient sensitivity in the relationship that my behavior will not be perceived as a threat? The work we are beginning to do in studying the physiological concomitants of psychotherapy confirms the research by Dittes in indicating how easily individuals are threatened at a physiological level. The psychogalvanic reflex—the measure of skin conductance—takes a sharp dip when the therapist responds with some word which is just a little stronger than the client's feelings. And to a phrase such as, "My, you *do* look upset," the needle swings almost off the paper. My desire to avoid even such minor threats is not due to a hypersensitivity about my client. It is simply due to the conviction based on experience that if I can free him as completely as possible from external threat, then he can begin to experience and to deal with the internal feelings and conflicts which he finds threatening within himself.

9. A specific aspect of the preceding question but an important one is: Can I free him from the threat of external evaluation? In almost every phase of our lives—at home, at school, at work—we find ourselves under the rewards and punishments of external judgments. "That's good"; "that's naughty." "That's worth an A"; "that's a failure." "That's good counseling"; "that's poor counseling." Such judgments are a part of our lives from infancy to old age. I believe they have a certain social usefulness to institutions and organizations such as schools and professions. Like everyone else I find myself all too often making such evaluations. But, in my experience, they do not make for personal growth and hence I do not believe that they are a part of a helping relationship. Curiously enough a

positive evaluation is as threatening in the long run as a negative one, since to inform someone that he is good implies that you also have the right to tell him he is bad. So I have come to feel that the more I can keep a relationship free of judgment and evaluation, the more this will permit the other person to reach the point where he recognizes that the locus of evaluation, the center of responsibility, lies within himself. The meaning and value of his experience are in the last analysis something which is up to him, and no amount of external judgment can alter this. So I should like to work toward a relationship in which I am not, even in my own feelings, evaluating him. This I believe can set him free to be a self-responsible person.

10. One last question: Can I meet this other individual as a person who is in process of *becoming*, or will I be bound by his past and by my past? If, in my encounter with him, I am dealing with him as an immature child, an ignorant student, a neurotic personality, or a psychopath, each of these concepts of mine limits what he can be in the relationship. Martin Buber, the existentialist philosopher of the University of Jerusalem, has a phrase, "confirming the other," which has had meaning for me. He says "Confirming means . . . accepting the whole potentiality of the other. . . . I can recognize in him, know in him, the person he has been . . . *created* to become. . . . I confirm him in myself, and then in him, in relation to this potentiality that . . . can now be developed, can evolve" (3). If I accept the other person as something fixed, already diagnosed and classified, already shaped by his past, then I am doing my part to confirm this limited hypothesis. If I accept him as a process of becoming, then I am doing what I can to confirm or make real his potentialities.

It is at this point that I see Verplanck, Lindsley, and Skinner, working in operant conditioning, coming together with Buber, the philosopher or mystic. At least they come together in principle, in an odd way. If I see a relationship as only an opportunity to reinforce certain types of words or opinions in the other, then I tend to confirm him as an object—a basically mechanical, manipulable object. And if I see this as his potentiality, he tends to act in ways which support this hypothesis.

Conclusion

In the early portion of this paper I reviewed some of the contributions which research is making to our knowledge *about* relationships. Endeavoring to keep that knowledge in mind I then took up the kind of questions which arise from an inner and subjective point of view as I enter, as a person, into relationships. If I could, in myself, answer all the questions I have raised in the affirmative, then I believe that any relationships in which I was involved would be helping relationships, would involve growth. But I cannot give a positive answer to most of these questions. I can only work in the direction of a positive answer.

This has raised in my mind the strong suspicion that the optimal helping relationship is the kind of relationship created by a person who is psychologically mature. Or to put it in another way, the degree to which I can create relationships which facilitate the growth of others as separate persons is a measure of the growth I have achieved in myself. In some respects this is a disturbing thought, but it is also a promising or challenging one. It would indicate that if I am interested in creating helping relationships I have a fascinating lifetime job ahead of me, stretching and developing my potentialities in the direction of growth.

I am left with the uncomfortable thought that what I have been working out for myself in this paper may have little relationship to your interests and your work. If so, I regret it. But I am at least partially comforted by the fact that all of us who are working in the field of human relationships and trying to understand the basic orderliness of the field are engaged in the most crucial enterprise in today's world. If we are thoughtfully trying to understand our tasks as administrators, teachers, educational counselors, vocational counselors, therapists, then we are working on the problem which will determine the future of this planet. For it is not upon the physical sciences that the future will depend. It is upon us who are trying to understand and deal with the interactions between human beings —who are trying to create helping relationships. So I hope that the questions I ask of myself will be of some use to you in gaining understanding and perspective as you endeavor, in your way, to facilitate growth in your relationships.

REFERENCES

1. Baldwin, A. L., Kalhorn, J., & Breese, F. H. Patterns of parent behavior. *Psychol. Monogr.*, 1945, 58, No. 268, 1–75.
2. Betz, B. J., & Whitehorn, J. C. The relationship of the therapist to the outcome of therapy in schizophrenia. *Psychiat. Research Reports #5. Research techniques in schizophrenia.* Washington, D.C.: American Psychiatric Association, 1956, 89–117.
3. Buber, M., & Rogers, C. Transcription of dialogue held April 18, 1957, Ann Arbor, Mich. Unpublished manuscript.
4. Dittes, J. E. Galvanic skin response as a measure of patient's reaction to therapist's permissiveness. *J. abnorm. soc. Psychol.*, 1957, 55, 296–303.
5. Ends, E. J., & Page, C. W. A study of three types of group psychotherapy with hospitalized male inebriates. *Quart. J. Stud. Alcohol*, 1957, 18, 263–277.
6. Farson, R. E. Introjection in the psychotherapeutic relationship. Unpublished doctoral dissertation, University of Chicago, 1955.
7. Fiedler, F. E. Quantitative studies on the role of therapist feelings toward their patients. In Mowrer, O. H. (ed.) *Psychotherapy: theory and research.* New York: Ronald Press, 1953, Chap. 12.

8. Greenspoon, J. The reinforcing effect of two spoken sounds on the frequency of two responses. *Amer. J. Psychol.*, 1955, 68, 409–416.
9. Halkides, G. An experimental study of four conditions necessary for therapeutic change. Unpublished doctoral dissertation, University of Chicago, 1958.
10. Harlow, H., & Associates. Experiment in progress, as reported by Robert Zimmerman.
11. Heine, R. W. A comparison of patients' reports on psychotherapeutic experience with psychoanalytic, nondirective, and Adlerian therapists. Unpublished doctoral dissertation, University of Chicago, 1950.
12. Lindsley, O. R. Operant conditioning methods applied to research in chronic schizophrenia. *Psychiat. Research Reports #5. Research techniques in schizophrenia.* Washington, D. C.: American Psychiatric Association, 1956. 118–153.
13. Page, C. W., & Ends, E. J. A review and synthesis of the literature suggesting a psychotherapeutic technique based on two-factor learning theory. Unpublished manuscript, loaned to the writer.
14. Rogers, C. R. The necessary and sufficient conditions of psychotherapeutic personality change. *J. consult. Psychol.*, 1957, 21, 95–103.
15. Quinn, R. D. Psychotherapists' expressions as an index to the quality of early therapeutic relationships. Unpublished doctoral dissertation, University of Chicago, 1950.
16. Seeman, J. Counselor judgments of therapeutic process and outcome. In Rogers, C. R., & Dymond, R. F. (eds.) *Psychotherapy and personality change.* Chicago: University of Chicago Press, 1954, Chap. 7.
17. Verplanck, W. S. The control of the content of conversation: reinforcement of statements of opinion. *J. abnorm. soc. Psychol.*, 1955, 51, 668–676.
18. Whitehorn, J. C., & Betz, B. J. A study of psychotherapeutic relationships between physicians and schizophrenic patients. *Amer. J. Psychiat.*, 1954, 111, 321–331.

chapter 21

The triumph of "achievement"
over inquiry in education

Herbert A. Thelen

Principals, teachers, parents, professors, or practice teachers who try to improve instruction in the classroom soon find themselves in a trap.

It is a fascinating trap built by people who know better. The fact that they built the trap very much against their will does not make the trap any less a trap. But it does show that one can get swept along by forces at work in the larger society.

In big, broad terms, the trap is the conflict between the Organization Man, who continually seeks to reassure himself of his place in society, and the Inquiring Man, who seeks to better himself and his society. In narrower terms, the conflict is between the way we try to teach children and the way we measure what they have learned. In middle-sized terms, the conflict is between education and achievement as school goals.

Close-up of a Trap

I should like to begin by describing the trap—by reporting on the conflicts and contradictions that make up the trap. So I shall talk about practices, not sentiments or theories.

My testimony comes mostly from thoughtful teachers who think wistfully about the possibility of improving their own courses. They are tired of just covering the ground, by which they mean exposing the pupil to a prescribed body of already organized ideas. They would like to get some

From *The Elementary School Journal*, LX(January, 1960), 190–197. Reprinted by permission of The University of Chicago Press.

inquiry going. They would like to see pupils study because there is something important to learn, something important to the pupils, that is.

As these teachers see it, the chief obstacle to making this shift is the way achievement is now defined by the public and measured by tests. The teachers perceive that their pupils are realistic enough to know that their job is to pass tests; this is what academic aspirations mean; this is what achievement means to pupils and to the public.

Of course, some of these teachers say, "We don't mark exclusively on tests. We take other things into account." But these "other things" are subjective and unconfidently known. At best, they merely blur the harsh outline of test results.

And here we can point to the heart of the conflict. Teachers try to set up learning experiences based on one set of views while they measure achievement based on a different set of views. The disparity can be disconcerting to pupils, parents, and concerned citizens as well as teachers. Let's look at some aspects of the conflict.

Pupils feel that testing puts them in competition with one another. But the teacher wants them to cooperate, not compete.

In class discussion and class projects, the teacher seems to want class members to share ideas. But on tests, pupils see their classmates as rivals who are required to get the better of one another.

There are even conflicting economic connotations here. In testing it is usually assumed that there are not enough A's to go around; in teaching it is assumed that everyone can have an A—if he earns it.

Our tests teach pupils that academic status, not learning, is the goal of education.

If learning were the goal, achievement would be measured as the difference between pretests and posttests on the material of the course. Since pretests are seldom used, the teacher has no way of knowing how much the pupil learned. The mark testifies to final status, not to what was learned during the course.

Pupils work for marks rather than in response to the challenge of the subject.

The purpose of learning is to gain status, symbolized in a mark, rather than to master the discipline of the subject. Good marks mean promotion and the regard of adults. Snap subjects and "soft" teachers are the sensible route to good marks. Moreover, acceptance or capitulation by the teacher to the mark-getting routine tends to free him from his professional obligation to make study meaningful in its own right.

Pupils study the teacher rather than the subject.

Often the main object of inquiry in the classroom is the sort of question the teacher is likely to ask, the bases he uses for marking, his biases and enthusiasms. This experience, over the years, has no doubt helped mold the Organization Man, who studies the boss for the same reasons that he once studied the teacher. In good teaching, the demands the pupil faces come from the problem situation, not from the teacher.

Learning becomes a kind of academic hit-and-run. The class hits the test and runs on to a new unit.

Once knowledge is tested, it can be safely forgotten. This notion directly contradicts the idea of education as a "deepening and enriching" experience. The unit plan, originally designed to organize learning into significant wholes, has become a package plan, with each package wrapped up by a unit test.

Pupils learn that specific information is an end in itself rather than the means to broad understanding of universal principles.

The easiest way to make a reliable test is to use a large number of independent, specific and separate items. This discovery about testing dealt a severe blow to the educational goal of understanding. The educated citizen is the quiz kid, not the wise man. And cramming for examinations, whether in school or on TV shows, is the basic learning process.

Pupils learn from experience with tests that all questions have clear-cut answers certified by authority. Such "thought questions" as the teacher uses are asked just to keep conversation going.

Compared with "getting the facts," the process of reasoning from data to probable conclusions is at best an intriguing parlor game. The teacher, himself conditioned by tests, may strive to be a walking encyclopedia rather than a guide to inquiry. We present to children a world in which all the lovely mottled grays of the adult world are squeezed into black-and-white certainties.

Post-Sputnik pressures, aided by the nationally standardized test, are rapidly turning the school into a processing plant rather than a place for inquiry.

In this processing plant, the teacher's role is that of a technician, not a professional. The professional, like the learner, must be aware of alternatives in a situation, choose among them, and test the consequences of his choice. The technician, like the rote learner, treats all situations alike, using prescribed rules and memorized procedures.

The range of choices that require mature judgment of the teacher is rapidly narrowing, and with this change the climate for inquiry is becoming less favorable. If we no longer trust the teacher, our confidence might be restored if we gave him better preparation, especially in his major subject. Detailed specifications for content, method, and activities were appropriate for wartime crash programs by the armed forces charged with the task of turning out technicians in quantity, but crash programs of this nature will not produce enlightened citizens and creative leaders.

The pupil is being taught to escape from freedom for the sake of material reward and social approval.

Freedom can exist only if self-knowledge is valued. Our procedures for measuring achievement do not help the pupil find out who he is or discover his strengths and weaknesses as a person. Our tests only tell us how well the pupil is conforming to a specified 1960 supertechnical model.

But we do have a conscience. Having conditioned the pupil, through awards and other forms of social approval, into submissiveness, we then propose to put him in a liberal arts college to develop his human spirit!

Our 1960 supertechnical model is defined by tests that give the pupil feedback about his growing strengths, his self-concept, and his abilities. These are expressed in terms that we prescribe, not necessarily in the areas where growth and development are taking place.

In teaching, we hunt for growth areas because it is through them that the pupil puts forth effort and gives attention. In testing, we have to disregard categories of information of unique importance to particular individuals, partly because we have to test everybody with the same instrument and partly because we simply do not know the ways in which children at various stages of growth relate to ideas and subject disciplines. Thus we teach the pupil that his own life and interests are irrelevant to education.

What do our present practices in measuring achievement contribute to education? Tests can be used to supply extrinsic motivation. This kind of motivation is considered undesirable by those who regard pupils as human beings rather than as manpower for technological enterprises.

Tests can also be used to spot children who need help. Many pupils have received remedial help because an appropriate screening test revealed their need. Most of us would agree that it is desirable to use tests in this way.

Tests can be used to guide teaching. But tests are generally given too late to serve this purpose. By the time the test results are known, the class has already moved on to a new unit. To help guide instruction, the teacher may, of course, devise short questionnaires of his own and use them at frequent intervals.

As diagnostic tools for helping the pupil understand himself and set his life goals, tests have little value for at least two reasons. First, what is past is past. We do not go back. We are satisfied to say how much the pupil learned, but not to help him master presumably important learnings. Second, achievement tests are not constructed to tell much about a pupil's unique strengths. This fact about our tests is an unfortunate one, since the pupil's strengths are all that he and the teacher have to build on.

Alternatives

Having described school practices in destructive, cynical, or perhaps honest, terms, I now ask: Do we have to be content with this kind of evaluation?

The answer is no, and many test makers would be the first to agree. Their responsibility for the present state of affairs is no more and no less than the responsibility of atomic physicists for Hiroshima. The bomb was dropped because of a complex alignment of social forces. The triumph of "achievement" over education is a sign of the times rather than the intention of educational evaluators. Moreover, like atomic energy, evaluation is taking an increasingly important place in our lives.

But the proper use of evaluation will not come about through the single-handed efforts of evaluators, teachers, or any other one group. Evaluation will contribute to education rather than to narrow goals in achievement only after widespread effort by many groups. As far as each school is concerned, the problem involves the attitudes, expectations, and goals of the entire community.

How can we return to the goal of education?

First, we could try to measure the pupil's growth as a whole, unique person, with his own goals, his own way of viewing people and the world. Individuals differ in their way of life. By *way of life* I mean the pattern of attitudes, abilities, and habits by which an individual lives and develops his strengths. If we could determine each child's general pattern, we could follow him as a whole person and help him make choices appropriate to the effective development of his way of life. We could be concerned with how he is organizing subject matter in his subjective world and the relationship between this world and his behavior in all situations.

But such evaluations can be achieved only if we start with children. We will not succeed if we start by asking: What does chemistry teach? What does history teach? We shall have to ask: How is the pupil assimilating the discipline of chemistry? Of history? How well is he mastering the method of the chemist? Of the historian? What do his learnings in chemistry and history mean for his way of life? This last question is the proper concern of the teacher, and it is a very different concern from the one that now motivates schools and communities.

My second suggestion recognizes that it is the purpose of education not only to develop individual powers but also to prepare effective citizens. Our schools have the responsibility of helping children live as self-realizing people, not in a vacuum or a hermitage, but in a complex society. In short, we recognize that children are going to have to take roles in a real world.

They are going to manage others; interpret the world around them; make discoveries; create social, political, and economic alternatives; ferret out facts; and persuade, promote, criticize, analyze, guide, console, and teach.

Education is at least partly an inquiry into the kinds of roles boys and girls may be fitted for. We must not seal off pathways before children's tendencies are thoroughly demonstrated, and we must always allow for unexpected changes in tendencies. But we can ask, as the Strong Vocational Interest Blanks ask in regard to occupations: What kinds of roles are children developing potential for? And we could keep records through the school years of profiles that show the child's aptitudes and readiness for certain roles.

Recommendations

The first thing we must do is to free the schools from the pressures that keep them from their proper job of educating boys and girls. We must reduce the pressures, so fashionable at present, for achievement, for covering ground, for mass production of pseudo-experts.

Let the schools concentrate on doing something for our children. Let the others—college faculties and employers—worry about what they are going to do about our pupils after the schools have done all they can. In other words, let's stick to our proper job of saying what has happened to our pupils and what goals they are moving toward. Let each college decide whether the student is ready to embark on its study program. Let the industrialists decide whether they want to hire him. Let the parents decide whether they are satisfied with him. These are their decisions, not ours.

Many of us in the schools know that our marks have always been monstrous. They try to signify two things that cannot be measured together. They try to measure the pupil's standing, judged against standards we have assumed (often erroneously) the higher school or college desired.

Marks also try to measure what the child has done compared with what he might be capable of doing. The criteria for measuring the pupil's standing must be the same for all pupils. Yet the criteria for measuring capability or growth of powers must differ from one pupil to the next.

The confusion over marks is a symptom of the larger confusion over the mission of the school. Let us commit ourselves to the educational job defined earlier, and let us find appropriate means for describing the results.

My second recommendation has to do with both the means and the measurement of education. Let us confront the pupil with the events, the ideas, the attitudes, and the practices that he must cope with. Let us help him cope with them, and from time to time let us assess his growth in the ability to cope.

In teaching let us use situations that are vital and lifelike, though not necessarily a slice of natural life. The situations we provide should have the validity of significant human activity. They should release the essentially dramatic quality of purposeful human endeavor. In testing, perhaps the simplest way of stating the recommendation is to say that more *complete* situations should be used.

I would like to see us experiment with sound movies. The pupil views a situation on the screen, tells what he would do in the situation, and justifies his response.

I would like to see us make much more use of role playing. Certainly one of the major goals of the disciplines of history, anthropology, and psychology is to develop the individual's ability to put himself in the place of people who lived at other times and other places. In role playing, we can watch the pupil as he tries to feel and understand situations from another's point of view. As we watch, we should be as interested in the child's actions and expressions as in his words. I would like to see these techniques used in our assessment of the pupil's powers as manifested in performance, not in puzzles.

I do not see any reason why we cannot use situations in the community to probe development. We have had a lot of talk about democracy. All right, let the pupil see a club or a board of directors in action. Let him come back and tell us about it. Let's note what he observes, what he responds to, what is important to him. Isn't this the sort of information we need to plan further activities and to assess educational growth?

I would like to get at the ideas to which the pupil is committed. What ideas are important to him? What causes is he nurturing? Is he developing any life goals? Any compelling purposes? Are his intellectual interests expanding?

To discover answers to these questions, we must occasionally give the pupil opportunities for free choice. In planning his work, we can offer him six or eight kinds of activities from which to choose. Which does he select? Why?

I maintain that this is relevant and interpretable information and that it has the feel of life. But let's let him choose among activities, not just among phrases written on a piece of paper.

The Doctor and the Detective

John H. Watson, M.D., wrote what may well be the longest and the most complete case study on record. His subject was Sherlock Holmes, the detective. In *A Study in Scarlet*, Watson attempts, after some weeks of acquaintance, to assess Holmes, and he writes out a report card in the best achievement tradition.

He certifies Holmes' knowledge of literature, philosophy, and astronomy to be nil. Politics—feeble. Botany—strong on poisons but weak on practical gardening. Geology—recognizes mud stains from various parts of

London. Chemistry—profound. Sensational literature—knows "every detail of every horror perpetrated in the last century." Anatomy—"accurate, but unsystematic." Good violinist, expert amateur athlete, "good practical knowledge of British law." And Watson, with rare insight into his own evaluative processes, labels the report card "Sherlock Holmes—*his limits*" (italics mine).

But with all this observation, which is quite accurate, Watson misses the essence of Holmes, and Sherlock has to tell him, finally, what his powers and abilities are and what social role organizes these powers and abilities into an effective personality and contributor to society.

What Watson missed, because he had never seen Holmes perform in an appropriate situation, was his intuition for unraveling crimes, his ability to apply special knowledge to problems, his conscious use of rules of deduction, his habit of observation. And the report card could never have led Watson to predict Holmes' role of "consulting detective."

Watson, I am afraid, embodies the achievement point of view in our schools. He represents the traditional, academic, propaedeutic view of education, which asks after achievement in its own categories but fails to comprehend, and therefore to educate, the child.

Sherlock is unique, as human personality is unique; and he represents that part of every man which must be understood within its own frame of reference and commitments. The categories useful for understanding Sherlock are not the categories most useful for understanding Watson.

Watson talks about his own education in language that is typical of certification and achievement. He "took his degree" and proceeded "to go through the course prescribed for surgeons."

Holmes never talks about his education. But he does talk about problems to be solved, inquiries to be conducted, and methods of thought that he values. For the most part, Holmes educated himself. His studies were "very desultory and eccentric, but he . . . amassed a lot of out-of-the-way knowledge which would astonish his professors." And the habit of inquiry —which the university could not stamp out—survived.

Can we say as much for our pupils?

chapter 22

Asking questions to trigger thinking

M. J. McCue Aschner

The classroom teacher probably devotes more time and thought to asking questions than anybody since Socrates. One might even say the teacher is a professional question maker.

Asking questions—in class discussion or on assignments and tests—is one of the basic ways by which the teacher stimulates student thinking and learning. And it is by asking questions and studying the answers that the teacher measures and evaluates the thinking and learning progress of his students.

Teachers regularly stimulate four main types of thinking activities by asking questions. These types are: remembering, reasoning, evaluating or judging, and creative thinking.

Definition: Memory Questions

Remembering is the most common thinking activity that goes on in a class-room. It is easy to ask questions that call for remembering. "Who was the sixteenth President of the United States?" is a typical memory question. So is "What is a noun?" and "What is a prime number?"

Some questions *appear* to call for another kind of thinking—until they are given a closer look. Consider, for example, the question, "Will you please describe the nitrogen cycle?" or "What is the difference between a mammal and a marsupial?" Just because these questions require more than

From *NEA Journal*, 50(September, 1961), 44–46. Reprinted by permission of the publisher.

a single word or a short phrase for an answer does not mean that the answer will be more than a recitation of what the student has remembered. Often when the teacher believes he is triggering a more complex type of thinking, he is merely asking a slightly more complicated memory question.

Such a teacher needs to develop skill in designing better questions. He needs to ask himself, "What kind of thinking task must my students do to answer this question? Of course, they must remember something to be able to answer any kind of question. But isn't there some way I can phrase this question to call for more than remembering?" Thus the first step in designing thought-provoking questions is to analyze and plan the task which a question can set for thinking.

Definition: Questions That Prompt Reasoning

Reasoning is called forth in such familiar questions as these: "If two men can lay floor tile for a five-room house in three days, how many men would it take to do the job in one day?" "Why did the metal strip bend when I held it over the flame?"

Or, consider the following social studies discussion:

Teacher—So why would you say that Jamestown settlers were unprepared?

Bill—Well, one book said that most of them were city people. And then they had never learned to do things for themselves.

Anne—Also, since it was a new land and nobody knew much about it, they didn't know what to expect.

Reasoning goes on when there is explaining to do, when computation is called for, when someone puts two and two together and comes up with four. Reasoning takes the "given" and works its way to the necessary conclusion. Bill and Anne used the facts they had learned about Jamestown as evidence that the settlers were unprepared.

But suppose we hear the following exchange:

Teacher—All right now why did Jackson veto the Maysville Road Bill?

Bob—Because he was against spending government money to benefit just one community instead of the whole country.

Was Bob reasoning or remembering? How can we tell? If we know—from what has gone on before—that Bob has a limited set of facts and *derived* from them the reason he gave for Jackson's veto, then we can be fairly sure he was reasoning. But if this is a review session, or if we know the class has already dealt with the full history of Jackson's decision, then we should assume that Bob is remembering, not reasoning.

To trigger reasoning, a question must call for an answer that is not retrieved but reached. It must be reachable on the basis of the "given," but not be itself part of the "given."

Definition: Questions Calling for Judgment

Evaluating or judging is an important thinking and learning activity. Students need experience in weighing alternatives, in judging and making decisions. They need to learn the ways of deciding whether or not a statement is true, a plan sound, or an action wisely taken.

This time our social studies teacher asks for evaluating:

Teacher—What do *you* think of Captain John Smith's "work or starve" policy for Jamestown? Was that a good idea?

Anne—Well, I think he just about had to lay down the law. If he hadn't forced them to build houses and gather food, they wouldn't have lived through the winter.

Dick—Yes, but that just means he was doing their thinking for them. I think he should have let them learn their lesson—even if some of 'em starved or froze to death!

Teacher—Let's get some more opinions here. How about you, Lee? What do you think?

Here the teacher asked his pupils to do their own judging. He did not frame their opinions in advance by giving his own or citing others' views. In the way he phrased his question, he provided for and welcomed differences of opinion.

But suppose a teacher asks, "What was the main reason why the Pilgrims came to the New World?" Is he asking for judging or remembering? If the teacher can be sure—before he asks the question—that the children have not yet encountered *any* evaluations (in textbook or class discussion) of reasons why the Pilgrims settled in the New World, then and only then can he also be sure he is asking them to judge.

Questions *can* be designed to elicit evaluation, however, even when other opinions and authorities have been studied.

Consider this way of designing the same question:

Teacher—We have seen that some historians think freedom of religion was the main reason the Pilgrims came here. Others think it was the desire for land or to set up their own government, and so forth. Now I want to hear your views on the matter. Tell me, what do *you* think? Give me *your own* opinion of what the main reason was the Pilgrims came over here.

This question signals clearly to students that they are being asked to evaluate; whether they do so or not is another question. Some students will always fall back on someone else's judgment. But at least when the teacher designs the question in this way, the students have a chance to do some judging; furthermore, they have the experience of being expected to do some judging.

Definition: Questions That Launch Creative Thinking

Creative thinking is thinking which produces ideas, proposes solutions to problems, invents ways of doing things. Creative thinking is something anyone can do, given the chance or the need to do so. In a classroom where a student is invited or required to act or think upon his own initiative, to seek instead of to receive knowledge, and to rely upon his own resources, creative thinking flourishes.

Here are some questions designed to stimulate creative thinking: "What would our world be like today if the Spanish had conquered England in 1588 instead of losing out with the Armada?" "What would happen if our nation's coal and oil reserve suddenly were to run out and go dry?" "How many ways can you get 12?"

Questions like these trigger brainstorming sessions. They are extremely useful when they are built into an over-all teaching strategy. Consider, for example, the English teacher who plans to develop his students' understanding of the structure of language. He says: "Let's invent a language for Martians. We'll give them a spoken language. Now, what will go into this language? What kinds of things must a language do so people can use it to communicate?"

In setting this problem, the teacher has accomplished much. First, with this off-beat approach, he has probably captured interest. Second, he has focused his students' thinking on the structure of language. Finally, he has put them on their own—he has launched creative thinking.

Helping Minds to Grow

Remembering, reasoning, evaluating, and creative thinking can—and should —go on in any classroom, at any grade or ability level, for thinking is the catalyst of learning.

To design a good classroom question, the teacher needs to begin by analyzing and planning the kind of thinking task to be set. Then he should fit the form and phrasing of the question or problem to this task. Precision and clarity in the wording of the question will focus thinking squarely on its task.

The teacher who is a skilled designer of classroom questions and problems is the teacher who helps young minds to grow.

chapter 23

The junior high school library develops investigative skills

Frederick R. Cyphert

An article in a recent professional publication contained the thought-provoking statement that one-third of all that we know came into being prior
to the year 1400; another third of the world's knowledge was discovered
between 1400 and 1900; and the final third of today's understandings is the
product of the twentieth century. If we, as educators, accept this geometric growth in the world of facts and ideas, we must recognize that a
school program geared largely to transmitting this accumulation of culture
to new generations is faced with an inextricable problem. The time has
long since passed when we should alter our instructional programs to place
increasing emphasis upon problem solving, research, and investigative
skills. It now appears that having the skill and ability for solving problems
as they are met, rather than carrying a set of answers preconceived about
our rapidly changing world, is the best equipment that we can give today's
youth.

The school library, filled with the treasures of the past and the promises
of tomorrow, becomes the key that unlocks this modern inquiring approach
to education. Unfortunately, in spite of the library's increasing importance,
recent research indicates that many schools are ineptly utilizing this materials center and are thereby minimizing its curricular contributions. What
can we learn from examining the strength and weaknesses of the junior
high school library programs of one of our major eastern states?

From *The Clearing House*, 33(October, 1958), 107–109. Reprinted by permission of the publisher.

Teaching the Skills of Library Usage

Virtually all junior high schools offer their students some type of pre-planned library instruction. This instruction is most often given in grade seven. The responsibility for the planning and execution of it is largely the librarian's.

It is reported that library skills are most often taught in isolation from the other learning experiences of students. Pupils find themselves assigned weekly to the library to consider such topics as book classification, card catalogue, library citizenship, and general reference books. There they are confronted with methods of instruction which consist chiefly of lectures, recitations, and questions covering duplicated explanations of library routine.

Is not such a formal approach to the teaching of library-usage skills as unrealistic as attempting to teach the fundamentals of basketball through the use of a rule book? Are not skills best learned through their successful application to real situations where their need is apparent to the learner? Most librarians and administrators believe that youngsters should become familiar with the school library, but they have not accepted the concept that understanding stems from intelligent use.

Teaching Practices and Library Use

Librarians say that the techniques of classroom teachers of greatest assistance in promoting library use involve devices calling for student inquiry. The assignment of individual reports to students and teacher emphasis upon research skills are considered to be superior to required book reports and encouraged personal reading. Many librarians are sympathetic to attempts by teachers to promote investigative skills because these activities fill the library with students.

However, there is evidence to indicate that both teachers and librarians at times promote research-demanding techniques without fully comprehending the consequences or evolution of such activities. Only one librarian in four is sufficiently familiar with the classroom activities of her school to analyze the teaching methods employed. Similarly, fewer than one librarian in five visits academic classrooms for planning with students. Also, on the average, the entire faculty in these same schools consume less than one-half class period per week in curriculum planning with the librarian. Furthermore, librarians, only superficially acquainted with the details of the school's instructional program, have to select the library's supply of new instructional materials because teachers fail to make their needs known. Problem-solving skills could be developed more effectively where teachers, students, and librarians work together in the logical planning of the objectives, learning experiences, and materials of instruction that promote these abilities.

Some Schools Do the Job

There are schools, however, which are effectively teaching the skills of investigation. The following example serves to illustrate the way in which one school organizes to teach these techniques of inquiry.

In this junior high school, each year's learning experiences are organized around a series of related problems, such as, "How does man earn a living?" The professional planning for each problem unit begins in a "little school" meeting with two core teachers, a math teacher, a geography-science teacher, and the librarian participating. After this preplanning, when the students have been confronted with the problem, the librarian joins the pupils in their classroom deliberations as a resource person to help organize the search for pertinent information.

Meanwhile, the "little school" of educators continues to meet weekly to coordinate teaching method and objectives. This enables the librarian to anticipate needs and to provide flexible scheduling so that entire classes, small groups, or individual students can visit the library to satisfy the need for additional information.

Some of these visits to the library, moreover, are devoted to the consideration of research techniques for which students and teachers realize the need. As the year progresses and the solution of one problem leads to further areas for investigation, librarian, teacher, and student alike come to grips with the strengths and shortcomings of their problem-solving abilities.

Pertinent Points in Planning

Developing investigative competencies in junior high school students raises some questions of teachers and librarians:

1. Are faculty members convinced of the need for having children develop these skills and abilities?

2. Have these skills and understandings been spelled out?

3. Do teachers direct their efforts toward a growing pupil independence and responsibility rather than a dependence upon teacher domination, thinking, and ingenuity?

4. Have channels of communication among teachers and between teachers and librarians been cleared so that each knows what the other is doing?

5. Do teachers and librarians have some time and place during the day to work together?

6. Are library materials selected by librarians, after an analysis of teacher and pupil needs and objectives?

7. Is the schedule of the library flexible enough for students to visit it as needed?

8. Do both librarian and the teachers approach the teaching of investigative skills by beginning with concrete situations?

9. Do we arrange for pupils to deal with problems and develop proficiencies commensurate with their abilities?

The Challenge

In today's world of ever increasing change, we cannot, try as we will, foretell what our children will need to think. We can, at best, give them a method for approaching the challenges of life. This task demands the utilization of all we know concerning the science of learning, and the effective integration of the library and the curriculum.

chapter 24

Homework

Lloyd McCleary

Reflection upon the subject of homework seems to open a Pandora's box for the educator. Pupils, parents, teachers, and administrators hold a wide range of beliefs and opinions relative to homework. Beliefs and opinions not only differ within and between each of these groups, but they also vary as attention moves along the line from practical concerns to the deeper philosophical questions which arise whenever problems of homework require attention.

As if this were not enough, opinions are likely to be affected by "side" concerns, for administrators *are* concerned about public relations; teachers *are* concerned about how "respectable" they appear to their colleagues; and parents *are* concerned about their child's readiness for College Boards. Since standard prescriptions of policy and practice are not likely to end the intense concern over this subject, perhaps an attempt in this article to indicate some of the major problems and some of the operating principles revealed by research and by current best practice may be of value to the reader.

The "What" and the "Why"

In an analysis of the topic of homework, we first face a semantic problem. To the uninitiated, perhaps it would appear that homework should mean work assigned by a teacher to be completed at home. This definition of homework is of little help in understanding what a given teacher is likely to mean by the term.

From *Educational Leadership*, XVII(January, 1960), 217–220, 225. Reprinted by permission of the author and publisher.

Because of the protests of some pupils, the author questioned an English teacher about the amount of homework she had assigned. The teacher in question denied vigorously that the required reading of a novel within a period of one week in addition to a strong dose of written work was unreasonable because the reading of a novel (although required) was not homework! Likewise, a Latin teacher became incensed with the author because he objected to the fact that she kept students after school each night to do the work she had assigned in class that day. She held many of her pupils until five o'clock almost daily because she didn't believe in having them do work at home! These are extreme but actual examples of the practices of teachers.

In the literature of the 1930's the term homework apparently had a very clear meaning. The assign, study, recite, test methods in common use gave rise to this parent reaction reported by Butler[1] in 1939. A parent wrote to a superintendent:

I have four little girls attending your schools. I am up at five o'clock in the morning to get them off to school and to get myself off to work. It is six o'clock in the evening when I reach home again, pretty well worn out, and after we have had dinner and have tidied up the house a bit, it is eight o'clock. Then, tired as I am, I sit down and teach the little girls the lessons your teachers will hear them say over on the following day. Now, if it is all the same to you, it would be a great help and a favor to me if you will have your teachers teach the lessons during the day, and then all I would have to do at night would be to hear them say them over.

Unfortunately, as late as 1950, Burton[2] reported an investigation which showed that four-fifths of the assignment procedures in the social studies classes studied were nothing more than page assignments of a single textbook.

Curriculum workers find the need to distinguish between formal or traditional practices and modern practices relative to teaching methods and techniques including homework. Very largely the distinction is based upon the degree to which practice is related to the findings of modern research dealing with individual differences in ability, in interests, and in rates of learning. The few statistical studies which have been made show that home study of the formal sort even when accompanied by questions, study guides and the like has little effect upon achievement. As teaching methods and

[1] Frank A. Butler. *The Improvement of Teaching in Secondary Schools.* Chicago, Illinois: The University of Chicago Press, 1939, p. 208.

[2] *Learning and Instruction.* The forty-ninth Yearbook of the National Society for the Study of Education, Part I. Chicago, Illinois: The University of Chicago Press, 1950, p. 227.

homework shift from the expository-memory type of activity to the problem-solving–independent-study type there will be many activities to be carried on outside of the scheduled class time. However, these homework activities do not resemble the "assigned textbook pages" kind of homework.

The "How"

The newer approach equates study with learning. The emphasis as far as homework is concerned becomes that of teaching pupils how to learn and how to become self-directing in their study. Continuity between classroom and out-of-classroom study is sought. Teachers know very well that the demands of the classroom will largely condition the approaches the pupil will use in independent study. If factual tests are a major element of the teaching method, memory will be the habit of study employed by the pupil. The habit of memorizing is likely to be employed as the means of study even in situations in which memorizing is completely inappropriate. Thus, classroom activities should require a variety of individual and group learning experiences which are completed outside the classroom. Examples of these activities are identifying and defining problems; analyzing problems through library, laboratory, or action research type of activity, interviews, visits, experiments, and the like.

Needless to say, this kind of homework emphasis does not reduce the range of opinion or the number of issues relative to homework. Rather the shifting emphasis to problem-solving and independent-study type of outside-of-classroom learning has introduced new problems and issues. The efforts to develop independent study have largely centered upon (1) the lengthened period with time devoted to the teaching of appropriate study techniques, (2) the development of separate how-to-study courses, (3) the use of special or remedial teachers such as a reading teacher to develop certain skills, and (4) the provision of supervisory help for the teacher in teaching study habits through regular class procedures. Within any given staff one will almost certainly find advocates of these various approaches. Obviously the direction of curriculum development being taken in a given school, administrative procedures, preparation of staff and the like will determine which, if any, steps are taken to alter the quality of homework and to prepare pupils to profit fully from it.

Regardless of the teaching methods employed, teachers need to understand and to recognize good study procedures and be able to diagnose cases of inefficiency in or ignorance of study procedures. Aids to the teacher in the form of books and monographs on effective study procedures, diagnostic tests, remedial materials, guides, inventories and the like are plentiful and are of excellent quality. In addition, the teacher can detect evidence of poor study habits through observation, examination of pupils' work, conferences, and self-constructed questionnaires.

Unfortunately, many schools attempt to initiate curricular changes without the proper preparation of the staff. The incidents of comic if not pathetic attempts are legend. In one school known to the author, the principal abolished all study halls and lengthened the class periods accordingly with the expectation that teachers would immediately begin teaching independent study techniques appropriate to their subject but with no preparation other than the announcement in a faculty meeting that this would be done.

During the 1940's a large number of controlled studies were conducted. The author was, however, unable to find a study which actually compared various techniques rather than various administrative schemes for facilitating study. A Project for the Improvement of Thinking, now being conducted by Professors Henderson and Smith of the College of Education of the University of Illinois, is an excellent example of a project which developed and tried out materials for improving pupil learning within the classroom. This study and others like it, however, have not directly investigated the aspect of independent study or the transfer of these learnings to use beyond the classroom. Soundly conceived experimental studies are badly needed in this area.

Although the nature of instruction and the development of sound habits of independent study are important to worthwhile out-of-class study, the assignment is a crucial element in productive homework. Regardless of the nature of the homework assignment, the pupil should clearly understand what he is to do and have definite leads to begin his work. There is ample research data to support the belief that pupil failure relative to study is as much caused by factors indicative of a poor assignment (frustration, lack of interest, failure to understand the relationship of the assignment to the classwork, etc.) than to poor study habits.

The "When" and the "How Much"

Definite answers to the "when" and the "how much" question are offered from many quarters. Generally these answers are not derived from the nature of a particular unit of school work or from the needs of particular pupils. Unfortunately, the professional journals contain just as many such answers as do the newspapers and popular magazines. In a 15-minute scanning of professional journals the author found seven separate (and each surprisingly similar) statements of the amount and timing of homework. Generally these statements were policies adopted and in force in some school system and apparently their publication implied their recommendation to the profession to be used as a standard for adoption in other schools. One such statement recommends: "In kindergarten to grade four: no homework; in grades five and six: one-half hour; in grades seven and eight: one hour; [and so on]. It is suggested that no homework be given over week-ends or holidays." Another article with the same time requirements is headed by the words "homework may harm the child's health and the school's public relations"!

These kinds of statements are not likely to be of much help to parents or to teachers. If such policies are taken seriously they may be a source of frustration to the teacher and a cause of irritation to parents that could defeat the public relations purpose which the statement professes to serve. Louis Brumer, the father of a pupil in a New York City high school, wrote his reaction to homework policy in the June, 1956, issue of *High Points:*

> Do responsible members of the high school teaching corps recommend 30–50 minutes (of homework) daily in each prepared subject?
>
> Do they believe students should be encouraged to give services to the school?
>
> Do they believe youth should be encouraged to attend school club meetings, and/or community religious group activities after school?
>
> Do they believe school children at the high school level should continue with music lessons, dancing lessons, or art lessons. . . ?
>
> Should children develop responsibility toward the home and family by performing special duties. . . ?
>
> Should families be encouraged to dine together nightly for an hour to review the day's events. . . ?
>
> Should there be an occasional free afternoon. . . ?
>
> Should at least one morning a week be assigned to formal religious devotions?
>
> Should time be set aside for shopping for a suit or dress, other wardrobe essentials, or an occasional birthday gift. . . ?
>
> Should any unscheduled time be left for an adolescent to read a *book of his own choice . . . ?*
>
> How many hours of sleep should a growing young man or lady require?

Some school-wide policies relative to homework seem to be required but it is doubtful that rather fixed time limits are either effective or meaningful. The most fruitful approach seems to lie in the direction of the study of the curriculum and the teaching procedures out of which the homework evolves. A knowledge of home conditions and the out-of-school experience of pupils should help teachers to devise learning activities which develop into stimulating out-of-class study and which can be tailored to individual needs.

Another avenue to independent study that is important to those concerned about homework is the use of the extended school day. Shops, libraries, science and language laboratories, work space and equipment for the use of tapes, television kinescopes and the like under the care of a para-professional teacher or a laboratory assistant are already available in some schools during out-of-class study time. Such facilities with proper provision for their use create excellent study conditions and do not involve the taxation of teacher time. This kind of activity meets many of the objections to homework held by parents and teachers. These activities could be incorporated with leisure-time pursuits, relieve the home of the burden of providing materials and equipment, enrich and extend classroom experiences and promote the development of independent study.

In an opinion poll of school administrators conducted by *The Nation's Schools,* 96 per cent of the administrators polled favored scheduled study during the school day; 95 per cent favored homework assignments for junior and senior high school pupils; 79 per cent favored homework at the upper elementary school level; and 31 per cent favored homework for pupils in the lower elementary grades. According to reports from the administrators involved in this poll, the average time spent doing homework was about three hours per week for elementary pupils and from four to six hours per week for high school pupils. If these reactions represent homework conditions generally, there is wide acceptance of the practice of assigning homework; and at least at the high school level, the average time spent doing assigned homework is the equivalent of one school day each week. If this time is to be employed effectively and if it can be invested to produce independent, self-directing students, the effort by teachers to improve the quality of homework becomes one of education's most compelling tasks.

chapter 25

Reporting to parents: why? what? how?

William M. Alexander

For some 25 years now, there has been widespread experimentation with newer types of reports. Reporting to parents has changed in many respects, mostly to the good. More information than percentage marks in the subjects is now commonly given in reports. Much effort is devoted to exchange of information and advice between parents and teachers. Many teachers try very hard to use the whole marking and reporting system as a means of helping their pupils to carry on self-appraisal and improvement.

But have those who are zealous to improve reporting sometimes confused parents, pupils, and even some teachers? In trying to communicate better with parents, are teachers sometimes making it more difficult for parents to understand later on when their children encounter other reporting practices? Have some fine efforts to aid pupil progress made it more difficult for pupils to judge their progress?

I would answer yes to these questions, because some teachers and interested parents have frequently overlooked two relevant if unfortunate facts:

1. Differences in reporting practices from level to level and school to school are not easily understood by pupils and their parents.

2. Try as many teachers and parents may to guide learning for learning's sake, there has been far more guidance of learning for the sake of grades and good reports.

From *NEA Journal,* 48(December, 1959), 15–18. Reprinted by permission of the publisher.

Perhaps further improvement in reporting would be aided by more common understanding of the logical answers to three questions: Why report? What to report? How report?

Why Report?

Any boy or girl can tell us why schools send reports home: so that parents may know how their children are getting along in school.

The newer practices have not reduced parents' basic interest in their children's progress. Indeed, informative reports may have whetted the interest of many mothers and fathers. Reporting systems that fail to convey to parents information they understand about their children's progress (or, perhaps more factually, their class standing) invite trouble.

Marks or grades have long been accepted reporting symbols. These marks found their way into school records as well as school reports, and so into college transcripts. From numerical marks or from point equivalents of letter marks, rank in class could be computed for high school seniors and used by college-admission officials.

Marks could also be reported to prospective employers. Thus, marks and reports became inextricably related, and their purposes were somewhat broadened, especially at the secondary level, to include prediction of college success and even of success in a job.

But the central purpose of informing parents about their children's school progress, and even the related purposes of informing colleges and employers about prospective students and employees, has frequently been subordinated to other purposes: Marks could also be used to decide on promotion and graduation.

Reports become the signposts of passing or failing. Although retardation has been drastically reduced in the past half century, marks still separate pupils by achievement in those schools in which a pupil's previous record determines his assignment to homogeneous groups or tracks.

In recent years, school people, pressed by many needs for better public support of the schools, have awakened to the public relations aspects of reporting. Here is one place, it was realized, where teachers and parents have a common interest and a reason for getting together. Therefore, reporting systems have been geared in many communities to their potential for interpreting the school and its needs to parents.

However, reports to parents were and are so widely used by both parents and teachers as clubs over the heads of children as to make the report card—and school in general—hateful to many. Are today's parents, whose own parents granted or withheld privileges on the basis of marks on the report card, likely to perceive their child's report as a happy symbol of the parent-teacher partnership?

Undoubtedly, one purpose of reports to parents has been to provide pupils with the incentive to do schoolwork that neither parent nor teacher knew how else to supply. However, indiscriminate clubbing through marks is known to have quite different results from those which well-meaning parents and teachers seek for children.

Of these various and frequently conflicting purposes of reporting systems, two seem clear-cut and justifiable:

1. Parents should have information about their children's progress and standing in school. If this information can be given in a way that promotes understanding of home and school, all the better. But the information needs to be sufficiently factual, even if disappointing, so that the mother and father can use it to understand and help their child. Certainly such information at the high school level should also be available to college-admission officials and prospective employers.

2. Ultimately, it is even more important that boys and girls have the best information available in understandable form about their own progress. To understand themselves, to capitalize on their strong points, and to remedy, if possible, their weaker ones, they need to know what these strengths and weaknesses are. Many types of evaluative data are needed for this purpose in addition to a six or twelve weeks' set of marks, but the accumulation and summary of facts at reporting time may be very useful in the pupil's own plan for continued, improved progress.

What to Report?

Differences of opinion and practice about the purposes of reporting seem almost minor as compared with those which exist about the content of reports. Great variations occur in the items on which information is reported and in the marking symbols. These variations are both vertical, from level to level, and horizontal, from school to school at the same level.

The educational philosophy in a school or system and especially in the classroom concerned would be expected to control the nature of the instructional program and the content of the report.

If achievement in subject matter is a central goal, the report card would report pupils' standing in knowledge of subjects of the curriculum. If behavior according to stated criteria of growth and development is a goal, then a description of relevant behavior would be reported. If progress in various work skills and habits is desired, then the report would indicate pupils' status or progress in specific skills and habits.

Since the instructional program typically serves more than one of these goals, the report may give a mark in the subjects and a check on various behavior traits and work habits. Sometimes, however, the philosophy is not clearly stated in the report or understood by either parent or teachers, and what the report is trying to report on is not really defined.

The dominant philosophy relates also to the basis on which standing and progress are determined:

Does an A, for example, mean that the pupil is doing top work with respect to his own potential or to the norm for the class? And if the latter, is the norm determined as an average of the distribution of marks in the class, or by the teacher's expectation of some standard of achievement, or by the norms of some standardized test? And does it describe the pupil's present standing or his progress since some previous time?

An A may mean any of these things in different communities, in different schools in the same community, or perhaps even in different classrooms of the same school.

Confusion arises, at least among some pupils and parents, when the items and underlying philosophies vary from level to level. The transition from elementary to secondary schools in many communities includes introduction to the use of letter marks for achievement and perhaps elimination of reports on behavior characteristics and work habits.

Even at the same level teachers may, and sometimes do, disregard in written forms the check lists or other spaces for reporting on items other than subject achievement. In oral reporting there may be even less uniformity in the items about which teachers and parents converse.

Lack of parent understanding may be increased by varieties in the symbols used in written reports and records. Elementary schools may use S and U, and perhaps also an E (excellent) or O (outstanding), or other symbols; and secondary schools, the traditional A's, B's, and C's. Or 1, 2, 3, 4 may replace A, B, C, D.

Ability grouping introduces still another problem: Does an A in the low section mean the same as in the high? Indeed, can A's be given in the low section? Actually, these are problems only if the report is focused on relative standing rather than individual progress.

I am not alarmed by these variations or even by the confusion they create for parents and pupils. Instead I see them as encouraging signs of genuine concern by American teachers for finding better ways of reporting to parents in the interest of helping individual pupils.

Although further experimentation with what to report is critically needed, would it not be well meanwhile, to stick to the two central purposes for reporting mentioned earlier?

Should not the school faculty be certain, first, that parents understand what their children's reports are intended to tell, and second, that the reports summarize data which pupils can use, and indeed have already used, in self-appraisal and improvement? If so, should not the report clearly distinguish between marks and comments related to present standing and those related to recent progress, and also among goals such as subject-matter achievement, work habits, and behavior traits?

How Report?

Where teachers are certain of the purposes of reporting and of what to report, the form of reporting seems to follow logically. Other articles in this feature show how careful studies of reporting by faculty groups help. Perhaps the great differences in reporting procedures are created by varying degrees of understanding by school faculties on the *why* and *what* of reports. School leaders might reduce confusion as well as the range of practice by providing for more thorough study of the problem.

Certainly our knowledge of communication methods brings into real question the use of written reports alone, especially when these consist of letter symbols and check marks only. Face-to-face communication seems to be as effective in reporting to parents as in other matters. My belief—which has been strengthened by many comments from parents and others—is that the single most effective reporting medium is the teacher-parent conference.

But whatever the method of reporting, there is still the question of how to express that which is to be reported. Marks and checks are simple to write but hard to explain.

The single hardest question to answer—and the one for which most parents would probably settle—is, "How is my child doing?" The complete record, plus samples of work, helps the teacher to explain Johnny's progress but may still fail to answer this question. The teacher, therefore, needs to explain two things to parents: First, how Johnny is doing in relation to his potential, as best it *can* be estimated (and teachers estimate it very freely among themselves), and second, how he is doing in relation to the class norm.

A satisfactory answer to the basic question in which parents are interested really means a two-way or dual marking system. In the elementary school, this system may be fairly simple. It may be enough, for example, to explain that Johnny is doing as well as he is expected to, although he is below the class average in arithmetic. But in the secondary school, marks are generally needed, and Johnny's status will probably have to be expressed by two sets of letter grades—one for progress or effort, the other for relative standing or achievement.

The Dilemma of Reporting

This overview of practices and problems in reporting may suggest that the situation has become hopelessly confused. To the contrary, I see it as having been hopefully experimental. However, we do need more widespread understanding of present variations in the *why, what,* and *how* of reports.

The perplexity of parents and others caused by varied reporting systems is real and must be recognized. Just as real and to be recognized, however, is the teacher's desire for better ways of helping individual learners.

This is the dilemma we face in reporting systems: A uniform system of reporting throughout the nation might eventually be more easily understood by everyone, but it might also greatly inhibit effective provisions for individual differences among both pupils and communities. In fact, providing for individual differences has already been adversely affected to some degree by greater uniformity of marking and reporting practices in high schools.

I believe that the following items are essential to improve the reporting system throughout the country: agreement among the teachers in each school as to the purposes of reporting and as to what is to be reported; careful explanation to each parent, both on the entrance of his child to school and repeatedly thereafter, of the reporting system used (and of its relationship to any previous systems the parent has known); and careful planning with parent groups as to the method of reporting most useful and convenient for both parents and teachers.

In addition, more systematic publication of relevant research findings, of results of experimentation with different reporting procedures, and of surveys of practices by local, state, and national educational agencies might help to bring about the understanding and spread of good practices.

chapter 26

What teaching machines can and cannot do

Robert B. Nordberg

Teacher, do you know these terms: Retractable Skinner Box, Single-door Lashley Jumping Stand, Graham-Gagne Runway, Pressey Multiple-choice Board? You will know them soon if not. They are varieties of teaching machines. Even in staid Britain, they represent a growing movement. A writer in *The Times* (London) complains that "chalk-and-talk still represents his [the teacher's] stock in trade as it did a hundred, or even a thousand years ago," and contrasts this situation with the efficiency of the modern push-button kitchen.[1]

This article will try to state what teaching machines can and cannot do, what opportunities and dangers they pose, what should be done about them.[2] There is no more pressing educational problem just now. These

[1] W. K. Richmond, "Teaching by Machine: British Indifference Criticized," *Times Educational Supplement*, MMCCCXXCV (February 3, 1961), p. 198.

[2] A general bibliography on teaching machines is published by the College of Education; University of Florida; Gainesville, Florida. 20¢. The following recent articles, not cited elsewhere herein, may be found helpful:

F. S. Cook, "Some Advantages and Disadvantages of Self-instructional Devices," *Balance Sheet*, XLII (December, 1960), 154–156.

J. F. Feldhusen, "Will Teaching Machines Produce Machine Teaching?" *Wisconsin Journal of Education*, XCIII (December, 1960), 18–20.

E. R. Keislar, "Potential of Auto-instruction," *American Vocational Journal*, XXXVI (February, 1961), 36–37.

P. K. Komoski, "Teaching Machines," *Instructor*, XXC (March, 1961), 32–33.

A. A. Lumsdaine and R. Glaser (eds.), *Teaching Machines and Programmed*

From *The Catholic Educational Review*, LIX(September, 1961), 361–367. Reprinted by permission of the author and publisher.

devices will be to the 1960's—for better or worse—what the standardized testing movement was to the 1930's.

The first patent on a teaching machine in the United States was given almost a century ago.[3] It was Professor Sidney L. Pressey, however, who did the most, and most fervent work in this field. Pressey began to build multiple-choice machines in the 1920's and reported optimistically upon their prospects.[4] By 1932, however, he abandoned the project and commented:

> The writer has found from bitter experience that one person alone can accomplish relatively little, and he is regretfully dropping further work on these problems. But he hopes that enough may have been done to stimulate other workers, that this fascinating field may be rapidly developed.[5]

Dr. Pressey's hope is being tardily realized.

Teaching and Machines

A machine is any contrivance of two or more resistant, relatively constrained parts, which can transmit and modify force and motion so as to do some kind of work. We shall herein mean, by "teaching machines," all such contrivances used as part of any instructional process. This includes such things as television programs, tachistoscopes, and the like, but especially devices designed to help the learner stamp in right responses and stamp out wrong ones. (Note the completely Thorndikean orientation.) To teach is to help another or others in acquiring facts, ideas, skills, or attitudes. In any but a mechanistic outlook, then, it is contradictory to speak of "teaching machines."

We might note that every tyranny the world has known—ranging from Orwell's fictitious *1984* (remember the "teaching machines" used to correct wrong thinkers in that superstate) to the real-life Communist empire—has

---

Learning (Washington: National Education Association, Dept. of Audio-Visual Instruction, 1960).

D. M. Schweickhard, "Electronics in Public Schools," *Minnesota Journal of Education* XLI (January, 1961), 20–21.

R. C. Snider, "Teaching Machines," *Nation's Schools,* LXVII (February, 1961), 70–73.

H. A. Tonne, "Ubiquitous Teaching Machine," *Journal of Business Education,* XXXVI (February, 1961), 192–193.

[3] U.S. Patent No. 52,758, granted February 20, 1866, to Halcyon Skinner.

[4] Sidney L. Pressey, "A Machine for Automatic Teaching of Drill Method," *School and Society,* XXV (May 7, 1927), 549–552.

Sidney L. Pressey, "A Simple Apparatus Which Gives Tests and Scores—and Teaches," *School and Society,* XXIII (March 20, 1926), 373–376.

[5] Sidney L. Pressey, "A Third and Fourth Contribution toward the Coming 'Industrial Revolution' in Education," *School and Society,* XXVI (January, 1932), 1–5.

enthusiastically adopted this mechanistic theory of learning and all that goes with it.

Communication Phases in Teaching

The writer has earlier developed a six-phase theory of communication and sought to indicate some of its procedural implications.[6] One need not accept this theory altogether in order to have a basis for highlighting the limits of teaching machines. Any really organismic approach will do. The six-phase theory provides a handy way, however, to analyze our problem. The reader is respectfully referred to the original presentation thereof for its fuller implications. Here, we shall simply sketch the phases briefly: (1) The sender (writer, speaker) has an idea or ideas to impart. (2) He selects symbols likely to convey his idea. (3) He actualizes these symbols in speech, writing, or otherwise. (4) These concretized symbols are encountered by the receiver (reader, listener). (5) The receiver identifies them as the symbols they are. (6) He associates meanings with them —not necessarily the meanings intended by the sender.

An idea is the direct representation in the mind of the nature of something. It belongs to the spiritual realm, as does the intellect that conceives it. A machine belongs wholly to the physical realm. Matter and spirit differ essentially. In terms of our six phases of communication, what can a machine do? It cannot handle phase one, because only a human or superhuman creature can have an idea. Neither can the machine handle phase two, because only an agent which can have an idea can relate a symbol thereto. The machine can take care of phase three *if* an intelligent being using it is taking care of the first two phases and programming the machine accordingly. It cannot take care of phase four except in the case of a machine talking to another machine—which we may yet live to see hailed as the most efficient and sensible type of conversation! The machine cannot take care of phase five, because it cannot contemplate a symbol in the abstract, but only rearrange concretized symbols. Nor can it take care of phase six, for that requires another intelligent being—the human receiver.

In sum, then, no machine, present or future, can deal with more than one (the third) of these six communicative stages, and only this at the hands of an intelligent being. In such hands, the machine can indicate to a pupil that he has, or hasn't, the "right answer," but it cannot deal with interpretive problems that might arise. If the pupil is so hopelessly unmechanized that he demands to know *why* this is the right answer, or isn't, the machine might paraphrase Chaucer:

I know not how these things may be;
I give the answer given to me.

[6] R. B. Nordberg, "Levels of Communication in Reading," *Catholic Educational Review*, LIV (February, 1956), 92–100.

Educational psychologists generally agree that the two best proofs of meaningful, solid learning are paraphrasing and application. Machines can deal with applications only in an isolated, superficial way, and they have yet to do much with paraphrasing. It takes a mind to judge a paraphrase. (From a great deal of teaching that goes on, one might sadly judge that it takes an exceptional mind to even attempt the job.)

For the most part, these devices tend with their whole force to operate under the stimulus-response psychology of Edward L. Thorndike. They fall short of any organismic treatment of the learner, and more short of the concept of a learner who, besides being an organismic whole, is a rational creature. Yet, as an example of their quick acceptance, one writer was able to say, "While there has been no thorough field demonstration of teaching machines, no reason exists to doubt that it could be done since the principles of programming are quite compatible with current educational theory."[7]

Our critique so far has been concerned only with a hylomorphic versus a materialistic conception of the learner. Another very important, related aspect concerns education for organization and expression of knowledge as against education for "checking the right answer." Surely everyone will agree that systematic arrangement of material and clear and effective articulation are "of the essence" in education. The creed of the machine, though—and, usually, of those who find machines fascinating—is that everything is the sum of its parts. Partly because the machine cannot think, cannot program itself, it cannot in the last analysis help us at all in the crucial business of teaching students to organize and express what they know. Even this is doubted by some. As regards a self-programming machine, one writer declared, ". . . only the ostrichist will dare to say that the thing is impossible."[8]

The problem of organization is taken up by E. Galanter of the University of Pennsylvania: "It appears that an AID can only teach associations, or rote materials, and therefore can never teach a child to be creative, and, in fact, may result in stultifying any creativity that he may have."[9]

Other Dangers

We have spoken of the superficial, mechanical, "right answer" concept of knowledge and of learning that teaching machines imply, and of their

[7] G. T. Kowitz, "Administering the Automated School," *American School Board Journal*, CXLII (February, 1961), 13–16. Mr. Kowitz is Coordinator of Experimental Programs, Research Division, New York State Education Department. The thoughtful reader will find this an interesting treatment of administrative problems likely to be encountered in the brave new world of push-button education.

[8] Richmond, 198.

[9] E. Galandter, "Two Models of a Student," *Teachers' College Record*, LXII (December, 1960), 194. The same issue of the same journal has an article by T. S. Eliot on "Teaching the Appreciation of Poetry."

total inability to deal with factors of organization and expression. There are other dangers in their use. One writer says, "Unfortunately, articles are beginning to appear . . . [implying] that teachers had better watch out lest robots take control."[10] This is not the point. There is no danger that robots will out-think their inventors; a robot stays a robot. The danger —indeed, the present and growing reality—is that many teachers will approach human learners *as if* they were robots, and thus will fail to utilize a whole world of opportunities for promoting insightful and integrated learning. The danger is that the preoccupation with trivia which has been the curse of schools since schools began will be increased incalculably by mechanical contrivances. The writer who scoffed at the scoffers went on to say, "The goal remains the improvement of educational practice." Since to improve is to come closer to a goal, this statement boils down to, "A goal is a goal." But, as the general semantics people would say at this point, $goal_1$ is not $goal_2$. No doubt we shall have numerous studies on how well machines can produce "improvement of educational practice," and no doubt these studies will mostly use the devices and the premises of the machine defenders. The capacity of behavioral scientists for evolving question-begging procedures is a great modern marvel. The only way to deal with their monumental irrelevancies, therefore, is to keep clearly in mind what education is supposed to be.

Another real danger is the nationalized (and almost certainly secularized) curriculum. "There can be little doubt that a rapid, uncritical adoption of automated methods would be the last step down the road towards a national curriculum."[11] A related problem is that of the commercial vested interest. One writer pointed out:

> The organization proposing to develop and market the machines and the materials stands ready to spend twenty million dollars on the project. The firm intends to recover this investment, and it would be most quickly recovered by the development of salable merchandise that would require no alteration for years.[12]

Educational theory is already being shaped partly by vested interests of companies producing the sixty million standard tests taken each year in this country. Probably, in coming decades, theory will also be shaped by vested interests of makers and sellers of so-called teaching machines.

We cannot exhaust the list of hazards, but one more is important. The significance of the sheer, metaphysical presence of the teacher in the classroom stands in increasing danger of being forgotten. Some of us remem-

[10] H. F. Silberman, "Teaching Machines," *Junior College Journal*, XXXI (February, 1961), 318. Silberman is listed as "a Human Factors Scientist, Systems Development Corporation, Santa Monica, California.

[11] Kowitz, p. 15.

[12] J. Ginther, "More on Teaching Machines," *Elementary School Journal*, LXI (February, 1961), 241.

ber the Hollywood gossip monger who used to end his programs, "Good-night to you; and I *do* mean *you*." The discerning listener could scarcely avoid the thought, "That's quite a trick, considering you never met me!" When a teacher is smiling at *me*, looking at me (not an *image* of a teacher on a TV screen or her alter ego in the gears and pulleys of a machine), this is something irreplaceable. A writer complained, "One of the weak-nesses in educational research has been the teacher variable—different teachers supplying enthusiasm or some other contaminant. . . ."[13] For reasons transcending research considerations—especially of the sort of atomistic research that usually leads to false conclusions anyhow—one hopes that "contaminants" of that sort are with us yet awhile!

Summary and Conclusions

Use of teaching machines is rapidly on the increase. Herein we set out to indicate in a general way what they can and cannot do, what teachers and schools should do about them. It was argued that such machines, regard-less of any degree of technical excellence, are *by nature* unable to rest on an educational psychology that stresses understanding as against condi-tioned reaction to "right answers" and are unable to deal with the im-portant considerations of organization and expression of knowledge. Other dangers in their use were also pointed out, such as a nationally standard-ized curriculum, vested interests of manufacturers, and a gradual neglect of the importance, for "humanistic" reasons, of the actual presence of the teacher.

This does not mean teaching machines cannot be of use. They can be of use in teaching cut-and-dried, completely unambiguous subject matter, such as spelling or simple computation, and only then when directed and actively supervised by a teacher and subjected to frequent review and criticism. The writer would strongly urge Catholic teachers—indeed, any teachers who are not mechanists and behaviorists—to use them only for that purpose, and to speak up bravely to all who make excessive and naïve claims for them. Those who opposed the excesses and absurdities of the testing movement in the 1930's were called anachronisms and die-hards. Many who then went all out for standard tests are now beating their breasts and confessing their folly. Must the whole cycle be repeated over machines?

We are often told that people are less efficient than machines. Let us hope, for the future of education, that those who oppose "the new mecha-nism" can be more *eloquent* than machines. Already, though, there is undoubtedly, somewhere, a well-trained machine which will step forward to protest (in suitably viscid prose) that this is not the issue at all.

[13] E. B. Fry, "Research Tools: Instrumentation in Educational Research," *Review of Educational Research*, XXX (December, 1960), p. 513.

chapter 27

Sharing teaching with television

I. Keith Tyler

The classroom teacher who uses instructional television must learn to share with the television teacher the responsibility of stimulating and nurturing pupil learning. What changes in role and function are implied?

Occasional use of television programs presents few problems to the teacher accustomed to using audio-visual materials. It is the systematic use of two to five telecasts per week in a given subject which requires major readjustments by the receiving teacher. He no longer is sole master of his school empire. He must share his functions with a studio teacher who may seem to eclipse him in the eyes of his students. He is likely to feel emotionally insecure and may respond with hostility, resistance, and overt or covert opposition.

The most difficult adjustment for the classroom teacher using instructional television is to relinquish curriculum autonomy. Teachers at all levels want to teach what they deem best, in the sequence that seems appropriate, in the manner they feel to be most effective. Instructional television, directed to many classes, necessarily limits curriculum autonomy by structuring the broad outlines of subject matter, the sequence of units and topics, and even the relative time to be devoted to each. It is only natural that teachers should resent this restriction upon their teaching freedom, even when television is employed in a single university or school system, and the most progressive teachers may be the most resentful.

The problem is further compounded, however, when regional, state,

From *The News Letter*, XXXVII(January, 1962), 1–4. Reprinted by permission of author and publisher.

or national instructional television is made available. This appears to represent a standardization of curriculum and teaching which ignores local and regional needs and interests. It may be viewed as a step toward centralization and regimentation.

Actually, of course, the teacher's curriculum autonomy is restricted by many factors. States and localities vary in the extent to which they prescribe detailed courses of study, adopt textbooks and administer uniform examinations. Textbooks themselves have proved so useful that some teachers have long since voluntarily relinquished curriculum control as they slavishly follow the scope and sequence of the book. For them, at least, using instructional television involves merely the substitution of one type of control for another.

Even the curriculum freedom needed to meet the peculiar needs of a state, region, or locality is more theoretical than real. The basic curriculum of American schools has a high degree of uniformity. Not only are much the same subjects offered from one section of the country to another, but even the grade placement of content material does not vary significantly. American schools have responded to broad trends in American society. They use textbooks distributed nationally and they benefit from ideas, practices, and research findings shared through national meetings and publications.

It seems clear, then, that teachers are not required by the systematic use of television to give up a large measure of curriculum autonomy. Their curriculum freedom is already greatly, and probably sensibly, limited by many factors. Indeed, those who rigidly adhere to the textbook are only substituting one form of organization for another. But those who have been able to follow their own course organization are required by the nature of instructional television to surrender this much of their classroom autonomy.

What do they gain in return? First, the television syllabus must represent the best organization of the course for the given grade level. It must be based upon competent curriculum research and authoritative opinion. It must be kept abreast of changing trends, emphases and subject matter. Teachers must feel assured that the television course organization and content are markedly superior.

Second, the day-by-day television presentations must be more efficient. The television teacher has much more time to prepare each presentation and he should be backed up by a team of experts in subject matter and learning theory. His presentation should take less time to cover the same ground.

Third, the television presentation must be more effective. It can use a greater variety of visuals, more extensive and expensive apparatus, and call upon authorities and experts where they may be needed. The impact or impression upon the pupil should be greater.

Where, then, does the teacher retain sufficient freedom of action to take into account the individual differences from pupil to pupil, class to class, and community to community? This freedom is exercised in the time allocated to the subject which is not consumed by the broadcast presentations. The appropriate relationship between the time devoted to television and that consumed by other learning activities will probably vary from subject to subject, and even from one grade level to another. Too little is known about this at the moment. There appears to be a trend toward reducing the amount of time devoted to television presentation and increasing the time for related classroom and individual learning activities, as teachers become adjusted to the new medium. The possibly disproportionate amount of time given to television in many instances was due to a failure to recognize the importance of individual and group learning activities on the one hand, and the efficiency and impact of the medium, on the other.

The second adjustment for the classroom teacher, made necessary by the introduction of instructional television, is to redefine his instructional role. If he conceives himself fundamentally as a purveyor of subject matter, he faces an imposing rival in the television teacher whose presentations are characterized by authoritativeness, efficiency and effectiveness. He feels reduced in status to a mere vassal who carries out the plans of the "master teacher." Worse, he feels degraded in the eyes of his pupils who may compare him unfavorably to the glamorous figure on the screen.

Unfortunately, in actual practice, some classroom teachers do spend an inordinate share of their time in doling out subject matter—in telling and showing. In higher education, for example, the lecture or lecture demonstration is the prevailing instructional activity—laboratories, tutorial systems, discussion groups and seminars to the contrary notwithstanding. In secondary schools, teacher telling and showing is also utilized to an extent not realized by the teachers themselves. And even elementary school teachers tend to consume more classroom time in talking than do all their pupils added together.

When, in a given subject, the purveying role is taken over by the television teacher, what roles remain for the classroom teacher? Basically the teacher as a professional has two essential roles which cannot be automated. He is a manager of learning situations and a counselor of individual learners. To discharge these responsibilities adequately requires a background of thorough professional training and, in day-to-day teaching, all the time available that is not consumed in the presentation of subject matter.

As a *manager of learning situations* the teacher must arrange appropriate situations in which pupils can learn—can achieve desired educational objectives. These may involve the entire class, groups within the class, individuals, or even several classes together. The situations may call for practice and drill, for reading and discussion, for research and investigation, for laboratory experimentation, for creative activity in music, composition, or the arts, or many other activities. A variety of media and learning aids may be utilized: radio, tape recorders, motion pictures, language laboratories, reference books and magazines, teaching machines, field trips, museum specimens, and laboratory equipment.

He must know his pupils well enough to be able to diagnose their needs, appraise their progress, and prescribe the appropriate learning situations. He must have a thorough background in subject matter so that he can relate it to effective learning activities. He must have a working familiarity with materials, media, and resources so that they can be employed appropriately. And finally, he must have a grasp of objectives and goals so that these can be related to his own pupils in terms of appropriate subject matter and learning experiences.

An important obstacle to the employment of more varied learning situations in the classroom is that teachers lack time to plan, arrange, and carry through such activities. They are typically burdened with the task of presentation—of purveying content. It is not alone the time consumed by presentation itself; even more important is the time involved in planning it. Television, by taking over the main task of telling and showing, can provide the teacher with more time for individual and group learning activities.

As a *counselor of individual learners* the teacher assumes a role always significant in education. The personal approach in teaching was never more important than it is today as society becomes increasingly depersonalized through mass media, urban living, and the changing nature of family life. Rising juvenile delinquency is attributed in part to the loss of emotional security by children who are victims of broken homes, parental neglect, migration of workers, and the tension, fears, and uncertainties of the world situation.

There is no mechanical or electronic device which can play this counseling role in education. Only the classroom teacher can study his pupils, ascertain their needs, and provide the appropriate emotional and intellectual guidance. Here again television can be an aid. While the television teacher tells and shows, the classroom teacher can be observing the reactions and symptomatic behavior of his pupils. When he operates as a manager of learning situations, he can provide also for appropriate guidance situations where needed.

Once teachers see their appropriate roles in the classroom as involving basically the management of learning situations and the counseling of individuals, they no longer look upon television as a threat. Presentation becomes one kind of learning situation which, when delegated to television, enables teachers to concentrate time and energy upon planning and executing other kinds of group and individual learning situations which take into account individual difference in needs, interests and levels of achievement. The television teacher whose specialty is telling and showing, becomes a teammate or partner in the total learning process. The classroom teacher alone is the all-around professional who studies his pupils, diagnoses their needs, and provides appropriate learning and counseling situations to enable them to achieve educational objectives. In this he attains his satisfactions, his fulfillment and his reward through face-to-face relationships with learners.

chapter **28**

The academic con men
Advice to young college professors

Francis J. Kerins

Eventually there comes to the average college teacher a disheartening awareness of his own limitations. The sophomoric visions of transforming society and shaking the world of thought fade in the harsh glare of the advancing years. And one realizes, with some regret if the awakening is fairly early in professional life, that he not only is not yet, but also never will be, a truly creative thinker or outstanding scholar. For the majority, genius is the goal, and frustration the reality.

At this point, the endless gray night of mediocrity threatens. The gifted few, of course, avoid it by their talent; the significant thinker, the authoritative scholar, the imaginative experimenter are, by definition, anything but mediocre. They are of no concern here. They do not really face the problem, since they solve it by being what they are; and they really deserve little credit. Anyone can be extraordinary, after all, if he has extraordinary ability. There is no trick to that.

The real challenge is for the rest—to become extraordinary, and well known, and revered, without unusual ability. Nor must it be thought that this is impossible; as a matter of fact, it is being done all the time. But it takes flair, and boldness, and a sustained effort in a carefully planned program. It is the remarkable achievement of the academic con man, the man who, despite a lack of striking originality or tremendous learning, becomes a luminary in the starry heavens of higher education. He is known

From *Journal of Higher Education*, XXXIII(June, 1961), 312–316. Reprinted by permission of the publisher.

at colleges throughout the land, he gives keynote addresses incessantly, he is referred to as one of the most important people on the contemporary academic scene. The young professor can do nothing more profitable for his career than carefully observe and emulate. To such a young man (or woman) are these remarks addressed, as an aid in the imitation of the con man's techniques on the road to the heady success which crowns his effort.

Your first step is to establish yourself. The genuinely gifted have already been excluded from the audience, so the objective is to become a "leading thinker," not in the obvious way, by doing leading thinking, but in the infinitely more difficult way of mental legerdemain. It is not so difficult as it may at first glance seem.

Achieving status is a basic requirement. For the beginner, perhaps the easiest method is name dropping. You must speak in public at every opportunity, and include in every talk highly personalized references to important thinkers. It is of great help to insert, parenthetically and with a faint air of apology, intimate anecdotes about the great men. For example, you might use the following: "As Toynbee has said—Arnold Toynbee [lingering affectionately over "Arnold"] has the most amusing habit of pulling on his left ear when he is grappling with a particularly vexing concept. . . . " It may well be that the ear pulling is really done by Michael Shayne, the detective, whom you know about from reading Brett Halliday's murder mysteries, and that you have never been close enough to Toynbee even to know whether he has a left ear. But the impact on the audience is incredible.

As you become more advanced, you can embellish your status by interspersing your talk with hints that the foundations are after you. "When we work out the details of the grant, we will be able to investigate this problem fully," does very nicely, for example. You can feel that you have really mastered this technique when the foundations really come after you, and really offer you grants. Inevitably, they will.

Another prerequisite for establishing yourself is to be highly versatile. Arrange with your home institution for an appointment to the department of general studies, or to the committee on curriculum integration, or some such ephemeral area, and never let anyone know what your field is. With this start, you will be able to become an authority in almost all the branches of learning.

The most efficient practitioners usually settle upon one theme, or gimmick, and devote themselves almost exclusively to its exploitation. This has the further advantage of eliminating much study and preparation; you can give the same talk over and over, in various places. Obviously, the choice of your theme is extremely important, and if you select an interdisciplinary vehicle, you will have done a great deal toward establishing your own versatility or universality.

The only other principle is that the more sweeping your vehicle is, the better chance of success you have. "The philosophy of space utilization and its impact on curricular research," for example, could serve as both field and title, and could last almost indefinitely. The philosophy of anything seems especially good, in fact, perhaps because no one seems to know what philosophy really is, and almost no one is willing to admit his ignorance.

Even more awe inspiring, and if possible more interdisciplinary, is the theology of something or other. This, of course, will limit your scope, since most colleges shy away from anything so medieval sounding. But it has its advantages, too; and if you are willing to restrict yourself pretty much to the church-related schools, you could found a fine career upon something like "The Theology of Group-centered Leadership."

Another effective method of attaining versatility is to refer periodically to esoteric items from vividly diverse fields. Post-Newtonian physics, cultural anthropology, and non-Euclidian geometry are especially fertile areas in this regard. Any address in which you mention curved space, fatting sheds in which South Sea Islanders imprison brides-to-be so that they can become obese before the wedding, and parallel lines which meet at infinity, is certain to overwhelm a convention. And you can use the references to prove anything at all, since few of the audience will know what you are talking about, and all will pretend that they do.

Finally, though this touch does require experience and the greatest finesse, versatility can be established by deference to specialists in the different disciplines. At a small college, for instance, the master con man might say: "Of course, your Dr. Jorgensen could explain this much better than I." You found out beforehand that Dr. Jorgensen heads the geology department; here you identify yourself with the institution and manifest a greatness of soul that only a true prophet could have. For, after all, everyone is acutely aware that, though you do not happen to be a geologist, you know much more about geology than poor old Jorgensen. So everyone turns to smile at him, thinking the while that your humanness virtually outshines your brilliant intelligence.

With your status and versatility solidly erected, you are ready for the next step in establishing yourself. This is to be a pioneer, to be on the forward, cutting edge of human thought, so to speak. Get ahead of the crowd, and they will never catch you.

For this purpose, have new information at hand at all times. Refer, for example, to very recent experimentation which more or less destroys all the concepts of classical aerodynamics; if anyone asks for references, simply tell him that the studies have not yet been translated. And consistently mention obscure books, even nonexistent ones. Thus you can overwhelm an audience by remarking, "As Sidney Wellenbach says in his new book, *The Charismatic Effect of Intermolecular Hypostatization*—really well worth the time and effort you may have to spend on it. . . . ." The real master will occasionally add the embellishment of having the book due off the presses next month. Sid sent you a copy ahead of time, and "watch for it."

It is also important that you be about to write a book yourself, when your thinking is crystallized. In general, it is better not to have published before, since this would lay your mediocrity bare for examination at leisure, and it is crucial to keep moving fast. But if you are going to publish momentarily, the progressive quality of your thought is emphasized.

But the most important phase of being a pioneer is to make your vehicle, or gimmick, an entirely new idea. And the more outlandish the idea, the more successful you are likely to be; the career of the academic con man is not for the fainthearted. Take any simple and homely item, and you can build your future upon it. Take haircuts. "The determinative influence of tonsorial mores upon cultural and industrial patterns of the past two centuries" is precisely the kind of stupefying theme you need, although, upon reflection, it seems slightly too intelligible to be really appropriate. However, that is the general idea. If your gimmick is sufficiently preposterous, you will be able to promote it by implying that your audience is psychologically incapable of absorbing it. "It is too *new*, don't you see? We have to go beyond the level of thinking to which we are conditioned by our civilization." The "we" is a nice touch. Actually, you *are* beyond that dull old level of thinking, and they are not. You know it, and they know it; but they will admire your humility.

Once you have established yourself, once you are a leading thinker, and versatile, and a pioneer, there remains only the relatively simple task of maintaining the delusion by impressing your audience. The key is to keep battering them and to keep shifting rapidly. One cardinal rule is to be obscure—consciously, conscientiously, and constantly obscure. The number of people who can distinguish between obscurity and profundity is startlingly, and for your purposes fortunately, small. You should develop a jargon of your own; either make up words yourself or use ordinary words in entirely new and unclear meanings. One proponent, for example, coined the word "civization"; his whole talk was about his new word and how it differed from the word "civilization." Typists invariably ruined his articles by substituting the real word for his unreal one. And this confused the whole issue. And so on. This is the same kind of misdirection which the manual magician achieves by having as his assistant a shapely young woman in a scanty costume. This man never even had to get to the point of defining "civization."

Above all, never organize a talk. This is fatal. Logic is your mortal enemy; and you must always leave your audience in a befuddled state.

Besides being obscure, you must be dogmatic. The goal here is a very humble infallibility; try to catch the gentle omniscient tone of a kindergarten teacher. Preface every sixth or seventh sentence with "I am convinced that." The personal element stresses at one time your humility (even though you speak as the repository of truth, you present it as your opinion), your pioneering (you alone are convinced because the rest of the world has not yet caught up with you), and your superiority (you disdain the techniques of the ordinary thinker, such as supporting your position with evidence).

For these effects, an accent helps immeasurably. "I am *conweenced*" is terribly impressive. However, if you were born in Oklahoma, you may find it impossible to develop the desired indeterminate but vaguely European speech impediments. In that event, at least use foreign expressions regularly, especially Greek. As for pronouncing them, remember that what counts is not accuracy but confidence.

Finally, be patronizing. Mention sources no one has ever heard of, and pretend that you think everyone has read them. Mumble a few lines of verse and add, "Prufrock, of course." Never translate your foreign expressions. Here you are acting as though your audience were educated; were they to remonstrate, they would simply prove what you knew all along, that they are illiterate. Your position is impregnable. And what better way is there to close your talk than, "As Xenophon said, ἐντεῦθεν ἐξελαύνει τρεῖς σταθμοὶ ἐπὶ τὸν πόταμον." You don't even have to know what it means. The few people left in the world who are learned enough so that they do know that it means "from there they went three stadia to the river" do not come to the sort of meeting at which you will be speaking. And even if one of them should wander in accidentally, rest assured that anything from Xenophon is music to his ears. And rare music indeed; he is on your side.

All of this is a very demanding program. To follow it, you will need dedication and discipline of the highest order. But the rewards are great. For those equal to its rigors, the life of the academic con man offers an international reputation, travel, adulation, and a steady and substantial income. For those who persevere, there will ultimately be a very high-salaried job in government or industry, as an expert on communicational effectiveness, interpersonal relationships, and the best use of human resources. What more could life give you?

part iv

The secondary school program

*What knowledge is of most worth? What skills, knowledges, and
attitudes should students learn in my class? What should I teach?
These are questions which all teachers have faced. Arriving at
answers demands the wisdom of a Solomon, yet these questions
must be answered daily. How does the serious student of education
determine what his subject matter should be and, with others,
what the program of the school will be?*

*Anything which is learned is the result of experiencing, that is
doing something. Learning does not result from merely the method
of doing; neither will content alone produce changed behavior.
An educational experience is the result of a unique interaction of
content and method, the what and how of teaching. Both the
inseparability of content and method and the organizational
convenience of considering them in separate sections, as this book
does, are illustrated in the following excerpt from Dewey's*
Democracy and Education:

*When a man is eating, he is eating food. He does not divide
his acts into eating and food. But if he makes a scientific
investigation of the act, such a discrimination is the first thing
he would affect. He would examine on the one hand the
properties of the nutritive material, and on the other hand,
the acts of the organism in appropriating and digesting. Such
reflection upon experience gives rise to a distinction
of what we experience (the experienced) and the experiencing—
the how. When we give names to this distinction we have*

subject matter and method as our terms. There is the thing seen, heard, loved, hated, imagined, and there is the act of seeing, hearing, loving, hating, imagining, etc. This distinction is so natural and so important for certain purposes, that we are only too apt to regard it as a separation in existence and not as a distinction in thought (pp. 195–196).

With this distinction in mind, we are free to consider the content and organizational ingredients of teaching-learning experiences.

The beginning teacher may feel that the author of his pupils' textbook was forced to make content decisions and that these decisions are good enough to determine the subject matter which his students should learn. Other teachers may delegate content selection to the principal, the supervisor, or a master teacher. Teachers who abdicate their responsibility for content selection are mere technicians, not professionals, for they forsake the creative role of designing learning experiences and adopt a routine application of techniques to packages of subject matter.

Part IV contains a series of papers centering around the foundations, issues, status, and problems of the programs of secondary schools. They are not specific how-to-do-it articles but deal with questions in their broader and more scholarly context. The reader, with the help of teachers and fellow students, must assume the task of deducing his specific guidelines for action from these more general presentations. This is the role of the professional: to consider data and explanatory theory, to define general principles of action, and to apply these principles with reasoned regard for the uniqueness of the precise situation with which he deals.

Putting first things first is a necessary prerequisite for efficient action. Fischer, in "The Priorities Question in Education," addresses himself to the queries: (1) Which of the purposes and needs of our society will the school be expected to serve? (2) How shall we distinguish between the peculiar functions of the school and those of other agencies? (3) With the time and resources at its disposal, in what order of emphasis will the school undertake its tasks? The thoughtful reader will be interested in the way Fischer relates schools and society, as well as in his concept of the teacher's role in this interactive process. A teacher must constantly seek to clarify

*instructional purposes and to ascertain the social desirability of what
he is teaching. Since the teacher serves both the public and his own
conscience, he must decide whether his lessons reflect current social
values or will seek to improve the ways in which people live. The
teacher, consequently, becomes a student of society.*

*Because of the proddings of pressure groups, the pleas of
subject-matter specialists, and the problems of providing education
for all, it is increasingly difficult for the public schools to develop
and maintain curricula which are well balanced and effective. Sand's
"Six Basic Issues in Determining What to Teach" poses questions
which must be answered before intelligent curriculum planning can
take place and indicates some answers. Does Sand's statement to
teachers that "a body of knowledge acquired in the conventional
way by a college graduate of 1961 is likely to be largely inadequate
by 1968 and, by 1985, quite obsolete" apply to professional as
well as substantive knowledge? What education does a teacher need
in order to be able to make the decisions delineated in this article?
The reader may want to check the periodical literature for further
reports from Project Instruction, a current and continuing major
undertaking of the National Education Association.*

*The third selection, Alberty's "Should the Modern Secondary
School Curriculum Be Experience-centered?" makes a case for the
inclusion of more firsthand experience in the secondary school
program. Can the reader recall from his own learning experiences the
roles played by vicarious and direct experiences? How does a teacher
determine an appropriate balance between them? Would it be
fruitful to postulate the probable effects of a number of approaches
to teaching a given objective? Perhaps in order to test Alberty's
hypothesis we should actually try these various approaches. Might
the reader agree with Alberty's description of the problem and
disagree with his proposed solution?*

*"Curriculum Decisions and Provision for Individual Differences"
calls for more thorough thinking on the part of teachers about their
objectives. Herrick illustrates how the teacher's perception of what
he is to teach affects his ability to accommodate differences among
students. The reader would benefit from (1) identifying objectives
which might reasonably be his as a teacher, (2) projecting potential
organizing centers for pursuing these objectives, and (3) measuring*

his organizing centers against Herrick's criteria. The concept of using subject matter as an end and as a vehicle is worth serious consideration. The superior teacher will try to select subject matter so that he can accomplish several objectives with the same content. He will also guard against teaching one concept which will inhibit the learning of a second principle. Can the reader identify illustrations of learning experiences as ends, vehicles, concomitant learnings, and curriculum conflicts?

Is it legitimate for a teacher to plan a lesson so that it leaves a residue of feeling or attitude change in pupils, or should the teacher restrict his efforts to imparting knowledge? Gould's discussion of "The Teacher's Impact on the Curriculum" is likely to produce an emotional as well as an intellectual reaction on the part of the reader, and this is consistent with his thesis. No one will deny that the teacher has a significant impact upon the curriculum of his classes, but much controversy arises concerning the real and desirable extent of this impact. Are algebra and history, for example, substantially the same regardless of who teaches them, or should courses be labeled "Whitehead I," "Whitehead II," and "Whitehead III"? What phases of a course of study are inviolate and what portions may be altered at will? Would the reader accept the oft-quoted phrase that teachers are free to use their own methods, but should not add to, modify, or omit specified content. The reader will enjoy Gould's clever sarcasm in the basic questions he raises.

The next three selections, "What Is a Comprehensive High School?", "The Secondary School Program of the Future," and "Education of Adolescents: 1985," contrast both implicitly and explicitly today's secondary schools with tomorrow's. They imply that school organization, as well as teacher and pupil personality, profoundly affects the curriculum. Have you considered what your high school education "added up to"? That is, what the residual impact of the institution was? Did classes build from preceding courses and relate to others in which you enrolled, or were some isolated, unrelated, and seemingly out of place? A secondary education is what a student has when he experiences the curriculum of a secondary school, and it is important that the curriculum is a meaningful whole. How does a teacher fit together the parts of a curriculum puzzle so that an integrated learning picture appears?

In "What Is a Comprehensive High School?" Gilchrist succinctly defines this type of school, which presently exists in a number of American cities. His portrayal represents a feasible ideal of many practicing educators. The reader will benefit from viewing the adequacy of this institution and its program in the light of his personal experience. Ways of ensuring that all students within a comprehensive high school get a comprehensive education and whether or not this is desirable might be considered. How does "comprehensiveness" affect a teacher's choice and use of subject matter?

Laughlin, in his paper "The Secondary School Program of the Future," discusses fifteen questions concerning trends in curriculum, organization, and administration of secondary schools. His predictions should be compared with those of Wiles in terms of feasibility and desirability. Will teachers do their best work with the kind of administrative leadership Laughlin believes is coming?

Wiles' revolutionary presentation shows a closer relationship between the nature of the thing to be learned and the method and organization used to facilitate learning. The four major categories of the school program should be analyzed and perhaps measured against other concepts of the function of secondary education. What appear to be the strengths and weaknesses of the curricular organization which Wiles proposes? How would this organization affect the teacher's role in content determination?

The reader might ask himself whether he has the courage to measure continually the effects of his daily teaching efforts. If pupil learning has not occurred, the teaching has not been successful. An examination score goes on the teacher's report card as well as on the student's. Obviously, a teacher must ascertain not only what pupils have learned, but also why some ideas have not been mastered so that he can vary his pedagogical strategies according to this analysis.

The concluding article in Part IV is Tyler's "How Can Effectiveness of Learning Experiences Be Evaluated?" This scholarly article discusses the need for evaluation, basic notions regarding evaluation, evaluation procedures, and using the results of evaluation. The careful reader will note significant differences between Tyler's theory of evaluation and what is generally practiced in secondary *schools. A serious student should profit from applying the principles explained to a series of lessons or teaching units of his own design.*

The educator has no more serious or crucial task than that of content selection and utilization. He must decide what portion of his teaching substance should be directly useful to students. He must determine whether some content which has survived the test of time is too important to be omitted from his classes. We will want to include knowledge which is essential to the pupil's understanding of the total discipline. How much attention should be devoted to subject matter in which students show a natural interest? The conflict between teaching what is and what ought to be presents an additional decision which affects the curriculum.

The necessity for building new learnings upon old ones dictates a sequential dimension to lesson planning and curriculum building. A teacher must know both the prior and subsequent competencies expected of his pupils. At the same time, he strives for utilization of knowledge by pupils, not for mere accumulation. The teacher must also know the level of abstraction with which his students can cope, so that he expects neither too much nor too little of them.

Planning the curriculum is further complicated not only by the necessity for determining what ideas to include or exclude, but also by the need for organizing what is to be taught into content both for the general education program (i.e., the required program, or what is needed by all and therefore required of each) and for the specialized education program (i.e., the elective program, or what is needed only by some because of specialized interests and abilities). It is obvious that the experts do not agree, but each educator, with his personal conscience and professional obligation, must arrive at justifiable decisions. In doing so, he must utilize all that he knows concerning the objectives and setting of education, the students he teaches, the methodological science of his profession, and curriculum theory, such as that expressed in the following selections.

chapter 29

The priorities question in education

John H. Fischer

The question of priorities in education is new only in the sense that all the important questions must be faced anew by every generation. Some years ago the problem of purpose in education was put this way:

> All people do not agree in those things they would have a child learn . . . from the present mode of education we cannot determine with certainty to which men incline, whether to instruct a child in what will be useful to him in life, or what tends to virtue, or what is excellent; for all of these things have their separate defenders.

That was Aristotle's summary of the matter. Twenty-three hundred years later "these things" still have their separate defenders.

But if the question itself is old, the context in which we now face it is unprecedented. More than ever before we depend upon our educational establishment not only to give us a steady and growing supply of experts and leaders but also to elevate the knowledge and competence of the whole people to the level required by the social, political, and technological conditions under which we live. It is this joint necessity, further complicated for us by the democratic ideal of equal opportunity for personal fulfillment, that now confronts us with a task that is truly new.

If our task were only to educate a minority to exercise social and political authority, as in ancient Athens, deciding what to teach and how to

From *Teachers College Record*, 61(October, 1959), 1–9. Reprinted by permission of the author and publisher.

rank the parts would be relatively easy. When to this purpose is added the broader but separate goal of teaching the common people the minimum skills of literacy and stopping there, the pattern from which European nations have only recently begun to depart, the priorities question is complicated somewhat, but the dual aims do not greatly conflict with each other.

Nor would it seem too difficult to establish satisfactory school programs in a culture where change comes slowly and the curriculum can be adapted only very gradually to new demands. If the monastery schools of the Middle Ages had curriculum committees, it is improbable that they felt any pressure to rush their reports.

Diversity Imposes Difficulties

But for us the problem is of a different order. "What tends to virtue" may not be too different now from what Aristotle would have approved; and in some respects, "what is excellent" continues to be permanent. But "what will be useful in life" seems to have changed a great deal in the past twenty-three centuries and with perhaps the greatest speed of all in the past twenty-three years.

At the same time that our culture has been growing more complex and the rate of change has been accelerating, both moral and material reasons have led us to extend the opportunity for education to more and more of our people. Indeed, so completely have we accepted the efficacy of universal education that we have gone beyond offering it as an opportunity and now compel virtually all of our children to attend school for eight or more years.

Consequently, the task assigned to the American school system exceeds in extent and diversity anything of the kind that has ever been attempted, much less accomplished anywhere in the world. To reach any sort of valid judgment on priorities within this far-flung structure and process, it is necessary to understand not only the present facts of the enormous diversity of our schools but also the social, political, economic, and philosophical origins of that diversity.

The present state of our schools is not the result of any one law, agency, movement, or conspiracy. It represents, rather, the slow accumulation of institutions and patterns approved from time to time by various segments of our people and successively adopted by other segments, as merit was found in one innovation after another. Each new addition to the curriculum has been made because some group, somewhere, considered it sufficiently desirable or necessary to make it the object of pressure for a new priority. Thus we have added vocational agriculture, home economics, instrumental music, varsity athletics, driver training, family life education, laboratory science, and elementary Russian.

Now, faced with new concerns and anxious about our place in the world, we are not so confident as we once were that the curriculum is best designed by the simple process of continuous addition. But the anxiety which stimulates us to reexamine our schools can hardly be said to improve the rationality of our thinking about them.

When we became disturbed because the Russian government managed its affairs so as to place a satellite in orbit several months ahead of ours, a number of well-publicized Americans concluded, by a curious sort of logic, that the later date of our own launching was determined not by administrative decisions but by a shortage of scientists; and that this condition was due to current weaknesses in the elementary and secondary schools. Some of us, continuing in confusion, then insisted that to beat the Soviets we should imitate the curriculum in which at that very time the Russians were preparing drastic changes because it was not meeting the requirements of a diversified economy and a varied population.

The place of foreign languages in the lower schools is another issue on which excitement compounds our confusion. So disturbed are we by the scarcity of Americans who are fluent in a second language that we ignore the facts from which correction must begin. We forget that until the end of World War II only a small percentage of Americans met even once in their lives the need to use a language other than their own. Many of these people—the children of immigrants—had actually been bilingual in their early years but had deliberately abandoned the foreign tongue as useless to them. A second fact which the critics overlook is that it is easier to get along with only English in many parts of the world than it is to decide which language is likely to prove most useful to a ninth-grade boy who has not yet the faintest notion of what he will do with his life.

This illustration is no argument against strengthening our language programs, for it is obvious that we badly need to improve what we are doing. To criticize any program, however, without reference to the context in which it was developed is not only pointless and irresponsible but retards improvement in the current context.

Old Schools and New Demands

Another example of criticism unencumbered by historical reference is the proposal that our elementary and secondary schools return to the simpler academic regimen that characterized the schools of the 1890's. No one could make such a suggestion seriously if he had considered in even the briefest fashion the development of education in this country. The obvious truth is that we could easily have retained the schools of the nineties. We had them at a time when the schools of education had not yet been created and the national professional organizations were in no position to dominate the educational scene as they are now accused of doing. Despite the absence of any organized force, one by one the schools of the good old days disappeared from the scene for the most natural of causes. They simply were not good enough to keep. Sixty years ago, when only the leading edge of the wave of twentieth-century industrialization had reached us, we saw that schools which offered only a single classical curriculum and which served largely as a selective screen for higher education could not meet the needs of the United States.

Such schools fell short in two major respects. They prepared no more than a minor fraction of young people for the roles they were to occupy in adult life; and they failed to offer opportunity for self-development to any but those with strong academic talents and interests. The American people wanted, in addition, schools that would prepare their children for the social and technological world in which they were to live, and schools in which the vast numbers of children not destined for professional or scholarly careers would find acceptance, opportunity, and if they earned it, success. The trouble with the old schools lay not in what they did, for much of it was good, but in what they failed to do to meet the new tasks laid upon them.

The shift away from the relative rigidity of nineteenth-century schools has not been pure profit. Modern schools, too, are imperfect. They are less effective than they need to be; they occasionally waste time and effort; they sometimes emphasize the wrong things; and in other ways they reveal their human origin and management. But despite their shortcomings they represent conscientious, competent, and, on the whole, successful efforts to serve the needs of our people and our times, and to employ in those efforts the best that is known about the development of children and the encouragement of their learning. In contrast to the restrictive policies of their predecessors, the chief fault of many modern schools is their tendency to accept almost any responsibility, whether or not it contributes to the pupils' education, and often with little regard for the effect of the new function upon the school's previous commitments. Clearly the time has come for a more realistic reconciliation of our expectation of the school with its capabilities.

In reconsidering the system of priorities by which the schools are now governed—or we might better say, since there is no master control over all our schools by which any one school is governed—we shall do well to examine what we now consider most important. We must ask whether we wish to depart from the framework of values upon which the present arrangements are based. To be fully responsible, we shall have to examine also the needs to which the current curriculum is a deliberate, rational response, and decide whether the needs are still relevant, or whether they can be better met by a revised program. Unless we do these things we may find ourselves looking for the baby when we had meant to toss away only the bath. Simple subtraction will serve no better than simple addition as a quick answer to the curriculum question.

Perspective and Balance

Much of the discussion about educational priorities starts with the assumption that there is now no orderly ranking of purposes in the schools, and that the curriculum is but one vast buzzing chaos. Those who know the schools best, know better. The issue is not whether we shall have order or chaos, but rather on what basis we shall alter the order we now have.

To consider the issue intelligently, we can raise three related queries:

1. Which of the purposes and needs of our society shall the school be expected to serve?

2. How shall we distinguish between the peculiar functions of the school and those of other agencies?

3. With the time and resources at its disposal, in what order of emphasis shall the school undertake its tasks?

Regarding the relation of the school to our purposes as a people a great deal has been said, but rarely has the essence of the matter been put as clearly as by President John W. Gardner of the Carnegie Corporation in his Annual Report for 1958, in which he called education "the servant of all our purposes." He wrote:

Most Americans honor education, but few understand its larger purposes. Our thinking about the aims of education has too often been shallow, constricted, and lacking in reach or perspective. Our educational purposes must be seen in the broader framework of individual fulfillment. It is time now to insist that this larger framework be universally explored and understood.

In a sense this is an obligation we owe to those great shapers of the Western tradition who taught us the importance of individual fulfillment. They gave us the blueprints for a cathedral but a good deal of the time we insist on referring to it as a tool shed. Now, while the nation is re-examining its aims in education—now is the time to see our purposes in a larger perspective.

What we need first of all is a conception of individual development which far transcends any popularly held idea of education. Education in a formal sense is only a part of the society's larger task of abetting the individual's intellectual, emotional, and moral growth. Learning for learning's sake isn't enough. Thieves learn cunning and slaves learn submissiveness. We may learn things that constrict our vision and warp our judgment. What we must reach for is a conception of perpetual self-discovery, perpetual reshaping to realize one's goals, to realize one's best self, to be the person one could be.

This is a conception which far exceeds formal education in scope. It includes not only the intellect but the emotions, character, and personality. It involves not only the surface but deeper layers of thought and action; it involves adaptability, creativeness, and vitality. And it involves moral and spiritual growth.

Any sound appraisal of American education in the light of our national purposes must consider the extent to which good schools are available to all of our children. High-quality schools are of value only to those children who can attend them. In a nation whose cornerstone of policy is the principle of equal opportunity, an imperative dimension of any public service, and most especially of education, is equality of access.

That so many of our children now fail to attain the development of which they are capable is not only a denial of their birthright but a grievous loss to the nation. In many instances this tragedy is directly due to the absence of good schools, but in other cases boys and girls who live within a short distance of some of the finest educational opportunities fail to profit from them. We must see to it as a nation that good schools are within reach of every child, but we can ill afford to stop there. We must also do everything we can to improve the conditions under which our disadvantaged young people now live, conditions which so warp their lives that they are inhibited even from looking up and reaching out, much less using the opportunities that others accept as a matter of course.

Part of the responsibility for such work rests in the school itself, but the larger part must be assumed by the home, the church, the playground, the law enforcement bodies, the health authorities, and the social agencies. Only as the school and these other forces learn to work together will our most grievously underprivileged children find the help they need or the willingness to accept it.

We come then to the second query: How shall we distinguish between the peculiar functions of the school and those of other agencies?

Surely there is no need to argue that our schools are seriously overloaded with tasks that have been urged upon them, often for no better reason than that the school has readily at hand a captive mass of children. Virtually everything the schools are asked to do seems useful and important to someone. From producing state championship teams (primarily, of course, for the character development of the boys) to supporting the Community Chest and buying United States Savings Bonds (always to teach citizenship of course, and never to increase the volume of collections), the schools are asked continually to extend the boundaries of their responsibility.

Concerning Our Educational Energy

Can any logically defensible lines be drawn to define the proper function of the school? If we are right in the view that the school is essential to our individual and collective welfare, that it should be protected and improved, then it must follow that its power should be neither wasted casually nor committed deliberately without careful consideration of the purpose being served. The resources of the school are so important to us that we can afford to use them only with discriminating economy on those tasks which belong peculiarly to the school and cannot be done as well by any other agency.

If we must be entertained by teen-age basketball teams and if we need to use other than normal financial channels to sell government bonds, means and agencies will doubtless be found to see that these things are done. It is extremely unlikely, however, that any other community group will be able or willing to teach reading or algebra when the school runs out of time.

In a world in which the systematic development of intellectual potential becomes increasingly urgent, and the orderly acquisition of knowledge, competence, and understanding is important for every child, we must be zealous to reserve the school's time and strength for what it can do best. For learning those things which require organization and practice, or where orderly observation and collection of data are involved, or where vicarious experiences must be carefully planned, or for lifting the student to experiences of a higher level than he would normally attain, or where the guidance of a specialist is needed to interpret experience and bring out its full meaning—for any such activity, the appropriate locale is certainly the school. It was for purposes like these that schools were devised, and until we find another institution better equipped to serve them, we had better give them the priority they deserve when we rank our expectations of the school.

But when we have settled on what the school should do, there remains the whole area of the procedures to be used. Rarely in discussing the problem do we remember that the means employed for any purpose is always and inevitably the nearer side of the goal we ultimately reach. When we choose our method we largely determine our objective.

It is one thing, however, to set a goal and another to have the pupil sense it, accept it, and reach it. The only real knowledge any pupil can have of his teacher's purpose for him is his actual experience in the classroom—what the teacher does to, for, or with him. The English teacher may purport to develop an appreciative understanding of poetry, but if his method of presentation leaves the student with only a clear knowledge of metrical patterns and no awareness of imagery, the teacher's purpose, for all the pupil knows, was concerned solely with meter.

Method and the Individual

In a world increasingly caught up in collective activity which more and more tends to submerge the individual, it is essential that in its procedures the school stand firmly on the side of individuality. But if we believe this we shall have to manage our schools and our classrooms to make this intention clear and to bring our purpose to life in the consciousness of our pupils. It will have to be accomplished not so much by the subjects we teach as in the methods we use, in the ways we touch the lives of children one by one.

For this reason, when we consider the assignment of priorities in education we may not restrict ourselves merely to fixing time allotments for the respective subject fields. Such allocations must be made, to be sure, but at least equal attention must be given to the ways we deal with children and young people. There can be little doubt that some of the more precious qualities of artist teachers are either innate or acquired quite aside from formal education. But it is equally true that no one is born with a knowledge of effective teaching technique, or the ways to motivate an intelligent boy whose only interest in school is to escape it. Nor are such competencies gained as by-products of a liberal education, any more than proficiency in surgery, engineering, or the law is so acquired.

For able pupils who have been favorably oriented toward formal learning from infancy, technical proficiency in their teachers is helpful but it is rarely a critical element in their lives. Such children come to school predisposed to learn and often need little more than opportunity. The extra benefit they derive from superior teaching should not be minimized, but high-quality instruction is for them an extra blessing rather than the basic necessity it is to others.

It is children who lack either ability or academic ambition for whom the absence of an effective teacher can mean educational disaster. Until we realize the fundamental importance of this relationship we shall achieve neither universal education in any genuine sense nor the conservation of our intellectual resources that is so urgently required in this country. In our scale of educational priorities a preeminent position must be given to the cultivation of the highest possible degree of professional teaching competence.

The third query I raised was this: With the time and resources at its disposal, in what order of relative emphasis should the school undertake its tasks?

Every good school, every good teacher, faces the problem of selecting from all the things that could be done those that are most worth doing. A good deal of the difficulty in which we now find ourselves stems from the fact that more and more work has been assigned to the school without a commensurate increase in the time available for its accomplishment.

We have, happily, made some progress by adding to the manpower of the school specialists and assistants to supplement and aid the teacher. Physicians, nurses, counselors, stenographers, dieticians, classroom and playground aides are now regular members of the school staff in many places, and these additions are all to the good. They make possible more kinds of attention to a particular child and they relieve the teacher of part of his burden. But extra help alone is not the answer.

The Personal Aspect

A parallel problem is the schedule of the child himself, which is even less elastic than the schedule of the school or the teacher. As we increase the activities of the individual pupil we must, if we are thoughtful of his welfare, ask at what point further additions to the quantity of his experiences begin to diminish the quality of his learning and the healthfulness of his development.

The priority question is no less important in the time table of the individual student than it is in the curriculum as a whole. It is a rare principal who has not been troubled by the effect on a particular student of the schedule conflict between band rehearsals and English classes, or the dilemma of arranging museum trips for the child who needs remedial reading quite as much as he needs to know about colonial furniture.

Wise and efficient use of the school's unique resources depends largely upon decisions that must be made separately in each school. Conditions and capabilities vary so widely in the American educational establishment that even in the face of overriding common problems and pressures it is not possible to issue from any central control point directives that will be equally valid in every local district, or even in all the schools of a single district. Although no school may properly disregard the general conditions to which universal education is expected to provide a suitable response, neither can it ignore its obligation to deal with peculiar local situations. Most of us know schools in which the first things to be done for children are to bathe and feed them. To argue that these services should not take the school's time or energy might be an interesting academic exercise, but not for the teachers who face those boys and girls in all their bitter poverty and shameful neglect. In such a school the priority question is answered in the only way it can be, by responsible humanity and common sense.

The question must be answered differently, of course, in the upwardly mobile suburban community where overambitious parents insist that 90 per cent of the students be in the top 10 per cent of the class, and simultaneously participate in half a dozen extracurricular activities.

In yet another form it arises in the town with little to boast of but its high school football team, and where scoreboard statistics rank higher in public esteem than college board results.

Every community must make its own decisions about how it will use its schools, and having made its decision, it must be ready to live with the consequences. But the outcome will turn less on the topics and the timing involved than it will on the values by which the policies have been set and the purposes toward which they are oriented.

No community accepting moral responsibility for the future welfare of its children can claim full freedom to choose its own curriculum. The conditions of modern life affect all parts of our country, and since no local school board has the power to alter these common challenges, the responses of all our schools must to a large extent be similar. No child can fairly be denied an adequate opportunity, for example, to learn to read, to become acquainted with the history of his country, or to discover the rising importance of science in the modern world. Any school which in the name of local autonomy denies its children such instruction in the basic fields of knowledge denies them the essential basis for participation in civilized life. It deprives them, moreover, of equal opportunity with other children and directly diminishes the nation's strength.

The Teacher's Role

Since it is fundamental with us that schools be controlled locally and by the popular will, it is pertinent to ask what role should be played by a teacher who is deeply concerned that the best use be made of the school and all it represents.

The work of the school being set by the society its serves, the teacher is, in one sense, a servant of that society. But the school is also the best hope the society has for its own improvement, for the school is its principal instrument by which it can release and develop the potentialities of individuals. The teacher, as a specialist in the art of education, must therefore be far more than a servant. He is also by virtue of his profession a leader, a counselor, and custodian of a particularly precious component of the culture.

The teacher has accordingly a moral obligation to his profession, and as a member of that profession, to the public, to give the best advice he can on the wise employment of educational processes and institutions, on the selection of purposes and the means to carry them out, on the setting of priorities and the appraisal of results.

The teacher's authority is of course limited. No one is required to accept what he says, for his words are worth no more than his wisdom, and his proposals have power only when his ideas are sound and persuasive. But if it is true, as many now believe, that this country is entering a period of educational renascence, and that beyond setting new priorities within our schools, we are about to give a new level of priority to the whole educational enterprise in our society, it is inevitable that the voice of the teacher will be heard in the land and heeded.

To the extent that the teachers who speak are informed and articulate, wise and humble, courageous and temperate, this will be a very good thing indeed.

It may help produce schools in which children who explore the atom and follow the astronaut can learn also "what is excellent" and "what tends to virtue," and so come ultimately to see for themselves that of all the things that can be learned, the long-lived values are truly the most "useful in life."

chapter 30

Six basic issues in determining what to teach

Charting a course for the instructional program

Ole Sand

Much has been written and spoken about plans for living in the *world* of tomorrow. Because science is turning the spotlight on history's greatest discoveries, we are now forced to plan for an existence in the *universe* of tomorrow. We are constantly confronted with new concepts demanding mastery even before old ones have been fully explored. Never before in man's history have dynamic forces of change spun with such incredible speed.

Upon every segment of our civilization new responsibilities are placed, but especially do the burdens rest heavily upon those who must help children prepare for their roles in the unfolding drama upon which the curtain has already gone up. At this critical moment in human history, no one can say with certainty whether we are at the brink of a colossal disaster or whether this is, indeed, mankind's shining hour. Certain it is that our profession—the profession of teaching—faces its greatest challenge.

From *Chicago Schools Journal*, published at Chicago Teachers College, 43 (January, 1962), 170–177. Reprinted by permission of the publisher.

New NEA Project Spotlights Instruction

As one means of meeting the challenge, the National Education Association has established The Project on the Instructional Program of the Public Schools.[1] It is the latest of several major NEA efforts designed to upgrade the quality of and give direction to American public education. Notable among other projects during the past half century have been the Seven Cardinal Principles of 1918, *The Purposes of Education in American Democracy* of 1938, and the recently published *The Central Purpose of American Education* of the Educational Policies Commission. The NEA feels that as the major representative of the organized profession it has a responsibility to state its conclusions at a time when so many other voices are being heard with varying definitions of what constitutes a sound program of elementary and secondary education.

Seek to Identify Problems and Indicate Solutions

The work of the Project can be summed up as follows: It has identified and clarified the concerns, the problems, the issues facing the schools as they seek to improve the quality of instruction. It is now in the process of analyzing these problems, drawing upon data from appropriate sources attempting to interpret the data in terms of clearly formulated values. Criteria are being developed for the solution of the problems, indicating possible approaches to their solution and suggesting the consequences of one or another approach.

The Project will recommend a course of action and take a position on certain issues; on others it will propose methods of inquiry by which local schools can make their own decisions or take their own positions. Four major publications, five bulletins, and some action recommendations will emerge from the study. For each of the tasks performed, use is being made of the vast skills and experience of six groups of people—students, teachers,

[1] A special committee was appointed for the Project from recommendations made by the NEA Council on Instruction and others. The fourteen members of the Committee are: Melvin W. Barnes, superintendent of schools, Oklahoma City, Oklahoma (chairman); Thomas G. Pullen, Jr., state superintendent of schools for Maryland (vice-chairman); Sarah C. Caldwell, high school teacher, Akron, Ohio (member of the steering committee); William M. Alexander, chairman, department of education, George Peabody College for Teachers, Nashville, Tennessee; Hollis L. Caswell, president, Teachers College, Columbia University, New York; Joe A. Chandler, executive secretary, Washington Education Association, Seattle, Washington; Rufus E. Clement, president, Atlanta University, Atlanta, Georgia; Marion Cranmore, elementary school principal, Ann Arbor, Michigan; Carol Douglass, elementary school teacher, Gainesville, Florida; Robert J. Havighurst, professor of education, University of Chicago, Illinois; James D. Logsdon, superintendent, Thornton Township High School and Junior College, Harvey, Illinois; Philip H. Phenix, professor of education, Teachers College, Columbia University, New York; I. James Quillen, dean, School of Education, Stanford University, California; and G. Baker Thompson, county superintendent of schools, Media, Pennsylvania.

administrators, scholars, and researchers in the discipline of education, scholars in the academic disciplines, and informed lay persons.

Study Reveals Six Major Educational Issues

The Project initially conducted seven surveys and held three conferences to determine the major areas of concern to the schools and the people. On the basis of this evidence, it was found that the issues fall in two major categories: *Deciding What to Teach* and *Planning and Organizing for Teaching*. Two of the four volumes to be published by the Project will deal with these topics, but in the meantime individual teachers and local groups would do well to ponder six major issues identified in the first category. These are discussed below so that teachers might organize their thoughts and experiences to meet them on the local level, where so many of our educational policies and practices are decided.

Many current criticisms of the schools focus largely on what is taught or is not taught—as, for example, "soft" subjects dominate in the curriculum; students are not made to work hard enough; basic subjects like reading and mathematics are not taught effectively; there is a serious lag between what is known by scholars and what is taught; process has been over-emphasized while substance has been diluted.

Although both educators and lay people vary in their reactions to such criticism, all will agree that the demands of a rapidly changing world, and especially the international situation, give new urgency to the need for wise decisions about what to teach.

Six major issues, it appears now, fall under the topic of *deciding what to teach.*

Who Should Make Curricular Decisions?

Issue one is: Who should make the decisions? Under study in this regard are such problems as legal and extra-legal forces affecting decision making in education; the quest for functional distribution of decision-making power; and equating local control, needs, and standards with what some believe to be an increasing need for national goals, standards, and planning. The basic question is "What kinds of decisions should be made at what levels of our political structure?"

Pupils Must Learn Structures of Subjects

Issue two poses this question: What are the implications of recent studies on the nature and structure of knowledge? A colleague of mine in a recent address said:

Not so many years ago it was possible for a single man to encompass almost all known knowledge, if he worked at it. Today we struggle just to keep abreast with one or two fields. Specialization, or knowing more and more about less and less, is indeed with us, and will be so to an increasing extent for the foreseeable future.

What are implications for the explosion of knowledge for education? For one thing, the problem of selecting content is complicated considerably.

Dr. Robert Oppenheimer and Dr. Joseph Schwab have estimated that the duration of a revisionary cycle in a median science is about 15 years. Thus a body of knowledge acquired in the conventional way by a college graduate of 1961 is likely to be largely inadequate by 1968 and, by 1985, quite obsolete.

Inquiries suggest that a curriculum planned to assist the student to comprehend the structure and methods of a subject field can greatly improve the quality and quantity of learning. At one time, facts alone were stressed. Then we had an era of concepts and generalizations. Current thinking indicates that students need to learn the *structure* of a field so they can "hang on" the *concepts* and relate the facts to concepts and structure in a meaningful way.

The Project also is focusing upon four interrelated questions related to the structure of knowledge and ways of knowing:

1. Does early presentation of the structure of a field make specific content of the subject more comprehensible to the learner, as has been suggested? Does it enable him to retain specifics longer or relearn them more quickly and easily?

2. Does early teaching of the structure of the subject enhance the student's interest and motivation for learning in the subject, and encourage continued study of it after formal schooling is completed?

3. Is transfer of learning facilitated by teaching the structure of the subject?

4. How can learners be helped to evolve flexible structures for the various fields of knowledge? Can creative thinking be encouraged by helping learners evolve flexible structures for the subjects they study?

Recommendations Concerning New Frontiers of Knowledge

A series of recommendations concerning the implications of recent studies on the nature and structure of knowledge are in process of being formulated by the Project. Here are some tentative recommendations in this area.

Recommendation 1. School systems that have not already done so might consider studying the contributions of the academic disciplines to the instructional program and take necessary steps to bring appropriate substance to it.

Recommendation 2. The total range of educational goals should be taken into account in planning revisions of the school curriculum.

Recommendation 3. School staffs should examine the content of each part of their instructional program to determine that recent findings in the related academic disciplines are reflected.

Recommendation 4. The school program should utilize content and ways of presenting content that will contribute to the pupil's development of structured (organized) learning at a level appropriate to his maturity and ability.

Recommendation 5. Teachers, administrators, academic scholars, and specialists in the various disciplines of professional education should cooperate in experimentation to determine how the school can best help children and youth to learn structures for the various subject fields.

Recommendation 6. The current interest and research in teaching for creativity hold great promise and should be pursued with reference to various fields of learning as they are developed in the school program.

Digesting Findings of Major Subject Area Studies

Issue three is: How can the schools most effectively use the recommendations from large-scale national studies in subject areas? In some fields of study, the basic content has been fundamentally altered in the past fifteen years; in all fields, the quantity of knowledge has increased in geometrical proportion. To mention a few large-scale studies in certain content areas, there are the American Institute of Biological Sciences Curriculum Study; the Chemical Bond Study; the Joint Project of the American Council of Learned Societies and NEA's National Council for the Social Studies; the mathematics projects at the University of Illinois, the University of Maryland, and Yale; the National Task Force on Economic Education; and the Physical Science Study Committee.

The basic question is: How can a teacher make intelligent use of the recommendations from such a variety of sources? Some tentative recommendations being discussed by the National Committee might help to answer this question.

Recommendation 1. In planning for any curriculum area, the need for balance in the student's total school experience must be an overriding consideration.

Recommendation 2. The need for a well-articulated curriculum from the kindergarten through grade twelve in every subject area must be kept in mind in applying the recommendations of current curriculum projects.

Recommendation 3. In applying the proposals and course materials that have been developed by a special curriculum project, the school staff must keep in mind the purposes and the student groups with which the project was concerned.

Recommendation 4. Schools must not permit the concern for the college-bound student that has dominated most of the nationally oriented curriculum projects in the academic fields to cause neglect of the responsibility to provide functional education for all children and youth.

Recommendation 5. Opportunities for advanced study should be provided for teachers, to enable them to work effectively in developing courses that utilize new approaches and new content.

Recommendation 6. Some means should be devised to provide continuing coordination at the national level of the various independently financed special curriculum projects, study groups, and other programs which are seeking to influence—and are influencing—basic curriculum decisions in the public schools of the United States.

Adapting Curriculums to Heterogeneous Groups

Issue four is: How can the curriculum be adapted to various groups in the school population? In a recent address, James B. Conant said, "I submit that the existence in the slums of our large cities of thousands of youth, ages 16–21, who are both out-of-school and out-of-work is an explosive situation. It is social dynamite." The dropout, the handicapped, the gifted, the culturally deprived, all of these give evidence that the question of *what to teach* needs added the phrase *to whom.* American education has moved rapidly in the past five years to better educate the academically talented. While continuing this important gain, American education also needs to focus more attention upon the serious problem outlined by Dr. Conant.

What to Include, What to Exclude

Issue five concerns what should be included and excluded in the school curriculum. Because this issue, in my opinion, is one of the central ones, it will be examined here in some detail. Most people believe it is the school's responsibility to teach the so-called "tool" subjects, referring to English and literature, the sciences, mathematics, and social studies. Controversy arises concerning the arts, personal guidance, driver education, home-and-family living, and the like.

Decisions on this important issue of inclusion-exclusion must deal with two components of what to teach—behavioral change and content. Once we have decided what is clearly the responsibility of the school, we still have to decide what content is of most worth. Good schooling depends today, as it always has, on mastery of subject matter, the "hard stuff" of the curriculum.

Subject Matter Alone Is Not Enough

I support this contention unequivocally, although I believe that mastery of subject matter is valid only insofar as subject matter is used as a vital means of learning—a means to purposeful thinking, feeling, and acting. The major jobs of education are to war on ignorance, to prepare youth for a life of creativity and freedom as individuals and for intelligent participation in the affairs of society, including gainful employment.

Concrete standards should be applied in deciding "what to teach" just as the purchaser of an automobile applies certain criteria in making his decision (styling has highest priority, gasoline mileage ranks fifth). Let us suppose, for example, that there are pressures in a school for adding French, German, and Norwegian to the curriculum of the third grade, or to push physics and geometry down into the first grade. The problem might be approached in three ways.

First, assume the school should do whatever the public wants it to do and add these subjects. The result is the "creeping" curriculum: "Never have so many learned so little about so much." A second way to approach this problem is to say, "Fine! We will add these subjects if you will tell us what subjects to remove from the curriculum."

Criteria for Deciding What to Teach

A third, and the professional, way to approach the problem of what to teach applies criteria. To assess the worth of any *single item* of content or behavior, the item must be analyzed in terms of four criteria: desirability, attainability, feasibility, and clarity of meaning. In appraising the worth of a *set of objectives,* as contrasted with a single goal, there also are four criteria: priority, comprehensiveness, balance, and consistency.

In reaching a decision on a problem such as foreign language in the third grade, at least five data sources would have to be consulted and weighted according to their relevance in resolving this specific issue. These are human growth and development, the psychology of learning, social forces and trends, the disciplines, and the real situation in schools.

Finally, these data must be interpreted in the light of explicitly stated values, values relating to the good life, the good society, the good school, and the role of the school.

How Many Responsibilities Can the Schools Assume?

A particularly important problem concerns the role of the school *vis-à-vis* other social institutions, such as the home, the church, and the out-of-school club. To what extent should the school accept responsibility for things that are important but not specifically educational in the usual sense? The resolution of this issue requires decisions about the basic educational responsibilities to be assumed by each of the major institutions mentioned above.

Ralph Tyler has suggested useful criteria for determining what the school ought properly to provide. Briefly stated, they are (1) learning that is based substantially on the arts and sciences; (2) learning of complex and difficult things that require organization of experience; (3) learning where the essential factors are not obvious to one observing the phenomenon; (4) learning that cannot be provided directly in the ordinary activities of daily life; (5) learning that requires more purified experience than is commonly available in life outside the school; and (6) learning in which re-examination and interpretation of experience are essential.[2]

Establishing Priorities in School Offerings

Issue six poses the question: How can priorities and balance in the curriculum be established? Is the contemporary emphasis upon science, mathematics, and foreign language redressing a former imbalance or creating a new imbalance? What about the humanities and the social sciences? Should electives be considered the "curricular dessert" or a means of meeting individual needs? What is the place of guidance when using electives to provide a balanced program? Should certain individuals probably have an imbalanced program? Thomas Edison might very well have been an ordinary person if his program had been balanced. Had he had formal education, the school as it too often exists might have stifled his creativity.

One word of caution is in order. Decisions in a professional field like teaching that deal with both ends and means are never made on the basis of data alone. Value judgments are always in order. Decisions equal data plus values plus the possible. One task of the Project is to make explicit the values that are used in interpreting the data.

We do not propose to study a purposeful, human enterprise with ends that are consciously willed as we would study a natural process like photosynthesis. This has been the error of too many "scientific" studies of education in the past. We are attempting to collect the best evidence available. But we are sufficiently in tune with reality to know that many field decisions still are steps in the dark.

Base Local Action on More than Research

In the final analysis, it is not so much the instructional program itself but the context of movement and mood through which the program was planned that will be of primary value. The Projects publications will, I hope, be useful to schools, but even more important will be what the publications suggest to the reader when filtered through his own vision, when fused with his own experience.

The recommendations we make will not be empty, flat, or devoid of meaning if school faculties interpret our recorded experience in the light of their own minds, their own personalities, their own knowledge—so they can say with Ezra Pound, "nothing matters but the quality of the affection that has carved the trace in the mind."

[2] Ralph W. Tyler, "Emphasize Tasks Appropriate for the School," *Phi Delta Kappan,* November, 1958, pp. 73–74.

How to Test Present Practices for Validity

In the meantime, I would propose the following basic jobs for teachers and administrators to work on to make certain decisions on what to teach are wise ones:

Justify what you teach in terms of facts about your learners, both from the research in growth and development and from studies of your own students.

Justify what you teach in terms of social forces and values, the needs of your state and community, and the reality situation in your school and also in terms of new developments in the disciplines (concepts, generalizations, structure, methods of inquiry).

Back up what you teach in terms of values, your philosophy. Decide what is of most worth, what is necessary, what should be taught ("ought" questions). Be sure your statement of beliefs deals with the good life, the good society, the good school, and the role of the school.

Back up what you teach in terms of the psychology of learning, what can be taught, what is feasible.

Define what to teach clearly in terms of behaviors and content, and in terms of the means necessary to achieve the goals.

The National Education Association and the profession in general are, in the judgment of this observer, rapidly moving toward a primary concern for the improvement of the content and the quality of instruction in schools throughout this nation and the world. If we sometimes despair of the formidable task ahead "in a mechanized, anxious world overshadowed by the threat of impending doom," and ask ourselves what any individual, however enlightened, or any educational institution, however dedicated, can do, let us remember that there have been dark days in the past. There was a famous one in New England in 1780 when the sun scarcely appeared at all. Thousands of people took it for the end of the world. Among them were many in the Connecticut Assembly, in which Colonel Abraham Davenport was sitting. It was proposed that the Assembly adjourn. Colonel Davenport said, "The Day of Judgment is either approaching, or it is not. If it is not, there is no cause for adjournment. If it is I choose to be found doing my duty. I wish therefore that candles may be brought."

chapter 31

Should the modern secondary school curriculum be experience-centered?

Harold B. Alberty

Experience is one of the many words in the literature of professional education which is subject to differing and sometimes conflicting interpretations. Sometimes the word is used loosely in its general dictionary senses as meaning the sum total or a portion of the "conscious events" which compose an individual's life. Thus when we say that a particular student's high school experience was very unsatisfactory, we are referring to the general character of all of the things that happened to him in high school. On the other hand when we use the term, *experience curriculum,* we may mean a curriculum made up wholly of pupil-planned activities, regardless of the nature of the activities. Between these extremes, needless to say, there are literally dozens of interpretations. Obviously, before any discussion of experience as a basis for the high school curriculum can have much meaning, it is necessary to make clear the precise manner in which the term is used.

THE NATURE OF EXPERIENCE

This discussion takes as its point of departure, the concept of direct experience developed by John Dewey many years ago.[1] In this sense ex-

[1] See *Democracy and Education.* New York: The Macmillan Company, 1916, pp. 163–164.

From *Bulletin of the NASSP,* 33(April, 1949), 115–124. Reprinted by permission of the publisher.

perience always involves a dynamic interaction between an organism and his environment. It involves a *doing* or *trying*—and an *undergoing*. The organism is said to have had an experience when the connection between the *doing* and the *undergoing* is sensed. Thus mere activity is not experience. It is what results when the activity is interpreted in terms of the "return wave of consequences which flow from it." The mere activity of touching a hot stove is not experience; neither is the suffering of pain. But when the pain is understood as the consequence of touching the stove, then a meaning has arisen which serves as a control of future action. This meaning we call experience.

Vicarious Experience

We need also to distinguish between personal, direct, firsthand experience, and vicarious experience. By this term we refer to understandings gained by an individual through the direct experience of another person or persons. This ability to control behavior by capitalizing upon the experience of others is what makes civilization possible.

Illustrations

Perhaps brief illustrations will help to make the differences between these two types of experience clearer.

Direct, firsthand experience	Vicarious experience
1. Eliminating your "slice" in golf by trying out the various "grips" and "stances" and observing the effect on the direction of flight of the ball.	Reading about the cause of the slice from a book written by a professional golf player.
2. Canning a bushel of peaches by the cold-pack method.	Reading about the method in a book, or hearing it explained over the radio.
3. Participating as one of the actors in a Shakespearean play.	Reading the play—or seeing it produced.
4. Determining the conditions under which a body will float.	Studying Archimedes' principle from the physics textbook.
5. Raising tropical fish.	Reading a book about tropical fish.

These illustrations may appear to be elaborations of the obvious, but they do, in a simple manner, illustrate the difference between direct and vicarious experience. It will be shown later that both kinds of experience have a real place in the educative process.

THE ROLE OF DIRECT AND VICARIOUS EXPERIENCE

It would, of course, be absurd to argue that all learning in the secondary school should involve *only* direct, firsthand experience. To do so would be to ignore the value of race experience, and to refuse to capitalize upon the enormous capacity of mankind to learn from the experiences of others. Without drawing upon these important resources, there could be little progress from one generation to the next. Perhaps the early "progressive" movement erred in this direction.

On the other hand, the ability of human beings to profit by vicarious experience has led to the plausible conclusion that effective education can take place almost exclusively by means of a study of logically organized race experience in the form of subjects or fields of knowledge. The assumption is made that these systems of knowledge can be "mastered" by the student, quite apart from individual firsthand experience. As Dewey points out, facts and principles are uprooted from their place in individual experiencing and placed in a new organization quite unrelated to the ongoing life activities of the person to be educated. The evils of this program are too obvious to need enumeration. Without a doubt, the high school has suffered from this false conception of the function of vicarious experience.

How has the traditional high school attempted to bridge the gap between these two partial interpretations of experience? At the risk of overgeneralization, it may be said that logically organized subjects with little use of direct experience have been retained in the "academic" curriculum for the bright, college-bound student, while programs involving a large measure of direct experience have been introduced for those of lower mentality. This has led to a vicious dichotomy, which has been given support by a certain school of philosophic thought.

THE ISSUE DEFINED

The issue which we face today is not whether the school should utilize direct, firsthand experience *or* vicarious experience. Rather it concerns the problem of which type of experience should be regarded as central and basic. In the first case, the scope and sequence of learning activities will be determined by the problems, needs, and interests of the learner, and will be carried forward by means of firsthand experiences enriched by all available resources, including organized race experience, and the ongoing experiences of people in the immediate and wider community. In the second case, the scope and sequence of learning activities will be determined primarily by the logical arrangement of subjects or fields of knowledge, enriched by the student's personal experience at whatever points and to whatever extent seems appropriate to the teacher. The first plan, in the judgment of the writer, is appropriately called the *experience-centered* curriculum, the second the *subject-centered* curriculum.[2]

ARGUMENTS FOR AND AGAINST THE SUBJECT–CENTERED CURRICULUM

The subject-centered curriculum has, of course, the backing of tradition. It has resisted rather successfully the attacks of critics over a period of many years. It is the prevailing type of curricular organization of most courses in higher education which are depended upon for the training of teachers for our high schools. It is the prescribed pattern of certification of nearly all of the state departments of education. A very large part of all available materials of instruction is designed for use in the framework of a logically organized curriculum. Why does the approach have such vitality? The reasons are not difficult to find. Let us examine them briefly.

Logically organized subjects or fields of knowledge have been built up by the specialists drawing upon the tested knowledge of long lines of investigators extending far back into history. Thus they represent the "highest perfection of knowing." These organizations of the specialist make it possible to interpret new knowledge as it is discovered. Such new knowledge in a very real sense tests the system, for if it doesn't fit in, the system has to be changed. Thus the principle of relativity revolutionized modern mathematics and physics. In a similar manner, new discoveries in history or anthropology change previous interpretations of events. Thus, we have continuous modification of human knowledge in light of the discovery of new facts and principles. Why then, if one purpose of education is to transmit the heritage of the race and to provide tools by means of which the individual can understand and interpret his world, should not these organizations of knowledge be made the center of the curriculum of the adolescent? The scientific curriculum maker, through vocabulary studies, has struggled long and successfully in bringing the material within the range of ability of students—or at least of many of them. What is forgotten is that *the organization of knowledge has little or no relationship to the way in which learning takes place*. It tends to assume that learning is an additive process, rather than a continuous process of reconstruction of experience. Hence, what frequently passes for learning (changes in behavior) turns out to be sheer memorization of facts and information which fail to function in the life of the student and are soon forgotten.

Without any disparagement of the value to the student and to society of logical organization of subject matter, it may be pointed out that on-going life activities, the problems which youth face in our confused society, are

[2] This point of view is developed more fully by the writer in Reorganizing the High School Curriculum. New York: The Macmillan Company, 1947, Chaps. IV and V.

not ordinarily cast in the matrix of organized knowledge, but rather have their roots in the daily lives of people as they go about the normal processes of living. It would, therefore, seem only common sense to start with these processes of living, and draw upon organized knowledge, whenever such knowledge is helpful to the student in solving his problems and in weaving unity and consistency into his design for living.

It must be conceded that much has been done in recent years to introduce direct experience into the logically organized fields of knowledge, thereby minimizing the criticism advanced above. But the fact remains that the scope and sequence, by the very nature of the system, are determined in advance and out of relationship to the learner, his nature, and needs. This accounts for the search during the past two or three decades for types of curricular organization more related to the demands of modern living.

EXPERIENCE–CENTERED LEARNING IN PRACTICE

Fortunately there is a large body of successful practice, ranging over a period of fifty years, with the use of experience-centered activities. Dewey's account[3] of the work of his laboratory school at the University of Chicago set the pattern. In 1911, a start was made in the field of agricultural education. Previous to that date, agriculture was taught mainly from the textbook. The principles were *first* taught, after which the teacher demonstrated them either in the classroom or on the farm. Since the above date, agricultural education has successfully followed an experience-centered program in which the student learned through carrying on concrete firsthand projects, bringing to bear logically organized subject matter upon the problem which he faced. Since that time, due largely to the work of William Heard Kilpatrick and his followers, experience-centered activities have become common in the better elementary schools and in areas of the high school, such as the arts, and to a less extent in English and the social studies. Undoubtedly the trend toward this type of activity is on the increase, held back largely by the widespread acceptance of textbook teaching.

An Illustration

The literature of modern education abounds in illustrations of the experience-centered approach. Accounts of activities in community schools, work experience, field trips, and the like all bear witness of the success of such activities. One such activity, which was rather well evaluated, will be described briefly in order to indicate the nature of direct experience. A group

[3] *School and Society.* Chicago: the University of Chicago Press, 1900. For a stimulating account of the work and contributions of this school, see Harold Rugg, *Foundations for American Education.* Yonkers-on-Hudson: World Book Company, 1947, pp. 545–557.

of seniors from the Lincoln School of Teachers College[4] planned an extensive study of the Tennessee Valley Authority and other agencies in the South. The group spent several weeks in careful preliminary planning under the direction of teachers representing appropriate fields of knowledge. The class then visited rolling mills in Pittsburgh and coal mines in West Virginia. They interviewed leaders in the fields of government, management, and labor. They studied, through firsthand data, schools, settlement houses, power plants, and homes of workers. The experiences of the trip were carefully planned and evaluated. Dr. Raths sums up the results as follows:

> The evidence collected suggests that carefully planned, direct experience may result in clarifying the beliefs which students hold; it suggests also that greater allegiance to human values, firmer faith in democratic principles, and a more flexible outlook on life which considers solution of social problems as tentative and not arbitrary, are some of the desirable outcomes which may come from educational experiences similar to the West Virginia trip.[5]

It will be noted from the above description that firsthand experience was utilized as the basis for the activity. It provided the plan, the nature of the investigation, the evaluation. Organized subject matter and various types of vicarious experience were used to enrich the meanings which the students gained.

ARGUMENTS FOR AND AGAINST EXPERIENCE–CENTERED ACTIVITIES

What are the values and possible weaknesses of the type of activity which has been described above?

Experienced-centered activities seem to have the following advantages: First, such activities when cooperatively planned afford excellent opportunities for teaching democratic values, for they represent a normal life process carried on as a part of the actual environment in which the day-to-day activities of people take place. The full consequences of action in terms of group welfare are easily seen. Second, they are consistent with the dynamic and organismic character of the learning process. When students are engaged in carrying out a project which they have planned, and in which they have a significant stake, the physical, emotional, and intellectual aspects of behavior are all unified into a coordinated whole. Third, when the school-community environment becomes the focal point in learn-

---

[4] See G. Derwood Baker, "An Eleventh Grade Field Study: The Coal Industry," *Educational Research Bulletin,* XVII, pp. 173–188(October 19, 1938) and Louis Raths, "Some Evaluations of the Trip," *Educational Research Bulletin,* XVII, pp. 189–208(October 19, 1938).

[5] *Ibid.,* p. 208.

ing, the barriers which traditionally have separated the school and community tend to be broken down, and actual living becomes the subject matter of the curriculum. Finally, since the needs, problems, and interests of the students grow out of an interaction of the student and his environment, experience-centered activities provide a direct means of further development along these lines.

It has been argued that facts and principles learned in the matrix of application are not permanently learned and do not transfer readily to new situations. This argument has much to support it if the teacher is not sensitive to the problem of the necessity of guiding learning to facilitate transfer and application. Again it is argued that the student does not achieve a logical organization of knowledge. This would be true if organized race experience were not continuously utilized in solving problems, and if the teacher were not aware of the need to help the student systematize his knowledge. If teachers are aware of the problems of transfer and system-building and move intelligently to solve them, these arguments would not seem very potent. It should be recognized that, whatever the type of learning activities employed, transfer is not automatic, and there is no guarantee that the student will achieve a workable organization of knowledge. It has also been argued, with some justification, that direct experience is too time consuming. A vast amount of time may be used in carrying out an activity with very little resultant learning. Some of the so-called community schools, for example, have the students spend a great deal of time in routine work experience. A recent report boasts that the students milk fifty cows daily, and put up 15,000 quarts of fruit and vegetables annually. Even the most ardent advocate of work experience would be hard put to explain the educational value of these activities *after* the processes involved have been learned. The criterion of growth in understandings, skills, and attitudes must always be applied to any sort of direct experience. If it cannot meet this test, it cannot be justified as a part of the curriculum.

WHAT BLOCKS THE EXTENSION OF THE EXPERIENCE–CENTERED CURRICULUM

If the merits of the experience-centered approach to learning have been amply demonstrated by extensive successful practice, why hasn't the movement gained greater headway in the American high school? Why has it been applied only in piecemeal fashion? The answer, of course, is to be found in the prevailing conception of the high school curriculum and its organization. High school education consists largely in the mastery of sixteen more or less separate and discrete units of subject matter, defined in terms of time spent and ground covered. Even that part of the program which is designated as general education—education needed by *all* for effective citizenship in our democratic culture—turns out to be a series of specialized courses, for the most part organized and taught as bodies of subject matter, each one sequentially arranged. Thus by their very nature, logically organized subject matter takes precedence over direct experience. To provide for direct experience, the school sets up an elaborate program of extra-class activities—usually quite unrelated to the day-to-day task of covering ground. To help students to solve their problems, an organized guidance program is provided—again unrelated to the main business of amassing the required sixteen units of credit. These vital aspects of a good learning situation thus become insulated from the curriculum. As was pointed out earlier, the teacher may succeed in introducing a good deal of direct experience into his teaching, but the center of emphasis remains the same. What is needed, of course, is a rather drastic reorganization of the curriculum, and all too few schools are ready to move in that direction. The relatively slight impact of the Association's bulletin, *Education for All American Youth,* on the high school provides documentation for this conclusion.

In the specialized aspect of the conventional curriculum, the situation is much more encouraging. The leaders of home economics and industrial arts have largely abandoned the idea that in order to be respectable their fields must be made scientific, systematic, and logical, and have centered their programs upon direct experience. The fine arts have followed suit. Vocational fields have always been more or less experience-centered. Undoubtedly this trend will continue and will gradually influence the academic fields. However, unless a frontal attack is made, progress is likely to be slow, for conventional subjects have become thoroughly intrenched vested interests supported by administrators, the teachers, the students, the parents, the colleges, and, last but not least, by the publishers of textbooks.

MAKING A DIRECT ATTACK ON THE PROBLEM

The movement toward the development of a program of general education based upon the needs, problems, and interests of youth in our society was well under way when nearly all curricular experimentation was halted by World War II. Certain high schools had developed core—or social living—curriculums which knew no subject boundaries. Students from these schools had been successful in college.[6] The processes by which these schools changed their curriculums to provide more functional learning had been described rather fully.[7] Leaders in secondary education had developed the "know-how" to transform the secondary school. The present stirrings in centers all over the United States indicate that school people are resuming

[6] See Dean Chamberlin *et al., Did They Succeed in College?* New York: Harper and Brothers, 1942.
[7] *Thirty Schools Tell their Story.* New York: Harper and Brothers, 1943.

the task of curriculum reorganization. In spite of the lethargy of teacher-education institutions in preparing teachers for service in core curriculums, schools are finding it possible through workshops and other in-service programs to overcome the obstacles to curriculum reform.

The thesis of this paper is that the program in general education as defined above should be organized in terms of the problem areas most directly related to the common needs of youth rather than in terms of organized knowledge. From these problem areas, learning units should be developed cooperatively by teachers and students with activities centering largely upon direct, firsthand experiences, utilizing all available resources, books, movies, recordings, and the like to enrich these experiences. Such activities should be built upon the "unit of work" concept of the modern elementary school and should occupy about one-half of the student's time during the six-year span of the junior-senior high school. The teaching of separate subjects should be entirely abandoned, though the development of basic skills, understandings, and the systematization of knowledge should be stressed. General guidance and many so-called extracurricular activities would become integral aspects of the program.

Each school would need, of course, to study its own situation and plan its own program in terms of available personnel and material resources. In the beginning, the correlation of subjects might be all that could be reasonably attempted in some schools. Others might adopt a unified studies approach. Still others might move rapidly to the program suggested above.[8] The important point is that schools study the problem of a more experiential curriculum and move as rapidly as possible in that direction.

There have been many formulations of problem areas potentially valuable in a program of general education. These are of material assistance to the curriculum maker. As an illustration, the following statement is presented. Due to space limitations, only the major categories are given.

1. *Problems of School Living:* How can we get most out of our school experiences?

2. *Problems of Self-understanding:* How can we know more about ourselves?

3. *Problems of Finding Values by Which We Live:* What means most to us and why?

4. *Problems of Forming Social Concepts in Terms of the Democratic Ideal:* What is our responsibility (individual and group) in facing and helping to solve the social problems of our community, state, and nation?

---

[8] For analysis of these approaches, see the writer's article entitled: "Developing a Curriculum That Meets the Needs of Junior High School Youth," *Bulletin of the National Association of Secondary-school Principals,* Vol. 31 (April, 1947), pp. 69–81.

5. *Problems of Employment and Vocation:* What are our opportunities for employment in the community now?

6. *Problems of Using and Conserving Natural Resources:* How can our natural resources be best developed and used?

7. *Problems of Education in American Democracy:* Why is education an important factor in our lives as citizens of a democracy?

8. *Problems of Constructive Use of Leisure:* How can we become more interesting and better adjusted people through extending individual and group interests?

9. *Problems of Family Living:* How can family living make for happier individuals?

10. *Problems of Communication:* How can we express our ideas more clearly to others, and how can we understand better the ideas of other people?

11. *Problems of Democratic Government:* How do we share in government in a democracy?

12. *Problems of Community and Personal Health:* How can we achieve and maintain healthful living for ourselves and all others in the community?

13. *Problems of Economic Relationships in a Democracy:* How can we become more intelligent consumers? How does the pattern of economic life relate to the ideal of democratic economic participation of all?

14. *Problems of Critical Thinking:* How can we develop skill in forming conclusions? What are the sources of information? What is a sound basis for forming conclusions?

15. *Problems of Achieving World Peace in the Atomic Age:* What are the contributions we can make toward world peace? How does atomic energy affect our living today?

16. *Problems of Intercultural Relations:* What are the factors involved in living democratically with many diverse social groups? What is our individual and group responsibility in becoming aware of and helping to decrease intercultural tensions?[9]

Obviously not *all* of the learning activities essential to the solution of the above problems could profitably be of the experience-centered type. Yet it would probably be fair to state that *most* of them could be so conceived. It is apparent also that such activities would require serious investigation and study involving many resources.

[9] These "*Suggested Problem Areas Appropriate for the Core Curriculum*" are a part of a research study being conducted by Lucile Lurry at The Ohio State University, under the direction of the writer.

For other combinations of problem areas see: Prudence Bostwick and Chandos Reid, *A Functional High-School Program.* New York: Hinds Hayden & Eldridge, Inc., 1947; William Van Til, *A Social Living Curriculum for Postwar Secondary Education.* (Unpublished Doctoral Dissertation) Columbus: The Ohio State University, 1946.

SPECIAL INTEREST AREAS

The remaining half of the student's time would be devoted to work in special interest areas selected in terms of his particular interests, problems, and needs. If he were expecting to go to college, naturally he would elect courses in specialized science, such as biology, physics, and chemistry, world history, languages and literature, plane and solid geometry, and algebra. Since, by hypothesis, these areas are selected because the student has already developed a special interest in them, the framework might well be logically organized subject matter, utilizing direct experience to enrich the facts and principles which are part and parcel of a particular field of knowledge. Teacher-student planning would continue to be employed but within the scope defined by the field of knowledge. Most of the other areas of special interests, such as arts, music, and the business, industrial, and agricultural fields would, as in the general education area, be largely experience-centered. As the student gained control over these fields, he would, with the help of the teacher, develop for himself logical systems of knowledge which would approximate those worked out by the race.

SUMMARY AND CONCLUSION

Should the secondary school curriculum be experience-centered? Direct, firsthand experience has clearly justified itself as the appropriate center for the organization of learning activities. If the teacher is sensitive to the need for helping the student to achieve logical organizations of knowledge, he will enrich direct experiences by using all available resources. Before the experience-centered curriculum can function effectively, the program of general education will need to be reorganized in terms of the needs, problems, and interests of the students. This suggests a core, or common learnings program, based largely upon direct, firsthand experience, with the so-called academic subjects serving as special interest areas. These should probably continue to be subject-centered. Most other special interest areas, such as the arts and vocational education, would, as now, be experience-centered.

chapter 32

Curriculum decisions and provision for individual differences

Virgil E. Herrick

A teacher makes a number of educational decisions when dealing with the problem of individual differences in his classroom. These decisions are in different classes.

One class of decisions has to do with the selection of objectives, the topic being studied, the organizing center being used, the instructional plan considered appropriate, and the nature of the evaluation desired.

A second class of decisions has to do with how individual children are recognized and respected, how teacher and pupil roles are determined, and how the interpersonal dynamics of the classroom are directed to more adequate personal, social, and educational ends.

A third class of decisions has to do with the way children and teachers are grouped, the way time and space are used, and the way instructional materials and resources are obtained and related.

Every teacher has to deal with all three of these classes of decisions in the teaching that he does. Most, if not all, of the provisions for dealing with individual differences in the classroom fall in these categories.

It is the thesis of this article that all these classes of decision making are important and related. No one class can be omitted from adequate educational planning for individual differences. Further, decisions in Class 1, which deal with goals and instructional strategies to accomplish them, and decisions in Class 2, which deal with individuals and with human dignity and respect, have first priority and should precede and control

From *The Elementary School Journal*, LXII(March, 1962), 313–322. Reprinted by permission of the University of Chicago Press.

rather than follow decisions in Class 3, where administrative arrangements for children, teachers, time, space, and materials are dominant considerations.

Too often we start with an administrative commitment to a teaching machine, to a teaching team and a group of ninety children (or for that matter, to a group of twenty-five children); and then we consider what directives these decisions have for instruction rather than vice versa.

This thesis can be documented by examining briefly two decisions in Class I that confront every teacher every day that he teaches. These two decisions have to do with determining the nature and the level of the teacher's instructional objectives and the nature and the characteristics of the organizing centers he selects for teaching and learning.

Several other decisions in curriculum could have been used for this discussion. The nature and the priorities of the screens for selecting learning activities and the nature and roles of the teacher and the learner in the evaluation process in instruction would have served equally well. The conclusions growing out of the two areas selected will illustrate the point being made.

One of our most ancient and most persistent notions about the teaching-learning act is that it ought to be purposeful—goal centered—and directed by significant educational objectives. Few disagree with this general proposition.

If this conception of the teaching-learning act is sound, a careful study of these objectives, their nature, and their use in making educational decisions should furnish many suggestions for providing for individual differences.

Nerbovig's (1) study of how teachers use objectives, Lund's (2) preliminary analysis of teacher-learning episodes, and our own studies of classroom behavior suggest several conclusions about how many teachers see and use objectives in their instructional practices.

1. Many teachers do not understand the difference between topics, areas, and objects as definitions of scope or of organizing centers for learning activities and important understandings and intellectual processes as definitions of instructional objectives. (*Addition* is a topic. *Chicago* is an area. The *earthworm* is an object.)

Teachers state their objective as "to teach Chicago" rather than seeing understandings like "Man works with other men to meet their common needs" as the objective and Chicago as a representative city that can be used to achieve some appreciation of this generalization.

Thus the phrases "to educate children," "to teach Chicago," or "to develop an understanding of the simple sentence" are not objectives. The first is a generality that states the total task of the school. The second is a possible organizing center to be used to develop certain understandings or objectives. The third avoids the issue: The objective is the understanding or idea of the simple sentence itself.

A teacher's statement of instructional objectives is more useful in making curriculum decisions if this statement does not include principles of learning, important organizing centers, a list of instructional materials, propositions about the good life, and the kitchen sink.

If a teacher can distinguish between important understandings and intellectual processes as objectives and the other necessary components of curriculum, he is freer to think imaginatively about the many different topics, areas, objects, and centers of interest that can be used to include the individual differences of children and yet deal with the important understandings and thought processes of the educational program.

In providing for individual differences in the classroom, teachers must realize that in any comprehensive teaching act, several important curriculum decisions have to be made. Determining instructional objectives is only one of these decisions. Equally important is the realization that objectives can perform certain curriculum functions and that they cannot perform others. Failure to make these distinctions creates obstacles to providing adequately for the individual differences of children.

2. Many teachers fail to distinguish between objectives seen as facts and specific skills, and objectives seen as major concepts of the subject area and as key intellectual and social processes.

How a teacher sees and defines his instructional objectives plays an important part in determining how he will provide for the individual differences of children.

Stenographic records of classroom episodes were used to examine how teachers perform their many instructional tasks. The records used were taken from schools in "Prairie City," a typical midwestern community studied by the Committee on Human Development of the University of Chicago, and from schools in communities in Texas, Michigan, Illinois, and Wisconsin. Our analysis of these records shows three important findings.

First, many teachers see their content objectives at the level of the specific fact and thus deal with such objectives as "Robins have red breasts," "5 fours are 20," "the letter *h* is formed with a straight line and a half loop," and "Chicago is on Lake Michigan."

When a teacher sees his instructional objectives in this way, adaptations for individual differences are forced in certain directions. The teacher may vary the speed with which children move through these particulars. The teacher may make adaptations in instructional materials—workbooks, drill exercises, flash cards—so that the child can work on those things which he does not know. The teacher may devise grouping procedures that will bring together children who are at about the same place in this hierarchy of things to know and to verbalize.

Some teachers see their objectives, however, at the level of such concepts as "a number may express either the idea of how many or the idea of relationship" or "the area of any rectangular surface is dependent upon the length of its base and height" or "man influences and is influenced by his environment."

When a teacher sees his instructional objectives on this more general level, his classroom provisions for individual differences tend to use a wider variety of related activities and experiences to help children deal with these understandings on many levels of conceptualization and in respect to many different sets of particulars. The teacher tends to see no single learning experience as having a one-to-one relationship to the mastery of these concepts. The way is opened for many possible adaptations in the learning experiences of children. If the teacher does not see how he can achieve his objectives through many possible instructional means, the only alternatives open to him for variation in his teaching are children, time, and materials.

With this latter perception of objectives, teachers are more likely to see these broader objectives as having meaning for both the kindergarten child and the high school senior. No time is spent in curriculum committees trying to define the level of understanding to be reached by first-, fourth-, or sixth-grade children. This important fact is always being defined by the children themselves. Thus, the child himself becomes an important agent in determining many of the necessary provisions for his own learning. Actually he is the only one who has much of the necessary information.

Second, many teachers who see their instructional objectives at the level of the fact tend to organize their instruction around these specifics directly and use instructional procedures that stress recognition, verbalism, and memory.

Thus, this kind of teacher sees no problem in teaching "3 fours are 12" as "3 fours are 12" or "air has weight" as the verbalism "air has weight." His objective, therefore, becomes the unit of instruction to be taught directly.

Our analysis indicates that when a teacher sees his instructional objectives as learning specifics, this perception limits the possible ways in which he can provide for pupils' individual differences.

Third, many teachers who see their instructional objectives at the level of the fact tend to ignore the importance of the whole array of skills— language skills, thinking skills, social skills, and skills in the use of instructional materials that are regarded as important instructional objectives in every curriculum program.

Again, our data seem to indicate that when a teacher sees process objectives as a necessary part of any classroom activity, he tends to organize his classroom instruction around organizing centers that properly include these skills. His organizing centers thus tend to be more comprehensive and provide more opportunity for various levels of skill use, for many different vehicles for skill development, and for many more appropriate areas of skill application—all important conditions that would make possible desirable instructional provisions for individual differences.

In our examination of learning episodes, the importance of the role of the organizing center in the instructional process soon became apparent. The more we thought about objectives and their nature and directives for instruction, the more we realized that if instructional objectives are important understandings and learning processes, then you did not teach them directly, but you had to select some vehicle or vehicles to provide the means for their accomplishment.

These vehicles—the questions the teacher asked, the example or problem posed, the objects to be examined, and the zoo to be visited and observed—all formed organizing centers to which the children and teacher related their activities and to which they applied their thinking, generalizing, and personal action.

An organizing center for instructional purposes is any object, idea, person, question, or instructional material used to relate and focus the thinking and the action of an individual or a group. Organizing centers can be defined better by their organizing functions than by their nature.

A picture is not an organizing center for instruction because it is a picture. Rather, it is an organizing center because the eyes and thoughts of a class of children focus on it and their learning behavior is related to it in some kind of active fashion.

If a picture is not the object of attention and educational action by some individual or group, it is not an organizing center. An object becomes an organizing center only when it becomes the focus for such action by these individuals. The nature of a center does not of itself make it a center; its nature merely permits and enhances such focusing and organizing behavior.

Nerbovig in her study found that teachers talked about teaching addition, the farm, electricity, and the seven basic foods as their objectives rather than identifying the understanding and the processes commonly assumed to be objectives (1: 122).

To us this finding indicated that many teachers start their educational planning with their organizing centers rather than with their objectives. Actually, this is a much more realistic and useful curriculum decision in their eyes than the decision that "a simple sentence is a single complete unit of thought."

These analyses forced the author to hypothesize that perhaps the most critical single decision a teacher makes about his teaching is the one dealing with the identification and the selection of a desirable set of organizing centers for giving meaning and scope to the learning activities of a group of children.

If an organizing center is to make it possible to meet the individual needs of the children who participate in its development, it should have the following characteristics:

1. *More than One Dimension of Accessibility.* If an organizing center can be attacked in more than one way by the learner, its power to provide for individual differences is increased.

If a teacher poses a question as a center for thought and action and presents the question orally, he limits its accessibility. If he asks the question orally and also writes it on the chalkboard, he increases the accessibility of the question for learning. None of the child's energy has to go into remembering the question so that if the question has any significance for him, he is freer to concentrate his full attention on studying and resolving it.

Even though the teacher speaks and writes the question on the board, if the necessary information to deal with the question is provided only by the teacher, he limits its accessibility to children. If, however, the necessary information to deal adequately with the question can be acquired by children through observation, manipulation, reading, and other sources of knowing, the accessibility of the organizing center to children for learning is correspondingly increased.

If the question is such that responses to it are limited to one word, *yes* or *no,* the capacity of the question to deal with individual differences is more limited than if this were not true.

If the map on the board is large enough for all to see and is placed properly, its accessibility to more than one child is increased. If the map is too small or is poorly placed, its accessibility for learning is decreased. Or, if work is to be done on the map, the map is more accessible to children if each child can have a copy than when this is not true.

An organizing center is more accessible to more than one child if it properly involves the participation of two or more individuals. Sending a note to the principal does not require the five children we sometimes send with it. One child can run this errand. We sometimes justify this action by claiming that the other four are getting better acquainted with their school environment. Organizing centers that consist of spelling words, vocabulary words in reading, combinations in arithmetic, seldom involve more than one child and thus permit only certain limited adjustments to individual differences.

All that has been said may sound simple-minded, but it has become obvious to me that irrespective of how we manipulate the variables of ability and accomplishment, the number of individuals involved, the pacing of the learning process, and the materials and physical space, unless the organizing center for the learning is accessible to the children, no real provision for individual differences can be made.

2. *More than One Level of Accomplishment.* If an organizing center is to have the capacity to provide for individual differences, it must have low catch-hold points and high ceilings. An earthworm can provide a challenge to a kindergarten child and to a college senior; to a child with limited experience and limited capacity to learn, as well as to a child with rich

experience and gifted capacities. This principle applies to organizing centers like the common and persistent problems of living in social studies, creative writing in language arts, and learning more about our weather in science.

Many teachers, however, use organizing centers that have narrow limits for knowing and learning, such centers as spelling the word *cat*, locating the capital of Illinois, naming the parts of speech, or working examples in arithmetic. Each of these centers limits the child to one level of accomplishment. Each provides little opportunity for individual differences. The teacher's alternatives are to try these specific centers until he finds one the child can do or to spend enough time on one until the child grasps the proper response.

3. *More than One Dimension of Mobility.* One of the most important problems in curriculum planning is to know how to ensure proper continuity in a child's learning. Every teacher wants one lesson in reading to contribute to the next one. Every teacher wants to help every child transfer his knowledge of his own community to his attempts to understand the lives of people more remote in space and time.

If a teacher can select organizing centers that have the capacity to move in time, in space, in cultures, and in logic, these centers have greater capacity to provide for individual differences than when this is not true.

In social studies, for example, such centers as great people, great documents, cities, states, or countries are commonly used as organizing centers, but they have limited mobility. It is hard to move Madison, Wisconsin, anywhere else. But social functions, common geographic characteristics, or the common and persistent problems of living, all have the capacity to move in time, in space, in cultures, and in logic. They have greater capacity, therefore, for providing room and opportunity for encompassing meaningfully differences in children's background, ability, and development than centers that lack this capacity.

If we checked proposed organizing centers in social studies programs against this criterion, we would go a long way toward providing a more effective instructional base for dealing with individual differences in this field. Unless instruction is organized around centers that provide room for individuals to vary and to zoom in understanding as far as they can go, few effective instructional provisions can be made for individual differences.

4. *More than One Degree of Organizing Capacity.* Some teachers favor a main organizing center that has several important subcenters that have to be studied if the children are to get a proper understanding of the whole. The *home* is one good example. As children study the home, such subcenters as the responsibilities of children and parents in the home; how such problems as food, clothing, earning money, and recreation are handled; how the different rooms of the house are used; and how the house is placed in a community of houses—all provide a means for in-

dividual and/or small group study and exploration. Yet all these enterprises are seen as important and relevant parts of the main area of concern. It was felt that this kind of organizing center provided many more opportunities for providing for individual differences than an organizing center like *pets*. Yet a center like *pets* provides greater organizing scope than naming locations, describing objects, and drawing up lists—centers commonly used by many teachers.

This examination of how decisions in two common areas of curriculum planning can contribute to more adequate provisions for individual differences suggests the following conclusions:

1. The decisions the teacher makes about the important components of curriculum direct and limit the nature of the provisions that can be made for dealing with individual differences.

2. Teachers who see their instructional objectives at the level of factual specifics tend to provide for individual differences through variations in time, in amount to be learned, in numbers of children, and in instructional materials. The things to be learned tend to remain constant at the specific level for all children.

3. Teachers who see their instructional objectives at the level of important generalizations and key intellectual and social processes are more willing to explore a wider variety of means for accomplishing those objectives and are more willing to accept a wider range of levels of understanding and accomplishment.

4. The capacity of a learning center to provide for individual differences depends on the extent to which such centers meet the following criteria: They need to have more than one dimension of accessibility, more than one level of accomplishment, more than one aspect of mobility, and more than a single degree of organizing capacity.

When these conditions are met, the teacher has an organizing base for instructional activities that will include more than one child, provide room for many levels of contribution, permit children to move in many important directions, and help them explore an adequate number of important relationships. To me, the provision of this kind of instructional base lies close to the heart of our problem of providing adequately for the individual differences of children.

REFERENCES

1. Marcella H. Nerbovig, "Teacher's Perception of the Functions of Objectives," p. 228. Unpublished Ph.D. dissertation. Department of Education, University of Wisconsin, 1956.
2. Virgil E. Herrick and Grace Lund, "The Curricular Analysis of Teaching-Learning Episodes," p. 25. Madison: University of Wisconsin, 1960. (Dittoed.)

chapter **33**

The teacher's impact on the curriculum

Samuel B. Gould

Any consideration of the impact of the teacher upon the curriculum must start with the kind of person the teacher is. A teacher who is primarily concerned with the humanizing aspects of education, who has the highest of standards and moral integrity, who can show students the close relationship between wisdom and humility, who practices his profession with dignity and good humor, who raises honest doubts and transmits to students his own fascination with the enigmas of life—such a teacher can have incalculable impact upon a curriculum, whether it has been constructed along the lines of a straitjacket or as the loosest kind of coverall.

Here is the greatest weakness, the greatest vulnerability of our profession. We plead again and again for high-minded, able, humane persons to join us in this greatest of all callings, yet how little we do systematically to search them out from their early years and persuade them into our ranks. And our failure to do this exposes us mercilessly to the dangers of mediocrity which creep like an undetected cancer into the very vitals of our educational system. We yearn for the gentle wisdom of the scholar but we settle all too often for the dull conformity of the pedant.

In such an age as this, with its unprecedented problems and its new frontiers of exploration, the teacher should be the great adventurer, the

From *School and Society,* 88(April 9, 1960), 175–178. Reprinted by permission of the publisher.

From an address at the 24th Annual Education Conference, Educational Records Bureau-American Council on Education, New York City, October 29, 1959.

intrepid and persistent seeker for the clues to man's survival. Such clues are to be found in the hearts of men rather than in the mechanics of existence. They are to be found in the broad reaches of the intellect coupled with a faith in man's individual destiny. The teacher so motivated is a worthy member of the profession, and the curriculum in his hands is a tool he uses with skill and judgment. He knows when to wield this tool and when to lay it aside. It is not a crutch or a refuge; it is, rather, an implement—only one implement out of many—for the gentle shaping of a life.

Perhaps it is essential, by the very nature of modern circumstances, that we surround our teacher procurement and development methods with legalistic safeguards, that we count carefully the credit hours and specify the areas of study for the prospective teacher. I do not challenge such a necessity. The sheer numbers to which we have grown and the increasing complications of our tasks make evident that we must assure ourselves of certain guarantees against ignorance or charlatanry. And so we turn to the tangible measurements which are easiest to apply to the teacher and which reflect the more obvious elements of his preparation. But somewhere in this process there must be provision also for judging him in terms of his human qualities, his ability to lead, to inspire, to persuade, to found his teaching upon verities that stand the test of every vicissitude of time. And if this provision were attended to first, how much more meaningful would be the rest of the process.

Surely we have the capacity to search for the quality components in a teacher in spite of the difficulty such a task presents. Is all our newfound knowledge of human behavior and human predictability of no avail when we are faced with the most important use which could be made of it? If we are so clever at penetrating man's mind to make him susceptible to our persuasions in the development of purchasing habits or in the acceptance of public images, are we incapable of applying any of these techniques to the evaluation of his humane attributes? Have we ever really, seriously tried to do this? Or must we always be content with the fulfillment of the merely technical requirements? Do we have the courage to reject those who, in their early teaching experience, show themselves manifestly unfit? Or do we excuse and postpone and procrastinate until it is too late and the incompetent has placed himself within the sanctuary of tenure?

My fundamental assumption, therefore, is the forerunner to everything else. And no matter how obvious it may appear, the assertion needs to be made again and again that first we must find the proper raw materials out of which the broadly educated, the skilled, the understanding teacher can be fashioned. Our primary essential is to search out men and women who are best qualified to become teachers. We must identify these people early in life—the earlier the better—and we then can have at least some reasonable assurance that we are devoting our training and educational energies to those who really should be in our profession. And there is no reason why this sort of process cannot be undertaken in an organized, systematic way. If it is possible to develop and maintain systems of recruitment in other walks of life, the same kind of approach is possible in recruiting teachers. In fact, *our* chances of success are greater because we have so much normal and regular contact with young people and because we inevitably come to know so much about them. The potential teacher sometimes can be identified at a relatively early age. He can be identified not only by the intellectual interest he displays, but by his relationships with those around him, particularly those contemporary with him or younger. But he may not be aware of the particular uses to which he ultimately ought to put these unusual characteristics of leadership, scholarship, and communication unless and until someone points out to him the possibilities they project. Proper identification of the teacher of the future is thus a vital prerequisite.

Now that we have agreed upon our teacher of quality, a person of intellectual ability, imagination, and persuasiveness, what should be his relationship to the curriculum which is his guide and teaching tool?

The first necessity of such a relationship from the standpoint of the teacher is an attitude of *irreverence*, complete and unequivocal. He needs to recognize the fact that the dicta of the curriculum are not sacred and that he is free to adapt and revise within reasonable limits. A strict constructionist view can lead to stultification and stagnation. The teacher ought to be free to cross departmental lines, to make judgments about what has become trivial or obsolescent, to reshape and redirect his plan according to the shifting requirements of students.

The fears that general disorder and even chaos are bound to ensue will be cited as ample reasons for the folly of my suggestion. It would appear that I am attacking a fine old American tradition of order, system, and organization in whatever we undertake. I am certainly not advocating chaos, but I am hinting that a little disorder now and then in our educational system would be refreshing. Our preoccupation in the business or industrial or even the social world with statistics and charts and tables of organization, with neat rows of figures that always balance correctly, with exact systems of procedure, or with proved formulae or standard practices has carried over into the educational area with almost frightening thoroughness. Just as in baseball the batting averages and various other records of the players sometimes can become more fascinating than the game itself, so in education we can, if we are not careful, fall into the error of thinking more about paraphernalia than about people. Nothing makes us happier than to see the automobiles coming steadily off the line at fixed intervals, or the bottles and cans moving with precision through their filling and capping and packing process. Nor are these proper places for deviation or innovation.

But education is something else again. Innovation and change and deviation and exploration are the red corpuscles of its lifeblood, keeping it healthy and pulsating with energy. The intangibilities and the immeasurables are somehow the elements that do not lend themselves too well to an orderly system, yet they may be the truly important components. If a curriculum makes the teacher timid, if it keeps him and his students marching in serried, unbroken ranks with everyone perfectly in step, if it creates in his classroom the happy and constant harmony of unchallenged agreement, then that curriculum is bad either in its construction or in the philosophy by which it is established.

A little irreverence now and then might therefore create some balancing factors against those which seem to be inevitable in the functioning of our school systems. Everyone at one time or another should have the rare and delicious privilege of thumbing his nose at someone or something. I submit that treating the curriculum occasionally in this impolite fashion will add in the long run to its vitality and validity. It is a discourtesy to be wished for devoutly.

Another element in the teacher's relationship to the curriculum should be his awareness of the values of serendipity—the out-of-the-way, unlooked-for treasures one stumbles upon, the unplanned-for by-products, the unsought augmentations to pleasure. To me, it is one of the happiest conceptions of life's promise, for it reflects the unpredictability and the unlimited possibilities of human existence together with some notion of the joy that comes from unexpected discovery. In the educational process, it is an unplanned ingredient that gives zest to learning and adds breadth to understanding. And it is an ingredient that is added not only by chance, but also by sagacity.

Still a third element in the teacher's relationship to the curriculum should be the "wisdom factor." Regardless of the subject matter involved, the whole should be surrounded by the aura of his personal values, his personal experience, his own wisdom. There is no way to put these into the curriculum outline, nor can the teacher purposefully plan when and where he can exert such influences transcending the course content. But if he is a certain kind of person and if he is motivated by a deep concern and love for youth, all this will become apparent to the student day by day. A new relationship will spring up in and out of the classroom, perhaps vague and unstructured but undergirded with a sense of mutual respect. When Alfred North Whitehead was asked what courses he taught, his reply was, "Whitehead I, Whitehead II, and Whitehead III." There is much in his answer for us to ponder.

I cannot refrain from making a plea for increased emphasis upon personality and basic motivations as we select our colleagues of the future, because we are so engrossed today in the problem of finding sufficient staff to meet the needs of the oncoming brigades of students. Under the stresses of immediate necessity, the temptation to compromise will be increasingly difficult to withstand. Because of the tremendous numbers we shall require, the methods of teacher selection will center more and more upon a check of those elements of the academic and professional backgrounds which lend themselves to easy evaluation. We shall have to be careful that even these methods do not become cursory. But in any case, the real essence of the teacher is not likely to be probed. Indeed, we have not done too well in this regard even under more favorable conditions. In the future there will be even less time to wonder what stimulative qualities, what horizon-stretching attributes, what spiritual insights the teacher will bring with him along with his formal credentials.

It is all the more urgent, therefore, that the curricula of the future take account, as far as it is possible to do so, of the increasing dangers of regimentation. They ought to be built with enough escape hatches for the curious, inquiring mind.

Under such circumstances, and assuming a teacher of quality, the resulting effects upon the curriculum cannot help but be significant. First of all, it will have characteristics of vitality and flexibility, provided by what the teacher puts of himself into its delineation and interpretation. The impact upon it of a vibrant and humane personality will give it life and verve and broad outreach. If that personality has, in addition, a wealth of knowledge transcending his own specialty, it will be possible for the student to draw all sorts of added dividends from his investment of time and energy. The teacher's impact will weaken the barriers of compartmentalization and correlate the branches of knowledge until the processes of interaction and distillation crystallize the raw materials into the beginnings of wisdom.

Furthermore, the impact of the teacher should cause the curriculum to be a shrewdly fashioned reflection of the contemporary and the timeless. In the hands of a skillful teacher, contemporaneous knowledge always can be reinforced by unchanging verities. Scientific and sociological facts fluctuate between acceptance and rejection and the net result is the progress of a civilization; but the need for the human attributes and the same ethical considerations remains constant for Western man. The methods of teaching may undergo tremendous adjustments because of modern inventiveness and increased skill in analyzing more and more accurately the elements of the learning process; but the discerning teacher still will know that matters which tie together the mind and the heart only can be transmitted personally and even intimately.

Finally, the teacher's influence should cause the curriculum to be a vast reservoir of unanswered and unanswerable questions. By his approach to teaching he can see to it that all answers and all solutions are only partial, leaving open doors through which the student must go, driven by curiosity or patient conscientiousness or pride or ambition or even infuriation. The curriculum is thus no more than a threshold, nor should it be represented to be anything more. There is something prophetic and saddening about the common expression used by students everywhere in speaking of their studies. "Last year I 'took' Shakespeare," one says, "and next year I expect to 'take' Chaucer." The word "take" has a terminal ring to it, a connotation of finality that later reflects itself in the intellectual habits of the adult population. Only by the influence of the teacher can this be avoided, for he must show himself able to translate the curriculum into an assisting instrument which encourages the student toward unattainable but exciting goals.

The Scriptures tell us in a beautiful passage that faith, hope, and love are the great attributes of life, and the greatest of these is love. The great attributes of education are the teacher, the students, and the curriculum, and the greatest of these is the teacher. Though I put the curriculum last, it is there none the less and, therefore, deserves the most meticulous treatment, a treatment which guarantees its breadth, adaptability, and relevance.

chapter 34

What is a comprehensive high school?

Robert S. Gilchrist

Ask any twenty educators and citizens for a definition of a comprehensive high school and you may get twenty different replies, each of which tells part of the story. Study the implications of the comprehensive high school ideal, and the pieces begin to fit into the larger picture. The danger in a restricted definition of the comprehensive high school lies in stressing one part or another of its program apart from the total purpose.

Comprehensive means inclusive or including much. A truly comprehensive high school provides learning opportunities for all normal adolescents within a range from barely educable to the gifted and talented. Its purpose is to enable each pupil (1) to develop to his greatest potential for his own success and happiness and (2) to make a maximum contribution to the American society of which he is a part.

To achieve this purpose, the comprehensive high school must affect positively the behavior of its pupils as adolescents and later as adults in all areas and aspects of living—not only as wage earners, citizens, and family members, but as unique human beings. This requires maximum intellectual development within a content of sound physical, emotional, and social growth.

Enough is known about human development, learning, the demands of living, and democratic values to describe the essentials of a comprehensive high school.

From *NEA Journal,* 5(November, 1962), 32–33. Reprinted by permission of the publisher.

Balance in the Curriculum Is the First Essential

Courses are offered at levels of difficulty to challenge all pupils in basic academic subject fields. Opportunities are also provided for each pupil to take elective subjects consistent with his interests, needs, abilities, and plans for the future. There are courses in the fine and practical arts as well as a strong health and physical fitness program.

Social learnings are recognized as important, because the surest guarantee of good adult citizenship is good adolescent citizenship. Student government, service clubs, social functions, publications, athletics, and other voluntary activities are a valuable supplement to curricular learnings.

Depth in the Curriculum Is Another Prime Requisite

No course merely covers the facts in a textbook. The ability to think through problems, to sense relationships, to generalize, and to develop and clarify values is essential to democratic living. Every subject and every activity can and should contribute to the ideal of democratic living.

Individualized Education Is a Characteristic of the Comprehensive High School

The home background, out-of-school experiences, abilities, interests, and plans for the future of each student are considered. A strong guidance program assists the student in clarifying goals, in assessing strengths and weaknesses, and in selecting a sound program. The student has opportunities to learn at a pace consistent with his abilities.

Functional Learning Is Essential in the Comprehensive High School

Each experience must have meaning for the student. Classroom learning must be related to life outside the classroom if education is to be effective. For this reason, a comprehensive high school is an integral part of the community, and the faculty works in close cooperation with parents and all youth-serving institutions. The total school environment, whenever feasible, encourages practice of whatever is learned in any subject.

Finally, the administration and organization of the high school are means to serve effective learning, never ends in themselves. Programs and schedules for students are determined by their relation to individual needs and abilities rather than by rigid timetables or classic academic criteria.

How important is it that boys and girls throughout America have an opportunity to attend a comprehensive high school? Here is what one mother says:

My daughters loved their high school, and we would not want them to have missed the opportunities for both the academic and the social learning that they had there.

It was an excellent comprehensive high school. It was multiracial, and its student body contained an economic and social cross section of the community; it had a fine academic tradition, an exceptionally good teaching staff, and an excellent library; it had good shop and vocational programs; and it offered outstanding opportunities in music, dramatics, and other arts. It had a continuation program of combined work and school. It was strong in athletics, had an enthusiastic student government, and a number of faculty-sponsored clubs.

In other words, it was strong both academically and socially. It trained for college or early job; gave opportunities for recognition and development of talent; and provided a framework in which young people from widely differing backgrounds could gain familiarity and some sense of communication with each other.

A student body that is limited to one classification gives limited preparation for living in a world where communication and understanding between people is of ever increasing importance. By my definition, a comprehensive high school believes in a comprehending program for a wide range of students. It provides academic challenge for the brilliant and seeks to raise the sights and stretch the minds of the less obviously gifted. It is dedicated to the premise that intelligence and ability cannot be categorized.

To what extent do American youth have an opportunity to attend comprehensive high schools? Although we have a right to be proud of our system of free public high school education, I believe we have a long way to go before we can say truthfully that most American boys and girls are attending comprehensive high schools.

Dr. Conant performed an important service when he stated clearly that our high schools should be comprehensive. But there are forces and pressures which are working against this development.

For example, because college entrance is determined largely by test scores in academic subjects, enrollments in the arts, in home and family living, and in physical education are decreasing in many secondary schools. Further, when financial limitations require budget cuts, courses for the pupils not going on to college are too often the first to be eliminated. Perhaps most damaging is the implication that the pupils not academically inclined are less important than the college bound.

America desperately needs the developed abilities of all its youth. Citizens and educators have, in the comprehensive high school, an exciting and valuable tool to fulfill America's needs for the future.

chapter 35

The secondary school program of the future

Hugh D. Laughlin

I have categorized the ideas about the future of secondary education into three major areas: curriculum, organization, and administration. In total, there are fifteen questions which I would like to raise with you. I grant there are many more, but these fifteen seem to me to be the ones of greatest import as we look to the future.

In the first area, curriculum, seven questions or topics bear consideration:

1. Who shall be responsible for making curriculum?
2. What is the future of the comprehensive high school?
3. What are the curricular relationships between secondary and higher education?
4. Will there be a continued upward extension of universal education?
5. Can we look forward to national standards and a national curriculum?
6. What are the responsibilities at the local level for experimentation in curriculum design and content?
7. What shall be the structure of the curriculum?

On the surface the first question, "Who shall be responsible for making curriculum?" seems to be one of the least important of all. I feel that it is one of the most difficult questions we face. To understand this question we must go back in history to see how curriculum at the secondary level was made in the past. At the turn of the century the curriculum in the secondary school was studied by many national committees of the NEA. This

From an unpublished manuscript. Reprinted by permission of the author.

was the period of the great committees. These committees, usually made up of school superintendents and college professors, attempted to standardize the high school program. These attempts at standardization often led to more uniformity of curriculum offerings and this uniformity frequently was effected primarily in the college preparatory subjects, particularly the classical languages and mathematics.

The Committee of Ten, appointed in 1892, studied the scope and function of secondary education in order to resolve the chaos which then existed. President Charles W. Eliot of Harvard University was the chairman. In its report, the Committee of Ten recommended four separate curricula: classical, Latin scientific, modern language, and English. The report was filled with such phrases as, "Subjects prescribed would all be used for training the powers of observation, memory, expression and reasoning," and "The goal was four years of strong and effective mental training." Little attention was given to the so-called practical courses.

Following the Committee of Ten, the Committee on College Entrance Requirements was organized. The most significant contribution this Committee made was to establish and define the Carnegie unit. In 1918, the Commission on the Reorganization of Secondary Education contributed the famous Seven Cardinal Principles. There were many other committees and commissions that worked during the first two decades of the century. The period was one in which experts met and studied, brought together their best thinking, reported their findings, and the high school curriculum was supposed to change accordingly. Needless to say, not much happened in changes at the grass-roots, classroom level.

Following the period of national committees came the scientific period of the twenties and early thirties. This was the period when Thorndike, the great psychologist, stated, "If it can't be measured, it doesn't exist." It was during this period that we saw the advent of standardized and objective tests. In the area of curriculum building, Bobbitt of Chicago and Charters of The Ohio State University were hard at work on the job-analysis approach to curriculum development. This approach provided that the school study the activities of people in great detail, then incorporate into the school program learning activities which were similar to the activities of people.

A third period of curriculum building followed the scientific period. This period could be labeled the experimentation and grass-roots period. In the scientific period and in the period of the great national committees, it was assumed that a postulation of appropriate curricula could be passed down from experts to teachers. This did not seem to be working, so attention was turned to reversing the direction of the flow of ideas. It seemed sensible that if curriculum ideas flowed from the bottom up, there would be more chance that ideas would get implemented in practice. It was felt that it was necessary to involve teachers, and any other people who were responsible for putting curricular ideas into practice, in the processes of curriculum development. It was during this period that the Progressive Education Association found large sums of money to sponsor the famous Eight-year Study. During the war years little attention was given to curriculum development. Immediately following the war the grass-roots movement was picked up again and we saw the development of such ideas as action research and the shift in nature of supervisory positions. These positions were reorientated toward greater responsibility on the part of the supervisor for leadership in the area of professional study, or in-service education programs.

Some say that we have not yet reached the zenith of this grass-roots period and that the future will see increased efforts to make curriculum building the function of teaching staffs. Personally, I feel that we are closer to the end of this period than to the zenith.

I believe there is evidence to suggest that we are entering a new period which I would label a period of administrative and organizational influence on curriculum development. We have spent almost two decades educating and convincing administrators that their primary purposes and objectives are to improve the instructional program. We now have a generation of administrators who are far more able and competent in the area of curriculum than we had in the past. Inasmuch as these people are normally in positions of status and authority, it seems logical to conclude that more and more sound curriculum decisions will be made by administrators. Here I include those people on both the line and the staff. These people will use teachers as resource persons, but not as the group that makes final decisions regarding the curriculum offerings, content, and methodology of the secondary school. I also cite the development of ideas such as national standards and the so-called Trump plan, both of which I shall mention later in more detail. These do not fit into the experimentation and grass-roots concept.

The second question is, "What is the future of the comprehensive high school?" I think that over a period of twenty to thirty years in the future we will continue to have what is called the comprehensive high school. In other words the trend and movement we have seen in the past two or three decades will be continued. However, I look forward to a change in the definition of the comprehensive high school.

Today we think of the comprehensive high school as an educational institution in which the offerings are broad and comprehensive. We test the comprehensiveness of the high school by looking at the courses offered or at the breadth of the program of instruction. We justify such a definition by saying that every pupil entering the high school will be able to find subjects which meet his needs. Conant used this general idea when he defined the comprehensive high school in his report, *The American High School Today.* He sees the comprehensive high school as any high school that offers a program which meets the needs of its pupil population. Under this definition, I submit that there are some communities in the United States where a high school would be called comprehensive under the definition, but would look very much like what we would call a vocational high school or perhaps an academic high school.

In the future, I think we will be testing the comprehensiveness of a high school by looking at the pupil who is the product. We will ask, "Have his educational experiences and learnings been comprehensive? Is he a well-rounded individual? Has he had opportunity to inquire in areas of instruction according to the needs of society, as well as according to his own individual needs?"

After some fifty years of talking about individual differences we are finally getting around to implementing the idea. This is evidenced, in part, by the present-day development of guidance programs. It suggests the logic of looking at the product, the individual pupils, rather than at the organization of the school program when deciding whether a high school is a comprehensive school or not.

The third question is, "What are the curricular relationships between secondary and higher education?" In the past five years we have seen the apple baskets of curriculum in the secondary schools and in the colleges upset. In the past, it was not difficult to determine what was a high school subject and what was a college or university subject. Geometry was a high school subject; calculus was college. General chemistry was high school; organic chemistry was college. Now we see that because of programs of acceleration and advanced placement at the high school level it is not as easy to establish a line of demarcation between the secondary school and the college. Our more able high school youth are being encouraged to go as far and as fast as they can in a given subject area. Note that this is also an implementation of the thesis of caring for individual differences.

Some years ago we saw the clear lines of demarcation between the elementary school and the high school start to disappear. At one time the elementary school was responsible for teaching all the fundamental skills. It was assumed that when the pupil came into the high school he would have the skills subjects in command and, therefore, would be able to move forward in his study of high school subjects. Now secondary school teachers, on the whole, are agreed that if the pupil, for example, has a reading problem, they will do what they can to help develop better reading competencies. I believe the clear-cut lines between high school and college are disappearing at the present time, which means that at the secondary school level we must be willing and able to offer courses which in the past were thought to be offered only at the college level.

Personally, I would like to see the colleges do a little more in assuming a responsibility for educating the young people, as these young people come to them. This means that instead of looking down their noses at remedial courses, the colleges would consider it an appropriate endeavor to offer students who are talented in one area enough to do college work, but who have lacks in other areas, those courses which will bring them along as quickly as possible. I am afraid that much of what goes on in the freshman year of college in many institutions is not as much *education* as it is *delayed selection procedures.* The freshman English course, for example, should be more than a proving ground in which the student shows what he has learned in the past, and qualifies or doesn't accordingly. It should be a course in which he is educated, meaning his knowledge is advanced and his competencies are improved. If this can happen, I am sure that we can see in the future a high school–college relationship which will look more like two combs joined by placing the teeth together, rather than a relationship which looks like an attempt to join the combs by placing them back to back.

I would predict that acceleration programs will become a very normal, rather than a unique part of the secondary school program. As this happens, the problems of advanced placement, which are primarily administrative problems, will be more readily resolved.

The fourth question is, "Will there be a continued upward extension of universal education?" I would say, *inevitably.* In spite of the attention which has been given recently to the problems of the "unwilling learners," the answer being to get rid of them, and the investigation of the proposition of lowering the compulsory school-age law, I believe that it will be impossible to reverse the trends of history which have been toward extending free public education upward. Personally, I think we have reached the high point in giving attention to the gifted group while giving little or no attention to the large mass of average pupils. We all know that just a few years ago our attention was focused on the slow-learning group. Then the pendulum swung and today we find ourselves giving attention to the needs of the gifted. I would not disapprove of this, for we must give due attention to the gifted. We must give due attention to every group of youngsters in our high schools. We must consider all of our pupils and give each the kind of program that will be best for him. I have noticed in recent months that there are more parents of average pupils speaking up. When we first initiated special programs for the gifted, we had many parents approving because most of them thought of their child as being at least high average, if not gifted. Simple arithmetic indicates that the majority of our parents have children who are in the average or below-average groups. I think that these good folk will ask that we provide for their children, giving equal consideration to them as well as to other pupils in the high school.

I also believe that five years from now we will spend more time talking about the talented pupils, or the talents of a pupil, rather than to set up a category of pupils known as the gifted. The concept of the gifted is too easily misconstrued as an across-the-board concept. Some psychologists have already thrown serious doubts on the idea that it is possible to segregate particular youth on the basis of general intelligence scores or on the basis of reading scores. We will learn to go deeper into an analysis of the particular and unique talents of a pupil, or the nature of his lack of talents.

There are other arguments which support the idea that universal education will be extended upward: (1) The demands of a technological society, with its complex economy, suggest the need for a better educated person if such a society is to continue to progress. (2) World tensions, which will probably be with us for many years, set a more important focus on ideas of citizenship education, or general education. Educating for democratic living cannot be done in a few years. It is logical to think it will be suggested that the number of school years for all youth be extended. Only a few school systems will provide this extension by instituting summer programs, eleven-month programs, or other programs, even though they do give better utilization of our building facilities, our educated professional group, and the time of the pupils. (3) Our economy is such that even in times of prosperity it is not feasible to place too many young people in the job market as competitors to those who have more adult responsibilities. (4) We have seen the worthwhile consequences of making it possible for many youth to go on into college. This was done through the GI Bills of Rights. I believe that realization will come that the monies so spent were very small compared with the human resource profit achieved for our democratic society. All of these reasons support the continued upward extension of universal education.

Question five, "Can we look forward to national standards and a national curriculum?" This is a question which interestingly enough would not have been given serious consideration five years ago. At the present time, however, there are outstanding educators who are suggesting that this is the best way to resolve the problems of upgrading the quality of our schools throughout the nation. Liberman attacks this problem and backs the idea of a national curriculum because of his concern for the upgrading of the profession. He argues that as long as we have a strong local control we will have a weak profession. Therefore, with a national curriculum there will be less local control and we will have a better profession. All very neat. Paul Hanna at Stanford University has written in recent months approving the idea of a national curriculum.

My own opinion is that we will not have a national curriculum, for I do not believe that it is in the value system of our people to release control of their schools entirely to the national level. I hear no one arguing that we should have federal aid *because* we want federal control and some form of national standards and curriculum. Those who favor federal aid, including myself, usually argue that it is not necessary to have federal control just because you have federal participation in the equalization of educational opportunity. Which side of the controversy one takes is not the important consideration at this point. What is important is that there exists one unanimously agreed on idea and that is that local control in a democracy is better than control at some higher level. On the other hand, I do not question but that we shall have higher standards in secondary education in the future.

I also suggest that the future holds more attention being focused on the raising of the quality of our efforts rather than our being satisfied, as we seem to be today, with raising quantitative standards. In raising quantitative standards, I am thinking of some of the peculiar things that are being done today in such areas as marking practices, grouping, and the attention which is being given to instituting a differentiated diploma. I do not see some of these practices as being consistent with the values of the American people. I do not argue against some of these practices from a social welfare position. I am thinking of them as being contrary to certain basic ideals and aspirations built into the values of the American people, which they will not negate, nor willingly give up. As a citizen, if I figure that the schools have given my child a certificate of attendance and have neglected to give him a fair chance, I will be one of the first persons in line the next time we have a board election, or there is a bond issue or levy to be voted on. This is exactly the way democracy should work.

The sixth question, "What are the responsibilities at the local level for experimentation in curriculum design and content?" I think the answer is that there will be greater responsibility in coming years for pilot studies and experimentation in the individual school. The total educational operation has become, in recent years, more scientific. I do not believe that this trend will be reversed. Even with the teacher shortage, we have a better informed professional group on pedagogical matters than we had in the past. Our public has become better informed. People are going to want to know whether a certain program or practice works or doesn't work. There is no way to find out other than through experimentation and research at the local level. The postulations of great national committees, a scientific period, even the experimentation that has gone on in campus laboratory schools has not had resounding results in changing curriculum in the secondary school at the local level. It seems that the proposition will be resolved in one of two directions; either the high school will continue the program it has had for so many years that we have forgotten its antecedents, or changes will be made as the local school moves out to try ideas which result from the reflection and study of its professional staff. I think the latter is the promising practice of the future.

Secondary education must change as society changes. It is inevitable that society will change; therefore, it is inevitable that the high school program will change. Changes, however, will be directed by demands of the community in which the pupils of a high school live. To know what changes are good, it will be necessary to experiment. Experimental projects must be tailored to the individual high school or the high schools of a particular school system. This, of course, makes it absolutely imperative that the person in the leadership role be skilled and competent in directing experimental programs within the school.

The last question under the curriculum area is, "What shall be the structure of the curriculum?" Little change has been made in the structure of the secondary school curriculum during the past fifty years. Usually schools have used an additive process when any change has taken place. Few courses have been dropped from the program, but many have been added. The advanced placement and acceleration programs have contributed to the large number of courses added to the program. The only structural changes which have been suggested during this period of time are the core curriculum and the idea labeled the Trump plan. More about the Trump plan later.

The core program is a basic curriculum revision, rather than a modification of the present program. Some people feel that this structure, which provides for general education, required of all pupils, in a block-of-time period, and special interest education, provided through an electives program, has been on the decline in recent years. I think it is not so much a decline as it is a matter of the core program not moving forward with as great momentum as it did a decade ago. Core classes, which are sometimes called self-contained classes, unified subjects, general education classes, etc., are not at all uncommon in high schools today, especially at the junior high school level. The problems in developing a core curriculum are unqualified teachers, our rigid adherence to the subject-centered curriculum, lack of familiarity of the public as to the nature of the program, and teacher and pupil resistance to any change. On the other hand, such a structure resolves many problems which now face us, especially those in the area of better citizenship education. It is a program that is closely aligned to modern pedagogical and psychology principles, and does provide for greater flexibility in the high school program. I believe this program will continue to grow, and as we observe the success we have with it at the junior high school level in the next decade more and more secondary educators will be inclined to incorporate it as part of the senior high school program.

The second category of ideas concerning the future of secondary education is organization. Here there are five questions to be asked:

1. What will be the size of the future secondary school?
2. What will be the vertical organization of the school system?
3. What is the potential of the Trump plan?
4. Is the team-teaching concept a desirable idea for the future?
5. Where does the community junior college institution fit into the organization of our school system?

Regarding the size of the high school of the future, it is obvious to almost everyone that schools will be larger, enrollments will be greater, and the program of instruction in any one school will contain far more elements than we find in most high schools today. Consolidation efforts and the present policies of the State Board of Education here in Ohio, regarding small substandard schools, lead us to this almost inevitable conclusion. Conant did not even consider the high school with less than one hundred pupils in the graduating class. The smaller high schools were quickly dismissed in his report.

Yet we will continue to have small high schools. The size of a school is not only dependent on the kind of program we want, but also on factors such as financial ability, population distribution, topography, and the vertical organization of the school system. It would be rather absurd to think that in the next few years we are going to eliminate completely small high schools. One hundred in the graduating class would mean about five to six hundred pupils in a four-year high school and approximately eight hundred to a thousand pupils in a six-year high school. Although most authorities agree that a high school of between a thousand and twelve hundred pupils is ideal, we will have to find ways of constructing good programs for schools with far fewer pupils.

To date educators in the small high schools seem to have expended much of their energy toward emulating the program of the larger high schools. In so doing, secondary educators in these small schools have taken on an almost impossible task and have ignored many of the advantages of the small school. It is in the small school that one can have more flexible scheduling from day to day. Many more special projects, which involve classes and the entire school are possible. Block-time scheduling is usually easier in the small school. There is greater opportunity for richness in the small-school program through the individualization of instruction. With a good staff and a high willingness to pay on the part of a community, I don't think you can beat the five-hundred-pupil high school. These smaller units are more educationally sound than the two- to three-thousand-pupil high school mills which we see in the very large metropolitan centers.

I believe our secondary schools will grow larger in size, but I do not think this necessarily guarantees a concomitant increase in the quality of education. The small school organization within the large school is an attempt to overcome the problems of the large school. Note that in this kind of school, the usual small-school unit is made up of five hundred or less pupils.

Many educators are talking about area vocational schools. Such ideas hold great promise if we do not limit ourselves to thinking in the present-day patterns of administration and organization. For example, it has been suggested that pupils might go to a small, general comprehensive high school for half the day. The specialized area high school would be used for scheduling the pupils' time the other half of the day. Such an idea is directly related to the development of the vocational part of the community junior college. The duplication of special facilities for the specialized high school is not necessary if we apply our administrative creativeness to the problems.

The second question is, "What will be the vertical organization of the school system?" We have been forced to the conclusion that there is no one ideal plan of vertical organization for all schools over the nation. Again there are many factors which determine the best vertical organization for a particular school system. Population concentration, topography, financial status are but a few. The most important factor of course is what the people of a given community think about the organization of the schools. The only generalization that I know which will stand up is that since pupils will be transferring from one school to another as they progress through the school system, a break will come at certain points during their school careers. Wherever these breaks come, there is the need for good articulation in order that the total twelve- or fourteen-year program is one which provides a continuity of learning experiences for children and youth.

Recently, attention has been given to a plan of vertical organization which is somewhat new. This is a 4–4–4 plan. It includes four years of elementary school, grades one through four, or kindergarten through four; four years of what is called intermediate school, grades five through eight; and four years of high school, grades nine through twelve. If the program is to be extended beyond the twelfth grade, either a separate two-year junior community college institution is added, or these two years are added as an upward extension of the secondary school to make a six-year high school. It seems to me that this organization has some merit and should be given careful consideration. It helps on some problems which have been perennial at the secondary school level. For example, the traditional three-year junior high school is only a three-year school in its organization and as an administrative unit. From the standpoint of curriculum, the ninth grade has not been a part of a three-year program. The 4–4–4 organization ties the ninth grade to the other high school grades where it probably belongs.

The third question is, "What is the potential of the Trump plan?" This plan gets its name from J. Lloyd Trump, formerly Professor of Education at the University of Illinois. He is now Associate Director of the National Association of Secondary School Principals and Director of the NASSP's Commission on the Experimental Study of the Utilization of Staff in the Secondary School. The Commission has produced a plan for the reorganization of the high school which is drastic and visionary. Essentially it focuses in at two places. One, the organization of the schedule and of class sections, and two, differentiated roles for the teachers and adults working in the high school. The plan abandons the traditional schedule, which includes five-periods-across-the-week classes. All pupils participate in three kinds of learning activities: one, large-group instruction; two, small-group instruction; and three, individual study. In the large-group instruction sections, approximately one hundred and twenty-five pupils come together to hear presentations by a teacher specialist. Approximately 40 per cent of the pupils' time during the week is given to this kind of instruction. The small groups are made up of no more than fifteen pupils with a general teacher observing and leading discussions on the content which has been presented in the large-group sessions. Approximately 20 per cent of the pupils' time is given to small-group instruction. The remaining 40 per cent of the time is spent by the pupil in individual study. Here he plans, initiates, and carries through individual projects under the guidance of teachers, counselors, and aids. It is at this point in the plan that the school provides each pupil with an individual carrell or study booth.

The Trump plan provides for a different organization of the teaching staff than we now have. It is claimed that this organization is no more expensive than our present staff. Teacher specialists work with the large groups. They are given time within the school day to prepare lectures and organize the work to use every known audio-visual device available at the present time. It is suggested that the teacher specialists receive an average salary of $8,000. The teacher specialist and the general teacher are both fully certified. The general teachers work with the small groups but are only paid an average of $5,500. In addition to the certified personnel, there are many teacher aids, for example, young people in the teacher education institutions who are doing cadet work, or well-educated people in the community who are willing to work on a half-time basis or on a more temporary basis than those people who are making teaching their career. There are also many clerical workers provided for in the plan.

As in the case of any plan which is suggested as a panacea, the Trump plan first mystifies us, then intrigues us. I predict, at a later date the Trump plan will leave us with certain residues which will be incorporated into secondary school programs. In some ways this plan is like the Dalton and Winnetka plans. These, along with such ideas as the Gary Platoon system, the Life Adjustment program and others, have left their tint on the present-day secondary school program. The Trump plan will do likewise. I doubt whether there will be many schools that will institute the complete plan as it is now postulated. This, in fact, would not be the challenge of the Commission. It would say, here are some ideas which need pilot studies and experimentation; if different schools will pick up different parts of the plan, we will find better practices for secondary schools.

Another concept, not unique to the Trump plan, but part of it, is the idea of the teaching team. The question is, "Is this a desirable organization of staff in the secondary school?" In the Trump plan the specialist teacher, the general teacher, the teacher aids, and clerical workers make up a teaching team for a given group, or grade, of pupils. This team, working to-gether, is responsible to see that the pupils in the group are given the best education for which the school can assume responsibility. The idea has great merit, and I predict that in the future we will give increased atten-tion to organizing the secondary school on a grade-level-staff plan rather than to forever hold to the idea of organizing the staff according to the subject matter fields. For example, there is far more profit in getting the teachers of the tenth grade together, those teachers who are working with the same pupils, to discuss the problems that the pupils have in the school, than to get the people of the same area together to discuss the problems they have in getting the same subject matter into the pupils.

The last question in this area of organization is, "Where does the community junior college fit into the organization of our school system?" This is one of the most important and pressing propositions before edu-cators today. The interest of public school people in the problem has been somewhat lacking. It is quite possible we are near the time when we will find we have been asleep at the switch. Something is going to happen, and happen quickly in this area of the community junior college. Funda-mentally, the problem is a choice of whether the community junior col-lege shall be an upward extension of secondary education, with local con-trol either on a school district or unified school district basis, or whether education beyond the high school shall be an outward extension of the in-stitutions of higher learning. This of course would mean control by these institutions and primary emphasis in the program on the college-parallel program. I suggest that within the next two years we will see things de-velop in this area which will occupy us in controversy for the next decade. Ultimately, community colleges will be established which include not only the college transfer course, but sound vocational-technical and adult edu-cation programs. I think the answer as to who shall control these insti-tutions is pretty much up to people such as are in this organization. If you are not interested, you won't be a part of the movement. If you are interested, you'd better get ready to do a little fighting.

The third category of ideas is administration. Three questions are im-portant in this area:

1. Are we to have higher standards for administrators of the secondary schools?

2. What new specialized positions will we have in the secondary school in the future?

3. How will we resolve the problems of college admissions?

At the present time we see a tremendous movement to raise standards of pupil achievement and performance. The new policies of the North Central Association indicate that we will not be satisfied, even though we might have to put up with, substandard teachers. I cannot help but believe that this will all be reflected in a need and requirement for more competent, highly trained administrators in the secondary schools. As you all know AASA finally decided that future members must have done more work at the graduate level than the former requirement of one year. I would look for this idea to give impetus to the same kind of requirement for the high school principals of the future. Within a decade, I would not be surprised if the high school principals, especially those in the better career positions, were required to do work at the doctoral level, or to qualify in one of the new programs leading to a certificate as educational specialist.

The second question is, "What new specialized positions will we have in the secondary school of the future?" We have seen in recent years a tendency to establish new specializations within the administrative team at the high school level. In the next few years the guidance counselor will be on the job in all high schools. In addition to the guidance counselor, I see the development of a position called the curriculum coordinator. Perhaps the principal will take over this role, in which case he will turn over to his administrative assistants the problems of administrative mechanics. If he does not, however, surely the high school will need some person designated as a specialist in curriculum development. In some systems we already have supervisors serving this function.

Another fast-developing specialization is that of the activities director. The extracurricular activities program has become so large that it is impossible in the ordinary high school for the single administrator to do the job alone. Therefore, a new position is being created which fortunately, in my judgment, has thus far not been limited to men, but gives opportunities for outstanding women to join the administrative team. As other specialization roles are developed we will see increased attention given to the concept of the administrative team. This is the group, in the future, which will administer the secondary school.

The concluding question I have to present to you concerns college admissions. It is, "How will we resolve the problems of college admissions?" In the future we will have an ever-increasing percentage of our high school graduates going on to college. This will be particularly true if we see the development of the community junior college. Last fall in the United States, 827,000 new students were enrolled as freshmen. By 1965, if present trends continue, the number will be between 1,300,000 and 1,400,000, an increase of 57 and 70 per cent. At present, this matter of college admissions presents the high school principal with his most exasperating problems. Everyone seems to want to test the junior and senior classes to see who is going to be eligible for college. The College Entrance Board has dominated the field for many years. Last year, a new group at the University of Iowa instituted a competing program. This resulted in the American College Test, or the ACT. To say that the two organizations are not happy with one another is to put it mildly. They do not even agree on what it is that should be tested. The college board people say the test should be made up of two parts, one part achievement, the other aptitude. The ACT people say there really isn't much difference between the two. The secondary school people get caught in the middle. They want to get their graduates qualified for acceptance into the colleges of their choice, so about the only thing they can advise is for the student to take any and all tests that come along.

Personally, I like the position taken by Havighurst at the University of Chicago. He advocates a scholastic aptitude test. He also thinks more attention should be paid to the candidate's personality and suggests that some colleges should even set up quotas for the less able student group. If this last position prevails, it will be because secondary school educators and administrators have finally raised so much objection to the present muddle that colleges and universities recognize they cannot continue to establish the ground rules alone, without consideration as to how their desires and decisions impinge on the high school.

chapter **36**

Education of adolescents: 1985

Kimball Wiles

Although it *is* possible that schools in 1985 will be used as instruments of thought control and social classification, the writer, nevertheless, is optimistic enough to believe there will continue to be a social commitment to freedom, creativity, and equality of opportunity. With this basic assumption, an attempt is made in the following statement to project the changes that technological advances and social problems will produce.

Purposes and Program: 1985

Planners of the education for adolescents hope that each pupil will: (1) develop a set of values that will guide his behavior: (2) acquire the skills necessary to participate effectively in the culture; (3) gain understanding of the social, economic, political and scientific heritage; and (4) become able to make a specialized contribution to the society.

The program of the school is designed to promote these goals and is divided into four phases: (1) analysis of experiences and values; (2) acquisition of fundamental skills; (3) exploration of the cultural heritage; and (4) specialization and creativity.

Analysis of Experiences and Values

In the school each pupil spends six hours a week in an Analysis Group. With ten other pupils of his own age and a skilled teacher-counselor he discusses any problem of ethics, social concern, out-of-school experience, or implication of knowledge encountered in another class he or any student

From *Educational Leadership*, XVIII(May, 1960), 480–483, 489. Reprinted by permission of the author and publisher.

brings to the group. No curriculum is established in advance. The exploration of questions, ideas, or values advanced by group members constitutes the primary type of experience.

The purpose of the Analysis Group is to help each pupil discover meaning, to develop increased commitment to a set of values, to provide opportunity to examine the conflicts among the many sets of values and viewpoints held by members of the society.

The membership of an Analysis Group is carefully selected to provide persons of relatively equal intellectual ability but varied social and economic values. The group remains as a unit throughout its high school program. Changes are made only when deep emotional conflict develops between students or between a student and the teacher-counselor.

The teachers of Analysis Groups are emotionally mature people. They were selected early in their teacher education program because they displayed a high degree of empathy and were warm, outgoing personalities that other people liked. They were given special training in counseling, communication, and value analysis. Each has been taught to see his role as helping others feel more secure, clarify their values, and communicate more effectively with their colleagues. If a teacher of an Analysis Group attempts to sell his viewpoint, he is considered unsuccessful and is replaced.

Each Analysis Group teacher meets three groups, or 33 students, during the week. His time beyond the 18 hours in the discussion groups is for individual counseling with the 33 pupils and their parents.

The Analysis Group is considered the basic element of the educational program. In the sixties it was recognized that unless citizens had values they accepted, understood, and could apply, the social structure would begin to disintegrate unless authoritarian controls were applied. To counter the danger of collapse of a democratic way of life, the school was assigned the task of making as sure that each child developed a set of values as that he could read. The Analysis Group evolved as the best means of performing the values development function.

Acquisition of Fundamental Skills

Citizens in 1985 must have fundamental skills far superior to those necessary in the late fifties to be considered literate.

In the home and in the elementary school, children learn to read, spell, and compute at their own rate of learning by the use of teaching machines. In the school for adolescents, mathematics, foreign languages, and many scientific processes and formulas are taught by machines supervised by librarians and a staff of technicians.

It has been proved that the machines can teach basic skills as effectively and efficiently as a human. The work of Skinner and of persons working with foreign language laboratories in the late fifties paved the way for this development. All the activities needed for teaching all fundamental skills have been programmed.

Each student planning a high school program is told the skills he must master. He works through the needed program as rapidly as he can. When he wants to work on a skill, he goes to the librarian, schedules a machine and a program, and goes to work.

Certain skills are needed by all citizens, and each adolescent's program includes the requirement that these skills be acquired. Other skills are considered vocational in nature and are added to a student's program if he indicates he has college entrance or a specific vocation as a goal.

Some students complete their basic skills work early in their high school program. Others work on them until they leave the high school.

Two librarians, one to issue programs and the other to help on request, and a staff of mechanical technicians supervise the work of 200 students. Disorder is at a minimum because each person works on his own level and on his purposes. Moreover, each student works in his own soundproofed cubicle.

The teaching machines laboratories for the various subject matter areas, mathematics, languages, grammar, are an integral part of the Materials Center of the school.

Exploration of the Cultural Heritage

The explosion of available knowledge in the first three quarters of the twentieth century confronts educators with the need for selecting, synthesizing, interpreting, and seeking better methods of transmitting it. The things that an effective citizen needs to know in 1985 are a multiple of the knowledge necessary in 1960. Textbooks with less than master teachers are not enough, and ways of bringing each student into a working relationship with the best teachers available have been sought. Basic knowledge from the essential fields is prepared in the most easily understood media and presented as dramatically and forcefully as possible. This knowledge from the humanities, the social sciences, and the physical and biological sciences is considered the Cultural Heritage.

Roughly a third of the program of each high school student is designed to help him acquire the basic knowledge of his culture. By exposure to the experiences, ideas, and discoveries of the past, it is hoped that the individual will become literate enough about the basic ideas of his culture to participate in discussions of them or to understand references to them. It is further hoped that the experience in the Cultural Heritage portion of the program will develop a desire to further enhance the values on which the society is based.

Classes in the Cultural Heritage program are large. Sometimes as many as 500 or 1,000 are in a single section.

Teaching is by television, films, or a highly skilled lecturer. No provision is made for discussion because ideas that produce a response can be discussed in the Analysis Groups.

Only one teacher and an assistant are needed in each subject matter field in each school. The teacher lectures or presents the material by an appropriate medium. The assistant prepares quizzes and examinations and records the marks made on the machine-scored tests.

The high pupil-teacher ratio in the Cultural Heritage area, 1 teacher for each 500 to 1,500 students, makes possible the low ratio, 1 to 33, for Analysis Groups and highly individual instruction for the exceptional student.

Teachers for the Cultural Heritage program are selected early in their teacher education program. They speak well, like to be before an audience, have a sense for the dramatic and are attractive persons. In addition to intensive work in their field, they are given work in speech, dramatics, logic, and mass media.

Specialization and Creativity

The Analysis Groups, the Cultural Heritage Courses, and the Fundamental Skills work constitute the program required of all. But, in addition, each student is encouraged to develop a specialization. It is not required, but the opportunity is presented.

Shops, studios, and working laboratories are available for specialized activities. All students who wish are encouraged to engage in some creative activities since the Cultural Heritage phase of the program is essentially a passive reception.

Writing laboratories are staffed to help students who want to develop creative writing ability. School newspapers, magazines, and telecasts are written in the laboratories.

Other students select work experience in various industries and businesses in the community. These students have decided they will not seek higher education and are using their specialized program to ensure a smooth transition to regular employment.

Special opportunities are available for the persons who qualify in terms of ability and intensity of purpose.

Seminars in the various content fields, and some of an interdisciplinary nature, are available for those who can qualify. Students must have displayed unusual ability and show evidence of a desire for individual investigation in a field before they are permitted to enroll.

Seminars are limited to 15 students. They meet for two 2-hour periods per week and the remainder of the time the students conduct independent research in the library or laboratories.

Small laboratories are kept open for full time use by the individual researchers from the seminars. In fact, students who are not expected to become scientists or technicians in an area do not use laboratory facilities. Laboratory experience was abandoned as a general education procedure in the mid-sixties.

In the specialized fields the pupil-teacher ratio is low, 1 to 40 or 50 pupils. Teachers give individualized supervision and plan with the Analysis Group teachers the experiences individuals should have.

No longer do the colleges blame the secondary schools for inadequate preparation. Graduation days have been eliminated. Students continue to work in the secondary school until they pass their college entrance examinations or move to a job. Most students enter the secondary school at 13, but some leave at 15 and others at 20. A student's decision to leave the program is conditioned by his completion of the Cultural Heritage experiences, his acquisition of fundamental skills, and his individual purposes.

The School Plant

The school plant has many different sized rooms. Analysis groups, specialized education classrooms, studios, and laboratories are small. Cultural Heritage courses are held in large halls equipped for lectures and mass media programs. Libraries and studios and shops are large. Areas where individuals work with teaching machines to perfect basic skills are divided into small work cubicles. Buildings with uniform size classrooms are obsolete.

Basis of Support

The program described above is paid for from federal funds. It was recognized in the late sixties that, with a population as mobile as ours, neither local communities nor the national government could afford to allow the great differences in educational opportunity to continue. No community was immune to poor education in another and the national government was thus neglecting a large percentage of its human resources.

Evolution of the Program

The program was not achieved without some difficult struggles. Many vocies arose in the late fifties and early sixties clamoring for a copying of a European educational system. Some wanted to use tests and allocate the pupil to a specialized curriculum as early as ten years of age and give him the required courses the experts deemed suitable for him. They proposed restricting the curriculum of the secondary school to the intellectual pursuit of information in certain areas of knowledge. Values and social development were to be left to the home and church.

However, increasing juvenile delinquency, more homes with both parents working, increasing mental and emotional disturbance could not be ignored. The secondary school program had to be made broad enough to deal with values, human relations, fundamental skills in communication, the cultural heritage, as well as work in a student's special field.

chapter 37

How can the effectiveness of learning experiences be evaluated?

Ralph W. Tyler

Since we have considered the operations involved in choosing and formulating educational objectives and in selecting and organizing learning experiences, it may appear that we have completed our analysis of curriculum development. Although the steps previously discussed provide the plans for the day-by-day work of the school, they do not complete the planning cycle. Evaluation is also an important operation in curriculum development.

The Need for Evaluation

The steps thus far outlined have provided us with learning experiences that have been checked against various criteria derived from educational psychology and from practical experience. We also have utilized criteria regarding the organization of these learning experiences. In a sense, then, certain preliminary evaluations have already been made of the learning experiences. We may refer to these as intermediate or preliminary stages of evaluation. The learning experiences have been checked to see that they are related to the objectives set up and to see that they provide for other important psychological principles, so far as these principles are known. However, this is not an adequate appraisal of the learning experiences planned for curriculum and instruction. The generalizations used as criteria against which to check the learning experiences are general principles applying to generalized characteristics of the learning experiences, and they are not

From *Basic Principles of Curriculum and Instruction* (Chicago: University of Chicago Press, 1950), 68–81. Reprinted by permission of the author and The University of Chicago Press.

highly precise statements of the exact conditions to be met in providing for the learnings desired. Furthermore, any set of learning experiences involves a number of criteria, each of which can only be approximated, so that we can only predict in general or with a certain degree of accuracy the likelihood that these experiences will actually produce the effects desired. Finally, the actual teaching procedures involve a considerable number of variables, including variations in individual students, the environmental conditions in which the learning goes on, the skill of the teacher in setting the conditions as they are planned, the personality characteristics of the teacher, and the like. These many variables make it impossible to guarantee that the actual learning experiences provided are precisely those that are outlined in the learning units. Hence, it is important to make a more inclusive check as to whether these plans for learning experiences actually function to guide the teacher in producing the sort of outcomes desired. This is the purpose for evaluation and the reason why a process of evaluation is necessary after the plans themselves are developed.

It should be clear that evaluation then becomes a process for finding out how far the learning experiences as developed and organized are actually producing the desired results, and the process of evaluation will involve identifying the strengths and weaknesses of the plans. This helps to check the validity of the basic hypotheses upon which the instructional program has been organized and developed, and it also checks the effectiveness of the particular instruments, that is, the teachers and other conditions that are being used to carry forward the instructional program. As a result of evaluation it is possible to note in what respects the curriculum is effective and in what respects it needs improvement.

Basic Notions Regarding Evaluation

The process of evaluation is essentially the process of determining to what extent the educational objectives are actually being realized by the program of curriculum and instruction. However, since educational objectives are essentially changes in human beings, that is, the objectives aimed at are to produce certain desirable changes in the behavior patterns of the student, then evaluation is the process for determining the degree to which these changes in behavior are actually taking place.

This conception of evaluation has two important aspects. In the first place, it implies that evaluation must appraise the behavior of students since it is change in these behaviors which is sought in education. In the second place, it implies that evaluation must involve more than a single appraisal at any one time since to see whether change has taken place, it is necessary to make an appraisal at an early point and other appraisals at later points to identify changes that may be occurring. On this basis, one is not able to evaluate an instructional program by testing students only at the end of the program. Without knowing where the students were at the beginning, it is not possible to tell how far changes have taken place. In some cases, it is possible that the students had made a good deal of progress on the objectives before they began the instructional program. In other cases it may very well be that the students have very little achievement before they begin instruction, and almost all of that noted at the end took place during the time the instruction went on. Hence, it is clear that an educational evaluation involves at least two appraisals—one taking place in the early part of the educational program and the other at some later point so that the change may be measured.

However, it is not enough to have only two appraisals in making an educational evaluation because some of the objectives aimed at may be acquired during an educational program and then be rapidly dissipated or forgotten. In order to have some estimate of the permanence of the learning, it is necessary to have still another point of evaluation which is made sometime after the instruction has been completed. Hence, schools and colleges are making follow-up studies of their graduates in order to get further evidence as to the permanence or impermanence of the learnings which may have been acquired during the time these young people were in school. This is a desirable part of the evaluation program. In fact, so far as frequency of evaluation is concerned, much can be said for at least an annual appraisal carried on year after year as the children move through the school so that a continuing record of progress can be obtained and evidence accumulated to indicate places where these changes are not actually taking place.

Since evaluation involves getting evidence about behavior changes in the students, any valid evidence about behaviors that are desired as educational objectives provides an appropriate method of evaluation. This is important to recognize because many people think of evaluation as synonymous with the giving of paper-and-pencil tests. It is true that paper-and-pencil tests provide a practicable procedure for getting evidences about several kinds of student behavior. For example, if one wishes to find out what knowledge students have, it may be easily obtained from paper-and-pencil tests if the students are able to express their ideas in writing, or can read and check off various items in a multiple-response test or other similar tests. As another illustration, paper-and-pencil tests are useful devices to get at the ability of students to analyze and deal effectively with various types of verbal problems, with vocabulary, with reading, and a number of other types of skills and abilities easily expressed in verbal form. However, there are a great many other kinds of desired behaviors which represent educational objectives that are not easily appraised by paper-and-pencil devices. For example, such an objective as personal social adjustment is more easily and validly appraised through observations of children under conditions in which social relations are involved. Observations are also useful devices to get at habits and certain kinds of operational skills. Another method which is useful in evaluation is the interview, which may throw light upon changes taking place in attitudes, in interests, in appreciations, and the like. Questionnaires sometimes serve to give evidence about interests, about attitudes, and about other types of behavior. The collection of actual products made by students is sometimes a useful way of getting evidence of behavior. For example, the collection of theses students have written may serve to give some evidence of the writing ability of students, or the paintings students have made in an art class may serve to give evidence of skill and possibly interests in this area. Objects made in the shop or in the clothing construction course are additional illustrations of the collection of samples of products as an evaluation device. Even records made for other purposes sometimes provide evidence of types of behavior or interest in terms of educational objectives. For example, books withdrawn from the library may provide some indication of reading interests. Menus checked in cafeteria may provide some evidence of the eating habits of students. Health records may throw some light on health practices. These are all illustrations of the fact that there are many ways of getting evidence about behavior changes and that when we think of evaluation we are not talking about any single or even any two or three particular appraisal methods. Any way of getting valid evidence about the kinds of behavior represented by the educational objectives of the school or college is an appropriate evaluation procedure.

Sampling is another basic notion of evaluation. Sampling is involved in many points. For example, evaluation assumes that it is possible to estimate the typical reactions of students by getting evidence about a sample of his reactions. We do not collect all the written work the students have ever prepared in order to get some estimate of their writing ability. We recognize it is possible to judge the writing commonly to be expected from this student by examining a proper sample of his writing. Correspondingly, with reference to a student's knowledge, we do not ask him all the questions about all the facts, principles, concepts, and the like that may be involved in his education, but rather we choose a sample of these things to question him about, and we infer from his reaction to this sample how he might react to the total set of items that might be involved in his knowledge. This holds for all types of human behavior, attitudes, interests, intellectual skills, appreciations, and the like. We assume that it is possible to infer the person's characteristic performance by appraising his reaction in a sample of situations where this reaction is involved.

Sampling is not only involved in appraising the individual's behavior, but it may also be involved in appraising the effectiveness of curriculum experiences in use with a group of students. It is not always necessary to find out the reaction of every individual in order to see the effect that the curriculum is producing. It is possible to take a sample of students, and if this sample is properly chosen the results with this sample of students may within small limits of error properly represent the kind of results which would have been obtained had all the students been involved in the appraisal. Thus, it is possible for an appraisal to be so designed that not too many students need to be interviewed or probed with time-consuming means in order to get some indication of what is happening to the students in terms of the behavior appraised by these means. Correspondingly, when follow-up studies are made to determine the permanency of the learning, it is possible to select a sample of graduates that will be properly representative of the total group and to concentrate at fairly intensive study of the behavior of the sample of graduates in order to draw some conclusions about the permanence of learning which is probably characteristic of the average graduate of the program.

These are some of the basic notions regarding evaluation which guide in the development of an evaluation program. There are other notions involved in evaluation, but these are among the most important ones. Their implications will be considered further as we examine the procedures for making an educational evaluation.

Evaluation Procedures

The process of evaluation begins with the objectives of the educational program. Since the purpose is to see how far these objectives are actually being realized, it is necessary to have evaluation procedures that will give evidence about each of the kinds of behavior implied by each of the major educational objectives. If, for example, one of the objectives is to acquire important knowledge about contemporary social problems, then it is necessary that the evaluation give some evidence of the knowledge students are acquiring. If another is to develop methods of analyzing social problems and appraising proposed solutions of them, then it is necessary that the evaluation procedures give us some evidence as to the skill of the student in analyzing social problems and appraising suggested solutions to them. This means that the two-dimensional analysis which served as a basis for planning the learning experiences also serves as the basis for planning the evaluation procedures. The two-dimensional analysis of objectives thus serves as a set of specifications for evaluation. Each of the behavioral headings in the analysis indicates the kind of behavior which should be appraised to see how far that kind of behavior is developing; and each of the content headings of the analysis indicates the content to be sampled in connection with the behavior appraisal. Thus, in the case of the objectives regarding knowledge about social problems, the two-dimensional analysis indicates that evaluation of knowledge must be made for the behavior, and the content headings indicate what areas of knowledge should be sampled in order to have a satisfactory appraisal of the knowledge being acquired by the students in this field. Correspondingly, an objective "Developing Interests in Literature" would require an appraisal of developing interests in students for the behavior aspect, and the content headings would indicate the areas in which interests might be expected to be developed and which should be sampled in order to see whether such interests are actually being developed. In this way a two-dimensional analysis of objectives becomes a guide to the evaluation of the curriculum.

It is, of course, assumed that these "behavioral objectives" have been clearly defined by the curriculum worker. They should have been defined clearly so as to provide a concrete guide in the selection and planning of learning experiences. If they have not yet been clearly defined, it is absolutely essential that they be defined in order to make an evaluation, since unless there is some clear conception of the sort of behavior implied by the objectives, one has no way of telling what kind of behavior to look for in the students in order to see to what degree these objectives are being realized. This means that the process of evaluation may force persons who have not previously clarified their objectives to a further process of clarification. Definition of objectives, then, is an important step in evaluation.

The next step in evaluation procedure is to identify the situations which will give the student the chance to express the behavior that is implied by the educational objectives. The only way that we can tell whether students have acquired given types of behavior is to give them an opportunity to show this behavior. This means that we must find situations which not only permit the expression of the behavior but actually encourage or evoke this behavior. We are then in a position to observe the degree to which the objectives are actually being realized. In some cases, it is easy to see the kinds of situations that give students the chance to express desired types of behavior. We are accustomed to stimulating students to express ideas through questions, and it is therefore possible in the question situation to evoke reactions of the students that involve knowledge and ability to deal with verbal materials. When we consider the whole range of desired objectives, we can see that the situations are not all of this type. If we are going to see how children are developing personal social adjustment, we must use those situations which give children a chance to react to other children. This may mean looking for evidence about personal social adjustment in the nursery school during those periods when children are playing and working together. It may mean that we shall look for evidences of interests in those situations where there is opportunity for free choice of activity. Students may, therefore, freely express their interests. If we want evidence of the student's ability to express himself orally, we must look in those situations which evoke oral expression. The principle is simple enough that any evaluation situation is the kind of situation that gives an opportunity for the students to express the type of behavior we are trying to appraise. Although the principle is simple, there are still many problems involved in finding situations that are sufficiently under control and permit the teacher or other evaluator to have access to them in order to see the types of behaviors the students are developing. In case some situations are difficult to handle, then one of the tasks of the specialist in evaluation is to try to find other simpler situations that will have a high correlation with the result obtained when the situation is used which directly evokes the kind of behavior to be appraised.

It is only after the objectives have been identified, clearly defined, and situations listed which give opportunity for the expression of the behavior desired that it is possible to examine available evaluation instruments to see how far they may serve the evaluation purposes desired. It is not really possible to look at a particular test and to decide whether it would do for appraising a certain educational program until the objectives of the program have been indentified and defined and until the kinds of situations that would give an opportunity for this behavior to be expressed have also been identified. After these steps have been taken, one can then examine particular tests and see how far they sample the types of objectives that are to be appraised and how far the tests either use situations which directly evoke the kind of behavior to be appraised or else they use situations which have been correlated with the situations that directly evoke the type of behavior. It has too commonly been true that persons have gone to test catalogs or have looked at sample tests and selected them without having these previous steps in mind to serve as the basis for making a wise selection. Just because Test A is the most widely used test in physics or Test B is commonly recommended for art or Test C has been prepared by some widely known specialist in mathematics, these are not indications that these tests may be appropriate ways of getting evidence about the particular objectives that are aimed at in a given educational program. It is very necessary to check each proposed evaluation device against the objectives that are being aimed at and to see whether it uses situations likely to evoke the sort of behavior which is desired as educational objectives.

When available evaluation instruments are checked in this way, it is quite probable that the curriculum constructor will find that there are available instruments which can be modified somewhat and made appropriate for certain other educational objectives, and finally, that there are some educational objectives for which no available evaluation instruments can properly be used. For these last, it may be necessary to construct or devise methods for getting evidence about the student's attainment of these objectives. The construction of evaluation instruments can be a very difficult task if the purpose is to get a highly refined instrument, but a great deal can be done of a less refined sort by collecting evidence in rather simple ways relating to these various educational objectives. We shall discuss illustrations of these a little later.

If it is necessary to construct an evaluation instrument for a particular objective, the next step is actually to try out some of the situations suggested as situations that give the student a chance to express the behavior desired. This tryout provides an opportunity to see whether these situations will serve as convenient ways of getting evidence. Thus, it may appear that the type of situation likely to give students a chance to show their ability to analyze problems is a situation in which a number of problems are presented in written form and the students are asked to analyze them. Situations of this sort can actually be tried out with students to see how far the responses obtained provide an adequate basis for checking the student's ability to analyze problems. Or, a situation that is likely to give students a chance to indicate their interests is to present a questionnaire in which a variety of activities are listed and the students are asked to check those in which they are interested and also to mark those in which they have no interest. If this appears to be a situation likely to give students an opportunity to show interests, then it should be used in trial form to see how satisfactorily it works. This step is a useful step in developing possible evaluation devices into forms where they can be satisfactorily used.

After deciding on certain situations used to get evidence about the behavior of students, it is then necessary to devise a means of getting a record of the student's behavior in this test situation. In the case of a written examination the student makes his own record in his writing. Hence, the problem of getting a record of his behavior is not a serious one. On the other hand, a situation that gives nursery school children a chance to play and work together may be a good situation to provide evidence of personal social adjustment but it is necessary to get some record of the children's reaction in this situation if there is to be opportunity to appraise this reaction after it has been made. This may involve making a detailed description of reaction by an observer, it may suggest the use of a motion picture or sound recording, it may suggest the use of an observer's checklist by which he checks off particular types of behavior that commonly appear, or it may involve some other means of getting a satisfactory record of the children's reaction. This is a step that must be considered in connection with each test situation to be sure that the situation not only evokes the desired behavior but that a record can be obtained which can be appraised later.

The next step in developing an evaluation instrument is to decide upon the terms or units that will be used to summarize or to appraise the record of behavior obtained. This method of appraising the behavior should, of course, parallel the implications of the objective itself. For example, if reading interests as an educational objective are to be defined as the development of increasingly broad and mature interests, it then becomes necessary to decide upon units by which a record of children's reading can be summarized to indicate breadth and to indicate maturity. Breadth may be indicated by a number which measures the different categories of reading material included in the youngster's reading for the year. Thus, a child who reads only Wild West stories and detective stories would have his reading list classified under two categories only and the figure 2 would represent a measure of breadth. This would be in contrast to a boy whose reading record could be classified under four categories such as adventure, romance, psychological, sociological. The fact that the second boy read materials classified under a wider number of categories would be represented by the number 4 in contrast to the number 2. Correspondingly, if different reading levels can be classified under different levels of maturity, it becomes possible to summarize a reading record in terms of its average level of maturity and thus to provide a measure of that aspect of reading interest. This illustration has been chosen because it is very different from the problem as it is usually viewed by the person who reads and scores the test; and yet, essentially all evaluation involves this problem, that is, the decision upon the characteristics that are to be appraised in the behavior and the unit to be used in the measurement or summarization of these characteristics. In the case of reading interests, the characteristics used were range and maturity so that the methods of summarization provided a rating for range and maturity.

The problem is a similar one in summarizing a typical objective-type test. Suppose it is a measure of knowledge. The question then to be faced is: Will knowledge be summarized in terms of the number of different items in the sample which the student was able to remember properly, or is it better indicated by some classification of the items so as to indicate which topics he remembered best and which less well, or is there some other way by which the objective of knowledge can be most satisfactorily summarized or appraised in order to serve the purpose of evaluation? Every kind of human behavior which is appraised for its part as an educational objective must be summarized or measured in some terms and the decision about these terms is an important problem in the development and use of evaluation instruments.

It should be clear that for most purposes the appraisal of human behavior should be an analytic one rather than a single-score summary. Simply to know that John Smith made a score of 97 and Mary Jones made a score of 64 on some evaluation instrument is not an adequate summary nor likely to be helpful for improving the curriculum. It is much more useful to have summaries which indicate the kinds of strengths and weaknesses, summaries at least in terms of each objective; and in many cases it may be desirable to have several scores or summaries for each objective so as to describe more adequately the achievement of this particular sort of objective. Thus, it is useful to know whether the students are making progress in developing a range of reading interests even though they may be making less progress in developing maturity of reading interests. It is helpful to know that students are making progress in their skill of interpretation in reading although their reading interests may not be as satisfactory as hoped.

This kind of analytic summary which indicates particular strengths and weaknesses is, of course, invaluable in using the results to improve the curriculum. It means that the plan for appraisal must be developed before scoring and rating is actually made. Decisions about these points are necessary decisions in developing an evaluation program.

The next step in the construction of an evaluation instrument is to determine how far these rating or summarizing methods are objective, that is, to what degree two different persons, presumably competent, would be able to reach similar scores or summaries when they had an opportunity to score or summarize the same records of behavior. If the scores or summaries vary markedly, depending upon who does the scoring or summarizing, it is clearly a subjective kind of appraisal and requires improvement in its objectivity in order to be a more satisfactory means of appraising a human behavior. Sometimes improvement can be made through clarifying the specifications for scoring, sometimes through getting a more refined record of behavior itself. It is beyond the scope of the present discussion to outline the various techniques for refining and improving the objectivity of the instruments. It is necessary, however, to recognize this problem and to attempt to get a more objective procedure when necessary. When these possible evaluation instruments have been tried out, one can not only check on the objectivity of the scoring or summary but also check upon the adequacy of the sample of behavior included in the instrument. In general, the size of the sample of behavior to be obtained depends upon how variable that behavior is. If one wishes to get evidence about the social attitudes of students and these attitudes are highly consistent in each individual, it takes only a few samples to get a rather dependable indication of the attitude of each student. On the other hand, if there is wide variability in each student's attitudes, for example, if he is highly selfish at some points and highly social at others, it takes a much larger sample of his behavior in order to infer reliably about the degree of his social or selfish attitudes. Hence, it is not possible to be sure in advance how large a sample of behavior must be collected regarding a given objective in order to have a dependable sample from which to draw conclusions about the individual's status. It is possible after trying out an instrument to find out what the variation among the items in the instrument is and thus to estimate how reliable the sample is and whether a larger or smaller sample would do satisfactorily. This is the problem of reliability of a test or other evaluation device; and, although it is beyond the scope of this discussion to describe methods of estimating reliability, it is important to recognize what reliability means and to realize that if a given test is too short to provide an adequate sample or if a given set of observations does not cover a large enough span of time to get an adequate sample of the student's behavior, it will be necessary to extend the sample before dependable conclusions can be drawn.

Since we have used the two terms for two of the important criteria for an evaluation instrument, namely, objectivity and reliability, it is necessary to emphasize the third and most important criteria of an evaluation instrument, namely, validity. Validity applies to the method and indicates the degree to which an evaluation device actually provides evidence of the behavior desired. Validity can be assured in one of two ways. One way is by getting directly a sample of the kind of behavior to be measured, as when one observes directly the food children are selecting as the basis for inferring food habits, or one obtains an actual record of reading done as an indication of reading habits, or one presents problems for children to analyze to get evidence of their ability to analyze problems. This is known as "face validity"—the evaluation instrument is valid on the face of it because it directly samples the kind of behavior which it is desired to appraise. The other way of assuring validity is through correlating a particular evaluation device with the result obtained by a directly valid measure. If it can be shown that the results of a certain reading questionnaire correlate very highly with the results obtained from an actual record of reading, then the reading questionnaire might be used as a valid indication of what children read. It would be valid because the results are shown by experimental methods to correlate highly with the direct evidence. In some cases, persons developing tests find that it is expensive or difficult or otherwise impracticable to get evidence by the direct method and they try out various possible ways of getting evidence which are simpler and easier to handle. None of these should be used, however, as a valid instrument until it has been shown to correlate highly with the evidence obtained directly, that is, from an instrument which has face validity.

These steps indicate the procedures followed in making an evaluation and in developing an instrument for an evaluation. In case the instrument is found to have too little objectivity or reliability, it is necessary to improve it. It is also necessary to make any other revisions indicated by the preliminary tryout, such as eliminating ambiguities in directions, dropping out parts of the instrument which got no significant reactions from students. In general, then, the result is a continually improved instrument for getting evidence about the degree to which students are attaining given educational objectives.

These instruments are used in order to obtain summarized or appraised results. These results may be in the form of scores, or descriptions, or both, depending upon the form which can be most satisfactorily used to summarize the behavior in terms that are appropriate for the objectives desired.

Using the Results of Evaluation

Since every educational program involves several objectives and since for almost every objective there will be several students in relation to this objective, it follows that the results obtained from evaluation instruments will not be a single score or a single descriptive term but an analyzed profile or a comprehensive set of descriptive terms indicating the present student achievement. These scores or descriptive terms should, of course, be comparable to those used at a preceding date so that it is possible to indicate change taking place and one can then see whether or not educational progress is actually happening. If it is found, for example, that the range of students' interests in reading is no greater at the end of the tenth grade than it was at the end of the ninth grade, it is clear that no appreciable change is taking place in reading interest. Correspondingly, if it is shown that the ability to interpret reading passages critically is no higher at the end of the tenth grade than at the end of the ninth grade, again, no educational change is taking place. It is, therefore, essential to compare the results obtained from the several evaluation instruments before and after given periods in order to estimate the amount of change taking place. The fact that these are not a single score, may complicate the process, but it is necessary for the kind of identification of strengths and weaknesses that will help to indicate where the curriculum may need improvement. For example, in connection with the curriculum program which involved the development of a core focused upon contemporary social problems, it was found that at the end of the first year, the students had acquired a great deal more information about these contemporary problems, that they had shifted their social attitudes slightly in the direction of greater social and less selfish attitudes, but that their attitudes were much more confused and inconsistent than before, that they had not gained any skill in analyzing social problems, and that their ability to interpret social data was worse because the students were drawing more unwarranted conclusions than before. Putting all of these things together gave the teachers the chance to see the kinds of weaknesses, which had to do with their greater inconsistencies, less ability to analyze critically and the like. This is more helpful in getting at the seat of the difficulty in this particular core curriculum than if there had been a single score which indicated a small amount of improvement but did not analyze this improvement into a number of different categories.

It is not only desirable to analyze the results of an evaluation to indicate the various strengths and weaknesses, but it is also necessary to examine these data to suggest possible explanations or hypotheses about the reason for this particular pattern of strengths and weaknesses. In the case just cited, after examining all the data available, it is suggested that this implied a great deal more ground was being covered and not enough time was being spent in careful critical analysis. This was checked against the actual amount of reading provided, which turned out to be more than 6,000 pages, and the number of social problems dealt with, which turned out to be 21, both of which in the light of these data seemed to be excessive and suggested that a possible explanation for these weaknesses was that too much material was being covered and not enough time devoted to critical analysis, interpretation, and application.

When hypotheses have been suggested that might possibly explain the evaluation data, the next step is to check those hypotheses against the present available data, that is, against additional data that may be available, and to see whether the hypotheses are consistent with all the data then available. If they appear to be consistent with the available data, the next step is to modify the curriculum in the direction implied by the hypotheses and then to teach the material to see whether there is any actual improvement in student achievement when these modifications are made. If there is, then it would suggest that the hypotheses are likely explanations and the basis for improving the curriculum has been identified. In the case just cited it was possible to reorganize the course for the coming year and to reduce the number of major problems from 21 to 7 and to reduce the quantity of reading material by more than half so as to utilize more time in interpreting, applying, analyzing, and otherwise treating the material dealt with. At the end of the second year, it was found that, although the students had not gained quite so much in the range of information acquired, they had gained greater consistency in social attitudes, had gained greater skill in analyzing social problems, and had become able to draw better generalizations from the data presented to them. This would indicate that the hypothesis that what was wrong with the course was that it covered too much ground seemed to be a sound one. This is a typical procedure that can be followed in using evaluation results so as to modify and improve the curriculum and instructional program.

What is implied in all of this is that curriculum planning is a continuous process and that as materials and procedures are developed, they are tried out, their results appraised, their inadequacies identified, suggested improvements indicated; there is replanning, redevelopment, and then reappraisal; and in this kind of continuing cycle, it is possible for the curriculum and instructional program to be continuously improved over the years. In this way we may hope to have an increasingly more effective educational program rather than depending so much upon hit-and-miss judgment as a basis for curriculum development.

Other Values and Uses of Evaluation Procedures

In the foregoing discussion of evaluation, we have concentrated primarily upon the use of evaluation procedures in identifying the strengths and weaknesses of the curriculum program. This is its main function in curriculum work. It also serves other purposes. The very fact that it is not possible to make an evaluation until objectives are clearly enough defined so that one can recognize the behavior to be sought means that evaluation is a powerful device for clarifying educational objectives if they have not already been clarified in the curriculum planning process.

Evaluation also has a powerful influence upon learning. It has been shown in the New York Regents' Inquiry that the Regents have more effect upon what is taught in New York State than course of study outlines as such. Students are influenced in their study by the kind of evaluation to be made and even teachers are influenced in their emphasis by the sort of evaluation which they expect to be made. This means that unless the evaluation procedure closely parallels the objectives of the curriculum the evaluation procedure may become the focus of the students' attention and even of the teachers' attention rather than the curriculum objectives set up. Hence, evaluation and curriculum must be closely integrated so that the effect will not be for the curriculum planning to be ignored in order for diverse objectives appraised by evaluation to be given major attention.

Evaluation procedures also have great importance in the individual guidance of pupils. It is not only valuable to know about students' background but also to know about their achievement of various kinds of objectives in order to have a better notion of both their needs and their capabilities. Any comprehensive evaluation program provides information about individual students that can be of great value.

Evaluation can also be used continuously during the year as a basis for identifying particular points needing further attention with particular groups of students and as a basis for giving individual help or planning individual programs for students in the light of their particular progress in the educational program.

Finally, evaluation becomes one of the important ways of providing information about the success of the school to the school's clientele. Ultimately, schools need to be appraised in terms of their effectiveness in attaining important objectives. This means that ultimately evaluation results need to be translated in terms that will be understandable to parents and the public generally. Only as we can describe more accurately the results we are attaining from the curriculum are we in a position to get the most intelligent support for the educational program of the school. Neither parents nor the public can be satisfied long with reports about the number of children enrolled and the number of new buildings built and things of that sort. Eventually, parents have a right to know what kind of changes are being brought about in their children. Now, most of the reports of this sort that they get are from appraisals that are not fairly made. We hear about the number of persons rejected because of lack of reading ability or lack of physical health in connection with Selective Service, but we have no means of tracing those cases back to particular schools. Increasingly, we must expect to use evaluation procedures to determine what changes are actually taking place in students and where we are achieving our curriculum objectives and where we must make still further modifications in order to get an effective educational program.

part V

Selected issues in secondary education

Societal changes have a tremendous impact on what schools are expected to do. Elder Americans look upon the school as a vehicle for communicating to young Americans the values that they believe should be fostered and perpetuated. School personnel are under continual stress to respond to the pressures exerted by local, regional, and national groups. What makes this problem especially difficult is that pressure groups are seldom united in what they want the school to do.

By very definition, an issue implies controversy. As soon as two or more groups have different proposals as to what course of action should be pursued by our schools, we have the makings of an issue. Some issues are centered around the nature of the educational process. Others revolve around the people who work in schools. But educational issues have one thing in common: They all attempt to influence, indeed determine, the roles to be played by school personnel.

In Part V, statements are presented on issues which are of great concern to future teachers, for how these issues are resolved will to a large degree influence the kind of work that future teachers will be doing.

Schools are frequently attacked because they are allegedly attempting to base their instructional programs on a particular philosophy of education unacceptable to the critic. Washburne's

*paper is concerned with the conflicts that must inevitably exist
between educational theory and educational practice.*

*The articles by Alexander and Hoover are related, in that they
discuss in some detail various facets of the teacher-learning
process. Alexander discusses some of the issues attendant upon
curriculum revision, and Hoover comments on the validity of
teacher-pupil planning.*

*The selections by Brix, Robinson, and Riccio and Peters are
concerned with what is an exceptionally controversial area: the
teaching of values related to the political order. Brix discusses the
teaching of communism. Robinson describes recent attacks on the
professional and political affiliations of teachers. Riccio and Peters
inquire as to whether we should attempt to promulgate cooperative
or competitive activity in our schools.*

*The last three articles are also concerned with heated
issues. Kohlbrenner compares the treatment afforded talented
students in America and in other nations. The report from
The Nation's Schools is concerned with whether we should teach
about religions in our public schools. Mott deals with the problem of
grouping students in terms of ability.*

*The issues presented are not intended to be exhaustive. They
are intended to be provocative. Some of the shorter pieces simply
state problems. The longer selections state problems, and suggest
solutions. The reader need not agree with the authors of the
articles; the materials presented are expected to generate discussion.*

chapter 38

Conflicts between educational theory and structure

Chandler Washburne

In a large, complex and confusing society like ours we have learned to accept the fact that things are often contradictory and working at cross-purposes. In fact, we frequently do not even notice it. This may be because we are used to the contradictions or have come to accept them, or it may be because the contradictions are subtle and not apparent at first glance.

Recently, when the writer was doing research into the position of the high school teacher, a number of contradictory elements emerged. As the work went on and more elements appeared, it began to be clear that they were all related to a general problem in the field of education.[1] As the character of this problem has become more formulated it has been found that it is not something unique to the educational field, but one found in many areas in our society.

What is this problem, or contradiction? Briefly, it is the struggle between *theory* and *social structure*. If we have a series of ideas, or a theory, concerning what man's behavior should be, or what he should be trying to reach, how do we realize it? Some sort of social organization is formed to carry out these ideas. Thus, as we look around us, we see any number of social structures, each struggling to reach their ends. For example, there

[1] Chandler Washburne, *Involvement as a Basis for Stress Analysis: A Study of High School Teachers* (Ph.D dissertation, Mich. State College, 1953).

From *Educational Theory*, VIII(April, 1958), 87–94. Reprinted by permission of the author and publisher.

are school systems or churches. We generally like to think that a structure is prevented from reaching its goals, or putting its theories into practice, by the opposition of other systems. This may not be the most important factor, and in the case of education one suspects that it isn't. There is a much more subtle contradiction frequently at work. It lies in the fact that the very social structure erected to implement the goals or theory may work at cross-purposes to them, because the structure has certain needs and aims intrinsic or inherent in it. The conflict then is one over *practice*. Theory dictates one thing and the very nature of the structure another.

Certainly, a very interesting analysis could be made of religious organizations, where they start with certain aims, and set up an organization to carry them out. Regardless of good intent, the structure may diverge in its aims from the theory. Take a typical religious idea, that of complete poverty —not having material goods, no social structure is likely to operate on that basis for long. This was a problem the Franciscan movement faced within the Roman Catholic Church. The history of the Christian churches is filled with men who have revolted against the structure, because they felt it was taking them away from the theoretical principles. In many cases this could be shown to occur because the inherent aims of the structure were moving away from the theoretical goals.

What Are Present Theory and Structure in Education?

In looking at the field of education, we need to ask two questions: What is present theory? What is present structure? Then we can proceed to determine what the contradictions may be.

When one looks at present theory in education from a very general standpoint, one notices that it is not a unique theory, but one shared by a number of other fields. It is part of a trend in modern thinking. Present educational theory is closely related to the types of theories found in modern science. The basic idea is very simple: things do not consist of isolated parts; they must be understood as a kind of whole. In educational theory, one aspect of this is the idea that we teach the "whole child," and we don't just teach him fractions or reading. In psychology we find *Gestalt* theory, which contains the same idea that things are seen as wholes. In the natural sciences there is "field theory." Things are not explained alone, but as they exist in a field of force, in relationship to all other factors around them. In fact, they are explained as no more than sets of relationships. In medicine, the idea of psychosomatic medicine with the idea that you treat the whole patient, has become prominent. In anthropology, there is the theory of functionalism which states that culture can only be understood as a functional whole. In all these theories there is the idea that things are related, and that only the study of the relationships will give us satisfactory answers.

When we deal particularly with educational theory there are additional factors beside the key one of "wholeness." Arising from this idea, however, is the concept that we must deal with the individual, we must personalize the educational situation to deal with his unique functional arrangement. We must suit the learning situation to the particular individual. This might be considered the idea expressed in the term used in modern educational theory: "the child-centered school." A further implication of the above is that we must allow each child to be unique, or follow his own particular pattern of development at his own rate in his own way. His own creativity and spontaneity must be used to work out his own particular problems. Further aspects of the theory can be dealt with below when the conflicts are analyzed. Something should now be said about modern social structure.

What is the typical structure created to carry out the theory of education? It is the *bureaucracy*. This type of social structure is one which is becoming dominant in our society. It carries with it certain principles of organization and certain values. There are some things it can do well, and some things it can't do at all. Those who direct the bureaucracy are generally likely to become concerned with the smooth running of the bureaucratic machine, and the spread of bureaucratic methods and techniques to all parts of it. This generates a whole set of values, and an interest in those techniques and methods which fit in with bureaucratic principles. There is no guarantee that the resulting bureaucratic factors will be in harmony with the aims of educational theory. It is the thesis of this paper that in many ways they conflict. Bureaucracy is not a completely flexible instrument that can be directed toward whatever aims you wish. In addition, it begins to change the individuals in it so that they hold new bureaucratic types of goals.

What is bureaucracy? There is only room here to point out some of the general characteristics that are relevant. The most general aspect is that it represents rationalization. This means the bringing of reason to social organization. The structure is made formal and objective, and there is the attempt to work out the whole structure along logical lines, rather than follow tradition or personal desire. There is the notion of efficiency in reaching goals. Most of the following points are related to the basic concept of rationalization.

As an aid in directing the activity of members of the bureaucracy, there are developed complex systems of rules, regulations, or laws. These rules are written to keep individuals from changing them, and to make them explicit to all. They are specific in the sense that they prescribe appropriate action for most of the recurrent situations faced by individuals in the bureaucracy.

The rules make action and consequence predictable, and prediction is a major value. For only by predicting can the complex system of organization be run. This interest ties in closely with science, in that science's aim is prediction.

Specialization is one of the most noticeable features of the bureaucracy.

It is closely related to the concept of rationalization and efficiency. The complex tasks of the bureaucracy are broken down into parts, each requiring someone to master the particular operations and obey the regulations applying to the particular position he holds. The individual need have no concept of the entire operation. This leaves the direction of the total operation to others who are specialists also. There is a complex hierarchy of authority, in which each person has authority and can make decisions in limited areas, and is responsible to someone higher up.

The position one holds is called an office. The bureaucracy is composed of a number of related offices, each responsible for a particular function, each governed by certain rules. This office can be occupied by any individual who meets the specifications. That is, it is not a particular spot created for a particular person; anyone who can carry out the rules and functions of the office will do.

The bureaucracy strives to put things in quantitative terms, and to replace qualities with quantities. This is necessary in the interest of prediction.

Those qualities that remain must not depend on personal factors, and the categories must be fixed by the system. Thus, we see the typical printed forms made by the bureaucracies, where one has to select one of the predetermined alternatives. If everyone reported something different, there could be no standard procedure in handling matters; and the system would bog down.

In order to maintain specialization and all the other factors in a bureaucracy, there has to be a certain minimum size to the system. As a general principle, one finds that with increasing size the bureaucracy increases in efficiency. Then more specializations can be made, meaning more skill in particular operations. Thus, there is an increasing tendency toward greater size.

Associated with the concept of office, as well as other aspects of bureaucracy, is depersonalization: that the individual as a *whole* is not important to the system, but only the *function* that he serves. One never need know what the person is like as long as he does what is required of him by the particular office he holds. The consequence of this is that the individual becomes segmentalized: that what he is at the office is only a separate part of him, not his whole life, or a realization of his whole personality. Acting in accordance with fixed rules laid down by someone else, he must conform whether he thinks it right or wrong, natural to him or unnatural. This leads to a distinction between the self and the job.

Conflict in Theory and Structure

Now that theory and structure have been discussed, one can look at the conflict between them. The conflict lies in the fact that theory, in a field like medicine, education, or sciences, may dictate one course of behavior and the bureaucratic structure, set up supposedly to carry out these ends, may dictate another. There are certain structural needs or pressures which may conflict with theory, yet they may come to dominate practice.

On a recent trip to a psychiatric hospital, the writer observed an example of the type of conflict described above. Theory might say that the patient needs to grow, to become more spontaneous and creative, needs contact and stimulation. Yet these things are rather dangerous, in the sense that the results are somewhat unpredictable, and the bureaucracy had become concerned with the caretaking aspects, with keeping individuals quiet and ordered, reducing stimuli, making them conform to the system. This made things run smoothly, and those who ran the system felt comfortable, and knew how to handle the situation according to the rules and regulations.

One could also look at general medicine. Increasingly, the theory has pointed to the fact that one treats the whole patient; just as in education one educates the whole child. We see this idea in the concept of psychosomatic medicine, where it is realized that mind and body cannot be thought of as separate parts. But, what is happening in practice? Increasingly we see the rise of specialists, who will have to take their place in the emerging medical bureaucracies. How can these specialists treat the whole patient? The patient is not a patient to him, but a heart or a lung. One could point out the consequences, which are many, of bureaucracy for medicine, but that is not our topic.

In education one sees the same basic conflict found in the above fields. Increasingly educators, especially those training teachers, are developing theories of education which are related to the various scientific advances (although a theory of education is not fully scientific in that it contains elements of value). At the same time, school systems are becoming bureaucratized as they become organized into huge, complex, formal systems. Bureaucratization is far from complete, but it is progressing at a rapid rate. The city school systems have gone furthest in this direction, but consolidation in the rural areas is producing the same organization. The schools have lagged behind business in the degree of bureaucratization, but even now business is moving further and further in the bureaucratic direction.

The educational bureaucracy, as a form of organization, has a series of needs, or tends to produce behavior in certain directions, which will increase the bureaucratic character of the system. It means that those concerned with developing the system are apt to develop certain appropriate values within themselves. The very fact of being in charge of a large complex system leads one to accept some of the following factors, if one is to do one's job. Naturally the technics one accepts, and the values underlying them, will be taken from similar successful models provided by our culture. Thus, one finds that a good bureaucratic administrator in one system can easily change to another, and be just about as successful. Applying this idea to education, one should find that it is possible to bring in a good administrator from business and have him be successful in running an educational system. The amount he might need to know about educational theory might be little. One can point to college presidents chosen in this way; and one suspects that things are moving in this direction, just as they have in other fields. The fact that education is a poorer paying field has probably slowed down the transfer. All this, of course, indicates that the bureaucratic structure and its needs, and associated values held by those who run it, can be something separate from educational theory.

Not only can theory become separate from structure, but there can be conflict. The points below are ones which stress the element of conflict. It doesn't mean that in all cases one will find this conflict, rather it is an indication of opposing directions taken by the bureaucratic structure and modern educational theory. This conflict will be more or less realized depending upon the particular situation studied. The points are quite interrelated, but for the sake of clarity they have been presented as separate factors.

1. Individual versus Mass. Bureaucracies, in the interest of efficiency, want to treat all the units in the same way, if possible. They want to develop a standard operating procedure; if there are exceptions these should be standard exceptions. The production line must move at the proper rate, and there is little room for unique responses. Increasingly, no one is held up on the line as it interferes with the system. This rate can be maintained in two ways: (*a*) concentrate on things which are simple enough for all to get; (*b*) don't worry about how much the individual gets, and think in terms of the same amount of exposure to whatever one is teaching. Educational theory stands in opposition by regarding every individual as unique, with unique problems and responses, which demand specialized treatment. Each child is a functional whole, and a difference in any one aspect makes the whole different. Operations cannot be standardized, but must be suited to the particular unit at hand: a craft concept rather than a mass production concept.

2. Necessary Time versus Fixed Time. The bureaucracy tends toward fixed time limits to accomplish particular tasks. In fact, they tend to think in terms of time, whereas time is not an important factor in educational theory. The theory would not be interested in the time aspect, rather it is concerned with the ends one must reach whatever the time. Moreover, this time will vary greatly depending on the unit you are dealing with, on its previous condition, ability, and the type of situation currently integrated. Modern educational theory would have each individual move at his own rate. This is in opposition to the bureaucratic concept of treating classes of objects, rather than unique individuals.

A further aspect of the time factor is the division of instruction into fixed class periods with the ringing of bells, etc.; consequently, whatever is going on must be abandoned to meet the fixed schedule of the system.

One has to pour so much into the student within the time, or you will be behind today, or at the end of the semester, or next year, and the student will not have enough to go on to the next unit. If attendance is compulsory at these fixed time class periods, there is apt to grow up the attitude on the part of the student that attendance is a magical thing giving him some automatic benefits, and, of course, it does in many cases where mere conformity to the rules is a heavy factor in grading. The bureaucracy would like to know where every individual is at every moment, and to know exactly what he is doing. The idea that one might become interested in a particular problem, and want to follow it through for a day or a week instead of shifting every forty minutes or hour to something unrelated, does not interest the bureaucracy. Learning theory related to educational theory indicates that constant shifting tends to cancel out learning. Thus, in terms of motivation and learning, bureaucratic needs of predictability in a time sense may run counter to educational theory.

3. *Creativity versus Predictability.* The bureaucracy is interested in predictability. It wants to know just what is going to happen, at any time, or in relation to any action. Only in this way can things be anticipated, can rules and regulations be made, supplies ordered, forms printed, etc. Now, if you regard each individual as unique, and the teaching situation integrated with him as something emergent, you do not have this kind of predictability. Creative ventures, because they are creative, cannot be too predictable as to when and how they will take place, and as to what will be the outcome. Not only are individuals—as viewed by educational theory —unique, but classes are unique, depending upon the particular selection of unique individuals and the current group situation. Thus, one has a creative emergent situation in this larger unit. The bureaucracy, not wanting its ordered existence disturbed by emergent and unregulated processes, is apt to concern itself with the more stable phenomena, such as discipline, promptness, memory work, "facts," forms, etc. It tends to produce a clustering about simple measurable phenomena that are predictable. It is apt to passively or actively discourage things which vary from the norm, which are unique or different from typical and predictable goals, which are creative or original and, therefore, untried and unanticipated by the system, nor does it generally encourage the critical.

4. *Unmeasurable versus Measurable.* Closely related to the above is the bureaucracies' concentration on measurable factors. This is part of the objection to the creative aspect above—that it is unmeasurable. The most clear-cut example of the desire for measurability is the objective test. It could be shown that this is just as subjective as the other type, but it offers several factors favored by the bureaucratic system. It treats all individuals in the same way—or better, as if they were the same—all similar responses are considered to mean the same thing to the people who made them. There is no room for unique and therefore unclassifiable responses.

The individual is forced to interpret and respond in the same way as others, while unique and critical responses are punished. The final result is a ranking of individuals from high to low, rather than a set of *different* approaches to a particular area of interest. The testing for measurable values and an exclusive interest in measurable values creates a situation where learning is stimulated in these areas, and ignored or punished in other areas. Educational theory would stress the presently nonmeasurable as well as the measurable. It would allow and reward variation, rather than mold in one form all thought in the interest of producing measurement and ranking.

5. *Qualities versus Quantities.* The distinction between measurable and nonmeasurable factors is a part of this distinction between qualities and quantities. An educational theory based on individualistic principles, developing unique individuals, responses, and situations, is going to be concerned with qualities. It will see things as qualitatively different. All bureaucracies have concerned themselves with the reduction of qualitative differences to quantitative ones. If one views differences as qualitative, then one cannot measure and rank, etc.; while viewing things in quantitative terms leads to measurement by such things as the objective test. The distinction should not be considered an absolute one here; it is just that the bureaucratic tendency goes further than educational theory would, and often sacrifices other values to achieve this end. It is necessary, if the administrator is to think about masses of individuals, that all their uniqueness is reduced to variations in degree in regard to a few variables. In educational theory, even after one measures certain variables, they should not be thought of in isolation, but in relation to the whole child—the functional unit determines the meaning of any particular score.

The interest of bureaucracies in treating differences as quantitative rather than qualitative parallels the interest of the sciences in this same problem. Sciences and bureaucracies have been most successful in dealing with physical factors where there is more homogeneity in the material. In dealing with personality and social factors, social sciences and bureaucracies have had more trouble; and they have had to incorporate more qualitative differences, because the material is more heterogeneous. Recently, business bureaucracies have been able to treat things more from the quantitative standpoint, whether individuals liked it or not. But the school system is faced with a unique problem in that, in some theoretical ways, it is committed to preserving individualistic differences and not jamming people into a common mold, which would be a natural tendency for bureaucracies to follow. For if the system is ordered and governed by rule and regulation, if things are predictable and regular, then deviation must be limited. Does the child adjust to the school or the school to the child? It is no longer a problem after a few years, as the school is creating the material it has to deal with, and in a few years it has created what it wants in the way of a student. Any teacher who has tried new methods will know that the student is a product of the particular system and closely adheres to the values stressed by it.

6. *Unique versus Formal.* Every bureaucracy is formal in character. That is, it wants action to be regulated by specific rules and regulations. It will have a large amount of written laws, which limit and direct behavior, and prescribe punishments for violations. They are made to ensure predictability of action, so that action can be integrated into the system of action involving many other individuals. Such regulations are only possible if one treats individuals and situations not as unique, but as belonging to classes or types. More subtle and variable phenomena which cannot be treated in this way, such as creativity or original thought, will tend to be ignored by the bureaucracy; it will receive neither punishment nor reward and will not be taught or learned. Teacher and student shift their attention to that which is the concern of the higher bureaucrats; and these bureaucrats can only deal with certain factors, using their methods of administration by rule and regulation, etc. It is thus that the values of the system may come to be different from those of educational theory, concerned with individuals, with their own special problems and contributions.

7. *Whole versus Segmental.* The bureaucratic approach demands segmentalization. Things must be broken down into parts. The various tasks that have to be performed are divided into parts each handled by a specialist. This makes for a higher level of competence and greater efficiency. It also makes it possible to replace any individual and still retain the same pattern of behavior. This has recently spread to the college level, as it becomes more of a mass, bureaucratic organization. The writer has talked with individuals who were hired to teach introductory courses, in an endless repetition, many times each day, of the same course. From the individual viewpoint this created a feeling of boredom, and of being involved in an endless and meaningless task. There was little joy in the completed product—the student—as one acts on only a minute section of it. The teacher deals with the student from a limited standpoint, and the endless masses of students who quickly pass through his hands cannot be understood, they can only be treated in a standardized, quantitative manner.

The same thing that happens to tasks happens to subjects: They become segmentalized into isolated bits which have to be treated in isolation, something like studying an engine by taking a course in the piston, then in the spark plug; and never one on the functioning whole. Educational theory would stress the interrelationship of the knowledge that an individual gains. There have been attempts to produce "integrated" courses, but these are generally a fixed integration of certain subjects: What theory demands is a dynamic interrelation of learning related to the unique individual—the idea that you teach the whole child. The bureaucracy can put any fixed collection of data together in a course, and, if necessary, have a number of different specialists teach it; this is not the answer to the theoretical problem of interrelating all one's knowledge into a dynamic whole.

Every bureaucracy demands more and more specialization as it becomes more bureaucratized. The idea of specialization is dominant, the bureaucracy is an organization of specialists; and specialists typically don't deal with the whole of anything. Increasingly everyone wants to become a specialist; it is the way to get ahead in the new bureaucracies. Specialization also *appears* more efficient, when measured by the values the bureaucracy considers important. When specialization occurs, one is less apt to think in terms of the whole student; and one's work seems less "a way of life" and more "just a job."

One could go on at great length about the various changes and conflicts now facing educational practice, but the general direction should be clear by now. The real problem, for those attempting to carry out educational theory, does not lie in the conflict, but in a gradual acceptance of the bureaucratic values without being aware of it. These values become more and more a part of the entire culture, and they are accepted without any clear awareness, and criticism of them thus becomes increasingly difficult.

chapter 39

Assessing curriculum proposals

William M. Alexander

We who would assess curriculum proposals are confronted by a dilemma, first of all, as to which of the multitudinous statements on education are "curriculum proposals." In addition to the many current curriculum studies and reports of substantial magnitude, hundreds of articles in both popular and professional journals continue to criticize and make suggestions about the curriculum. The NEA Magazine Report reviewed, for the first quarter of this year alone, 142 articles on education in national magazines and newspaper supplements. The first issue for this school year of the NEA newsletter, *Education U.S.A.*, noted 12 articles in popular magazines for September. The majority of all of these articles relate in one way or another to the school program and very frequently present somebody's proposal for curriculum change.

If we add the suggestions by thousands of lay and professional committees and by citizens in general, the number of "proposals" approaches infinity. Many are duplicates, of course, and if a test of novelty were applied, probably only a small group of proposals would require assessment. Nevertheless, it is undoubtedly good for American education for there to be such widespread interest in curriculum improvement, regardless of the extent of duplication and repetition of ideas. What is important for school people is that they be aware of this plethora of proposals and that there be orderly processes within our school organization for assessing all suggestions and recommendations, whatever their source and nature.

From *Teachers College Record*, 63(January, 1962), 286–293. Reprinted by permission of the author and publisher.

Adapted from an address presented to the Teachers College Conference on the Curriculum at Teachers College, Columbia University, on 31 October, 1961.

Two aspects of such orderly processes are considered here: *speculation* about the possible results of putting a proposal to work, and *evaluation* of actual results when the proposal is implemented. Extended attention is first given to current curriculum change and change agents. If we are to assess, as we must, proposals for curriculum change in terms of their potential or actual results, then we must understand as best we can what proposals actually turn into practices and the processes and sources of this momentum.

Current Curriculum Change

We know more about the extent to which curriculum proposals are being made than the extent to which they are being implemented. But we also know more about the extent of implementation than about the nature and extent of the speculation which preceded or the evaluation which accompanied implementation. It seems unhappily probable that many proposals are put to work with little preliminary speculation or concurrent evaluation.

To aid in this analysis of the realities of curriculum change, I would like to introduce some data regarding current changes and forces very recently compiled by the NEA Project on Instruction. These data indicate that rather substantial change is taking place and further suggest that the chief influences on change are considered by school principals to be state and local school leadership. The latter point strongly supports my own belief that the assessment process must be closely identified with state and local leadership.

In beginning work on the development of guidelines for local groups interested in improving instruction, the Project on Instruction found it necessary to secure some facts about the extent to which change was occurring in the instructional programs of public schools. With the help of the Research Division of the NEA, a study was made in 1961 of the status of the curricula of elementary and secondary schools and of certain changes which have occurred in the past five years or are expected to occur in the next five. The findings, now in process of publication, indicate quite clearly that many types of change have been quite pronounced and are expected to continue.

Some Findings

Note the following selection of views reported by relatively large numbers of the elementary school principals included in the stratified sample used by the Research Division:

1. Twenty-nine per cent of the principals stated that "much change" had occurred in their schools since 1955–1956; 53 per cent reported "some change." The three highest ranking changes reported in response

to a question calling for the "one most important change" were "emphasis on subject areas" (38 per cent); "methods and techniques" (28 per cent), and "teaching materials" (14 per cent).

2. Seventy-three per cent of the principals believed that too little emphasis had been placed upon science in the elementary school five years ago, and 32 per cent too little emphasis on mathematics; 63 per cent believed the emphasis is "about right" today in science and 79 per cent in mathematics, with corresponding reductions in the percentage believing there is still "too little" emphasis.

3. Forty-five per cent reported that some subjects (principally mathematics, science, and cursive writing) had been moved downward in the past five years.

4. Twenty-two per cent of all districts represented and 51 per cent of large school districts now offer a foreign language; many other districts expect to do so in the next five years.

5. Forty-six per cent of the respondents reported an increase in their schools in grouping by ability or achievement.

6. The percentage of elementary schools with "all self-contained classrooms" had decreased from 66 per cent in 1955–1956 to 55 per cent in 1960–1961. It is expected to decrease to 34 per cent by 1965–1966.

7. Fifty-one per cent of the principals believed their schools expected more work from pupils than five years ago.

Some similar findings from the secondary school survey follow:

1. Offerings in foreign languages have markedly expanded. Small high schools have added one or more languages; larger high schools have added the third and fourth years of one or more.

2. Sixty-three per cent of the principals believed "too little" emphasis was placed upon science five years ago and 55 per cent on mathematics. Only 17 per cent believe this situation still exists in science, only 16 per cent in mathematics.

3. Fifty-two per cent of the principals reported that some subjects (principally science, mathematics, and foreign languages) had been shifted downward during the past five years.

4. Sixty-three per cent of the principals said that grouping by ability or achievement had increased in their schools. The same percentage expected further increases during the next five years.

5. Thirty-one per cent of the principals expect to have team teaching ("a plan whereby two or more teachers are jointly responsible for the instruction of a group of pupils") in 1965–1966, although only 12 per cent (in contrast to 5 per cent a year ago) report having it now.

6. Forty-nine per cent described as "none" their use of TV programs

in 1960–1961 (3 per cent, "much use" and 48 per cent "some use"), as compared with 82 per cent for "none" in 1955–1956 (1 per cent "much" and 17 per cent "some"), and only 14 per cent anticipated "none" in 1965–1966 (21 per cent "much" and 65 per cent "some").

7. Sixty-eight per cent of the respondents believed their schools expected more from pupils today than five years ago.

Causes and Influences

The NEA survey did not seek information directly as to procedures employed in assessing changes. It did investigate the principals' opinions about the causes, influences, and results of some of the changes. In general, the replies indicated a high degree of satisfaction. Thus, the percentages who considered the present increased emphasis on science and mathematics "about right" were high compared with similar percentages estimated for 1955–1956. As another example, 60 per cent of the elementary principals thought that the expectation of work for pupils was "good" (only 3 per cent thought it "bad," the remainder having mixed feelings or being uncertain), and 68 per cent of the secondary principals felt the same way, (only 2 per cent "bad," the remainder mixed or uncertain). Also, only small percentages of principals reported negative feelings among teachers toward various innovations. Apparently, such assessment as has been done and was reported has been quite favorable toward the various instructional changes.

The survey also yielded some data as to the principals' beliefs regarding the sources of change in the instructional program. The elementary principals ranked highest as influences on the instructional program in 1960–1961 the following: (1) "local school officials (superintendent and staff)," (2) "the school faculty," (3) "research studies on learning, child growth, and development, etc," and (4) "state officials (state superintendent and department of education)." "National programs sponsored by the government," "national studies in the subject areas," "prominent studies associated with individuals," and the "large foundations" were ranked considerably lower than the top four, although the rankings of each of these latter items for 1960–1961 was higher than for the past five years. The secondary principals also ranked as highest the influence of local school officials (first), and the school faculty (second), but placed national studies in the subject areas third and gave the same ranking of fourth to state officials and national government-subsidized programs, with prominent studies associated with individuals next and close in rank. Replies to a question as to the influence of selected national projects on the secondary school program revealed that several presumably significant studies had "had no effect": 51 per cent so replied regarding the Staff Utilization Study (Trump), 67 per cent with respect to the Chemical Bond Study, and 48 per cent for both the Biological Sciences Study and the Physical Sciences Study. Fifteen per cent of the principals stated that each of three projects had "caused important changes": the Advanced Placement Program, the Conant report, and the National Mathematics Study.

The principals' rankings of the usefulness of various educational resources also give some insight into the effects of their influence on the curriculum. "The textbook" was ranked highest by both elementary and secondary principals. The following resources constituted the next highest four for both groups, although the rank order differed: "curriculum materials prepared by faculty of this school," "local workshops and curriculum study conferences," "curriculum materials prepared by local superintendent's staff," and "courses of study and curriculum guides prepared by state department of education." The secondary principals gave higher rankings than the elementary principals to the usefulness of national studies in various subject areas and to reports associated with prominent educators.

Change Agents

Probably the chief conclusion to be drawn from this NEA survey is the obvious one that change has been occurring quite extensively in the instructional program for the past five years. But there seems to be adequate warrant for other inferences of greater significance:

1. Very little resistance on the part of principals to current changes or to their expansion during the next five years is indicated.

2. Principals give little weight to the influence of national organizations, nationally publicized reports, and national projects of various types. They do attach great importance to the textbook, itself a national and major curriculum force.

3. The change agents recognized most frequently by both elementary and secondary school principals as being most important are the local school system staff, the individual school faculty, and the state department of education.

The central point here is that principals tend to perceive state and local leadership as the real agents of change in their schools. We who would assess curriculum proposals need to recognize that the ideas most likely to affect practice are the ones which get into the mainstream of communication in state and local school systems. Generally speaking, even the most ambitious curriculum research and evaluation projects are not communicated through professional or lay publications to school faculties. Locally and state-produced materials are the influential ones.

Granted that a principal may overestimate the real influence of his superintendent and state department of education, his perception of the importance of this leadership remains a powerful factor in bringing about or blocking change. Furthermore, the principal's own attitude toward change is known to be highly critical in faculty decision making. Perhaps it is his estimation of his own influence which causes the principal to rank so highly the power of his faculty! Certainly, the principal must be a primary focus in the evaluation of curriculum proposals.

Assessment and Communication

So far, our chief attention has been given to curriculum change and its agents, rather than to proposals for change and their assessment. The relation is direct, however: Change results from somebody's efforts to put into effect somebody's proposal of something different. The "somebodies" may be the same, although I believe they are usually different. That is, some individual or group makes a proposal which is accepted, rejected, or ignored by some (other) individual or group responsible for the school program.

If we have belabored the survey and its interpretation, the fact remains that local and state leadership *are* responsible for curriculum change. I can recall few significant changes in schools which were not at some point sanctioned by immediate status leadership. The central problem, therefore, is whether this leadership can be trusted to assess curriculum proposals from all sources. If not, a related problem is whether assessment done by some other source can be adequately communicated by the local decision-making group.

As to the first problem, it is my own judgment that many present state and local decision-making groups *do* need help in the assessment of curriculum proposals. The range of competence in such groups is, of course, considerable. In some situations, persons of great and varied abilities could be readily assembled, but in many circumstances, there is a real dearth of curriculum leadership. Very frequently, other pressures are so great that status leadership has little freedom to speculate with deliberation about the possible consequence of curriculum decisions or about designing experiments to test consequences.

The second problem, communication between the sources of help and the status groups, is a highly complex one. It could be solved by making the assessment process an integral part of the official curriculum planning procedure and by involving in the process adequate representatives of the status leadership at the state and local level. A way of systematizing speculation about the possible consequences of a curriculum proposal may now be described.

Systematizing Speculation

Observation of decision making by many state and local school leaders suggests that curriculum proposals are all too often accepted or rejected without careful consideration. Deliberate efforts to size up the consequences are frequently impossible, and adequate bases for evaluating proposals are lacking.

To systematize the processes of speculation, I propose that the governing body of each state school system establish a State Curriculum Evaluation Commission. Each such commission might have some of the functions and composition of the National Commission for Curriculum Research and Development recently urged by Paul Hanna (4) without his geographic scope and its resultant difficulties of communication and action. Granted that the fifty commissions might at times be considering the same curriculum proposals, each commission would be operating within the special framework of a particular state and with clear channels of communication to its schools.

A common pattern for the state commissions is as unlikely as is their immediate establishment. Fortunately, most states already have state curriculum committees of some sort. The first step interested officials should take is that of reviewing the work of these existing committees in the light of the urgent need for deliberate, informed evaluation of curriculum proposals from many sources. Such questions as the following might well be considered:

1. Is there a group responsible for screening curriculum proposals?

2. If so, does the group have status such as to enable it to present recommendations that will be responsibly considered at state and local levels?

3. Does the group have sufficient budget to pay the expenses of its members, employ an adequate executive and secretarial staff, and on occasion compensate needed consultants?

4. Does the membership include able representatives of the educational specialists, the practicing schoolmen, and the interested laymen of the state?

5. Does the group have an adequate set of critera by which to select curriculum proposals for tryout purposes?

Systematizing speculation about curriculum proposals would involve early and continued concern with the last question. Certain criteria by which proposals have frequently been somewhat casually judged in the past seem inadequate for the orderly processes now needed: (*a*) the ease with which the proposal can be adopted, (*b*) the prestige or educational experience of the author of the proposal, (*c*) the extent to which the proposal departs from tradition, and (*d*) the amount of possible resistance to the proposal. Although such considerations may properly be weighed by the curriculum evaluation commission, other criteria are of greater importance. First of all, the probable *significance* of each proposal needs careful review—its relation to accepted educational purposes, the scope of its applicability, and its timeliness. Second, the criterion of *appropriateness* must be broadly applied—to the functions of various types of schools, to the various communities, to learners, and to the present curriculum. Third, the *utility* of the proposal must be considered in the light of the ability of the people concerned to put the idea to work, the possibilities of adequate evaluation, and the extent to which local school systems can make choices about the proposal.

Obviously, commissions of this sort would need excellent communication channels and media. Interchanges among the various state commissions would be useful for the sharing of proposals and their evaluations. Reports and recommendations by national projects and organizations should be of major concern to each state commission, and proposals from local school systems and local leadership should be welcomed and encouraged. Many larger school districts might well have curriculum evaluation commissions of their own which could profitably work in close cooperation with the state body.

Local Experimentation

A major function of the state curriculum commission should be that of stimulating careful experiment and evaluation in local schools. As Conant (3) has pointed out, "competition among educational ideas is continuously going on," a fact which underscores the role of the local school groups in assessing these ideas. Said Conant:

> The guarantee that society will be well served consists in having the many official tribunals that make decisions as honest and effective as can be—ready to call in consultants, to listen to expert witnesses, and to weigh the evidence presented.
>
> All of which means, of course, a continuous effort by all concerned with curriculum research and development to press forward with trying new ideas and subjecting the consequences to the most painstaking analysis.

I believe that local school faculties can do more than share opinions about the consequences of proposals they have tested, important as this may be. They can also collect some factual evidence to be "weighed" in the procedure Conant describes. Recently, William B. Brownell (1) made a strong plea for more "what-happens-if experimentation," which he illustrated as follows:

> My first concern is that in our growing preoccupation with the more complicated forms of research we shall not overlook the virtues of—

indeed, the need for—simpler kinds. Note that I did not say easier kinds. To make clear what I mean, let us suppose that our problem is to determine the effectiveness of Method A (whatever that is) in teaching a particular segment of subject matter in Grade 5.

In research simple in design, we could select a reasonably large sample of Grade 5 children, determine their characteristics in detail, and teach them as planned. We would then note carefully what occurs from day to day—which children progress rapidly, and which slowly, *and why;* at what points in the sequence of subject-matter topics, learning difficulties arise, what they are, *and why.* Our procedures would be those of testing, interviewing, and observing.

Brownell's comment that " 'what-happens-if' experimentation *can* contribute a great deal of vital information about many kinds of educational problems, and the pity is that it is not more popular than it is" seems particularly relevant to the evaluation of curriculum proposals. More careful collection of more relevant data about what happens when new ideas are put to work in schools is sorely needed as we attempt to assess these ideas.

Coordinating Inquiries

Long-range research in curriculum matters is also greatly needed. President Hollis L. Caswell of Teachers College has for some years been calling to our attention the paucity of such research undertakings. His address (2) at the 1950 ASCD Conference was influential in causing this organization and other groups to undertake more cooperative curriculum research. The Horace Mann-Lincoln Institute he established has led the way in many significant studies. At the 1961 ASCD Conference, President Caswell spoke against a national curriculum agency, but once again he cited the need for more systematic long-range curriculum research, proposing that the federal government establish four to six centers, probably at nationally recognized institutions, for the study of curriculum plans and the development and use of instructional materials. At the same meeting, Conant (3) urged as a preferred class of evidence about education the "results of systematic studies involving large numbers of individuals, carefully designed and analyzed with the use of modern statistical devices." He specifically suggested that "the members of the educational research community might well get together to design a set of specific experiments and to persuade the federal government to support a mammoth project" (dealing with class size, the research need Conant was illustrating). These arguments for federal support of coordinated, large-scale research are very convincing. With the interest in educational research shown by the federal government in recent years, such a program may well be a next step.

Such undertakings should feed their findings into the state curriculum evaluation commissions I am proposing here. These commissions could usefully reciprocate by gathering valuable data and helping through regional research organizations established voluntarily by interested states. The model of the Southern Regional Education Board could well be considered in such instances. This Board, established and supported by the state governments of the South, has rendered a large number of significant services, especially to higher education.

Disseminating Data

Regardless of how well the speculative and evaluative processes are carried on, the data yielded are easily lost, not understood, or ignored. The work of an official state commission should be of real value in disseminating and clarifying such information. For the job to be effectively done, however, the commission must be genuinely representative of the best educational leadership of its state. Its publications must be prepared by persons who can be heard with respect, presented clearly and in an attractive style, and introduced to local groups by well-informed representatives. Professional associations must be actively interested and involved, so that their meetings, journals, and representatives may also help in the communication of evaluative data about curriculum proposals. Finally, the mass media can be of great value in informing the wider public, and effective evaluation commissions will undoubtedly find ways to work collaboratively with the press and broadcasters.

I have not attempted to deal with the technical problems of research and evaluation regarding curriculum proposals and innovations but to make still another proposal—to establish state curriculum evaluation commissions which would have official responsibility to assess curriculum proposals in general. This proposal represents a middle ground between arguments for some new and powerful national commission to serve such purposes and other arguments for continuing local autonomy in curriculum matters. It is offered, however, not as a compromise between these extremes, but as a realistic way of strengthening present decision-making processes at the local and state levels. Obviously, the idea needs much more complete development and discussion. It is offered here for the same kind of speculative assessment suggested in this paper as desirable for curriculum proposals in general.

REFERENCES

1. Brownell, W. A. Educational research in the decade ahead. Address to the American Educational Research Association, 15 Feb., 1961, at Atlantic City, N.J.
2. Caswell, H. L. Research in the curriculum. *Educ. Leadership*, 1950, 7, 438–445.

3. Conant, J. B. *Trial and error in the improvement of education.* Washington, D.C.: Association for Supervision and Curriculum Development, NEA, 1961.
4. Hanna, P. Proposed—a national commission for curriculum research and development. *Phi Delta Kappan,* 1961, 8, 331–338.

chapter **40**

Learning through teacher-pupil planned activities

Kenneth H. Hoover

A glance at almost any general-methods or principles text for secondary school teachers will indicate a plea for democratic classroom procedures. The following cliches are common: "Let the learner assist in goal formulation; plan with your students; guide individuals in self-evaluation."

The college instructor who conceives secondary education as a process of directing the learning activities of boys and girls usually emphasizes democratic procedures. Too frequently, however, his students, when they become teachers, resort to "task-setting" and "textbook teaching." Why is this? The prospective teacher, while intellectually accepting the idea of "democratic" procedures, tends to believe eventually that his former teachings were purely "theoretical" or at least not very practical. He may be vaguely aware of scientific research studies which support joint teacher-pupil planning of class work but shrugs them off with the excuse that his situation is different. If pressed he is likely to admit that he actually lacks specific understanding of how to involve students in direction of their own learning activities.

College students who have generally experienced "task-setting" and "textbook teaching" at both high school and college levels of education will tend to revert to such instruction *unless they experience other approaches in sufficient quantity and quality to cause a reconstruction of unconsciously*

From *The Journal of Teacher Education*, XI(March, 1960), 50–54. Reprinted by permission of the publisher.

held values and concepts.[1] Indeed, it has been established that the degree of transfer of ideas to related situations is dependent upon the number of similar elements which the learner perceives to exist in both situations.[2]

The evidence now available clearly indicates that students will transfer their learnings to other situations if they are taught by methods which favor transfer.[3] Trow seems to sum up the issue when he says:

> . . . if abilities, attitudes, and skills in general, and ability to think in particular, are to be transferred *outside* the structure, the emphasis must be shifted to the other kinds of situations in which they are to be used. Methods of teaching are thus of the essence. . . .[4]

Beginning with Thorndike and Woodworth's 1901 experiments,[5] evidence has accumulated which conclusively demonstrates that methods of learning and instruction are of prime importance. Trow concludes that "Such conclusions as these, derived again and again from experiment after experiment, are strangely at odds with the current effort to de-emphasize methods in teaching."[6]

These findings seem to suggest a need for application of democratic procedures in college classes, especially those classes which are concerned with teaching principles or techniques. Therefore, the purpose of this paper is to suggest how such techniques may be applied to teaching and some of the advantages which are often associated with such a teaching method.

Identifying and Clarifying the Problem

The *general* goals or purposes of a course are usually determined through the school or department. Students must be thoroughly familiarized with these goals. Specific goals can be formulated by students, however. And certainly learning methods may be determined by students! Let us illustrate by specific example.

As many high school classes are of an exploratory nature, let us assume the general problem confronting the college class is that of exploring the teaching profession. The teacher usually needs to restate the general purpose to be investigated in the form of a problem. To illustrate: What prob-

[1] For a more complete exploration of this thesis the reader is referred to Kenneth H. Hoover, "Teaching Methods of Teaching by Demonstration and Application," *Clearing House* 33: 90–91; October, 1958.

[2] William Clark Trow, "The Problem of Transfer—Then and Now," *Phi Delta Kappan* 40: 68–71; November, 1958.

[3] Lee J. Cronback, *Educational Psychology* (New York: Harcourt, Brace and Company, 1954) p. 258.

[4] Trow, *Op. Cit.* p. 71.

[5] Edward L. Thorndike, *The Psychology of Learning* (New York: Teachers College, Columbia University, 1913) p. 359.

[6] *Loc. Cit.*

lems and opportunities may be encountered in the teaching profession? The general problem becomes one of specific problems (goals) when students are given an opportunity to present questions for investigation. These questions can, then, serve as a basis for teacher-pupil formulation of interest areas. After inspecting their original questions, one group of college freshmen decided that they had suggested seven such areas of interest. These were: teacher welfare; professionalization of teaching; requirements for teaching; school support; general expectations of teachers; teaching in American territories and in foreign countries; and educational trends.

Planning and Developing Learning Activities

The areas of interest form a basis for formulation of committees. These committees, thus, become "democratic" units which have the responsibility of devising plans for solving their particular problems.

Each group, first, restates the problem as a question of policy. To illustrate: How may the welfare of teachers be effectively improved? What should be the teacher's responsibility with respect to the professionalization of teaching? What action should parents take to alleviate the problems of school support?

As one of the critical stages of solving any problem is the formulation of meaningful questions, the instructor will need to move from group to group in a guidance and consultant capacity. His greatest assistance may come indirectly—through his own questioning techniques. In the final analysis, decisions must be reached by the students themselves. The instructor, having previously introduced students to a method of problem solving, now guides each group in making an appropriate application of problem solving to its particular interest area.

In any question of policy there are a number of questions of value.[7] In the problem "How may the welfare of teachers be effectively improved?" the investigators must, first, thoroughly understand the present state of affairs (facts); then there will be differences of opinion (value) as to what can be done about the status quo; finally, it is hoped that an agreement may be reached. Thus, each group becomes actively engaged in solving problems which are related to a particular area of interest.

Collecting Data

While other class activities are proceeding as usual, each committee will be collecting data which are important to its particular area of investigation. (In high school classes much of the work may be accomplished during class time.) Not only will those involved need to investigate a variety of written sources of information; they may also desire to interview people, write for

[7] Waldo W. Braden and Earnest Brandenburg. *Oral Decision-Making* (New York: Harper and Brothers, 1955) p. 43.

supplemental authoritative reports and the like. The desirable leader will want to encourage the use of as many informational sources as possible while, at the same time, encouraging development of appropriate techniques for their evaluation.

Sharing Research Findings

Although a group may have accomplished a great deal in planning and directing research activities, the value to the total class group is dependent upon how well the findings are presented or shared. At some point in the operation the entire class may want to establish standards for this phase of the project. One class listed, as guidelines for committee reports:

1. Materials presented should relate to the goals established or the questions asked.

2. Presentations should involve all members of the reporting group in some way.

3. Presentations will be brief—preferably not to exceed one class period.

4. Presentations should not be read.

5. Other class members should be given an opportunity to ask questions. If a key question cannot be answered, some member of the group should be designated to find the answer.

6. Technical material should be omitted from the presentations. If it is, nevertheless, important, it should be duplicated for the class.

7. Sources of information should be made available.

8. Contradictory evidence should be presented as impartially as possible.

The instructor continuously encourages the development of group creativity as to unusual methods of presentation. The ultimate criterion is not what the instructor would prefer, but what the groups believe would be most interesting and worthwhile to their peers. If one class period is scheduled for each presentation, it is usually desirable to allow at least one-half of the following period for a teacher-led discussion of problems raised and additional concepts which need developing.

Evaluation Activities

Evaluation actually begins with the advent of teacher-pupil planning. When students are encouraged to formulate meaningful questions, they are asked to evaluate. When a problem is being solved an individual is continuously evaluating, deciding if this or that procedure would be preferred, whether the sources of information are available and the like.

The progress report is frequently evaluative in nature. The instructor and students continually want to know: "What difficulties have we encountered today? What are our plans for today? Are there any anticipated problems?" Each committee may need to devote a specified amount of time each day (four to five minutes, perhaps) in reflecting upon current difficulties. These may then be written out and submitted to the teacher if assistance is needed.

One of the most satisfactory schemes developed in classes which the writer has directed is amazingly simple in its development. Each committee and each member therein is identified on a sheet of paper with the request that (1) the committees be ranked or evaluated and (2) members of each committee be ranked or evaluated by its members. Since teacher-pupil planning is a joint activity, the instructor evaluates each group. The combined student evaluations may be averaged with the instructor's rating.

The writer has accumulated some preliminary evidence which appears to support the validity of evaluation by the peer group. In nine different classes over a two-year period, students have been required to "indicate the three or four individuals who appear to have made the most valuable contributions to group progress." Seventy-two per cent of all "A" students in these groups were among the most frequently mentioned by students. The number might have been even higher but for the fact that in at least one class no "A" was administered. It seems likely, however, that teaching method may be a key factor in determining the validity of such evaluations. The instructor, in this case, tended to emphasize the experience type of learning. Assuming that one's general teaching approach is fairly consistent, it seems possible that many teachers could rely upon student judgment to supplement other evaluative techniques. Perhaps even more important, however, is that some such scheme appears to be consistent with the democratic ideals upheld in teacher-pupil planning and direction of class activities.

When the project is completed some teachers ask students for written suggestions in directing such activities. This not only enables the teacher to see himself through the eyes of students, but it indicates to students a teacher's willingness to improve teaching procedures. The reader will recognize that, in a sense, the teacher is at this point doing problem solving of his own. Because of the tendency of students to tell their teacher what they think he wants them to say, certain precautions are in order if validity is to be assured. Some sort of multiple-choice response items should be constructed. This enables students to respond by checking their answers. Under such circumstances the papers should not be signed. The teacher may wish to leave the room while the papers are being marked. Then, if additional suggestions and comments are desired, they can be written on a separate paper.

Evaluation which evolves from teacher-pupil planning takes on a broader picture than the typical procedure of relying heavily upon written tests. An important function of the teacher is to assist students in becoming aware of this change. For example, a student's recognition of growth in his ability to get along cooperatively with others may be highly significant. Carefully prepared evaluation forms, made in terms of the original purposes, may assist immeasurably in this area.

Among the more important advantages of joint teacher-pupil planning at the college level of instructions are the following:

1. It tends to be consistent with sound educational theory, i.e., the instructor is more likely to "practice what he preaches" than in traditional settings.

2. It gives prospective teachers an opportunity to experience democratic procedures prior to their own teaching.

3. The procedure enables students to formulate and solve their own problems.

4. The student is given an opportunity to assume important responsibilities in presenting materials to a class. This, in many respects, approaches the reality of teaching.

5. A greater variety of class activities may be utilized than would be possible by one instructor. To illustrate: In one class (of 40 students) involving eight committee presentations, the following activities were utilized: (*a*) three resource speakers, some of whom, in all probability, could not have been secured through the efforts of any one person, including the instructor; (*b*) one panel discussion; (*c*) one class forum; (*d*) two movies; (*e*) one presentation which involved the use of the opaque projector, charts, and pictures; and (*f*) one symposium, based upon personal interviews and findings of experimental research.

6. By assuming responsibility in directing his own learning, the student is encouraged to bring his creativity and originality to bear upon the solution of a real problem. These are values which are cherished in our democracy and are important characteristics of "good" teaching.

Today it is generally assumed that the best training for a democratic way of life is to live it—in school, community, work, and home. Most educators would agree with John Dewey's observation that the school *is* life rather than a mere preparation for life. Such a thesis certainly applies to college life as well as that of elementary and secondary schools. The college classroom could be a "proving ground" for those who desire to apply democratic procedures to classroom instruction.

chapter *41*

What, when, how should we teach about communism?

Arnold J. Brix

Storm clouds are forming on the horizon. Old skeletons are rattling in the closet and the ghost of fear past is about to walk the path called education in Ohio. When should we teach about communism? Should we teach about it at all, or bury our heads in our grade books and hope that it will go away?

Whenever I read that interested groups are questioning the present Ohio law in this matter, I am reminded of a quote from *Boswell's Journal*, dated in London, England, on the 26th of July, 1763.

> We talked about the education of children and what was best to teach them first. Sir, there is no matter what you teach them first, any more than what leg you put in your breeches first. Sir, you may stand disputing which is best to put in first but in the meantime your backside is bare.

If we are charged with the responsibility of fitting human beings for life in a world which has suddenly crystallized into a single community, I don't see how we can avoid teaching our students about communism. We are engaged in a gigantic struggle with the forces of communism. Many leading Americans are convinced that we are losing this battle. Educators must take their share of the blame for this initial setback.

But the cause is not to be found in when we teach about communism

From *Ohio Schools*, 40(March, 1962), 19. Reprinted by permission of the publisher.

but in what kind of a job we are doing in American history and American government courses now being offered in our Ohio high schools. We must admit that untrained or poorly trained people are pressed into teaching service in this field. Some administrators have accepted the erroneous philosophy that anyone can teach social studies. Quite often competent people are discouraged from pursuing a major in this field because they are told the field is overcrowded.

There can be little doubt that before students are exposed to alien philosophies they must be well grounded in their American heritage. It is not enough to be against something. Good Americans must know what they stand for. They must be taught the reasons our forefathers chose freedom and they should fully understand the basic safeguards they built into our governmental system to preserve freedom and the identity of the individual.

The Matter of Contrasts

Our American philosophy is that the personality of the community resides in its individuals and not in the state idol. This philosophy starts not with the fact that every man is full of conceits, faults, and delusions but that he is a living collection of natural rights and a prospective harvest of reasonable deeds and virtues.

The decisions of men and women as citizens and as voters rest in large part on the basic education they receive in our schools. Our society will stand or fall by our quality as a nation of citizens. With the above in mind, I can't see any argument against teaching American history first, last, and always.

Now what about communism? Basically the question is not "when we should teach about it." I think common sense dictates the answer that question requires. The major problem that presents itself is "what are we going to teach about it." What source material are we going to teach about it and how are our present social studies people equipped to handle this subject?

I am quite sure that many of our people are against communism not knowing whether it is a philosophy, an economic system, a religion, or a new virus. I wonder how many of our teachers have read Marx, Engels, Lenin, and Stalin. How many of our teachers have been teaching collectivist nonsense and downgrading capitalism with little or no conception of the close tie between economic freedom and political freedom?

We seem to be willing to rush to the barricades against a thing we have labeled communism not knowing the nature of the animal we want to destroy. We must face the fact that too many of our people are not prepared to handle the dialectician we will have to grapple with in our preparation. It should be obvious that the preparation of teachers to do battle is the first order of business rather than when we should engage the enemy.

I firmly believe that the best way to equip students to resist this new menace to freedom is to give them knowledge about it. Knowledge will destroy the myth of communist invincibility. The philosophy is not so irresistible that we need fear its ultimate success. Its defeat will only come however when we have a dedication to our cause equal to the communist's dedication to his.

chapter 42

The teachers
take a birching

Donald W. Robinson

The attorney, member of a leading Phoenix law firm, smiled with obvious relish as he said, "We've got them on the run, and we're going to keep them on the run." "Them" referred to Communists, Socialists, and liberals, all of whom he lumped together as dangerous. He considered liberals most dangerous, because "they are so firmly entrenched in government and education and because they pave the way for the Communists."

Speaking of teachers, he said, "A few of them are Communists, and a great many are sympathizers. It's not their fault. They are just the products of the thinking on which they were raised. That's what we've got to change. The liberals have captured the state university, all except Dean Shofstall, who sponsors 'Students United against Communism.'"

This attorney helped to lead the successful fight for the dismissal of a teacher who in a PTA meeting had criticized the film "Operation Abolition" and had defended the American Civil Liberties Union, of which he was a member. The school board confesses that it was deluged with demands for the dismissal following the furor at the PTA meeting, but insists that the cause of the dismissal was that "the teacher-pupil relationship maintained by this teacher had not met the professional standards required of teachers in the district."

The record is clear, however, that the PTA meeting where the trouble began was attended by scores of John Birch people who did not reside in

From *Phi Delta Kappan*, 43(February, 1962), 182–188. Reprinted by permission of the publisher.

this school district. At this meeting one woman cited the ACLU as "closely affiliated with the Communist movement in the United States whose main function is to protect the Communists." The leading Phoenix newspaper reported that "she received a roar of approval when she said, 'I do not approve of teachers who belong to Communist front organizations teaching my children.'"

Two students, one the president of the senior class, the other the president of the student body, arose in the same meeting, identified themselves as Barry Goldwater conservatives, and proceeded to rebuke the crowd for its discourtesy in booing and jeering the teacher who was the invited speaker. This action was referred to by subsequent speakers as proof that the students had been brainwashed by this "subversive" teacher.

Following the dismissal, a citizens' committee declared, "We cannot allow devoted teachers to be pilloried, libeled, slandered, and then dismissed for taking stands, as responsible citizens, on controversial issues." The committee was of course powerless to affect the decision of the school board regarding retention of a probationary teacher. A woman active in the Birch Society told this reporter with obvious pride, "Well, we got one teacher fired!"

Another Phoenix patrioteer said simply, "Our job is to root out socialism from the schools. We don't want teachers who are corrupted by the American Civil Liberties Union. Dr. Schwartz' study groups are no good because they just stay with the theory. They don't go into the local problems. The schools use all this double-talk about making students think for themselves, but they really make the students think the way the teacher thinks, and too often that is the wrong way. We had a student last year who really stood up to his teacher and stuck by his conservative views. If he had got a lower grade because of this we were going to make an issue of it, but he got an A. We had this student take notes about the teacher, so we had the evidence. We have no children ourselves. It's the parents' responsibility. The parents must arise."

Another teacher, with years of successful teaching but without tenure, was forced to resign because she was "too controversial." This also followed a public meeting, at which, after an address by Morris Ernst, she defended the activities of the American Civil Liberties Union, of which she too was a member.

Phoenix affords an example of the extremist conservatives at loggerheads with the schools, but not a typical example. The Phoenix area, recently characterized in the *Washington Post* as "The Valley of Fear," is one of the strongholds of conservatism in this country. Here the extremists are backstopped by a phalanx of highly respected hard-core Americans who publicly deplore the vigilante methods of the heckling crowds, but who nonetheless sincerely believe this country is going down the drain because of the domination by liberals, and whose consistent antipathies include Harvard, the A.D.A., the income tax, Erich Fromm, and the United Nations.

The forces that have conspired to create the vehement Phoenix conservatism include the large proportion of well-to-do retired persons in the population, its Bible Belt fundamentalism, its own-paper conservative press, its tradition of frontier individualism, and Barry Goldwater—all reinforced by the same undercurrent of fear and anxiety prevalent everywhere.

The Citizens Information Center in Phoenix, supported by donations, boasts that the day following a one-minute spot commercial it received two hundred requests for information on how to fight communism. The director, who concedes that Gerald Smith and Rockwell and McGinley are extremists, but denies that Robert Welch and Fred Schwarz are extreme, says the apathy of the public is our most serious problem and the education of the public to an awareness of our perils is the answer. "Our goal," he says firmly, "is a return to constitutional processes. Aid to our enemies, including Poland and Yugoslavia, is treason and should be dealt with as treason. The pseudo-liberal erodes our liberties. The welfare state destroys them."

The articulate, respectable conservatives in Phoenix, the pillars of society, some of whom are Birchers and some not, sound eminently reasonable and ready to protect the civil liberties of all, as one listens to them one at a time. But they do not check the rabble-rousers. They do not use their considerable prestige to halt the pressures on teachers and school boards, because they are in sympathy with the objectives of these pressures, even though they might personally flinch from using the extremist tactics.

An editor of the conservative *Arizona Republic* says, "The conservative position is being dusted off and restored to respectability. The John Birch position is not respectable and should not be. Nothing is stronger than ideas. If we, the conservatives, can win the colleges, we can win the battle and reverse the 200-year-old trend in this country."

He believes we should not limit, restrict, or dismiss liberal teachers, but should provide an equal number of conservative teachers, and make sure that all teachers respect academic freedom, that is, the freedom for ideas other than their own to permeate the classroom. Today, he insists, there exists no balance in teaching. Harvard parades its Schlesingers and Galbraiths, but no conservatives.

His paper published nothing in defense of the teacher who was dismissed except a brief editorial statement, "The Man Should Have Been Heard," referring to the fact that in the public dismissal hearing the accused was refused the right to make any statement.

Phoenix conservatives agree, when pressed, that the American people are not likely to be persuaded to choose communism, but that the internal danger is still crucial, not only because of the nature of Communist subversive tactics, but, as the editor suggested, "the welfare state may not lead to communism, but it has always led to a nation's downfall." Perhaps the most serious indictment of the literate conservative position is its deviousness in this sort of deliberate confusion between anti-liberal and anti-Communist campaigns. In order to enhance the patriotic appeal, it plays up fear, and it associates liberal ideas with Communist threats when it does not seriously believe that connections exist.

It is not easy to assess the effect this conservative crusade is having on Arizona teachers. Arizonians are tough. They don't scare easily. They relish a contest, which is in the frontier tradition. So teacher morale has probably suffered less than it might have in some communities farther removed from the old frontier. And perhaps Arizona teachers are a bit more conservative than some others to begin with. A leading Bircher said, "They don't teach much about the United Nations around here because they know we don't like it."

An official of the Arizona Education Association, while deploring the Birch-type activity, admits that it may have had one beneficial side effect in training teachers to be more discriminating and more objective in their statements.

Liberals feel disquiet in the Phoenix area, but not panic. Some think the peak of the aggressive extremist activity has passed, for the time being, but they know it is not dead, and they know it is likely to be revived at any time, so long as the cold war continues.

The spirit of the alarmist patrioteers and the level of its appeal shines forth in this piece of doggerel published in the *Arizona Republic* over the name of Agnes Daniel:

When I was a child I loved to hear
Of the midnight ride of Paul Revere,
Who helped decide our nation's fate:
But now I fear he's out of date;

If such a man should now appear,
They'd say that he was "spreading fear,"
They'd call him a "disciple of hate,"
And never give him a chance to relate

A story which only could spread alarm,
"Dividing folks" and "doing much harm."
They'd turn him away and bar the door
Cover their heads and sleep some more.

Four hundred miles west, in the Los Angeles area, the tone is somewhat different, not because the Welch-Schwarz-Hargis campaigns are less virulent, but because here they lack the support they enjoy in Phoenix of a monopoly conservative press and a tradition of respectable conservatism. In the Los Angeles area the school incidents seem to assume that bizarre coloration that has become associated with this part of the Golden State. Some examples:

In nearby Santa Barbara, the Freeborn Club, identified by its vice-president as a front for the John Birch Society, mailed to the entire eleventh- and twelfth-grade student body of the San Marcos High School an announcement titled "Will You Be Free To Celebrate Christmas in the Future?"

In the same city the American Opinion Library distributed various pieces of conservative literature overprinted with telephone numbers to call for "The Voice of Freedom." Whoever dialed those numbers heard a recorded message opposing the extension of teacher tenure and recommending a certain conservative local radio commentator.

A San Diego State College history professor stated in a letter to the *Los Angeles Times*, "I know one teacher who was reprimanded by her principal for stating in class that the USSR is larger in area than the United States; a parent had complained."

A Los Angeles grand jury issued a report questioning the objectivity and value of a mock UN Assembly conducted by seventh-grade students. As the *Los Angeles Times* pointed out editorially, "For some reason the original critics of the mock assembly did not bother to present their arguments to the school board. Their complaint—which may be entirely valid—was given instead to the grand jury. They went to the wrong place."

At Garden Grove in notorious Orange County a local citizens' group campaigned for the revocation of the teaching credential of one teacher because of a questionnaire circulated in a sex education class. Properly, the State Department of Education was involved and stoutly refused to revoke the credential.

In Paradise a social studies teacher was attacked in an anonymous leaflet for inviting students to attend a conference on human rights at Asilomar, sponsored by the Friends Service Committee. The leaflet spoke of "an organized activity to weaken the souls of our children," and the leader of the group said she was concerned because the Asilomar conference "is the work of internationalists and United Nations spokesmen—all Communist fronters."

In Fullerton, California, a counselor was subjected to a persistently abusive campaign of letters, phone calls, and demands for his dismissal, based on three charges: (1) membership in the American Civil Liberties Union; (2) former membership, while an undergraduate, in American Youth for Democracy; and (3) permitting a controversial figure to address a meeting of the ACLU in his home. This attack was so severe that it prompted a joint investigation by the California Teachers Association and the NEA's Commission for the Defense of Democracy through Education. The report of this joint commission applauds the Fullerton school board and administration for their continued support of this counselor in the face of repeated attacks.

The organized nature of the attack is indicated by the testimony of one school official who reported that a member of the John Birch Society had assured him that if the board got rid of the counselor he would "call off about fifty people who are going to the newspapers" about the case.

In Fullerton, when some junior college students published a student newspaper off-campus in apparent competition with the official campus paper, which they considered intellectually sterile, the editors were approached by two members of the John Birch Society with offers of literature, advice, and financial aid. When the editors refused to be taken over by the Birchers they were subjected to a public attack by citizens who attended board meetings and even attended student council meetings to protest the authorization of a literary club to provide outlet for the literary expression of these student editors.

Other teacher incidents have occurred in other parts of the state, notably Antioch and San Carlos.

Although Southern California is a major stronghold of Birchism, officials of the Southern Section of CTA feel that it does not constitute a major menace. They are watchful but not worried. These leaders recommend a selectively aggressive policy, saying, "We cannot answer every John Birch letter, but we must meet every important attack." They add, "Teachers are less afraid in general than they were in the McCarthy era, for this movement is so extreme it is beyond the pale of respectability. The Birchers are hanging themselves by their own incredible statements." One schoolman obviously reflected the sentiments of others when he said, "This is a very lucrative racket. The crusaders are getting rich."

Compulsory Instruction Programs on Communism

In a state where the anti-Communist clamor is so strong, it was inevitable that a demand should arise for the state-wide compulsory adoption of an approved outline for the teaching of the virtues of capitalism and the vices of communism. Two states, Florida and Louisiana, have adopted rather drastic compulsory instruction programs on communism, and twenty-one states have some legislation on the subject.

In California a thirteen-man commission is now wrestling with the problem and appears to be thinking along the lines of preparing suggestive but not prescriptive materials, including bibliographies, a possible course outline, criteria for book selection, and suggestions for teacher preparation.

As soon as it was announced that the state was officially interested in teaching about communism in the schools, the State Department of Education was deluged with letters, mostly prescriptive, and mostly critical of the laxity of the schools in their anti-Communist posture.

One of the complaints was directed at a music book which included a song containing the phrase "Swing the shining sickle," because it was "as obvious a case as I have ever seen of Communist infiltration." The song in question is an old harvest song which has been popular in our songbooks since 1897.

Another correspondent proposed that we forthwith cease all reference to the American Revolution, since immature students might associate the same virtuous qualities of the American Revolution with the Russian Revolution. Instead, he suggests, let us refer always to the War for American Independence.

The flow of letters continues at the rate of about 300 per month, most of it of the "What have you done to fight communism today?" variety. When a conservative commentator in Southern California reported that the legislature was about to remove the requirement of a daily pledge of allegiance in the schools, the department was flooded with 6,000 letters, nearly all of them protesting vehemently against the rumored change.

The problem of patriotism and of the content of instruction relating to democracy and communism is a serious one, not to be taken lightly. Since our schools will inevitably devote more attention to the subject of communism, the question of the materials and methods to be used becomes a significant issue. It is inconceivable that we could achieve complete agreement on the seriousness of the internal Communist threat or on the proper posture to assume toward the external danger. This is one of the great issues of our time, and we are engaged in working through the attendant problems. All viewpoints should be expressed—though they cannot all be accepted—but all action and propaganda should be within the framework of our accepted notion of democracy and fair play.

Some teachers are exasperated or wrathful at the amount of time they must spend preparing materials to explain their teaching of democracy and communism, "just to satisfy these fringe critics." Teachers had better be willing to spend a great deal of time rethinking their teaching of democracy and communism, not only because much of it has been casual and patchwork, but because this is one of the central issues of our age and deserves thorough and painstaking thinking and rethinking.

Dr. Richard M. Clowes, who as assistant state superintendent in charge of curriculum bears much of the brunt of the extreme pressures in California, says, "I hope that twenty years from now we can look back and say we were not pressured by hysteria into unwise action, and what we did was sound by any sensible criterion."

Another manifestation of the conservative pressures bursting out of bounds is the rising fever of book banning, which has reached such a pitch that in Kent, Washington, alleged Birch-front groups protested the morality of *The Red Badge of Courage*. In Pontiac, Michigan, a group of parents sought to have *The Good Earth* and *Drums along the Mohawk* removed from the reading list as obscene.

In one state a group of civic leaders presented to the governor and the legislature a petition that they remove from the approved textbook list, as subversive, such standard texts as *United States History*, by Fremont Wirth; *Geography and World Affairs*, by Jones and Mirphy; *This Is America's Story*, by Wilder, Ludlum, and Brown; *Magruder's American Government*, by McClenaghan; and *World History*, by Boak, Slosson, and Anderson.

The cases cited by no means constitute a complete catalog of the instances where the patrioteers have attempted by pressure tactics to influence the operation of the schools, but they probably represent a fair sampling of the kinds of incidents occurring in many communities. They place in focus a number of extremely thorny questions.

Who Is a Patriot?

When do we ignore and when do we respond to accusations from the lunatic fringe? Where is the dividing line between active citizen participation in school affairs, which we encourage, and vigilante pressures or meddling, which we resent? How far should we go in acceding to community pressures to decide what constitutes proper patriotic procedures in the schools? Who is a patriot?

The answers are not simple, and in many important particulars they will vary from district to district.

It seems almost futile to join the chorus of hortatory voices pontificating on the subject, but since the democratic process requires that all views be stated and restated and restated, it might be appropriate here to recall a number of the caveats with which we are already familiar.

Schoolmen should retain a sobering awareness that they have not yet succeeded too well in their goal of education for responsible active citizenship. Both the leaders and the followers of extremist groups are, by and large, products of the public schools, products who were precocious in some of the less commendable qualities, exaggerating pride in self-expression at the expense of intellectual effort. They are still shirking the intellectual job and deriving a vicarious sense of participation from their presence in the jeering section.

Schoolmen should learn to accept criticism and dissent, perhaps even personal attack, as evidence of a functioning democracy. Granted that teaching efficiency is reduced when teachers are made to feel defensive or pressured, teachers should be able to absorb some criticism—even some sharp and unfair criticism—without crying "foul." When teachers too quickly admit to feeling pressured, they are confessing a lack of faith in their administrators, school boards, professional associations, and in the ultimate good sense of the American public. Any teacher who is fearful of having his teaching reviewed in the court of public opinion just may be deficient in his faith in democracy—and that is the same charge he is leveling at the Birchers.

It is interesting to note that in nearly every community where the film "Operation Abolition" became a source of controversy, neither the defenders of the film nor its critics trusted adult American audiences to analyze and interpret the film for themselves. Both sides felt impelled to have speakers accompany the film to be sure that the audience was "given" the desired interpretation. Lack of full faith and confidence in the ultimate good sense of the people is always a matter for concern, the more especially when it emanates from staff members of a democratic school system.

The muzzling of teachers must be prevented, but not by the muzzling of the patriotic groups. The name-calling campaigns must be countered, but not by name calling. The emotionalized hate-fear attacks must be met, but not in kind.

The dedicated member of a liberal group, bristling with anger when it is labeled a Communist front, is sometimes the loudest in retorting with charges of fascism. We must be fearless in reply, but we must be precise and accurate. Otherwise the careless slinging of slanderous terms makes a basic philosophical struggle between liberal and conservative forces degenerate into an offensive mudslinging contest. Let ardent liberals inquire whether by objective standards it is less proper to criticize the recent decisions of the Supreme Court and to seek the ouster of its chief justice by constitutional means than it is to mock the activities of a committee of the Congress and lampoon some aspects of the defense and security programs.

It is essential for the democratic process and for effective education into the democratic process that there exist at least two authentic alternatives on every issue. The current revival of a confident and articulate conservatism in this country is a wholesome development, though it is most unfortunate, especially for conservatism, that so many of the leaders at present are so "way out." We must no more judge conservatism by the extremists than we should judge liberalism by its crackpots. But we must meet school-community situations as they arise, and today they are frequently the result of John Birch Society activities. The Birchers are the conspicuous examples who are providing the popular image of the conservative in action.

It is the situations created by these extremists that place the strain on community relations, on school effectiveness, and on democratic faith. For even when a teacher under attack receives the standard expressions of support from his school board and his superintendent, he is still subject to inner pressures. He becomes the victim of a war of nerves and is incapable of devoting his whole energy to teaching. This teacher can never be sure when the pressures on the superintendent may become too strong, or when the board will withdraw its support in order to mollify an important segment of the community. This teacher, if he has not attained tenure, cannot foretell when he might be told with regrets that through no fault of his own he has become too controversial and his usefulness to the community has come to an end.

This has happened to a number of teachers and has been a genuine threat to a great many more. This is the pressure from the conservative organizations that is causing some concern. Wherever the John Birch Society commences an irresponsible attack, it should be met with the most responsible rebuttal that can be offered. If any teacher is unfairly dismissed, the responsibility rests squarely with the superintendent and the board. They were selected to meet pressures and to administer the schools fairly. If they have failed in an important instance, and if the democratic process is healthy in the community, they will not be chosen for another term.

The joint CTA–NEA commission which investigated the Fullerton, California, situation offered a clear set of recommendations to the board of trustees which might profitably be adopted elsewhere:

1. Adopt a clear-cut policy regarding academic freedom and rights of teachers.
2. Establish regular procedures for airing citizens' complaints.
3. Seek general understanding of the school's program and goals.
4. Take prompt action on all complaints, supporting the staff fully until facts are presented to justify withdrawal of support.

Dealing with Tensions

Intelligent administration of wise policies, such as the one proposed by the CTA–NEA commission, can reduce but cannot remove tensions. Tensions always accompany change, and today the tempo of change continues to accelerate.

The birth of the atomic age in 1945 complicated our loyalties by making more imperative the relaxation of traditional concepts of national honor and survival in favor of a new commitment to human honor and survival. The 1957 demonstration of superior Soviet technical skill provided impetus to the new trend to include a study of communism in the schools. A substantial reason for including in the curriculum well-planned instruction in the facts of communism is to reduce the necessity for reliance on other sources for this instruction. The report of the Fullerton investigation refers to the four-day "Anti-Communist School" sponsored by the Anti-Communist Crusades in Orange County in March of 1961 and includes the testimony of teachers who attended to the effect that the program was poorly planned and conducted and the speeches appealed to the emotions rather than to reason. "Many students and adults were left with the belief that there is a definite Communist threat, but without any guidance as to how to meet the threat. The fear this engendered has created a climate for acceptance of irresponsible criticism and unjustified attacks on the schools."

Such a comprehensive plan as that implied in the suggestions for attention to communism in the curriculum, clearly formulated policies for dealing with citizen complaints and for assuring teachers of support, plus a positive policy of honestly encouraging the dignified airing of differences of conviction can lead to satisfactory handling of tensions in any community where they arise.

The tragedy is that we learned to build the bomb before we learned to control our own emotions. If we are to meet our challenges successfully— the Birchers, the Soviets, and the bomb—we must learn fast how to examine our own inner feelings and act confidently at a rational level, free of the compulsive fears, enervating guilt, and irrational hostility that permeate so much of human behavior.

chapter 43

Needed: cooperation and competition in the school program

Anthony C. Riccio and Herman J. Peters

Twenty years ago the American public school was excoriated by its critics for compelling students to compete for unrealistic goals. It was alleged by social reformers of various stripes that much psychological damage was wrought upon children who failed to do well things that were not worth doing anyway. Today the public school is attacked because, in the opinion of some of its more vocal critics, it is sabotaging the American system of free enterprise by leading students down the pink path of collectivism. It is held that students whose education consists of nothing but wishy-washy cooperative experiences are not in a position to take an active and productive role in the American economy. Obviously, Americans are not agreed on the role that competition should play in education. In view of this problem, should the secondary school stress competition, cooperation, or both, and under what circumstances?

As commonly employed, the word "competition" refers to the procedure by which individuals or groups *contend against* each other for a particular goal; "cooperation" denotes individuals or groups *working together* for a common goal. The phrases of obvious importance in these concepts are "contend against" and "working together," for implicit in them is the nature of the respective acts. But the word "goal" is also of great consequence. Competition and cooperation are morally neutral; it is the end toward

From *Phi Delta Kappan*, 40(November, 1958), 97–99. Reprinted by permission of the publisher.

which these processes are focused and the conditions under which they operate that determine the value and/or desirability of either. Competition can lead to positive self-appraisal or a nervous breakdown. Cooperation may help produce a well-adjusted individual or a spineless, other-directed neuter.

Philosophers of most major schools agree that man is a social being. Obviously, competition and cooperation require a social context in which to operate. Man will inevitably come into contact with both forms of endeavor repeatedly during his lifetime. Moreover, because man is by nature potentially cooperative *and* competitive, it behooves the school to assist the individual to realize the development of these potentialities in a desirable fashion.

It has been suggested further that man lives in two worlds: a vocational world that is generally competitive in nature and an avocational world that is for the most part cooperative.[1] The school can assist the youth in the first instance by teaching him some means of competing in the economic arena. Vocational curricula are examples of what the school can do to help the individual meet selected competitive demands. But the avocational interests of a student must also be fostered, and this is probably best done through cooperative methods. Boys and girls cooperate to make a success of the school dance; husband and wife cooperate to make a success of a steak fry held on a patio cooperatively designed and constructed by the whole family.

The instances in school and adult life in which cooperation is a prerequisite for competition are numerous. Interscholastic athletes cooperate during gruelling practice sessions in order to compete successfully against another group of schoolboys who have done likewise. In fact, it is difficult to think of a social situation in which there is not at least a modicum of competition or cooperation. The problem is not whether the school should discontinue competitive or cooperative practices, of course, but whether it should place more stress on one of them.

A perusal of the literature reveals that very little is published pertinent to the positive value of competition in school living. Emphasis is generally placed upon the dangers that result from unhealthy competition or the beneficial cohesiveness gained from using cooperative procedures in group work. One would gain the impression that cooperation is *the* method of the democratic school setting and that competition is to be shunned whenever possible. The inevitability of competitive experiences demonstrates the impracticality of such an outlook.

The literature indicates that competitive behavior has ambivalent effects. Researchers have reported that although competition reduces group solidarity, it increases individual output. Notwithstanding studies citing the importance of competition as a powerful motivating factor, it must be re-

---

[1] H. A. Davidson, "Competition, the Cradle of Anxiety," *Education*, November, 1955, pp. 165–166.

membered that "only those compete who feel they have a chance of winning. The rest ignore the competition."[2]

The implications of pertinent research findings are readily stated. The schools must provide situations in which the student can gain competitive experiences that are not harmful and cooperative experiences that make it possible for a student to retain his individual character. Although much has been written on the various methods of providing students with beneficial cooperative experiences through such activities as teacher-student planning, little has appeared as to what the school can do to establish a healthy setting in which to provide competitive experiences. Alberty has listed a number of criteria that a competitive activity must meet to be educationally sound.[3] Among other things, he states that a competitive activity must provide for a number of "winners," must be engaged in on a voluntary basis, must have goals that are intrinsic to the activity itself, and must have rewards that are commensurate with the activity. Needless to say, if such criteria are to be met the secondary school must have a broad program of specialized activities—curricular and cocurricular. Logically, Alberty's position suggests that intramural athletics should receive more attention than is currently the case and that sponsors of such activities as debating and dramatics should critically examine their objectives and methods of selecting participants.

If the school provides competitive and cooperative experiences consonant with the findings of educational research, teaching methods will doubtless be affected. The teacher must note which students like to compete in certain activities and provide for them. Conversely, the teacher must also know the harm that can be done by compelling children to compete when they either do not wish to compete or would be foolish to do so. Further, a class in social studies might well consider the relative merits of competition and cooperation in a democratic society. They might even decide cooperatively on the kind of competitive experiences that the school should provide for students.

If sound experiences of a competitive and cooperative nature were provided for students, the work of the school counselor might be modified. Cooperative endeavors would in all probability reduce the number of social isolates, and the counselor might well devote more time to what Robinson has termed "higher level adjustment skills."[4] The counselor in conjunction with the curriculum coordinator could aid in establishing conditions favorable to meeting the needs of individual students in the areas of competition and cooperation. The guidance point of view would indeed prevail if stu-

[2] Arthur W. Combs, "Myth of Competition," *Childhood Education*, February, 1957, p. 265.

[3] Harold Alberty, "Some Criteria for Evaluating Competitive Learning Activities in High School." Unpublished material.

[4] Francis P. Robinson, *Principles and Procedures in Student Counseling*. New York: Harper and Brothers, 1950, pp. 231–259.

dents could develop their competitive and cooperative potential in a series of specially constructed experiences.

The goal, then, is one of balance between competitive and cooperative experiences with a eutectic quality of success permeating both. The recognition by today's pupil of the larger framework of standards which most people support and the competitive opportunity to achieve excellence in some phase of living should do much to give the pupil a sense of responsibility for becoming a productive person rather than a sense of expectancy of receiving much with a minimum of responsibility.

chapter **44**

The talented student
in a democratic society:
historical perspectives

Bernard J. Kohlbrenner

It is important in addressing ourselves to this subject that we notice, first, that we in this country have not had a democratic society very long and that even now we do not have, if we ever shall have, a completely democratic society. It is not necessary here to stress the very great progress that awaits to be made in the near future, to attain this objective, but it may be helpful to reflect on some aspects of the story as we have developed up to the present and to look very briefly at the contemporary scene.

Although the basic foundations for a republic were laid in the Constitution of 1787, the Bill of Rights was not part of the original document and was added as the first Ten Amendments only because of the resistance found in the States when they were not guaranteed by our fundamental charter. And even though they were added and the new Federal government went into effect within two years, still that government was a Federal government of delegated powers. The control of many of the aspects of life that would bear directly on citizenship, equality, and opportunity was in the hands of the several States. Here were lodged the regulations on the right of suffrage, the various arrangements that gave preferred status to some religious denominations, and the laws or the lack of them that would provide for a system of common schools. And here in the various states would be prevalent the many customs that would determine in large measure the

From a paper presented at the University of Notre Dame, July, 1961. Reprinted by permission of the author.

field of opportunity for the many social, economic, religious, and national language groups that inhabited the States. Although we did not have a caste system (except in the South with the institution of slavery), we did have a class-conscious society for many generations, as, indeed, we still have such a society in several respects.

But, in general and in great contrast to many other parts of the world, this country became a beacon for the millions who came from everywhere until the virtual end of immigration in the 1920's. These great waves of newcomers led to concern for their Americanization, the development of the common school, the encouragement of like-mindedness rather than uniqueness. Native movements untouched by the coming of the foreigners had led to the Jacksonian revolution, the spoils system in government, the halo put around the "self-made" man, and the esteem accorded the "school of hard knocks." Although Thomas Jefferson regarded himself as a democrat, he was an aristocratic democrat, but even he was unsuccessful in his attempt to reform his *alma mater*, the College of William and Mary, and to institute a system of public education that would ensure complete education for at least a few poor but able boys.[1] (It might be recalled that even he referred to the boys who would be drawn off from the system of schools at the first level as the "rubbish," a term that would not later be acceptable to the egalitarian sentiment.) Benjamin Franklin, who has often been called the first civilized American but was a completely self-educated man, proposed the reform of the middle schools, and academies such as he had espoused did become established and did prove to be popular but at most they became semipublic, rather than outright public institutions.[2] When George Counts came to give his interpretation of schools and education as the "road to culture," although he listed what he found to be ten of the controlling aims in the American effort to attain culture, he did not list respect for the talented as one.[3] This has not been in our culture.

Gradually, however, and after strenuous opposition even from those who might benefit most from them, we did obtain a system of public schools from the first grades to the universities. But the rise of the high school as, first, a popular and, later, a common school came slowly. Although begun in the 1820's, it was a select school until late in the century and was often referred to as "the people's college." Entrance examinations were commonly required until accrediting procedures began toward the end of that period. In the post-Civil War period, William T. Harris, who was then the most active and influential city superintendent of schools, always referred to them

[1] The best detailed account of his plans is found in Roy J. Honeywell, *The Educational Work of Thomas Jefferson*, Cambridge, Harvard University Press, 1931.

[2] I. L. Kandel, *History of Secondary Education*, Boston, Houghton Mifflin Co., 1930, pp. 391–422.

[3] George S. Counts, *The American Road to Culture*, New York, John Day Co., 1930.

as intended to produce those with "directive power" in society, a term which today would probably be translated into "leadership."[4]

Slowly at first, and then more speedily in recent years, the fulcrum has moved up from the high school, to the college, the university, and for many purposes to postdoctoral study. The frontiers of knowledge and scholarship have moved so far and so fast that it has become difficult for teachers, for example, to be abreast of the new knowledge in their fields. Recently a committee of scientists recommended that teachers of physics in high school have at least the doctor's degree in order to become sufficiently competent for their tasks. And a friend of mine who is the author of a high school textbook in history tells me that he has to make accommodations in his book to satisfy a state-wide examination requirement that is thirty years behind the scholarship in the field. We have really proceeded from the colonial ideal of vocational training for the mass of men and literary education for the few, and have gone from the concept of the rudiments for everyone to substantial education for all, but the communication of this substantial knowledge and the preparation of the teachers of this knowledge are still largely unsolved problems.

It is interesting and, I think, revealing, to note that the Educational Policies Commission published *Education for All American Youth* in 1944, and *Education for All American Children* in 1948, but *Education for the Gifted* in 1950, and *Education for All American Youth: A Further Look* in 1952.[5] This sequence puts, I think, in brief and perhaps not altogether fair form, the history of our concern over the education of the many and the education of the few, especially the few who are gifted. Our great overwhelming problem for several generations was to found and spread a school system for the masses—the brick-and-mortar stage—to get the laws passed, to provide the revenues, to establish the machinery, and obtain and prepare the teachers on at least a minimum level, to attract and to retain the pupils. In this effort, anything beyond the elementary school was for several generations regarded as possible only for the few, not always the intellectually gifted few, but too often, I fear, for the few whose families were in affluent social and economic circumstances. The pace-setting colleges held their own entrance examinations and recruited their freshmen classes from a small number of preparatory schools. But the states, through either their departments of education or their universities, began in the late nineteenth century to accredit high schools within their borders. Graduation from such schools became tantamount to admission to many colleges. And at a little later date, the voluntary accrediting associations began their work in collaboration with both the high schools and the colleges.

---

[4] *Nineteenth Annual Report* of the Board of Directors of the St. Louis Public Schools, St. Louis, 1874, pp. 61–65.

[5] All published in the respective years by the National Education Association, Washington, D.C.

But then, a little later, at about the turn of the century, the leading colleges began to stiffen their requirements for admission mainly through the work of the College Entrance Examination Board which they organized. Now even the colleges with the most and the oldest ivy have many students admitted from public high schools, and the much less prestigious colleges are requiring their applicants to take the CEEB examinations. Needless to say, the cutting scores required in the two classes of colleges are not identical, but it is revealing of what has happened in the selection of college freshmen to find admissions officers and deans all over the country rather suddenly speaking of means, medians, quartiles, and percentiles, not always, I fear, with understanding, but with at least superficial sophistication. It is sometimes rather flippantly said that any high school graduate may be admitted to a state college or university within his state. I do not need to tell you people who work in guidance how untrue that statement often is. It would be far more accurate to say that there is probably a college somewhere that will take almost any student who wants to go there, but such a college is often not a public institution. The state colleges may differ among themselves and between themselves and other colleges and universities but practically all are sharing the same concern about getting and retaining good students.

In the contemporary world many societies are becoming democratic even though all do not define democracy in the same way. And all are concerned over the problem of quality and quantity in education. The problems differ because of differences in elements of history and culture, and hence, the solutions will differ. In general, most European countries have had a variety of types of secondary schools for special classes of pupils. Such classes may be determined by type of education desired but the general distinctions have been made more on social and economic status of the family. All these nations have attempted to break the financial block to higher education of the poor but talented by providing, first, scholarships and, second, free education for all able pupils. All have types of secondary schools that, because of history, tradition, and types of pupils who have attended them, are vastly more prestigious than others. Paradoxically, as Goodwin Watson points out, it is the U.S.S.R. that has recently been most interesting to Americans bent on obtaining a more stimulating and more demanding education for able American pupils. This is the one nation that, on principle, does not adhere to the notion of innate individual difference, but their pupils do differ in accomplishment and motivation and in the length of schooling they receive.[6] A broad generalization might be made to the effect that the Europeans have attempted to make more available sec-

---

[6] Goodwin Watson, "Ideas from Secondary Education in the U.S.S.R.," in Samuel Everett (ed.), *Programs for the Gifted; A Case Book in Secondary Education,* Fifteenth Yearbook of the John Dewey Society, New York, Harper, 1961, p. 55.

ondary and higher education to those formerly not considered, whereas we have the problem of strengthening and deepening the educational opportunities of the more able pupils and students. Theirs is, fundamentally, more of a social and economic problem whereas ours is more strictly speaking an educational problem. Despite strenuous efforts in England to promote schools that roughly approximate our comprehensive high schools, the Great Public Schools and the grammar schools are still the most prestigious, and, as King points out, it is highly important for the higher careers that students attend schools where the proper speech and accent are used.[7] The student of the French *lycée* and the German *Gymnasium* generally has an education equivalent to what our *best* students do not complete until after two years of college. And only about 30 per cent or less of *Gymnasium* students proceed to the *Arbiturium,* the entrance examinations for the universities.[8] It is estimated that only about 14 per cent of French adolescents are in secondary schools,[9] an estimate that is not too wide of the mark for continental Europe generally.

But comparisons between American and foreign educational practices are notoriously difficult to make and more difficult to make meaningful. And the comparative practices are often misleading because of basic differences in educational philosophy and concepts. Even such terms as "secondary" and "higher" as used in accounts of education in various countries do not carry with them the same denotations and connotations, and often the latter are more important that the former. Mr. Conant has pointed out, however, one striking similarity amid many apparent dissimilarities that have a significant bearing on the education of the talented. He calls attention to the fact that, although something like one-third of young Americans are "going to college," and only about one-fifteenth or one-twentieth of young Europeans are university students, actually the contrast is not as great as would appear. This is true because the vast majority of these American students are not *university* students in the European sense; that is, they are not students preparing for careers in the higher professions. The group that is so preparing for such careers is, and this is the significant thing, about the same in the United States and abroad, namely only about 6 per cent of the age group.[10] So far as the secondary level is concerned, at least one major contrast is found and is likely to persist—the Europeans generally have a variety of types of secondary institutions whereas we have a commitment to the general or comprehensive high school. To be sure, we have a num-

[7] Edmund King, *Other Schools and Ours,* New York, Rinehart and Co., 1958, p. 87.

[8] Christian O. Arndt, "Ideas from the German Gymnasium," in Everett, *op. cit.,* p. 72; J. F. Cramer and G. S. Browne, *Contemporary Education,* New York, Harcourt, Brace, p. 456.

[9] King, *op. cit.,* p. 37.

[10] James B. Conant, *The American High School Today,* New York, McGraw-Hill, 1959, p. 3.

ber of highly regarded specialized types of secondary schools, the preparatory academic schools, highly specialized technical and vocational schools, and special schools for gifted students in the arts and sciences. But these are not numerous and they will probably never be found except in the largest centers of population. For good or for ill, the problems of developing proper education for the talented youth in this country will be solved, for the most part, in the same schools where the problems of the proper education of the average and the slow learner will be solved, in the comprehensive high school.

I should like to come now to a brief consideration of a few aspects of our recent history as they bear on the question of the education of the talented. There is little doubt about the concern over this question being largely determined by the social, political, and economic development of the country—it has not been the case of educational theorists sitting down to do some arm-chair philosophizing about the problem. As Havighurst has stressed, any rapidly changing society such as ours is likely to have a series of educational crises, and we have had three such crises since 1930.[11] The period of 1930–1940 was a period of economic depression and, hence, a period when there was no need for young people in the labor market. This was, therefore, a time marked by strenuous efforts to retain pupils in school and a period when curriculum interests lay along the lines of nonvocational education, with stress on the attempt to teach pupils to become better citizens, parents, and consumers. This was likewise a time when college students tended to major in the social sciences because of the impact of the current social and economic factors.

Then came the crisis of World War II which had great need for not only men but many women in industry and the military services. This was a time when dropouts of both boys and girls were common because of the allurement or the necessity that was found outside the schools. This was a time, I can vividly recall, when critics were urging the colleges for women not to undervalue their obligation to liberal education at a time when the men students were either drawn away from college or were concentrating on the courses that had immediate utility. This period came to an end, of course, and this was about 1950.

From then to the present time there has been a dearth of young people in a period of, generally, an enormous economic boom. There was, of course, the economic slowdown or depression of this past year from which we now seem to be recovering. It is important to note the smaller percentage of young people in the general population during a period of economic growth, a smaller percentage due to the low birth rates of the

[11] Robert J. Havighurst, "The Impact of Population Change and Working Force Change on American Education," *Educational Record*, 41, No. 4 (October, 1960), 346–356. The discussion of these crises which follows is based on this analysis by Havighurst.

1930–1940 period, which produced small numbers of young adults for the 1950's. But an increase in the birth rate beginning in 1946 made the elementary schools bulge in the 1950's, creating problems of school housing and teacher supply. The cold war with the U.S.S.R. gave a spurt to programs of military and economic aid to our allies or hoped-for allies as well as to the propaganda war. Colleges and universities were asked to prepare students for both. We are all familiar with some of the changes in educational emphases that occurred during this period—the increase of enrollments of men in college, both in relative and absolute numbers, the increase in enrollments in physical sciences, foreign languages, and engineering, the popularity of the idea, at least, of "tough" education, and attention to the development of programs for gifted students in college and pupils in high school. Havighurst points out, significantly, that the gifted were now defined as the top 10 or 15 per cent of the age group whereas they had been defined as only the top 1 or 2 per cent of the age group in the 1920's, which was also a time of high interest in the talented.[12]

Havighurst also points out how our very concepts of talent and its so-called wastage are dependent on the socioeconomic factors in the society of the time. In the 1950's there was a great amount of talk about the wastage of talent primarily because of the great need our society had for large numbers of engineers, scientists, and teachers. But there was actually less waste of talent then than in the 1930's when there was a smaller proportion of able students in college. But at that time there was no dearth of youths and hence no talk of the waste of talent. In the attention given to the education of the gifted in this period, the gifted were defined almost always as those who were intellectually superior, an emphasis brought about, no doubt, because of our need of scientists, engineers, and teachers. But there was little attention given to the gifted in the fine and literary arts. The emphases that were found in this period were, as Havighurst says, forced on us:

> It is hard to see how education could have avoided its emphasis on the gifted, its stress on mathematics and science and tough pedagogy, its concern over wastage of talent, and its program of expanded opportunity for youth of minority groups or low economic status. This ideology may have been no more than the noise people made as they did what they were bound to do.[13]

So far as the coming crisis is related to some aspects of the education of the gifted, Havighurst refers to the commonly recognized effort of most colleges to become more selective in their admissions but those that are presently most selective can scarcely become more so with respect to just

12 *Ibid.*, p. 348.
13 *Ibid.*, p. 350.

intellectual factors. The best of the colleges can now fill their freshman ranks with the most intellectually talented youths available in the total population. These colleges will undoubtedly turn increasing attention to personality factors and special interests of applicants. Other colleges will undoubtedly raise the levels of the student bodies as determined by school records and test scores. But will it be vocational education or general education for the talented? Will the emphasis of the 1950's on the production of scientists, engineers, teachers, and business executives be continued? We are now training 80 per cent more engineers than in 1951 and it should become possible to balance the concern for vocational preparation with at least an equal concern for good and superior education for good and superior students. As Terman insists, the current spirit of our society and our time pointed up the need for more scientists and engineers but the *Zeitgeist* should likewise be directed to prepare the way for future appreciation of needs not yet recognized.

By encouraging the development of all kinds of special talent and of aptitude for every kind of leadership and scholarly achievement, the *Zeitgeist* itself would, in time, be molded along more liberal lines and to the appreciation of whatever enlarges the spirit of men.[14]

To speak of only the two comprehensive means of adjustment for the education of the talented student, acceleration and enrichment, it has been the latter that has been most favored in American schools.[15] But in recent years, with the Advanced Placement Program and the Early Admission to College Program, there has been some attention given to acceleration and to the combination of acceleration and enrichment. But neither has found much acceptance so far in large numbers of our schools. In order to increase the number of schools that will involve talented students in these programs and will devise other ways and means of developing the talents of their most gifted students, both the schools and the larger society in which they work will have to fight against the cult of mediocrity, the folklore that stresses its fear of the superior in such terms as "ivory tower" and "egghead." They will have to contend with a materialistic civilization that stresses the acquisition of wealth and in which careers of doing rather than thinking are esteemed. They will have to resist the social climate in

[14] Lewis M. Terman, "What Education for the Gifted Should Accomplish," in *Education for the Gifted,* Fifty-Seventh Yearbook, National Society for the Study of Education, Part II, Chicago, University of Chicago Press, 1958, p. 17.

[15] In 1950 some 4 million pupils, representing 20 per cent of those enrolled, were grade-retarded and of these more than 1.6 million were two or more grades retarded. In the same year some 1 million were grade-accelerated. Eleanor H. Bernert and Charles B. Nam, "Demographic Factors Affecting American Education," in *Social Forces Influencing American Education,* Sixtieth Yearbook, National Society for the Study of Education, Part II, Chicago, University of Chicago Press, 1961, pp. 104–105.

which the short work week and the long weekend, guaranteed vacations, and even selected travel guaranteed in advance for military enlistees are prominently featured. Most of the resistance to the scientist has been broken down, broken down so much and so far that he is often popularly surrounded with an aura of irrational awe and deference. But the resistance to the importance and the necessity of other contributors to the national welfare and the enrichment of human life is still great.

This resistance cannot be broken down by the schools alone; it is a task of our whole society. Indeed, the schools may prepare gifted students for a life of frustration if our society does not parallel the higher standards of the schools with higher standards of individual and group life. Indeed, the advantages that some foreign countries have in the promotion of superior education for superior students come more from the climate of public opinion than from the technical work of the schools. In our country there is no doubt that schools and teachers could do more in a similar effort if they were assured of support from the larger society. But nothing less will save us. We have too many unresolved problems of individual and social life to leave unexploited any talents our students possess. The great contributions of all history were made by talented individuals. We have abundant evidence that many of our talented students are not developing their potential. Other societies have created climates which accent and stimulate the gifted. We can do no less than establish a similar climate for the good of the individual and for the common welfare.

chapter 45

Schools should teach "about" religions but are doing enough on moral values

Editors of The Nation's Schools

Public high schools should find a place in the curriculum to teach *about* religions. Except for this addition, schools are doing all they reasonably can be expected to do in the teaching of moral and spiritual values.

These views were expresssed by the majority of administrators responding to September's opinion poll.

Fifty-two per cent favor instruction *about* religions in the high school curriculums. Taking the long view, a Michigan schoolman commented: "I believe knowledge of the various religions—their basic beliefs and objectives—can be of significant value in helping to further national and world understanding."

A superintendent from Missouri favors teaching about religions in the high school "if the material is carefully planned and taught by persons who could maintain an unbiased and objective point of view."

"Every high school student should be taught about religions," stated a Texas administrator. Then, adding this prayer, said: "God help the teacher, however, who runs afoul of the bigots and crackpots in the community!"

Perhaps the 45 per cent who are against teaching about religions thought of this; at any rate, most of them anticipated trouble.

An Ohio official predicted that "the word 'about' would soon be lost and there could be trouble."

Some prefer that "comparative religions" be taught at the junior college level, where the subject might be chosen as an elective. Others contend that history courses offer enough teaching in this area for high school students.

Enough on Spiritual Values

Whether moral and spiritual values are taught or "caught," as one administrator suggests, public schools are doing as much as can *reasonably* be expected in this area, believe 61 per cent of the respondents.

Said a Washington superintendent: "With pupils' school environment restricted to a maximum of about 1,080 hours during the school year, the best the school can do is *supplement* the teaching of moral and spiritual values, not assume the major responsibility."

"Already, schools are teaching good sportsmanship through supervised playground activities; various classes are presenting the ideals of citizenship," mentioned a Nebraskan. "Teachers act as examples and indirectly teach values to students," said an administrator from Minnesota. Schoolmen from Maine and South Dakota reported that their schools are participating in a program of released time for religious instruction in local churches.

Going a step farther, a Wisconsinite offered: "Knowledge of what is right does not necessarily lead to right conduct. The problem is how to bolster knowledge with a desire to *do* what is right. This calls for more practice and example."

Some respondents contend that the schools are doing their share in teaching moral and spiritual values, but other agencies are not. Said an Iowa official: "Perhaps it is a worn-out statement, but I still believe that the home should do most of this teaching."

One group of superintendents invoked the doctrine of separation of church and state. "I think all of us teach moral and spiritual values, but I can't see that the school should infringe on or take over the work that rightfully belongs to the churches," stated a Kansan.

"Probably the schools are doing all that it is reasonable to expect, considering the crowded curriculum, the wide variety of standards concerning spiritual values and the time-consuming duties of a noninstructional nature that are required of teachers," commented a Texan. "Nevertheless, results are not being obtained."

Thirty-eight per cent of the respondents would probably use the Texas superintendent's last statement as a reason for saying that schools should do *more* in teaching moral and spiritual values. A second administrator from the Lone Star State declared: "Tomorrow's citizens must be stronger spiritually to withstand the tempestuous onslaught of isms."

A Minnesota schoolman would accomplish this through "teaching by example only and entirely without words"; a New Yorker by "discussing questions of moral significance with individual pupils as pertinent situations arise"; a Wyoming official by "emphasizing fair play and honesty in all classes."

Before schools attempt to assume more responsibility, there are changes that must be brought about, caution some respondents. "Until we reach some reasonable standards on moral and spiritual values, the public schools are on shaky ground even if the teachers teach unofficially," maintained a Massachusetts schoolman.

Opinion Poll Findings:

1. Are public schools doing as much as can reasonably be expected in the teaching of moral and spiritual values?
   Yes . . . 61%   No . . . 38%   No Opinion . . . 1%

2. Should there be a place in the high school curriculum for teaching about religions?
   Yes . . . 52%   No . . . 45%   No opinion . . . 3%

Based on a 4 per cent proportional sampling of 16,000 school administrators in continental United States, this survey brought a 36 per cent response.

chapter *46*
The case "for" ability grouping

Kenneth Mott

A decade in the classroom—elementary, high school, and junior high school —has left some very firm impressions in my mind concerning grouping policies which are practiced in our schools. What I have to say on this subject is *not* from the standpoint of an "educationist" who has elaborate courses of study in pedagogy to his credit and little classroom experience. I speak from the classroom teacher perspective. What I have to say is based on personal findings derived from having worked directly with children of high, low, and average mentality. No elaborate quotation of "expert" opinion accompanies what is said here. I speak candidly on a much-debated subject without the blessings of a "known" educator.

What I have to say is based on actual experience with pupils in the classroom, and not upon test results which were the result of research by an outsider. No elaborate research procedure was used other than keeping accurate records and observations, which were a part of normal activity. However, I firmly believe that my presentation reflects the problem in its true light and implies the correct policies that should be followed in meeting the problem.

Democracy and Grouping

Educational bulletins are filled with articles about and educational texts devote many chapters to grouping. Ability grouping, social, emotional, and maturity grouping, as well as various other types of grouping are expounded upon. Some authors are against grouping of students under any circum-

From Bulletin of the NASSP, 45(November, 1961), 50–54. Reprinted by permission of the publisher.

stances according to ability because such grouping might tend to create what is termed "special elite groups." They say that ability grouping is undemocratic. This is a major defense of the opponents of ability grouping. Although there are several avenues of approach to the problem, let's look at this "democratic" aspect first.

Isn't there a muddled interpretation of democracy involved here? Does democracy in education mean that all children must become "equal" in *every* respect? Does it mean that every school child should be compelled to go through the identical process or course of study to ensure that all receive the same treatment? Does democracy have its basis in group dynamics? Does democracy in education mean that the social adjustment of the individual is of supreme importance? Does democracy in education mean that everyone must be given "passing marks" simply if they do their best? Or does this indicate that the creator made people differently in the first place, and that they therefore must be treated accordingly?

Does "democracy" mean that some pupils should be allowed to progress on through elementary, junior high school, and senior high school when they show no capabilities of mastering the curriculum which they are required to follow? Should these pupils be given the same diploma as the more intellectually capable? This has happened in the cases of many "slow" students so that they would not "feel differently" from the others in their class.

Our democracy has lasted because it was founded on the idea of individualism, not upon the idea of the "common mold." Our democracy's initial strength lay in the strength of the many individuals who were very desirous of a chance to be able to grow, learn, and prosper by using the abilities which they possessed as individuals. Abraham Lincoln believed this about democracy. He stated it in unequivocal terms when he said:

> The prudent, penniless beginner in the world labors for wages for a while, saves a surplus with which to buy tools or land for himself another while, and at length hires another new beginner to help him. This is the just, and generous, and prosperous system which opens the way to all, gives hope to all, and consequently energy, and progress, and improvement of conditions to all.

However, somewhere along the line of educational reasoning in the last four decades, "democracy" began to take on some new aspects. It came to mean that each child should not only have an equal *chance* to an education, but also that he must be "pushed" through an identical mold so that little or no individual motivation or incentive existed. It came to mean that there should be no such thing as "failure" in school. If a fellow tried at the mastering of a course of study, but failed in its mastery, he should be promoted anyway for "trying," and be given the same diploma as his more intelligent classmates. To deprive him of that diploma would be showing that he was different from others—and that would be undemocratic. If these "new" interpretations are true, then Mother Nature was undemocratic.

To those who say that we should not group pupils according to their abilities and/or intellectual capacities which they possess, because it is undemocratic, I address this question: What is undemocratic about finding the God-given qualities and abilities in all students and giving them the divine privilege of associating and working as nearly as possible with the type of people with whom they have equal mental ability and desire? This is *not* social grouping. Remember, *many* of our more capable students come from families which fall in the low-income bracket and, consequently, on the low social scale.

We do not hesitate to extoll much praise upon the founders of our great democracy. In what scholastic group did they fall? In the average or middle group? Of course it is common knowledge that Franklin, Jefferson, *et al.* rose to the top. But what would they have achieved if they had been exposed to some of our grouping procedures where individualism on the part of intellectual students is buried in a classroom of mediocre and below-average students? What would they have achieved if they had been exposed to the modern leveling practices? What if their interest and enthusiasm had been squelched in their youth by the "egghead" label?

On the other hand, what would the effect have been on the average and below-average students, in the early days of this country, if they had been forced by a state law to "learn" with their more intellectually able counterparts? Would these nonintellectuals have gone on to fill their vital roles in the founding of our great democracy as they did? Or would they, like the slow and average groups of today, be rebellious against being placed into a situation in which they could neither excel nor see any immediate hope of firm progress? What would have happened to their initiative if all of these apprentice artisans and tradesmen had been robbed of their individual rights to learn to be good smithies or clerks even if they could not fathom the depths of mathematics, science, and the classics? What if these fellows had been forced to sit in Latin classes which they could not begin to comprehend, or in mathematics classes which were beyond their abilities to master, when their heart's desire was to be a good smithie or clerk like father?

Today in most of our schools, these two groups of students are forced together in the same classes. Both the slow and rapid learners are required the same courses of study in junior high school and senior high school. The slow learner is unable to master the work, so he is "put up" with his social group or his age-level group. The rapid learner can comprehend and master the required work, but in all too many cases he does not work up to his capacity because he knows that the slow learner is being put up. So why shouldn't he be also?

Is either group receiving just and fair treatment? Figures show that only about 5 per cent of all students are delinquent. This 5 per cent is composed of a mixture of people from the "low" and the "top" intelligence brackets. In school, the dull or slow students rebel against school work which is intended for the average group, but which they are expected to do. The top intellectuals rebel against the same work, which is fitted for the average, because it is too easy for them. *This common mold is the crux of our problem.*

Individualism: A Prime Factor to Be Considered

I wonder if this business of grouping has really been considered from a logical and practical standpoint; or has it been approached largely from a theoretical point of view which has a few test results as its basis? Let us actually consider grouping at the grass-roots level—from a common-sense point of view—from the classroom teacher's perspective wherein the problem must be met face to face.

A principal who is an acquaintance of mine, and who incidentally favors the recognizing and dealing with individual ability whether it be high or low, told me recently about the visit of a state supervisor to his school. In the course of their conversation the supervisor said, "Mr. M . . . told me you were trying ability grouping in your school, but I said that I knew you better than that. I knew that you would *never* try such a thing."

The principal replied that he had been trying it, and that success was being experienced. However, this principal was reprimanded. He is only one of many who will dare step aside from contemporary policy—that of grouping wide ranges of ability in one classroom environment.

Through such attitudes on the part of our administrative superiors, we teachers have been soothed into a professional state of mind in which we are hesitant to recognize and promote individual ability in pupils. Do we not speak of "Education for All Children," and "Education for the Whole Child," and then glorify the common at the expense of the uncommon or *vice versa?* Have we hesitated to bring intelligent students into contact with that which is challenging and difficult, just because the majority of the students are unable to cope with and master difficult things satisfactorily? Likewise, haven't we, by administrative requirement, neglected the bottom group (or slow learners) by putting them through the same program as the average and above?

Ability or intelligence grouping (homogeneous grouping) is a natural and inevitable consequence of God's creation. Not only by divisions of the animal and plant kingdom, but according to strength, stamina, intelligence, ineptness, laziness, and countless other criteria. Ability grouping according to classes in school is merely an aid to and the carrying out of the basic plan of God and nature.

If a thousand people were each given a million dollars, (someone has said) in a short time, most of the billion dollars would be controlled by the top 1 to 5 per cent of the people to whom it had been given, and the rest would be in varying amounts distributed among the remainder of the people. Thus, although an effort might be made forcibly to equalize opportunity by making all alike, the individual will, personality, God-given intellect and other factors tend to lead those individuals with the larger amounts of these characteristics, to the top of the heap. They are able to lead and control their fellow men, and their fellow men succumb to their effort.

Let's consider this example from nature: I have often noticed a group of young pine seedlings in an old field. They are, at first, as thick as weeds. As time passes, some of them die before reaching one foot in height. Others reach a few feet higher before dying, and only few of the originals reach maturity. The majority are smothered from lack of sunlight, having been deprived of it by the stronger and more highly developed trees. Foresters call this "natural" selection. Would the foresters, however, ever recommend that all of the strong vigorous trees be cut so that the spindly ones could grow? Or on the other hand, would the forester level all of the seedlings to struggle together with no regard to their differences? If they were all left together (both the strong and weak) the strong would no doubt triumph and grow to maturity. But, the strong ones would also be adversely affected by the presence of the weak ones in large numbers, and their growth would be slower. Of course the weak would gradually die out as they were forced to do by the persistent growth of the strong.

This same principle applies to the area of human relations. If students are compelled to work closely together without any real consideration being given to their individual abilities, the result will be the same with them as with the trees—complete and full growth will not result unless some selectivation is done.

This selectivation can be done in the classroom without difficulty if it is understood and dealt with properly. It should be recognized that a child's abilities in some areas vary with time, or maturity. We can call this the maturation factor. An example of this factor will illustrate its significance: A one-year-old child does not have the ability to catch and throw a baseball accurately. He masters this (or gains ability to do it) somewhere between the ages of two and seven. Just because one child can catch with accuracy at the age of five, and another at seven or eight, does not necessarily mean that the first child is innately more intelligent than the other. It simply means that his maturation level for that activity was reached sooner. This may also be the case in other areas. So when a child is grouped in a class according to his reading ability, this is not an indication of innate intelligence, but one of maturation or readiness to do. Therefore it may be necessary that a child remain in the same ability group only long enough to improve himself to the point where he is ready to go on higher. He may not have to remain in the same ability group all through his school career. He may show progress (and he will if taught on his level within his group) and, when he does, he should be promoted to the next ability group.

Many educators disagree with this outlook on grouping. They say that educational experiments have proved that no real change results in learning for either the slow or fast groups when they are separated. That was probably true in the experiment or experiments as they were conducted. Do you know why no difference in learning resulted? Because both groups were given identical programs with which to work, and no individual consideration was given to the students. I have found by experience, that learning skyrockets when individuals are treated as individuals and are motivated and challenged with school work of a type that produces some measures of success and interest in and for the individual. The child must be taken where he is and helped to progress toward the goals that he is expected to reach. Those goals should not be any lower for one group than for the other.

In the practice of forestry, this idea of individualism is a basic factor. Selective cutting is carried on in an effort to help all of the seedlings progress at a rapid rate. Trees which are sure to die before maturity is reached are pruned early. They are put to use as posts or other uses which require small-sized trees. In the nursery while they are still in the small seedling stage, the strong ones are weeded out of the beds and placed in a larger area where they may grow without being crowded by their neighbors.

An application of this principle in school may be illustrated thusly: Let's suppose that two boys each have the very same opportunity and environment so far as socioeconomic factors are concerned. However, they go in opposite directions after leaving junior high school. One goes on through high school and college and becomes a doctor, the other becomes a common laborer after having stayed in school eight years. Why did this occur? Because of individual differences. They have separated themselves *naturally*.

In a very large percentage of the cases of this kind, the boy who quits school could be greatly helped if he were pruned early, preferably in the upper elementary grades or junior high school, and given the opportunity to remain in school and study the curriculum which he is able to master, and which may prepare him to do whatever his abilities permit. If it is found that he *can* do high school or college work after he has had more elaborate background work in the basic subjects, then he should be able to do so.

It is obvious that, in a situation of this type, one boy has the ability *and* the desire to become a doctor; the other might have had the desire to become a doctor but the ability to become only a laborer. Ability is the dominant factor in the consideration of what life holds for each of us. Desire without ability is void so far as our contribution in this life is concerned. If the boy who became a laborer had been pruned early, and given an opportunity to take a special course which would enhance his ability, in all likelihood, he would have not quit school, neither would he have been a possible problem on society. However, to achieve this, the way must be paved for the student's acceptance of proper attitudes toward the idea of individual differences which exist in the abilities of everyone.

Paving the Way for Acceptance of Individual Worth

Pupils can be taught to love and respect all learning whether it be calculus, or a vocational trade, Greek, or home canning. Pupils should be taught that all learning is highly desirable. They should be taught that each effort put forth by any individual to learn any worthwhile activity or to gain any bit of worthwhile knowledge is a dignified and sacred process which involves the spiritual and physical makeup of the human being. He should be taught that his ability represents his possibilities for adjustment in this world environment, and that, effectively to do so, he must look upon all forms of work, however lowly in the eyes of man, as deserving of the same dignity as any other.

He must be taught that he must find his place in life and work with all of his might to achieve success in it. To do less is to make a mockery of the divine privilege of being a human being with superior intellect. However, let's face the issue squarely: We are *not* all alike in ability any more than we are in appearance. The creator did not make us all alike, so why use a common mold for all pupils in this all-important business of teaching and learning?

We educators *could* take a good lesson from the forester. But who is to do the pruning of the intellectual "high-flyers" from the "low-flying" intellectuals? That is, who is to undertake the job of separating the sheep from the goats? (Now I am not talking about the economically or socially underprivileged. Remember, some of our most intellectually brilliant pupils come from economically underprivileged homes.) Who is to guide both of these groups of pupils into accepting their roles in society and making the most of their individual abilities and capacities? Who shall dare draw a line between the average and above average?

Ability grouping by classes can be achieved easily through the efforts of the classroom teacher and the school administrator. Teachers can recognize intellectual and scholastic ability, so their voices should be heard strongly in determining the more intellectually inclined students whose abilities are above average. In order to do this, all teachers must assume the proper attitudes regarding the program. If teachers do not respect and have confidence in an ability-grouping program, it is doomed to failure. Therefore, it will be necessary to begin such a program in college where future teachers are shown the feasibility of such an undertaking. If we educators are really as professional as we like to be considered, we would have very little difficulty in dealing with this business of pruning students according to ability. We would already have a sound and workable program. The main reason that such a program is not in existence, is that most teachers are afraid of criticism which is based on the idea that it is undemocratic and is not the *popular* thing to do.

We need to be professional about it. We must face this problem realistically and prune our higher abilities from the lower abilities, and challenge them. Strong students *must* be grouped together and challenged with the highest possible standards. Slow students should be placed in a situation with a curriculum adjusted to their abilities, and yet should be guided by the same high standards or goals as the others. Then if their abilities in academic subjects show change for the better, they should be allowed to progress to the "strong" group. This possibility was proved in the recent experiment in New York City in an "asphalt jungle" situation. The principal, Daniel Schreiber, found that IQs actually improve when children of greatly underprivileged homes are subjected to cultural and intellectual pursuits, and students were challenged with new higher goals in life and shown that they *could* be attained.

We must prune those whom we are very sure will drop out of scholastic or academic work early, challenge them with intellectual pursuits, and if there is still no response, help them to learn the vocation for which they aspire, or for which they are best fitted. Only ability grouping according to subject matter or intellectual lines can be successful here. I don't mean to "cram it down their throats" and reap poor results which is now happening on a widespread scale. An undertaking of this type would require parent-teacher teamwork. Parents would have to recognize each child for exactly what he is. Thus an orientation program would be required.

Several articles which I have read about grouping maintain that even when grouping is done according to ability, there is still a wide range of differences in physical, social, vocational, and other areas. The authors further maintain that if this wide range still exists in a supposedly homogeneous group, perfection has not been reached and, therefore, no effort should be made if all pupils are not exactly alike. How absurd! Of course there are differences within a class. There is no such thing as absolute homogeneity. The creator did not intend it to be so. Those guilty of this kind of confused thinking simply refuse to see the forest because of the trees. Ability grouping should not be considered from that angle. We educators must be realistic about it. We must act in the interest of the students.

Definite criteria must be set up which will establish a person's general scholastic ability. As previously stated, experienced teachers can very easily classify students according to general performance and achievement, so their opinions should stand out prominently in determining these criteria. The situation where two or three pupils are scarcely able to write their names, fifteen or eighteen pupils are barely average, and two or three pupils of outstanding intelligence are all placed together in the same classroom must be eliminated wherever possible. This can be done easily in the larger schools where the population is above five hundred or so. In a class situation such as that just described, the slow students are unable to do their best, as they are adversely affected by the bright ones and *vice versa*. Let me explain why this is so.

During my decade in the classroom, I have witnessed the complacency of many students with very high intellectual abilities. I have watched them wither on the vine from the lack of proper challenging and from the lack of proper instructional procedure made necessary by improper grouping. I have watched many of the intellectually alert students cringe and slump in their seats when a fellow student asked a question which seemed too immature and juvenile to them. I have also heard their acid replies to those questions which were far below their level, but which were meant for average and below-average students. And, in turn, I have seen these bright pupils become discipline problems because they were not challenged. I have also seen the slow students forced to sit in English grammar classes and in algebra classes when they could scarcely write their names, much less work eighth- or tenth-grade mathematics or English. These became discipline problems too.

These were the results of the common mold. These attitudes could have been eliminated by helping the students recognize individual abilities, and then separating them according to those abilities. Many educators claim that the low-ability group of students would envy the high-ability group, and the high group would become the elite. This would not happen if the perpetuators of the program of grouping have the correct attitudes toward the program, and inculcate these ideas into the personalities and philosophies of the students.

The Problem in Focus

Critics of my statements will probably ask, "Why don't you as a classroom teacher do something about the situation which you describe?" "Why don't you as a teacher create a classroom situation which will provide the best opportunity for all degrees of intellect or ability which exist in your classes?" The answer to these questions is this: "I have done something."

I have spent many hours in extra work, trying to perfect a method in my classroom procedure, whereby I might give equal time and help to the several *very* slow learners, the average learners, and the several *very* alert students which usually make up a typical classroom. I am sure that thousands of other teachers have done the same. I have had to resort to various grouping procedures within my own classroom, in an effort to deal with those students in the top intellectual ability group on their levels. This I did so that they might not become completely bored to distraction at the procedure which must be used with other groups, and so that the slow learners might have proper attention.

Handling this type of classroom setup is somewhat like a hypothetical case which we might describe as follows: Suppose a swimming instructor is assigned a class made up of five husky perfect physical specimens, who are eager to learn to swim; twenty healthy little fellows who have varying degrees of aquaphobia; four or five chaps who suffer types of paralysis, and one or two paraplegics. The instructor is told that this is an ideal class according to some expert, and that he must teach the entire group to swim all at one time. Should he devote as much time to the paraplegics as to the strong vigorous aquatic lovers? If he neglects the strong ones, who will more than likely be the best swimmers, they will probably learn by themselves. But how about their form? How about learning proper breathing and stroking? Does that come naturally? Will the instructor have time to teach these things effectively to all three groups? If this instructor has one hour per day, how is it to be divided among these groups? How would a swimming instructor handle such a group? What about the fellows with paralysis? What about the little ones with aquaphobia?

Ridiculous? Of course it is. No physical education expert would recommend such a situation. However this is *exactly* the same dilemma that the average academic classroom teacher is forced to face. She must deal with these intellectual paraletics and paraplegics. She must try somehow to find time to strike the middle group, and if possible, teach and challenge the husky intellectuals. This could not, and cannot, be done effectively any more than the swimming instructor could effectively teach all of his students on the same level at the same time in one classroom.

In a situation where a teacher must divide her time in the classroom between the above, middle, below, and far-below students, there is an extra amount of effort required, not only in preparation and hard work, but in mental and physical strain. Some pupils are bound to be neglected, and this usually turns out to be the bright ones. This is because—in the words of many teachers today—"They can root for themselves. They will *get* it anyway. We must use most of our time helping the 'slow' ones, because they have so much trouble learning."

Will they "get it anyway"? Let me put the record straight. Am I saying that we should neglect the dull students in favor of the bright ones? *No.* I am simply saying that we cannot give either the low or high group (not to mention the average masses) a fair chance unless we do something about the way they are grouped, and unless we create more practical classroom procedures. These procedures should be designed for individual needs instead of the needs of one level, and this can be accomplished only by grouping students by ability according to subject matter and other areas, or by assigning a teacher per pupil. The latter is obviously unthinkable. Ability grouping will help eliminate the "common mold" idea and put learning on a sound basis so far as the classroom climate is concerned.

Let us look at what must go on in a classroom where several ability groups exist, and then consider the implications which involve education as a whole. In a classroom situation where the teacher must deal with three or more ability groups (which I have already indicated), she must plan in detail for dealing with the different groups. That is, she must do this if she is really interested in giving each of the groups an equal chance. She must be sure that a fair amount of time is spent with each group, if it progresses at the rate that it should. Here the teacher can't afford to give more of the same "stuff" to the bright pupils, while the average and dull are trying to master what the alert ones have already mastered. The "bright" pupils must be given advanced material and guidance—challenging work—and the slow ones must be met on their level. This requires actually dealing with what amounts to three or four classroom situations within the walls of one classroom, all at the same time.

This is the situation which *had* to exist in the old one-room country school where only a few students were in each class, and there was only one teacher. However, *must this anachronism exist in modern schools which have facilities for not only meeting the present needs of each pupil, but for preparing him so that his education will meet his needs as a grown-up in society?*

Where three or four widely varying ability groups exist in one classroom, the teacher must divide her time to the extent that the frustration point is reached. I know from experience. I know that when the teacher must deal with several groups, a poorer quality of teaching results. I know, because I have taught all the types of classes mentioned in this article. The below-average group that I taught afforded an enjoyable experience, just as the bright group did. I say this because in each case I was able to strike a medium of procedure and deal with the entire class at once. Several people appraised my handling of this slow group. According to those who made the appraisal, more progress was made with my handling the slow pupils as a group than under other situations in which they had been placed in the school program.

After having taught low, high, and mixed ability classes, and after having weighed the results which concern both teacher and pupil, *I must declare in favor of ability grouping, by subject matter or otherwise*. It is of unlimited help in enabling both teacher and pupil to do a better job.

It follows then, that if poorer teaching results from improper grouping, an inferior product in the form of student output will result. It is needless to say that tons of literature have been printed which deal with the "inferior quality" of students in this country. Although I do not agree with all that is said on this subject, I do believe firmly that a much better educated and a much better trained individual would result if ability grouping by class were carried on in the junior and senior high schools of our country.

to say that tons of literature have been printed which deal with the "inferior quality" of students in this country. Although I do not agree with all that is said on this subject, I do believe firmly that a much better educated and a much better trained individual would result if ability grouping by class were carried on in the junior and senior high schools of our country.